CASE

OF

THE BLACK WARRIOR,

AND OTHER

VIOLATIONS OF THE RIGHTS OF AMERICAN CITIZENS

BY

SPANISH AUTHORITIES.

WASHINGTON:
BEVERLEY TUCKER, SENATE PRINTER.
1854.

IN SENATE OF THE UNITED STATES.

MONDAY, JUNE 26, 1854.

Resolved, That two thousand copies of House Document No. 86, relating to the seizure of the steamer Black Warrior, and other cases of alleged wrongs to American citizens, by the authorities of Cuba, be printed for the use of the Senate.

Attest: ASBURY DICKINS, *Secretary*.

MESSAGE

FROM

THE PRESIDENT OF THE UNITED STATES,

TRANSMITTING

A report in regard to Spanish violations of the rights of American citizens, &c.

To the House of Representatives of the United States:

I transmit herewith to the House of Representatives a report of the Secretary of State, with accompanying documents, in further compliance with their resolution of the 10th March, 1854.

FRANKLIN PIERCE.

WASHINGTON, *April* 5, 1854.

DEPARTMENT OF STATE,
Washington, April 4, 1854.

The Secretary of State, to whom was referred the resolution of the House of Representatives of the 10th ultimo, requesting the President, "if not inconsistent with the public interest, to communicate to this House any information he may have received relative to the detention of the steamer Black Warrior, the seizure of her cargo, or the imprisonment of her officers; also any information in reference to any other violation of our rights by the Spanish authorities," has now the honor, in addition to the papers communicated on the 15th ultimo, relative to the case of the Black Warrior, to lay before the President a copy of the documents specified in the accompanying list, in respect to other complaints against the Spanish authorities, which, with the documents previously communicated to Congress, also referred to in the said list, are believed to embrace all important papers connected with the cases.

Papers in reference to other cases of like complaint are in the course of preparation, and will be laid before the President as soon as they are completed.

Respectfully submitted:

W. L. MARCY.

To the PRESIDENT OF THE UNITED STATES.

LIST OF DOCUMENTS ACCOMPANYING THE REPORT OF THE SECRETARY OF STATE TO THE PRESIDENT, OF THE 4TH OF APRIL, 1854.

Case of the Crescent City.

Mr. Morland to Mr. Webster, enclosures, September 23, 1852.
Mr. Roberts to the Secretary of State, October 6, 1852.
Mr. Moreland to the same, enclosures, October 7, 1852.
Mr. Conrad to Mr. Roberts, October 8, 1852.
Same to Mr. Sharkey, October 11, 1852.
Mr. Sharkey to Mr. Conrad, extract, October 11, 1852.
Mr. Morland to Mr. Webster, enclosures, October 18, 1852.
Same to the Secretary of State, October 20, 1852.
Mr. Roberts to the Acting Secretary of State, enclosure, October 21, 1852.
Mr. Law to the same, October 23, 1852.
Mr. Conrad to Mr. Law, October 25, 1852.
Mr. Law to Mr. Conrad, October 27, 1852.
Mr. Morland to same, extract, October 27, 1852.
Mr. Conrad to Mr. Barringer, enclosure, October 28, 1852.
Mr. Morland to Mr. Conrad, October 29, 1852.
Mr. Conrad to Mr. Law, October 30, 1852.
Mr. Calderon to Mr. Conrad, enclosure, November 5, 1852.
Mr. Sharkey to the Secretary of State, extracts and enclosures, November 8, 1852.
Mr. Everett to Mr. Maxwell, November 13, 1852.
Same to Mr. Calderon, November 15, 1852.
Mr. Kennedy to Mr. Everett, enclosures, November 16, 1852.
Mr Sharkey to Mr. Everett, enclosure, November 17, 1852.
Mr. Calderon to same, November 17, 1852.
Mr. Sharkey to the Secretary of State, November 17, 1852.
Mr. Everett to Mr. Sharkey, November 30, 1852.
Mr. Sharkey to Mr. Everett, extract, December 1, 1852.
Mr. Everett to Mr. Barringer, enclosure, December 4, 1852.
Mr. Calderon to Mr. Everett, December 10, 1852.
Mr. Barringer to same, enclosures, December 14, 1852.
Mr. Roberts to same, enclosure, December 14, 1852.
Mr. Everett to Mr. Sharkey, December 30, 1852.
Mr. Roberts to Mr. Everett, enclosure, January 4, 1852.
Mr. Barringer to the Secretary of State, extract and enclosures, January 5, 1853.
Mr. Everett to Mr. Barringer, February 4, 1853.
Mr. Barringer to Mr. Marcy, April 7, 1854.

Cases of the steamer Ohio and Schooner Manchester.

Mr. Marcy to Mr. Barringer, enclosures, April 19, 1853.
Mr. Barringer to Mr. Marcy, extract, June 10, 1853.
Same to same, extract and enclosures, July 8, 1853.
Same to same, extract and enclosures, July 16, 1853.

Same to same, extract and enclosures, August 18, 1853.
Mr. Soulé to same, extract and enclosures, March 8, 1854.

Case of John S. Thrasher.

Mr. Webster to Mr, Sharkey, extract, January 9, 1852.
Mr. Barringer to Mr. Webster, extract and enclosures, January 14, 1852.
Same to same, enclosure, January 15, 1852.
Mr. Sharkey to same, extract and enclosure, February 9, 1852.
Same to same, enclosure, February 13, 1852.
Mr. Graham to same, February 21, 1852.
Mr. Thrasher to same, March 22, 1852.
Mr. Webster to Mr. Sharkey, July 5, 1852.
Mr. Everett to Mr. Brooks, January 8, 1853.
Mr. Hayes to the Secretary of State, enclosure, March 10, 1853.
Mr. Marcy to Mr. Hayes, March 12, 1853.
Same to Mr. Lawrence, April 12, 1853.

Case of the steamer Falcon.

Mr. Owen to Mr. Webster, enclosure, August 17, 1851.
Mr. Derrick to Mr. Calderon, September 13, 1851.
Mr. Calderon to Mr. Derrick, September 29, 1851.

Case of the schooner Lamartine.

Mr. Worrell to Mr. Marcy, enclosures, February 25, 1854.
Same to same, enclosure, March 4, 1854.
Same to same, enclosure, March 9, 1854.

Case of Rey, alias Garcia.

Mr. Barringer to Mr. Clayton, extract, January 9, 1850.

Case of Pedro Raices.

Mr. Robertson to Mr. Marcy, extract, November 7, 1853.
Same to same, December 1, 1853.
Same to same, enclosures, January 11, 1854.
Mr. Marcy to Mr. Robertson, February 9, 1854.
Mr. Robertson to Mr. Marcy, extract, February 20, 1854.
Same to same, extract, March 5, 1854.
Mr. Marcy to Mr. Magallon, March 15, 1854.
Mr. Magallon to Mr. Marcy, March 18, 1854.
Mr. Robertson to Mr. Marcy, extract, March 21, 1854.

Case of Charles Peter V. Esnard.

Mr. Campbell to Mr. Clayton, enclosures, February 1, 1850.

Case of John Salinero.

Mr. Morland to Mr. Webster, enclosures, April 7, 1851.

Case of Captain Larrabee—Delays in judicial proceedings in Cuba. (Report on tribunals annexed.)

Mr. Trist to Mr. Forsyth, extracts and enclosures, Sept. 29, 1853.
Mr. Robertson to Mr. Marcy, March 9, 1854.

Case of the annulling of the Cuban Decree of October 7, 1844.

Mr Buchanan to Mr. Irving, enclosures, May 9, 1845.
Mr. Irving to Mr. Buchanan, extract, June 25, 1845.
Same to same, extract, July 10, 1845.
Mr. Barringer to Mr. Marcy, extract, August 11, 1853.

Case of Michael D. Haraug.

Mr. Gallaher to Mr. Forsyth, extract and enclosure, March 2, 1839.
Mr. Forsyth to the Chevalier d'Argaiz, February 28, 1840.
The Chevalier d'Argaiz to Mr. Forsyth, March 2, 1840.
Mr. Forsyth to Mr. Gallaher, March 4, 1840.
Mr. Gallaher to Mr. Forsyth, extract and enclosures, April 11, 1840.
The Chevalier d'Argaiz to same, December 24, 1840.
Mr. Vail to Mr. Webster, extract and enclosure, May 2, 1841.
Same to same, extract, July 24, 1841.
Mr. Webster to Mr. Vail, extract, September 1, 1841.
Mr. Vail to Mr. Webster, November 2, 1841.
Mr. Webster to Mr. Vail, extract, January 31, 1842.
Mr. Webster to Mr. Irving, extract, July 30, 1842.
Mr. Irving to Mr. Webster, enclosure, October 8, 1842.
Same to same, extract and enclosure, November 5, 1842.
Mr. Calhoun to Mr. Irving, April 30, 1844.
Same to same, extract, May 29, 1844.
Mr. Irving to Mr. Calhoun, extract, June 24, 1844.
Same to same, extract, July 14, 1844.
Same to Mr. Buchanan, extract and enclosures, August 23, 1845.
Mr. Buchanan to Mr. Saunders, extract, December 6, 1847.
Mr. Saunders to Mr. Buchanan, enclosure, February 8, 1848.
Same to Mr. Clayton, extract, July 7, 1849.
Same to same, extract and enclosures, September 25, 1849.
Mr. Barringer to Mr. Webster, November 8, 1852.
Same to the Secretary of State, enclosures, February 23, 1853.
Same to same, extract and enclosure, March 8, 1853.
Same to same, enclosures, March 26, 1853.
Mr. Gallaher to Mr. Forsyth, November 23, 1838.

Case of the seamen belonging to the barque Jasper.

Mr. Robertson to Mr. Marcy, enclosures, July 6, 1853.
Same to same, enclosure, July 11, 1853.
Same to same, July 13, 1853.
Commander J. F. Gerry, U. S. N., to Mr. Dobbin, July 15, 1853.
Mr. Marcy to Mr. O'Conor, enclosure, July 19, 1853.

Case of the Black Warrior.

Opening of the mails of the United States by the authorities of Cuba.

Same to Mr. Everett, enclosure, February 21, 1853.
Same to Secretary of State, extract and enclosure, March 12, 1853.
Mr. Robertson to Mr. Marcy, August 29, 1853.
Same to same, enclosure, August 29, 1853.
Same to same, extract, September 13, 1853.
Same to same, extract, October 14, 1853.
Mr. Marcy to Mr. Pierce, February 1, 1854.

Case of the Contoy prisoners.

Mr. Campbell to Mr. Clayton, extract and enclosures, May 19, 1850.
Same to same, extracts and enclosures, May 22, 1850.
Same to same, enclosures, May 31, 1850.
Same to same, May 31, 1850.
Mr. Clayton to Mr. Campbell, May 31, 1850.
Same to same, June 1, 1854.
Mr. Campbell to Mr. Clayton, June 4, 1850.
Same to same, June 8, 1850.
Same to same, enclosure, June 19, 1850.
Same to same, extracts, June 19, 1850.
Same to same, extract, June 27, 1850.
Mr. Clayton to Commodore Morris, June 29, 1850.
Same to Mr. Campbell, June 29, 1850.
Mr. Campbell to Mr. Clayton, extracts, July 3, 1850.
Same to same, July 8, 1850.
Same to same, enclosure, July 12, 1850.
Same to same, July 16, 1850.
Same to same, extract, July 19, 1850.
Commodore Morris to same, enclosures, July 23, 1850.

Note.

For previous correspondence relating to the case of *John S. Thrasher*, see House Ex. Docs. Nos. 10 and 14, 32d Congress, 1st session.

For previous correspondence in the case of *Rey, alias Garcia*, see Senate Ex. Doc. No. 13, 31st Congress, 1st session.

For previous correspondence in the case of the *Black Warrior*, see House Ex. Doc. No. 76, 33d Congress, 1st session.

For previous correspondence in the case of the *Contoy prisoners*, see Senate Ex. Doc. No. 41, 31st Congress, 2d session.

For correspondence in reference to the seizure and imprisonment of Captain Thaddeus Beecher, and his officers and crew, of the schooner North Carolina, see House Ex. Doc. No. 29, 33d Congress, 1st session.

For correspondence relating to the imprisonment of James H. Weston, see Senate Ex. Doc. No. 46, 33d Congress, 1st. session.

CASE OF THE CRESCENT CITY.

Mr. Morland to Mr. Webster.

[No. 13.] CONSULATE OF THE UNITED STATES, HAVANA,
September 23, 1852.

SIR: Since my last communication, (No. 12,) under date of the 25th ultimo, the only circumstance that has occurred which renders it proper to communicate to you, is the steps threatened to be taken by the Captain General towards the mail steamships that come to this port, announced to me only on the 21st instant, although he had issued his orders on the 4th, and the "Crescent City" had come in and departed in the interim.

I enclose herewith a copy of the Captain General's communication, (containing the Political Secretary's letter to the consignees of that ship,) and my answer thereto, by which you will see that he is determined to refuse entry to any ship with any person on board who may have written "calumnious" charges against his government. Such a proceeding may cause very serious injuries to the commerce of the United States connected with this place, and interrupt the course of the mail.

I take this opportunity of stating that in the only two cases wherein I have deemed it my duty to appeal to the Captain General in behalf of American citizens who have been arrested and imprisoned for violating the regulations of the port, &c., he has evinced a disposition to be just and conciliatory; and finally both were released, and one fine was remitted.

I have the honor to remain, with great respect, your obedient serv't,
JNO. MORLAND, *Acting Consul.*

Hon. DANL. WEBSTER,
Secretary of State.

[L. S.] POLITICAL SECRETARY'S OFFICE, SECTION 1.
Havana, September 21, 1852.

The Secretary of this Superior Civil Government has, on the 4th instant, communicated, by my order, to the firm of Drake & Co., merchants of this city, what follows:

"A person named William Smith, who seems to be an employé on the steamer 'Crescent City,' has published, on the arrival of said steamer, her last voyage, at New York, the grossest calumnies against the government of this island, taking advantage, to give a greater appearance of truth to his impostures, of the frank hospitality extended to foreigners in Cuba.

"This act, which the whole world will know how to judge and qualify with its true colors, has very seriously called the attention of his excellency the Governor and Captain General, which superior authority, although he despises the ridiculous assertions made against his administration, to occupy himself even for a single moment in refuting them, deems it a duty to let the author understand that her Majesty's government will not permit that acts of that nature shall be reproduced with impunity.

"In virtue whereof, proper orders have been issued, that immediately that the steamer 'Crescent City' arrive at this city, a police officer shall go on board for the express purpose of preventing said Smith from coming on shore. And by order of his excellency I state it to you; adding, that if in future said individual should return in any of the steamers of the company, or any other person employed on them should take the liberty to abuse in a similar manner the privileges that the Spanish authorities offer him in the ports of the island, this sole act will be sufficient not to allow entry to the vessel conveying him, whatsoever the losses may be that such a measure may accrue to the company; for although the company have it not in their power to prevent their subordinates from committing such excesses, their honor and interest must oblige them to immediately withdraw their trust from any one that should attempt to compromit them foolishly."

Which I transmit to your lordship for your information and proper effects, in case that it should be attempted to oppose the orders of this superior government, which I am firmly resolved to carry into effect.

God preserve your lordship many years.

VALENTIN CAÑEDO.

To the CONSUL OF THE UNITED STATES *in this city.*

CONSULATE OF THE UNITED STATES, HAVANA,
September 22, 1852.

MOST EXCELLENT SIR: I had the honor to receive your excellency's official communication of yesterday, containing a copy of a communication from the secretary of the superior Civil Government addressed to the mercantile house of Drake & Co., by your excellency's order, on the 4th instant, on the subject of some gross calumnies on your excellency's conduct published in the United States by William Smith, an officer or employé on board the United States mail steamer "Crescent City." The secretary says, "that although your excellency despises such ridiculous falsehoods, you still deem it a duty to make it known to their author that her Majesty's government will not permit things of this nature to be reproduced with impunity," and that your excellency "has issued orders that immediately the said steamer 'Crescent City' shall arrive in this city, a police officer will be sent on board with an express order to prevent the landing of the said Smith;" and that "in future, if this individual shall return, or any other person employed in the steamers belonging to the company shall take the liberty to abuse in a similar manner the privileges extended to them by the Spanish authorities in the ports of Cuba, this sole fact will be sufficient for the vessel conveying such person to be refused an entry, whatsoever may be the losses that may accrue to the company; as, although it is not in their power to prevent their subordinates from committing such excesses, their honor and interest ought to oblige them to withdraw immediately their trust from any one who may attempt to compromit them foolishly." And your excellency advises me that "you are firmly resolved to carry into effect, in case any opposition should be attempted, the order of the superior government."

As the secretary's communication to Drake & Co., was made under date of the 4th instant, seventeen days since, they state that they have advised the owners of the steamers of the import thereof for their government. And as your excellency now states to me your firm intention to carry into effect the determination your excellency has come to in this matter, it remains for me merely to communicate the same to my government. I cannot, however, refrain from expressing my deep regret that anything should have occurred to induce your excellency to take such a step, particularly as it will involve other persons entirely innocent of such offences in much loss and difficulty. And besides, as the steamships "Crescent City" and "Empire City" are the bearers of the United States mail, any interruption, caused by your excellency's government, in the progress of their duties, will result in much harm, and be anything but conciliatory with the federal government of the United States.

I have the honor to be, respectfully, your excellency's, &c.,

JOHN MORELAND, *Acting Consul.*

His Excellency Señor D. VALENTIN CAÑEDO,
Governor and Captain General, &c.

Mr. Roberts to the Secretary of State.

OFFICE OF THE U. S. MAIL STEAMSHIP COMPANY,
New York, October 6, 1852.

SIR: I have the honor to state to you, that we learn by telegraph from New Orleans, this afternoon, that the U. S. mail steamship "Crescent City," Captain Porter, United States navy, on her arrival at Havana from this port, whence she sailed on the 27th ultimo, with mails, passengers, and freight, was not permitted to enter that port, or was ordered out of the harbor forthwith. She was, accordingly, compelled to proceed, with her mails, passengers, and freight, to New Orleans.

This is not the first instance in which the ships of this company, and the American flag, have been subjected to injury and insult by the Cuban authorities. The "Ohio," commanded by an officer of the United States navy, and conveying the government mails, was ordered, without cause or provocation, and against the protest of her commander, to an unsafe and hazardous anchorage, under the guns of the Moro Castle, or forthwith to leave the harbor, without being allowed to deliver her mails or freight, or to obtain her usual supply of coals. The "Falcon," also, commanded by an American naval officer, was fired upon and boarded on the high seas, by a Spanish vessel of war. The "Philadelphia," also bearing the United States mails, entered the port of Havana, (her usual place of coaling and obtaining supplies,) in distress, destitute of coal and provisions, and with many of her passengers sick. After being ordered to quarantine and having proceeded thither, she was ordered several miles outside, and then peremptorily driven from her anchorage, without being allowed to receive on board her coals and provisions, then alongside, for the want of which her passengers and crew were suffering, and was compelled to go to sea, to the imminent danger of the safety of the steamer and mails, and with fatal consequences to many of the persons on board. And this systematic course of insult and outrage has been followed up, by driving the "Crescent City," in the service of the government of the United States, and commanded by an American naval officer, from the harbor of Havana, without being allowed to deliver her mails, to land her passengers or freight, destined for that port, or to obtain her supply of coals.

The conduct of the Cuban authorities in these repeated and wanton acts of hostility, not only causes a serious interruption to the due delivery of the mails, but is a great detriment and loss to this company, in disturbing its business and its contract arrangements with the government; a serious annoyance and injury to American citizens, passengers, and shippers, and to the trade and commerce between the two countries; and is calculated, if not designed, to disturb the amicable relations heretofore existing between the two governments. More than this, we cannot but regard it as a gross insult to the American flag, derogatory to our national character, and in violation of our national rights.

The pretext on which this last outrage has been perpetrated, is the allegation that the purser of the "Crescent City" made a publication in an American newspaper, of some of the statements of which the Cuban authorities complain. The allegation is unfounded; but, if it were true, we know of no right on the part of a foreign government to dictate to an American citizen, in his own country, what he shall utter or abstain from uttering, through the journals of his own country.

It has ever been the aim of this company to avoid the semblance of anything that could give offence to the Spanish authorities of the island of Cuba. Its commanders, and all persons in its employment, have been uniformly instructed to abstain from all interference in the affairs of that government, and I have no reason to think that these instructions have not been fully complied with.

We have forborne to call the attention of our government to the insults by the Cuban officials to which the ships of this company and the American flag have been heretofore subjected, from a desire to avoid everything that might lead to irritation between the two governments, and from a belief, that a knowledge of the unfounded nature of the allegations on which they pretended to act would prevent their repetition. But we feel it due, not less to the public interests confided to our charge, than to our own interests and the interests of American citizens engaged in a peaceful and lawful commerce, to bring these facts to the consideration of the American government; and to ask, as American citizens in the service of the government, and required by it to deliver its mails, protection and redress; or to be allowed to redress the grievance and repel the insult to our national flag, with such means and in such manner as we can, and shall deem equal and due to self-protection.

I have the honor to be, with high respect, your obedient servant,

M. O. ROBERTS,

By order of the United States Mail Steamship Company.

Mr. Morland to the Secretary of State.

CONSULATE OF THE UNITED STATES, HAVANA,
October 7, 1852.

SIR: Since my last dispatch, No. 13, under date 23d ultimo, and on the 3d instant, at a little past three o'clock p. m., the United States mail steamer "Crescent City," commanded by Lieutenant Porter, of the United States navy, arrived here with the mails on board, and sixty-five passengers, to be landed in this city, and, agreeably to what was threatened by the Captain General, in his official communication of the 21st ultimo, to me, copy of which was transmitted to you, he was peremptorily ordered to leave the port, without being permitted to land either mails or passengers.

Captain Porter was permitted to send me his protest, under cover, against the authorities here, which, owing to the shortness of the time he stayed, I was not enabled to send to the Captain General, with a communication from myself, before his departure; neither was I able to communicate with Captain Porter, but I sent the document to the Captain General early next morning, since which I have not heard from his excellency.

I accompany herewith a copy of Captain Porter's protest, and of my note to the Captain General when the same was sent to him.

I have the honor to be, sir, with great respect, your obedient servant,
JOHN MORLAND, *Acting Consul.*

CONSULATE OF THE UNITED STATES, HAVANA,
October 4, 1852.

MOST EXCELLENT SIR: The accompanying document I received last evening, to be sent to your excellency, from Captain Porter, of the United States mail steamer "Crescent City," who was ordered out of port immediately, before I could have time to comply with his request. Captain Porter has been obliged to take with him the mails intended for this port, and upwards of sixty passengers destined for this city.

I have the honor to be your excellency's obedient servant,
JOHN MORLAND,
Commercial agent, in charge of the Consulate of the United States.

OCTOBER 2, 1852.

Whereas the Spanish authorities in Cuba have issued an order to prevent the entrance of the United States mail steamship Crescent City into the port at Havana, to which the said steamship is bound in the pursuit of her legitimate business, no offence having been committed, on the coast of Cuba, against the laws of Spain, by the officers or crew of said vessel, and the said order being in direct contravention of the treaty stipulations between the two countries, I do therefore strongly protest, in the name of the United States Mail Steamship Company, whose interest I represent, and also in the name of the government of the United States, whose officer I am, against a proceeding so arbitrary.

The Spanish authorities in Cuba, for the extraordinary course taken by them, profess to hold the United States Mail Steamship Company responsible for newspaper articles published in the United States, and which are alleged to have been written by the purser of the Crescent City.

It has been distinctly declared by me, (though no such declaration was called for on my part,) that Mr. Smith, the purser, had no agency in composing or publishing any such articles. I protest against the United States Mail Steamship Company being held responsible for the publication of any articles in the newspapers of the United States, as such matters are wholly beyond the control of said company, as well as of the officers of the ships connected therewith.

The press of the United States acknowledges no direct censorship from any quarter whatsoever, and is amenable only to the laws of the government. I protest against an American citizen, and an officer of the ship, being held responsible for such publications, and being treated with personal disrespect; such conduct is unworthy a nation that professes to have attained the highest degree of civilization.

I protest against the non-admission of this ship into the harbor of Havana, as it is a deep injury to the United States Mail Steamship Company, who are thereby disabled from complying with their contract to the government of the United States, and which company have already received most serious injuries from the hands of the Spanish government by having their ships driven out of the harbor of Havana.

Respectfully submitted:

DAVID D. PORTER,
Lieut. U. S. N., and commanding U. S. mail steamship Crescent City.

To the AUTHORITIES OF CUBA.

Mr. Conrad to Mr. Roberts.

DEPARTMENT OF STATE, WASHINGTON,
October 8, 1852.

SIR: Having occasion for a personal interview with you, I will thank you to come to this city for that purpose as soon as may be practicable.

I am, sir, &c.,

C. M. CONRAD,
Acting Secretary.

M. O. ROBERTS, Esq.,
President of the U. S. Mail Steamship Company, New York.

Mr. Conrad to Mr. Sharkey.

DEPARTMENT OF STATE, WASHINGTON,
October 11, 1852.

SIR: I have to acknowledge the receipt of the dispatch from the consulate, No. 13, accompanied by its correspondence with the Captain General of Cuba, occasioned by an alleged publication in the newspapers of New York of intelligence relative to that island, by William Smith, the purser of the United States mail steamer Crescent city. Since your dispatch reached the department, a letter has been received from the president of the Steamship Company, stating that the "Crescent city had been forbidden to land her passengers and mails at Havana, and had been ordered out of that harbor. The letter also states that the Cuban authorities had previously committed similar acts of inhospitality towards other steamers of the same company.

The public journals have also recently represented that United States vessels generally, at Havana, have been subjected by the authorities to various annoyances; that they have been searched; that police officers have been placed and kept on board of them; and that their letter bags have been opened and letters taken therefrom, &c. The department has no means of judging of the truth of this statement, especially as your dispatches are silent on the subject. You will therefore lose no time in collecting and transmitting accurate information on the subject.

I am, sir, &c.,

C. M. CONRAD,
Acting Secretary.

To Wm. L. Sharkey, Esq., *&c., &c., &c.*

Mr. Sharkey to Mr. Conrad.

[Extract.]

Vicksburg, *October* 11, 1852.

Sir: * * * * * * * * *
A new cause of difficulty has now occurred in consequence of the course pursued by the authorities of Havana towards the steamer Crescent city. This affair will doubtless command the attention of the government, and, it is hoped, be adjusted without difficulty. Allow me to say that a new treaty with Spain might possibly be the best means of producing a permanent good understanding between the two governments. I hope to be in Havana by the first of November at furthest, and will be happy to observe any instruction the department may think proper to give.

With great regard, I have the honor to be your obedient servant,

W. L. SHARKEY.

Hon. C. M. Conrad,
Acting Secretary of State of the United States.

Mr. Morland to Mr. Webster.

[No. 15.] Consulate of the United States, Havana,
October 18, 1852.

Sir: The arrival of the "Crescent city" here on the 14th instant caused very considerable sensation. This vessel was suffered to lie, but not permitted to land her mail or passengers, or to have any communication with the shore; but the government boats went alongside and communicated with Captain Porter, who desired a communication to be delivered to me, but was refused. Believing there was something that might require action on my part, I went personally to the Captain General to get his permission to go and receive it. On arriving at the country seat of his excellency, I found there one of the consignees of the vessel, (who had been, as I understood, alongside with the authorities,) who represented to the Captain General that there was a package for me on board, and that he understood Captain Porter to say that it was a communication from the American government, which induced his excellency to give his permission for me to communicate with Captain Porter, and to receive the dispatch, which was done; but on opening it, I merely found another protest, (copy of which is herewith enclosed,) and which I transmitted to the Captain General, informing him likewise that Captain Porter had stated that he had come by express orders of the Postmaster General.

Having in my previous communication of the 4th instant stated the fact of the "Crescent city" being the bearer of the United States mails, and officered by officers of the navy of the United States, no notice was taken until the 16th, when, at 10 o'clock p. m., I received a communication, (copy of which is herewith enclosed,) under date of 15th instant, wherein you will notice he rebukes me for acting in affairs foreign to my functions.

Considering the "Crescent city" very different from a common merchant vessel, as a vessel chartered by the United States to carry the mails, and officered by officers from the Americen navy by permission of government, I had no hesitation in sending Captain Porter's protest, in both cases, and shall make such explanation to the Captain General.

I have the honor to be, very respectfully, your obedient servant,

JOHN MORLAND,
Acting Consul.

Hon. Daniel Webster,
Secretary of State, Washington city.

Consulate of the United States, Havana,
October 14, 1852.

Most Excellent Sir: Having, by your excellency's permission, gone alongside of the American mail steamer "Crescent city," to receive from Captain Porter a package said, as I understood Mr. Morales to say to your excellency, to contain dispatches from the government of the United States, I received from Captain Porter a package containing only an extension of his protest, (which I herewith send your excellency,) made on the former occasion of his being refused entry here; but I have to state to your excellency that Captain Porter could not have received dispatches at New Orleans from the United States government, there not being sufficient time, but that the agent of the mails at New Orleans did receive a telegraphic communication ordering the "Crescent city" with the mails to come to this port, and deliver them, if permitted; if not, to proceed on to New York. This I believe is what the captain communicated to Mr. Morales, as those orders were from the Postmaster General of the United Statee, who is a member of the Cabinet. These vessels bearing the United States mail are hired for that purpose, and officered entirely by officers of the navy of the United States.

I have the honor to be, with great respect, your excellency's obedient servant.

JNO. MORLAND,
Com. Agt. in charge of the Consulate of the United States.

His Excellency Señor D. VALENTIN CAÑEDO,
Governor and Captain General of Cuba, &c., &c., &c.

Protest.

OCTOBER 14, 1852.

Whereas the first article of the treaty of amity between Spain and the United States declares there shall be a firm and inviolable peace and sincere friendship between his Catholic Majesty, his successors and subjects, and the United States, and the citizens, without exception of persons or places. Article 6th of the same treaty promises mutual assistance and kindly acts towards the ships of either power when in the ports of the other, which engages to defend and protect them to the extent of jurisdiction by land or sea; and article 9th secures to the citizens or subjects of each free access to the courts of justice of the other in *all cases*, and provides that all cases be prosecuted by order and authority of law *only*, and that the parties shall have liberty of counsel and defence.

How far the Spanish authorities in Cuba have conformed to this treaty is apparent from the fact that they have arbitrarily, and without any form or process of law, caused a United States Steamship engaged in the pursuit of a legitimate and peaceful business to be turned from their port on one occasion, and refused communication on another, for an *imputed* offence committed in the territory of the United States, and which offence, if actually committed within their own territory, the Spanish authorities had no right to punish an American citizen for.

On two occasions the undersigned has, in plain terms, denied that Purser Wm. Smith wrote anything against the Spanish government in the newspapers of the United States, but the word of an officer (who has heretofore enjoyed the confidence of his government and the company he serves) has been as entirely disregarded by the Cuban authorities as if they were ignorant of the polity which governs civilized nations.

On the contrary, they have pursued a vindictive course, which must, if persevered in, inflict great and serious injury on the commerce of the United States, and against which course, as applied to this vessel or any of the company's vessels, he, the undersigned, once more most strongly protests.

The undersigned begs leave to draw the attention of the Spanish government in Cuba to the fact that the Crescent City sailed from New York with a large number of American and Cuban passengers on board, *every one* of whom had with him a *passport from the Spanish consul at New York*, granting permission to sail *in the Crescent City*, *for the port of Havana*, with a guarantee of safe landing on the shores of Cuba; moreover, that the Spanish consul at that place did not inform the passengers, or give any notice to the United States Mail Steamship Company that there was a likelihood of the Crescent City being prevented from entering the port of Havana.

It is true that a "manifesto" was issued to the undersigned; but the company were in no wise bound by such a "manifesto," having perfect right to consider it as the hasty and ill-advised act of a subordinate officer, Martin Galiano, by whom it was signed, which act, if persevered in, would interrupt the friendly intercourse of the two countries, and which they would likely not repeat after the disavowal of the imputed offence of the undersigned.

The Spanish authorities in Cuba have, in the most arbitrary course pursued by them, violated the treaty of amity existing between the two countries—have inflicted serious injuries on private individuals, and on this company. Interests of large amount are likely to suffer by the non-deliverance of the mail intrusted to the government officer of a friendly nation, and the wheels of commerce, as far as regards this ship, are entirely at a stand.

Mr. Smith, the officer in question, has been a long time employed in the company's service by the full knowledge and previous countenance of the Spanish authorities, who have driven him from their harbor; and it is a well known fact that the undersigned, and those under his command, have always abstained from any acts of interference with the affairs of the island, either bv speech or act, though it might naturally be supposed that they could not help but sympathize with the misfortunes of captives.

In conclusion, the undersigned takes this opportunity to protest again, in the strongest terms, against the indefensible disregard of the treaty of amity and law of nations by which American citizens are, without notice and legal accusation of offence, or opportunity offered to defend themselves, subjected to proscription and severe mercantile loss—the flag of the United States treated with scorn and contempt, and the government treated with disrespect, in the person of its officer, who, though commanding a ship owned by a company, is placed in his position by a written order of the United States government, and by a law of Congress of the United States.

The undersigned also protests against not being allowed to make known to the American consul the situation in which he is placed, having been refused, most positively, permission to communicate with the representative of the United States in the island of Cuba. An appeal to the consul of a country is even respected among the Barbary Powers, of whom a knowledge of the law of nations is not so much to be expected.

Respectfully submitted:

D. D. PORTER, *Lieut. U. S. N.*

To the SPANISH AUTHORITIES OF CUBA.

[Translation.]

[L. S.] POLITICAL DEPARTMENT, SECTION FIRST,
Havana, October 15, 1852.

SIR: With your communication of the 4th instant I have received the document which is addressed to me by one Porter, captain of the merchant steamer "Crescent City," comprising the protest which he thought proper to make on his arrival at this port the day before.

Neither on account of the character of the contents of this document, nor in consideration of the unusual form in which it has been drawn, can I permit myself to enter into any reply in regard to it, and therefore I confine myself to state that I have acquainted my government with the matter to which it refers, and I hope, in future, that you will abstain from addressing yourself to my authority concerning matters which, like the present, are foreign to your functions.

God preserve you a thousand years.

VALENTIN CAÑEDO.

To the COMMERCIAL AGENT
of the United States at this place.

CONSULATE OF THE UNITED STATES, HAVANA,
October 18, 1852.

MOST EXCELLENT SIR: Your excellency's communication of the 15th reached me on the 16th late at night; and as your excellency is pleased to rebuke me for sending to your excellency Lieutenant Porter's protest, and consider the "Crescent City" as a mere merchant-vessel, I beg leave to state that the "Crescent City" and "Empire City" are both vessels freighted by the government of the United States, and are commanded by officers of the navy of the United States, placed there by permission and with the approval of the government. Hence it was that I considered it my duty to forward to your excellency Lieutenant Porter's protest, without any wish or intention to enter into any questions that might be considered foreign to my functions; and I now merely give your excellency this statement, believing that your excellency may not have been aware of the true character of the "Crescent City;" and I was in hopes the positive denial of Lieutenant Porter that William Smith, the purser of that vessel, had ever given *anything* to the press in the United States, of *any* nature whatever, would have had some influence in producing a more favorable view of the supposed act.

I take this opportunity of acknowledging the receipt of your excellency's communication relative to Samuel Harme, (dated 18th instant,) for which your excellency will please receive my thanks.

I have the honor to be your excellency's obedient servant,

JNO. MORLAND,
Commercial Agent in charge of the Consulate of the U. S.

His Excellency Señor Don VALENTIN CAÑEDO,
Governor and Captain General of Cuba, &c.

Mr. Morland to the Secretary of State.

[Extract.]

[No. 16.] CONSULATE OF THE UNITED STATES, HAVANA,
October 20, 1852.

SIR: My dispatch No. 15, under date 18th instant, sent per mail schooner *via* Charleston, contained sundry documents touching the affair of the "Crescent City." I now have the honor to enclose herewith duplicates of my said dispatch, and of the papers accompanying it. I likewise transmit a copy of my answer to the Captain General's communication of the 15th instant, which I had no time to prepare for transmission by that vessel, as she stopped here but a few minutes after it was written.

* * * * * * * * *

I have the honor to be, sir, with great respect, your obedient servant,
JNO. MORLAND,
Acting Consul.

Mr. Roberts to the Acting Secretary of State.

OFFICE OF THE U. S. MAIL STEAMSHIP COMPANY,
New York, October 21, 1852.

SIR: I have the honor to enclose, herewith, an affidavit made and subscribed by Mr. William Smith, purser of the United States mail steamship "Crescent City," by which it will be seen how utterly unfounded have been all the charges in relation to calumnious publications alleged to have been made by him against the government of the island of Cuba, or of any interference in its affairs, and how causeless has been the high-handed course of its authorities in this respect.

I have the honor to be, with high respect, your obedient servant,
M. O. ROBERTS,
Agent of the U. S. Mail Steamship Company.

UNITED STATES OF AMERICA,
Southern District of New York. } *ss.*

I, William Smith, purser of the United States mail steamship "Crescent City," being duly sworn, depose and say, that the allegation contained in a certain order or manifesto, signed "M. Galliano," an officer of the government of the island of Cuba, dated at Havana the 4th day of September, 1852, and repeated in the official paper at Havana, that I had "published the most gross calumnies against the government of said island," and the further allegations, which I understand have been made unofficially to the government of the United States, that I had held communication with disaffected persons in the port of Havana or the island of Cuba, and had been the bearer of letters or messages to and from such persons, are all utterly without foundation. I have never written or published anything against the government of the said island of Cuba, nor have I ever carried letters or messages to and from disaffected persons in said island, or held any communication with such persons, or in any manner interfered with the affairs of the said island, or the proceedings of its authorities. I have confined myself strictly to the discharge of the duties of purser of the ship, and have demeaned myself accordingly. Furthermore, it has been the express command of Captain Porter, and of the Mail Steamship Company, that no officer or person employed on the ship should be allowed to carry letters outside of the mail, other than those belonging to the ship's business; and, when letters have been sent on the steamer after the mails have been closed and received on board, they have been placed in charge of the purser, and in all cases delivered to the postmaster at Havana.

I also further depose and say, that I have never been in any manner connected with any association or expedition for hostile purposes in relation to the island of Cuba, or for annoying, resisting, or interfering with its authorities.

WILLIAM SMITH.

Sworn to this 21st day of October, 1852, before me,

JOSEPH BRIDGHAM,
U. S. Com. Southern District of New York.

Mr. Law to the Acting Secretary of State.

OFFICE OF THE U. S. MAIL STEAMSHIP COMPANY,
New York, October 23, 1852.

SIR: Mr. Roberts had the honor to address you on the 6th instant, in relation to the course of the authorities of the island of Cuba towards the steamships of this company, and especially in relation to the "Crescent City."

I await your reply to his communication, to determine the course of the company. The 27th instant being the sailing day of the next steamer for New Orleans, via Havana, we are daily inquired of whether mails and passengers can be allowed to land at Havana, and whether the Cuban authorities are to be permitted to continue the course towards the ships of this company, of which the government of the United States have been heretofore apprized.

I have the honor to be, very respectfully, your obedient servant,

GEORGE LAW, *President.*

Mr. Conrad to Mr. Law.

DEPARTMENT OF STATE,
Washington, October 25, 1852.

SIR: Your letter of the 23d instant has been received. No intelligence has reached this department from Cuba since that which was received by your steamer. It has no means of knowing the intentions of the authorities of the island other than what you possess, and cannot, therefore, inform you whether mails or passengers will be permitted to land there or not. It may, however, be inferred, from the last proceedings of the authorities, that the mail and passengers conveyed in the steamer Crescent City will not be permitted to land them, in case the individual named, William Smith, should remain on board of her.

I am, sir, very respectfully, your obedient servant,

C. M. CONRAD, *Acting Secretary*.

GEORGE LAW, Esq., *New York*.

Mr. Law to Mr. Conrad.

OFFICE OF THE U. S. MAIL STEAMSHIP COMPANY,
New York, October 27, 1852.

SIR: I had this day the honor to receive your letter of the 25th instant.

On the 6th instant we addressed the Department of State a letter, detailing at some length the grievances of which this company feels it has a right to complain in relation to the course on various occasions of the authorities of the island of Cuba towards the ships of this company; and we respectfully requested to be advised as to our own rights, and whether the government of Cuba were justified in pursuing the course above alluded to.

Our motives in writing that letter were to bring to the notice of our government, which we felt bound to do, certain acts of a foreign government which we could not but regard as oppressive and unjust towards this company, and to American citizens and shippers engaged in lawful commerce with that power, and also as an insult to the flag of our country. The company suppose that the authorities of Cuba had no right to dictate to our own government or to the owners of American ships who should be employed on board of them, or to make a compliance or non-compliance with their dictation in this respect a pretext for excluding such ships, with their passengers and mails, as did not conform to their directions in relation to the employés on board of them. If these impressions were not well founded, we supposed that we should be so advised by the Department of State. If they were well founded, we had, as we supposed, a right to expect from our government protection against the injury. We have as yet received no reply from the Department of State to our letter of the 6th instant, although addressed in duplicate both to Washington and Marshfield; and the letter of the Acting Secretary of State of the 25th instant, in reply to my letter of the 23d, fails to afford us the desired information. Every day's delay is, and has been, a great loss to this company, extremely detrimental to the commercial interests of the country, and, more than all, subjects us, if correct in our impressions, to the humiliation of submitting to a wrong.

I desire respectfully to say that it was less our intention to inquire what course the government of Cuba would pursue than to ascertain what interpretation our own government gave to the rights of American citizens and of this company, and what course was expected of the company, in order to know how far we would be able to comply with it.

I have the honor to be, very respectfully, your obedient servant,

GEORGE LAW, *President.*

Hon. C. M. Conrad,
Acting Secretary of State.

Mr. Morland, Acting Consul, to Mr. Conrad.

[Extract.]

[No. 17.] Consulate of the United States, Havana,
October 27, 1852.

Sir: I have had the honor to receive your dispatch of the 11th inst., by U. S. steamship Powhatan, which arrived in this port on the 23d, having on board the minister to Mexico and Commodore Newton. I now beg leave to reply to the several questions contained in your said dispatch, by referring you to my communications, Nos. 13, 14, 15 and 16, relative to the affair of the U. S. mail steamship "Crescent City."

As to the "El Dorado" steamer, the treatment whereof by the authorities here has been brought to the notice of the Department of State, I have to say that the affair occurred when Mr. Sharkey, the consul, was here. I learn, however, that she came here from Aspinwall on the 19th day of July last, with 290 passengers, five having died on the passage, and three being sick with fever on arrival, but no cholera. This vessel was not allowed to have fuel, provisions, or water sent to her, (of which she was in great need,) but these articles were taken to her outside by the "Empire City" steamer, belonging to the same company. The "El Dorado" was allowed to make fast to a buoy one mile outside the Moro, until the health officers had visited her, when the Captain General called a meeting of the Board of Health, which decreed that the ship must immediately leave the port, not permitting her to lie at anchor a moment longer, or to have communication of any kind with the shore. She therefore proceeded to Key West. These facts appear in the records of this consulate, in a protest entered by the agent of the company owning the "El Dorado."

The other complaints made by our merchant ships are, particularly, the placing on board police officers and soldiers on two or three of them, to prevent any obnoxious person from landing, and also to prevent such parties as are accused of being connected with the supposed attempt at revolt from escaping out of this island. This, of course, is annoying enough. The custom has been more particularly exercised in the case of American steamers, where so many passengers come and go, that it is very easy for parties to effect their escape; and I have heard, from good authority, that many have so escaped. A police officer is placed on board of every merchant vessel that brings passengers. It is an annoyance, no doubt, but I do not think it is in any way prejudicial to the interests of American commerce.

I will now state, in obedience to your directions, the details of the late occurrence relative to the barque Cornelia, Captain Ward, of New York, which appears to be the most important case excepting that of the "Crescent City." That vessel had cleared and was proceeding to sea, when a government boat went alongside to search for a suspected person, and some dispatches supposed to have been sent under his care from the disaffected here to certain people in the United States connected with them. The person was found on board; and although he had his passport, he was taken out of the Cornelia and brought ashore, and he has been in prison ever since. The officer likewise found a Mr. Samuel Harme, or Hearkness, an American engineer, secreted on board, as he had no passport; he was also brought on shore and imprisoned, but allowed his liberty in a few days at my request. The captain of the Cornelia came to the consulate and noted his protest, but did not extend it. He stated to me that the captain of the port demanded the dispatches which Guzman (the other person alluded to) was supposed to have, and that he had answered that he could not swear whether he had received them or not, as he was in the habit of throwing into a drawer all letters sent on board not in the letter bag. He spoke of abandoning his ship, but I told him that would never do; and I question whether it was anything more than a mere threat, without any serious intention to do so. He complained of the violent and insulting language which he asserted the captain of the port had used towards him on his denying a knowledge of the existence of the dispatches sought after. Captain Ward proceeded to sea on the next morning with his letter-bag. There is no doubt but the letter-bag, which had been taken out of the ship by the officers, was examined, and some packages directed to suspicious persons abstracted, as the Captain General gave notice through the newspapers for the persons who may have written those letters, giving the address of each, to call at the palace and witness the opening of the said letters; and some did go, but how many I know not; and as mere reports are less to be trusted here than anywhere I have ever been, I shall not venture to give any. Under these circumstances, when the laws were violated on the one hand, and the government was protecting itself on the other, I did not deem it a case in which I had a right to interfere; therefore I made no official report of it to the department.

* * * * * *

I have the honor to be, sir, with great respect, your most obedient servant,

JOHN MORLAND, *Acting Consul.*

Hon. C. M. Conrad,
Acting Secretary of State, Washington.

Mr. Conrad to Mr. Barringer.

[No. 64.]

Department of State,
Washington, October 28, 1852.

Sir: An incident connected with our relations with Spain has recently occurred, which is of so grave a character as, in the opinion of the President, to require that it should be immediately laid before the government of that country.

In the year 1847 a company was formed, under the auspices of this government, for the purpose of conveying the mails in steamships from New York and New Orleans to Havana, there to connect with another line to the Isthmus of Panama. The law under which the arrangement was made required that the steamers should be placed, to a certain extent, under the control of the government, and should be commanded by officers of the navy. Under this arrangement the mails have been regularly carried from New York and New Orleans to Havana and back. By another arrangement the mail is carried from Charleston to Havana. All this has been done with the full knowledge of the Spanish government and of the local authorities. (See the instructions of Mr. Buchanan to Mr. Saunders, No. 16, and Mr. Saunder's dispatches to the department, Nos. 26, 27, 28, 33, 47, 49, and 51; see also copy of a letter from Mr. Campbell, United States consul at Havana, to Mr. Buchanan, dated November 17, 1847, which is hereto annexed.) These documents all refer to the Charleston line alone, but the New York and New Orleans line went into operation about the same time, and the same facilities have, it is understood, been extended by the local authorities to both lines.

The mails carried by the steamers are placed in the charge of an agent of the Post Office Department on board, and, on their arrival at Havana, are delivered to the postmaster of that place on his receipt, and the return mails are received from him.

On the 3d instant the Crescent City, one of the steamers employed in this service, on her voyage from New York to New Orleans, touched, as usual, at Havana to land the mail and the passengers (65 in number) destined for that port. She was not permitted to land or send the mail ashore, but was peremptorily ordered out of the harbor, although it was then threatening a gale.

This government has deferred taking any action in relation to the matter until the facts could be fully ascertained. This has been done. The reports of the acting consul at Havana, (the consul himself being then absent,) and of the captain of the steamer, have been received. From these documents, copies of which are hereto annexed, it appears that on the preceding voyage of the Crescent City to Havana—to wit: on the 4th day of September—the agents of the company (a commercial firm in that city) were informed, by a letter from the secretary of the Superior Civil Government, that an individual of the name of Wm. Smith, the purser of the vessel, had, on his arrival at New York from the preceding voyage, published the grossest calumnies against the government of the island; and that if that individual should thereafter return in any of the steamers of the company, or if any other person employed on board of them should venture to abuse, in a similar manner, the privileges granted by the Spanish authorities in the ports of the island, that fact alone should be sufficient to prevent the vessel which brought him from entering the port. No notice of this order was given to the American consul until the 21st of September, when a copy of the letter addressed by the Superior Civil Secretary to the agents of the company was sent to the acting consul by the Captain General, although in the interval between the two dates the steamer had arrived at Havana, and again departed for New York; consequently, the acting consul had no means of notifying this government of its existence in time for it to take any action in the matter before the return of the steamer to Havana; nor was any notice given to the government through the Spanish minister in this country. The consequence was, that the steamer returned to Havana with the obnoxious individual on board, and, as has already been stated, was prohibited from landing, On her return voyage from New Orleans to New York, and before this government was apprized of the fact, she again put into Havana to land the mail, and, for the same reason, was again denied permission to do so. You will observe, that the secretary of the Superior Civil Government, in his letter to Messrs. Drake & Co., the agents of the company, declares that it was the intention of the government to persist in the course adopted towards the Crescent City, and that if any person employed on board of one of the steamers of the company should commit a similar offence to that with which the purser of that vessel was charged, that fact alone would be a sufficient cause for excluding such steamer from the port.

It may be well to add, that Wm. Smith, the individual whose alleged calumnies against the government had occasioned these proceedings, has, since his return to this country, made oath that this charge is entirely unfounded, and that he has "never written or published anything against the government of the island of Cuba." (See copy of his affidavit, herewith enclosed, marked A.)

The President directs that you lose no time in communicating these facts to her majesty's government, and in expressing his surprise and regret that they should have occurred.

You will state that this government does not question the right of every nation to prescribe the conditions on which the vessels of other nations may be admitted into her ports. That, nevertheless, those conditions ought not to conflict with the received usages which regulate the commercial intercourse between civilized nations. That those usages are well known and long established, and no nation can disregard them without giving just cause of complaint to all other nations whose interests would be affected by their violation.

That the circumstance of an officer of a vessel having published, in his own country, matter offensive to a foreign government, does not, according to those usages, furnish a sufficient cause for excluding such vessel from the ports of the latter.

That, moreover, the Crescent City was at the time of this occurrence employed in the transportation of the mail, which is everywhere a matter of great public concern.

That, in this country, the duty of providing for this object, whether at home or abroad, devolves upon the executive branch of the government; and although it is invariably discharged not directly through its own officers, but through the medium of contracts with individuals, the government is responsible for the proper performance of this duty. Any measure, therefore, tending to impede its fulfilment, cannot be viewed as directed against the agents to whom its execution is intrusted, but against the government itself.

That the steamers employed in transporting the mail from this country to Havana, being in the employment of government, and placed by law, to a certain extent. under its control, partake, in some degree, of the character of public vessels.

That, although no positive arrangements exist between this government and that of Spain, relative to the mail service between their respective countries, that government was fully aware that mails were regularly conveyed from the United States to the city of Havana, and the local authorities, so far from objecting to this practice, had not only acquiesced in it for a series of years, but had, in various ways, sanctioned and encouraged it.

That, under these circumstances, this government had a right to expect, that if the Captain General of the island should see fit to impose new and unusual conditions upon the continuance of these mails, due notice of these conditions would be given to this government before proceeding to enforce the penalties attached to their non-observance. But before it was possible for this government to have any official knowledge of the Captain General's intentions, the mail was sent away, and the vessel that conveyed it was, in a manner unusually harsh and offensive, driven from the harbor. All this was done, not for any violation of the laws of nations, or of Spain, but for an act alleged to have been done by a subordinate employé of the company, in his own country, and of which there is every reason to believe he is entirely innocent.

That the President cannot but consider this proceeding, under all its circumstances, as not only a violation of the usages of civilized nations, and of the tacit understanding which may fairly be said to result from the long acquiescence of Spain in the transportation of a mail to Havana, but as an act of marked discourtesy to this government. If the Captain General thought that a vindication of his character, or his dignity, required that he should notice anonymous attacks made on his government by the newspapers of a foreign country, the means employed for that purpose should, at least, have been consistent with justice, the usages of nations, and the courtesy due to a friendly government. That some apology might have been found for it in the irritation caused by a supposed insult to the government; but that, from the letter of the Captain General to the acting consul of the United States, it would seem that it was the result of a deliberate policy, and that it was the determination of the government to apply to the mail steamers of the United States a system of treatment different from that which was applied to all other vessels.

The President will not permit himself for a moment to believe that her Majesty's government will sanction an order which amounts almost to a declaration of hostility to this government; but, on the contrary, confidently anticipates that it will receive its prompt and decided disapprobation. Should he be disappointed in this expectation, this government will then be called upon to determine what course a just sense of what is due to its own dignity and interests requires it to pursue.

In conclusion, you will remind her Majesty's government that in the efforts it has constantly made to restrain any portion of the inhabitants of this country from disturbing the peace of her Majesty's dominions, this government has unequivocally manifested its anxious desire to cultivate the most friendly relations with that of Spain. That an additional proof of this desire has recently been afforded by this government in making an exception to the usual practice of most nations, by taking steps towards indemnifying the subjects of her Majesty who had sustained losses by the acts of a mob in one of our cities. That, on the other hand, in the clemency extended by her Majesty towards a number of misguided citizens of this country, who had justly incurred the penalty of her laws, this government had beheld a gratifying evidence that these kind feelings were reciprocated by her Majesty's government.

You will assure her Majesty's government that this government is disposed to make every allowance for the distrust naturally engendered by past events, and for the desire of the local authorities to adopt all reasonable precautions to prevent their recurrence; but that if the measures recently adopted by them were designed for that purpose, they are calculated to defeat their own object, as they must manifestly tend not only to encourage those who are engaged in unlawful schemes against the island, but to awaken the just resentment of the sober and intelligent citizens of the country, and seriously to compromit the peace of the two nations.

I am, sir, very respectfully, your obedient servant,

C. M. CONRAD,
Acting Secretary.

D. M. Barringer, Esq., *&c., &c., Madrid.*

Consulate of the United States, Havana,
November 17, 1847.

Sir: On the evening of the 15th instant I had the honor of receiving your official communication of the 20th of October, which was brought by the ship Norma from New York. The subject of mail steamers shall, as you request, receive my best and most energetic attention. I had previously been unofficially informed of the contemplated enterprise, and set myself to ascertain what privileges would be conceded, and am authorized (as yet not officially) to say they will immediately be placed on the same footing with the British mail packet steamers. The concessions to the British steamers were obtained at Madrid by the English minister, when Espartero, the friend of England, was prime minister. I shall certainly use every effort to obtain still greater concessions than those already conceded, to wit:

1st. The steamers will be exempted from the payment of all the contributions always charged at the custom-house, in case they come and depart in ballast, or when they bring cargo that no operation is made upon.

2d. They are exempted from custom-house charges when they only land passengers, baggage, packages of samples, newspapers, and other effects of the same kind.

3d. When they import, export, or receive from on board other vessels, articles of commerce not exceeding three tons, of which, however, the respective duties must be paid.

4th. When they import, export, or take to or from other vessels merchandise exceeding three tons, they shall pay like other vessels the duties for visits, registering, and others established, likewise the tonnage and ponton dues on all free room, excepting that part occupied by the machinery and coal. The above I have over the signature of the intendente, but not communicated to *me* officially.

You will thus perceive that, for all purposes of mail steamers, the concessions are ample; as freighting vessels and common carriers, they would have to pay as such when laden. I shall, however, endeavor to obtain greater concessions, in conformity with your instructions, although such concessions would, as freighting ships, give them very great advantages over the sailing vessels and steamers engaged in the freighting of goods to and from the States, as a vessel paying $1 50 per ton could not compete with those passing free of tonnage dues.

I have the honor to be, with great respect and esteem, your most obedient servant,

ROBERT B. CAMPBELL.

Hon. JAMES BUCHANAN,
Secretary of State.

Mr. Morland to Mr. Conrad.

[No. 18.] CONSULATE OF THE UNITED STATES, HAVANA,
October 29, 1852.

SIR: Since my communication of the 23d instant, (No. 17,) nothing worthy of notice has occurred here.

The United States steam-frigate Powhatan, with the minister to Mexico and Commodore Newton on board, sailed yesterday morning for Vera Cruz.

Judge Conkling informed me that the affair of the mail steamer "Crescent City" had been arranged between him and the Captain General unofficially; that the steamer would be allowed on her arrival, even if she had Lieutenant Porter and Purser Smith on board, to land the mails and passengers, and also to receive both; but that neither the lieutenant nor the purser was to come on shore. But it is understood that neither of them is coming in the "Crescent City."

I have the honor to be, &c.,

JOHN MORLAND,
Acting Consul.

Hon. C. M. CONRAD,
Acting Secretary of State, &c., &c.

Mr. Conrad to Mr. Law.

DEPARTMENT OF STATE, WASHINGTON,
October 30, 1852.

SIR: Your letter of the 27th instant, has been received.

That of the 6th instant, to which it refers, was addressed to this department by Mr. M. O. Roberts.

In consequence of the information it contained, that gentleman was requested to repair to Washington. He did so, and had a long conversation with me in relation to the occurrences at Havana. He is therefore fully apprized that the subject has engaged the attention of the department.

I have only to add, in reply to your own letter, that, as soon as the department could obtain authentic information of the occurrences referred to, they were made the subject of a communication to the government of Spain. When an answer to that communication is received, it will probably be made public.

In the meantime, I must be excused from giving you any information or advice on the subject.

You may rest assured, however, that neither the honor nor the interests of the country will be neglected.

I am, sir, &c.

C. M. CONRAD,
Acting Secretary.

GEORGE LAW, Esq., *New York.*

Mr. Calderon to Mr. Conrad.

[Translation.]

LEGATION OF SPAIN IN WASHINGTON,
November 5, 1852.

His excellency the Captain General of the island of Cuba, Don Valentin Cañedo, informs the undersigned, in various communications lately received by him, of all that has passed with Captain Porter, of the Crescent City, on his entrance into Havana on the 14th day of October last, and on his presenting his second protest, dated the same day.

General Cañedo at the same time gives an account of the friendly and confidential interview which the honorable Judge Conkling had with him, while stopping at that port on his way to Mexico as envoy extraordinary and minister plenipotentiary from the United States to that republic.

In compliance with the request of the General, as well as with a view of making known the facts precisely as they occurred, the undersigned proceeds to give the honorable Mr. Conrad, Secretary of State *ad interim*, the substance of the above mentioned communications.

The Crescent City returned from New Orleans (after having been refused admission into Havana, from persisting to have on board the purser, Mr. Smith, on the 14th October last. The day had not yet dawned;

and, breaking through the custom observed by all ships, whether national or foreign, the Cresent City entered the bay, refusing to give any reply to the questions put to it from the Moro castle, concerning this proceeding, and the reasons for entering before daybreak, thus infringing the regulations of the port, known to all, and respected by all.

When it had cast anchor, the captain of the port made known that the ship must remain without communication with the shore, if the purser, Smith, were on board, although it might continue in the bay all the time which was considered necessary.

Señor Morales, representing the house of the consignees, Drake & Co., then presented himself to the Captain General, requesting permission, which was granted him, to go and speak to Captain Porter. A short time after, the said Mr. Morales returned, accompanied by the vice-consul of the United States, and informed the General that Captain Porter was bearer of a dispatch from his government to the said vice-consul which the latter also affirmed to the General, although referring to the testimony of Mr. Morales. His excellency consented that this dispatch should be received, out of respect to the government of the United States.

The Crescent City immediately took its departure, firing a gun as it passed the Moro castle—a demonstration which, although puerile and in bad taste, was considered significative and offensive.

The Cresent City having left the port, the vice-consul, Mr. Morland, addressed an official letter to the Captain General, dated this same 14th of October, in which he enclosed the second protest before mentioned of Captain Porter, who, in order to insure its reception, had employed this unworthy artifice, which the government of the United States will no doubt condemn. General Cañedo enclosed to the undersigned a copy of the said communication of the vice-consul, (translated,) in which is the following: "But I have to make known to your excellency, that Captain Porter could not have received dispatches in New Orleans from the government of the United States, because there was not sufficient time for him to have done so; *but that the mail agent in New Orleans received a telegraphic communication* containing the order that the Cresent City should go to Havana with the mail, and should deliver it, if permission were given to that effect; and if not, should continue her voyage to New York. This is what, I believe, was communicated by Captain Porter to Mr. Morales, *this order being from the Postmaster General of the United States, who is a member of the cabinet.* As these vessels carry the mail of the United States they are freighted accordingly, and the *officers* belong *exclusively* to the navy of the United States."

The undersigned leaves it entirely to the upright judgment of the Hon. Secretary to qualify as it deserves the stratagems employed by Captain Porter for insuring the reception by the Captain General of his irregular protest, and the assertions of the vice-consul, Mr. Morland.

Without making any commentary, or entering into any further details, it appears to the undersigned that the above is sufficient to justify the antipathy of the inhabitants of Havana towards Captain Porter, and the universal conviction which is there entertained that he is of the number of those who have proposed to themselves to bring about a misunderstanding between the two countries, notwithstanding the sincere desire of the governor of the island of Cuba not only to avoid all disagreement, but to preserve the most cordial harmony; a desire which his excellency repeatedly expresses in the most unequivocal and sincere manner in the communications alluded to by the undersigned. Nor will the Hon. Secretary of State be surprised, if, foreseeing some disagreeable occurrence in regard to Captain Porter and Purser Smith, arising from the public exasperation, however much this would be regretted by the General, and however severely he would punish its authors, that he should have earnestly desired the undersigned to endeavor to persuade this government that prudence and the friendly relations subsisting between both countries render it advisable that the irritation likely to be produced by the presence of these individuals in Havana should be avoided.

Of the attention and politeness with which General Cañedo has received the Hon. Judge Conkling, and of their non-official interviews and conversations, it is probable that the Hon. Secretary of State *ad interim* has already received circumstantial accounts. The undersigned having received from General Cañedo a detailed account of the conciliatory result of these interviews, under date of the 29th of last month, and believing that no abstract can give so clear an idea of the circumstances as his excellency's own communication, encloses herewith a literal copy of the dispatch for the Hon. Secretary of State.

The Hon. Secretary will observe that out of respect to the wishes of Judge Conkling, and to show his consideration to the government of the United States, and his high esteem for his excellency President Fillmore, the General has granted permission to the Crescent City, which left New York on the 27th, to disembark the passengers and the correspondence, but not to land either Captain Porter or Purser Smith, should they be on board; but with the understanding that this permission merely extends to this voyage of the 27th, unless, these obstacles being removed, the governor of the island may alter, as he is desirous to be able to do, his dispositions in regard to the Crescent City, without failing in the sacred duty imposed on him of maintaining tranquillity in the island, and of not permitting his authority to be despised.

The undersigned offers to the Hon. Mr. Conrad a renewed assurance of his distinguished consideration.

A. CALDERON DE LA BARCA.

Hon. C. M. CONRAD,
Secretary of State of the United States.

[Translation.]

SEAT OF GOVERNMENT OF THE ISLAND OF CUBA,
Havana, October 29, 1852.

MOST EXCELLENT SIR: The steamer Prometheus, which sailed from this port for New York on the 27th instant, at 4 o'clock in the afternoon, has taken out a parcel, under cover, to the Spanish consul at that port, whom I have directed to transmit the same to your excellency without delay, containing communications of mine, dated respectively the 22d and 27th, (this very day.)

Your excellency will have seen, by these communications, all that has taken place on the occasion of the second arrival of the Crescent City, and the confidential interview I had, on the 25th, with Judge Conkling, the appointed minister to Mexico.

I will then relate to your excellency the continuation of my intercourse with this diplomatic functionary, together with whatever the state of the question may suggest to me, both in regard to the conferences which have taken place here, and in relation to what your excellency has been pleased to say to me, in your polite communications of the 9th, 15th and 18th, which I received on the 27th, in order that your excellency may signify to the government of the United States my honest intention to preserve the friendly relations which the latter maintains with the government of Spain, and my firm determination at the same time, not to allow any want of what is due to this nation, on account of her power, perhaps not well understood, and, above all, on account of the good faith and generosity which characterize her proceedings with other friendly countries.

I told your excellency, in my communication of the 27th, aforementioned, that in order to avoid the effects of any mistake in regard to the true understanding of the reasons laid down in the conferences which I had held with Mr. Conkling, I had asked him to give me a small memorandum, without signature, recapitulating what he had stated to me in that conference; that on receiving this document I had noticed a certain reservation in regard to the censure he had cast on the reprehensible and inexcusable conduct of Mr. Porter, captain of the "Crescent City," during the interview, and that he had likewise omitted to mention the offer he had made to ask his government, although confidentially, for the withdrawal of said Porter. Being desirous to clear away all doubt, and to leave no room for concealment, I sent to entreat the Hon. Mr. Conkling that he would have the kindness to come to see me. He did so the day before yesterday, and when I had informed him of the difference I had noticed between his conversation and his written statement, he replied to me, that notwithstanding the want of explicitness in the latter, on those points to which I have alluded, his fixed determination was to ask his government for the removal of Porter, whose conduct he had pronounced, and still designated, as *reprehensible* and *inexcusable*. I said to him, in return, that in order to avoid all complication and disagreement between what had been spoken and written, I thought it better for him to withdraw the memorandum, if there was no obstacle to his doing so; and having cheerfully acceded to my proposition on his part, I proceeded to inform him, that according to what was stated in a confidential letter of your excellency of the 19th, neither Porter nor Smith would return to Havana, as it had been declared by the American Secretary of State, whose assurances to this effect were moreover confirmed in a telegraphic despatch which was sent from Washington to Charleston on the 23d, and brought here by the captain of the Isabel. His reply to this was, that such measure would harmonize with the system of government pursued by President Fillmore; adding, "that it was full time these individuals should retire into private life, as they had been the cause of sufficient mischief."

Notwithstanding this, he said to me, that in order to avoid all conflict for the future, and in case—which was not a probable occurrence—the "Crescent City," whose departure from New York was announced for the 27th, should have those individuals on board, he begged that I would have the condescension to allow, for this time only, the passengers and the mail to land, although I should prohibit the crew, comprising the persons in question, from landing likewise, because, in doing so, I would not only prevent any injury being done to commerce and to the passengers, but that I would lessen the embarrassment which these occurrences were occasioning to his government. Mr. Conkling being entitled to some civility, on account of your excellency's especial recommendation, and even to my sympathy for his judicious and upright deportment during his interviews with me, and with a view, also, of not increasing the difficulties which at this moment harass the worthy President Fillmore, I promised that his wishes should be complied with; but I took good care to remark to him, that neither Captain Porter nor Purser Smith would be allowed to land at Havana—that my agreement to allow the mail and passengers to land would be for this occasion only, in case the government should not have had time to forward instructions in relation to them; and that after that, I should enforce my original measures, adopted, as they have been, after a thorough examination of what it behooves me to do for the security of the island, and in virtue of the indisputable rights with which the authority I exercise has been invested.

The Hon. Mr. Conkling evinced his appreciation of the act by many expressions of gratitude, and went away from me satisfied, and yesterday he sailed once more for his destination.

In thus making your excellency minutely acquainted with what has passed, I desire, in the first instance, to show my respect for the actual government of the United States, my deference for an old and respected diplomatic functionary, who has come here, in a confidential mauner, to obtain a thorough knowledge of the disagreeable occurrences of the past, and finally to make known that if the Mail Steam Company, abusing my forbearance in these considerate proceedings, should again send to this place the persons who have been the cause of these lamentable evils, I shall be compelled to sustain the dignity which has been conferred upon me by her Majesty the Queen, by positively prohibiting the entrance into this port of the "Crescent City."

God preserve you, &c.

VALENTIN CAÑEDO.

The Most Excellent
MINISTER PLENIPOTENTIARY AND ENVOY EXTRAORDINARY
of her Majesty in Washington.

Mr. Sharkey to the Secretary of State.

[Extracts.]

[No 19.] CONSULATE OF THE UNITED STATES, HAVANA,
November 8, 1852.

SIR: During my absence Mr. Morland kept you advised of the condition of our relations with this island. Having no dispatches to reply to, I can only inform you what has occurred since my return on the 30th ultimo, which was duly announced to you. On my arrival Mr. Morland informed me that Judge Conkling, our minister to Mexico, had called here on the business of the difficulty with the steamer Crescent City, and that a temporary arrangement had been entered into betwen the Judge and the Captain General, by which that vessel should be permitted to land her mails and passengers and receive others, but that neither Captain Porter nor Purser Smith should be permitted to land. This arrangement, however, was understood to be but a suspension of the prohibition which had existed towards that vessel. The Crescent City arrived in this harbor on the 2d instant with Purser Smith on board, under the command of H. R. Davenport, esq., and was permitted to land her mails and passengers. Soon after her arrival I had the honor of an interview with the Captain General, in which his excellency stated to me the purport of the agreement with Judge Conkling, but said it only extended to the present visit of the ship, and that, as Purser Smith was still on board, she could not be allowed a similar privilege on her return from New Orleans, unless he could be assured that Smith should not be in her. His excellency expressed much surprise that the purser was still retained, after the assurances given by the Secretary of State to the Spanish minister at Washington. He stated to me that he had received a communication from the Spanish minister to this effect: that the Secretary of State had assured the minister, in the most positive terms, that Smith should not return on the vessel, and authorized the minister to make that statement known to the Captain General. This letter was exhibited, and that portion of it translated by my secretary. Deeming this fact one of importance, I forwarded a statement by the Crescent City, to be communicated to you by telegraph from New Orleans. I was not prepared to reply to this intelligence, and could only suggest to his excellency that probably Smith was not an officer of the government, and therefore not subjected to its control, which I afterwards learned to be true, as he was there by contract with the owner of the vessel. I informed Captain Davenport of what had occurred, and stated to him what might be expected on his return. I cannot be positively certain whether his excellency said the ship should not enter the harbor, or only that she should hold no communication with the shore. My secretary is under the impression that he only intended to interdict communication with the shore. The difference, however, seems to be of little consequence. This affair has produced a very unpleasant state of things, and I have only to hope that the government will give it prompt attention.

* * * * * * * * *

I herewith forward a copy of a letter from Mr. Morland to the commander of the Crescent City, and one from Mr. Morland to me, together with a note from the Captain General. I had not time to prepare this dispatch to be forwarded *via* New Orleans by the Crescent City, but avail myself of the earliest opportunity which will be afforded by the Black Warrior.

I have the honor to be your obedient servant,

W. L. SHARKEY.

To the Hon. SECRETARY OF STATE
of the United States.

CONSULATE OF THE UNITED STATES, HAVANA,
November 1, 1852.

SIR: I have to advise you that Judge Conkling, who called here on the business of the steamship "Crescent City," has come to an understanding with the Captain General on the difficulties lately existing in relation to that ship, which is arranged so that that vessel may enter port, deliver her passengers and mails, receive others in return, and proceed as usual heretofore; but that Captain Porter and William Smith, esq., shall not land here. I give you this information for your government; and am

Your most obedient servant,

JNO. MORLAND, *Acting Consul.*

To the COMMANDER
of the United States Mail Steamer "Crescent City."

HAVANA, *November* 4, 1852.

DEAR SIR: In answer to your note of this morning, I have to say that I had no occasion, and therefore did not see his excellency the Captain General after the departure of the Powhatan, and therefore did not receive from him anything on the subject relative to the "Crescent City;" but Judge Conkling informed me that he had arranged the matter with the Captain General, and that the "Crescent City" was to be admitted with Captain Porter and Mr. Smith on board, who were not to land, but that the mails and passengers were. He added that it was a suspension of his former order, but named no limits.

I remain yours,

JNO. MORLAND.

Hon. JUDGE SHARKEY.

P. S.—Judge Conkling said that the Captain General had suggested the necessity of writing a letter, or rather that Commodore Newton should do so, to Captain Porter, to be delivered to him, explaining the arrangement, which was not done, as I understand from the harbor-master.

[Translation.]

HAVANA, *November* 2, 1852.

[SEAL.]

To the captain of this port I have said, under yesterday's date, the following:

"In view of the friendly explanations that have been given me, when he touched at this port, by Mr. Conkling, minister plenipotentiary of the republic of the United States near Mexico, for the remote case that the steamer 'Crescent City' might still make one voyage, having on board Mr. Porter as captain, and Mr. Smith as supercargo, that I should condescend to permit the landing of her passengers and mails, I have deemed it proper to accede to his wishes, as a proof of consideration to his person and to the respectable recommendations he was the bearer of. You will, therefore, should the case referred to occur, which is not probable, allow the passengers and mails to land, but with the express prohibition that it should be done by Smith or Porter, whose conduct I have qualified as notoriously suspicious for the security of this island; and I must add to your lordship that this concession is understood to relate only to the next voyage of the said steamer."

And I communicate it to your lordship for your information, and the effects it may be useful for.

God preserve your lordship many years.

VALENTIN CAÑEDO.

Señor CONSUL OF THE UNITED STATES *in this place.*

Mr. Everett to Mr. Maxwell.

DEPARTMENT OF STATE,
Washington, November 13, 1852.

SIR: Official information has been received at this department that there is a law or regulation of the island of Cuba forbidding the entrance of any vessel into the port of Havana after nightfall, and before a certain hour in the morning; and that it is the duty of the officers stationed in the Moro castle to fire upon any vessel attempting to enter the port in violation of this regulation or law. On the occasion of the arrival of the "Crescent City," on the 14th ultimo, she entered the port within the prohibited hours, notwithstanding, as is alleged, that she was hailed three times, and required to desist.

The sentinels, whose particular duty it was to fire upon a vessel under these circumstances, have been imprisoned for failing to perform their duty on this occasion; and the Governor General of the island informed Mr. Conkling, the American minister to Mexico, on his visit to the island, that he had given peremptory orders, that should an attempt again be made by the commander of the "Crescent City" to enter the port of Havana at an unlawful hour, she should be fired upon from the Moro. The President requests that you would bring these facts to the knowledge of the owners of the "Crescent City."

I am also directed to inform you that the Spanish minister has communicated to the department a copy of a letter from the Governor General of Cuba to himself, from which it appears that the suspension of the order of the Governor General, forbidding the entrance into the port of Havana of the "Crescent City," if Lieutenant Porter or Purser Smith should be on board, was not designed by the Governor General to be a permanent suspension, as understood by Mr. Conkling, but to apply only to the then next expected arrival of that vessel. You will also be pleased to inform the owners of this correspondence.

I am, sir, &c., &c.,

EDWARD EVERETT.

HUGH MAXWELL, Esq.,
Collector of the Customs at New York.

Mr. Everett to Mr. Calderon.

DEPARTMENT OF STATE,
Washington, November 15, 1852.

SIR: You have already, I believe, been informed that this department had reason to think that the information received by the Governor General of Cuba, relative to Purser Smith of the "Crescent City," was erroneous. To show you, in a perfectly satisfactory and authentic manner, that such is the fact, I take the liberty to enclose you a copy of an affidavit made by Mr. Smith, in which he disclaims, in the amplest terms, everything that has been laid to his charge. A copy of this document has been already transmitted to Mr. Barringer, to be communicated to her Majesty's government.

In the mean time, as the sole objection to the abrogation of the order of his excellency the Governor General, of the 4th September, is understood to be the want of a personal assurance on the part of Mr. Smith that he is entirely innocent of the matters laid to his charge, I persuade myself that your excellency, by communicating this document to the Governor General, will enable him, without delay, to restore the intercourse with the island to its accustomed amicable footing.

I avail myself of this occasion, sir, to renew to you the assurance of my distinguished consideration.

EDWARD EVERETT.

Señor Don A. CALDERON DE LA BARCA,
&c., &c., &c.

Mr. Kennedy to Mr. Everett.

NAVY DEPARTMENT,
November 16, 1852.

SIR: In compliance with the request contained in your communication of 13th instant, to be furnished with a copy of the statement of Captain Porter, of the United States mail steamer Crescent City, relative to his conduct in the recent refusal of the Spanish authorities of the island of Cuba to permit that vessel to land her passengers or mail at the port of Havana, I have the honor to transmit herewith an additional copy of said statement, it being the third which has been furnished by this department.

I have the honor to be, sir, with high respect, &c.,

JOHN P. KENNEDY.

Hon. Edw. Everett,
Secretary of State.

Saturday, *October* 24, 1852.

Sir: Agreeably to your order, "that I should communicate to you in writing a statement of the events which lately took place in Havana in relation to the steamship Crescent City," I have the honor to give herein a detailed statement of facts as they occurred:

I sailed from New York on the 27th of August for New Orleans, *via* the Havana, anticipating no difficulty of any kind, and arrived in Havana on the 3d of September; was boarded by the health officer, custom-house officer, and police officers, who examined the passports, and the ship admitted all the privileges of the port; two hours after I anchored, and while asleep in my cabin, one of the police officers entered my room, and informed me that it was the Captain General's order that Mr. Smith, purser of the ship, should not be permitted to go on shore. Not being perfectly awake at the time, I did not ask the reason why Mr. Smith could not go on shore, but simply replied that I would attend to it. I accordingly gave Mr. Smith an order not to go on shore, intending to obtain further information on the subject; but the ship's sailing soon after, drove the matter from my mind. On my arrival at New Orleans, I saw an extract from the "Diario de la Marina," (the government paper,) accusing Mr. Smith of writing calumnies against the Captain General, and accusing him of having written them over his own signature. This explained to me the cause of Mr. Smith's not being permitted to go on shore. I returned to Havana on the 14th of September, and after being at anchor for a short time, the captain of the port came alongside in the health boat, and after the usual courtesies were passed, the captain of the port desired to see our shipping articles, which I ordered Mr. Smith to bring to me: after looking down the list, the captain of the port came to Mr. Smith's name, and in rather an irritable manner ordered the person to be kept on board the ship. I asked of what particular offence he had been guilty. He replied, in a passionate manner, that he could not go on shore.

I informed him that the order should be obeyed, and asked him if he had any further commands. He said he would like to see Mr. Smith; the latter person was alongside of me at the time, and I pointed him out, when the captain of the port, in a great state of excitement, not at all called for by the occasion, called up the police boat, and in a loud voice ordered the police officer to "mark Mr. Smith," meaning, to notice him well. I asked if he desired anything further with Mr.

Smith, and on receiving a negative reply, I retired up the ship' side, somewhat astonished at the injustice and want of courtesy of Spanish officials. One hour after this occurred, I received a communication from the house of Drake, enclosing an order from Martin Galliano, the political secretary, informing me that no vessel belonging to the company would be permitted to enter the port of Havana with Mr. Smith on board, or any other person who made use of his position in the line to write abusive articles against the Captain General, and informing me, at the same time, that a police officer would be detailed on board the "Crescent City" to watch over Mr. Smith. I immediately wrote to Mr. Drake, and assured him, on the honor of an officer, that Mr. Smith had never written or composed any article against the Captain General in the newspapers of the United States. I informed them, at the same time, that under the circumstances of the case, I would not permit any police officer to remain on board the ship for the purpose of taking charge of any officer; that I intended to sail at 4 o'clock, and that they would be held responsible if they attempted to prevent me. I sailed at the usual hour without molestation, and concluded that my disavowal had been satisfactory. On my return to New York I laid the matter before the company, assuring them at the same time that Mr. Smith was perfectly innocent of the accusation, and explained to them how the charge against Mr. Smith originated, viz: from the accusation of the correspondent of the "Diario de la Marina." I beg leave to state here that Mr. Smith is an old man, sixty years of age, and is retained in his position more owing to his great integrity of character, than from any abilities he may possess for the arduous and intricate duties of his station. It was at my solicitation that he was originally ordered to the "Crescent City," and I desired to have him from the fact that he attended solely to his own duties, meddling with nothing which did not relate to them, and assumed no responsibility without consulting me.

I sailed again from New York on the 27th September, and arrived at Havana on the evening of the 3d of October; it was blowing a gale of wind at the time; and as I knew no boat could come far enough outside to us to get a pilot from, I made no signal for one, but stood into the harbor. Near the mouth of the harbor the pilot was waiting for us; I ran close to him, slowed the engine, and hove him a rope, but, owing to the high sea, he failed to get hold of it. Close to the pilot boat, and fast to the buoy, was the health boat, inside of which I recognised the captain of the port, who made signal to me to back out, which signal I paid no attention to. As I passed him he ordered me "to stop the ship," which I refused to do, as it was a very dangerous place to stop a ship in, and within fifty feet of a reef of rocks on our lee-beam.

I accordingly proceeded to my usual anchorage within. I was followed by the captain of the port; when he came alongside, he demanded why I did not stop the ship at the mouth of the harbor when he ordered me. I replied, that it was not a proper place to stop a ship in, especially a steamer with a single engine. The explanation seemed satisfactory. He then demanded to see the ship's articles; and on seeing the name of Mr. Smith, he told me to proceed to sea at once, by the Captain General's order. I asked him if he had not received my letter disavowing the charge made against Mr. Smith; he said yes, that the letter had been received, but that I must go to sea at once. I told him I must make my protest to the American consul, and I refused to lift my anchor until I had done so. After some discussion, the captain of the port concluded to take my protest to the Captain General; but it was returned to me again, with a message that it must be sent through the consul. I accordingly sent it to the consul by our agent, who was permitted to come alongside to get the communication. After sunset, the captain of the port again came alongside, and informed me that the consul was some distance out of town, that the Captain General had not time to answer my communication that night, and that I must proceed to sea at once. I represented to him the great responsibility of so treating a ship on such frivolous charges, pointed out to him the breach of faith with the passengers who came to Havana with passports from the Spanish consul at New York, and also the inconvenience to the community from the non-deliverance of the mails. I received no satisfaction on these points. My mails and passengers were refused; and finding no hopes of communicating with the consul, I proceeded to sea, with every appearance of a gale of wind, and blowing so fresh at the time in the harbor that I had to cut the cable by which the vessel was secured to the buoy, as they offered me no assistance to cast it off. A pilot was offered me, but I declined it.

Previous to my sailing from New Orleans, I received instructions from the company's agent, by telegraph, to proceed to Havana and offer the mails; and if they were refused, to extend my protest and return to New York without delay.

I accordingly proceeded to Havana, where I arrived on the 14th of October, at daylight, was permitted to enter, and anchored in my usual place. The captain of the port came alongside, and on finding Mr. Smith on board, informed me that the vessel was "incommunicado;" that is, not allowed communication; that we would not be turned out of the harbor, but that no intercourse of any kind would be allowed.

I requested permission to send a protest to the consul, which was positively refused. We were then surrounded by guard-boats, and I ordered the steam to be let off, intending to remain some time to see what turn matters would take. Seeing that I had no intention of going to sea, two guard-boats were detailed from a frigate, preventing the approach of any boats towards the Crescent City. At 9 o'clock, Mr. Morales, of the house of Drake & Co., came alongside. I informed him that I had letters for him from the company, which ought to satisfy the Spanish authorities, but that I was not to deliver them. He asked me if I had made an explanation. I told him yes, and assured him that Mr. Smith was perfectly innocent of any offence, of which opinion he was himself. He then suggested that Mr. Smith should write direct to the Captain General, denying the charges against him. He said no official communication had been made to the Spanish government. I told him that I had made an official communication, which had received no attention. He said my communications were not considered official, but that from Mr. Smith would be.

I told him that my instructions were to present a protest, which was all I desired to do, and that I thought the protest would satisfy them on all points, as I had stated plainly all the grounds of complaint, and again disavowed the offence on Mr. Smith's account, or rather referred in it to my two former disavowals. This Mr. Morales seemed satisfied with, and proceeded to the shore, where, through his influence, the American consul was permitted to come alongside, in charge of the captain of the port, accompanied by an interpreter. I presented my protest to him in person, and he advised me to go to sea at once, as nothing more could be done with the authorities. I accordingly got under way at once, and proceeded to sea; hoisted the American flag at the fore, and fired a gun as I passed the Moro.

These are the exact circumstances connected with the matter. Of course, sir, I cannot describe the feelings or the expression of the different parties, which add weight to circumstances of this kind. Suffice it to say that the conduct of the Spanish authorities was unfriendly in the extreme. The conduct of officials, it is true, was more courteous towards the last; but it could not have been otherwise with people boasting of anything like civilization, for my conduct towards them throughout the whole difficulty, until I got under way, was courteous and respectful in the extreme, as I determined to give them no cause of complaint.

I have herein confined myself to the simple facts; but will take this occasion to say that I have always been instructed by the company to cultivate the most friendly feelings with the Spanish authorities; and I take pleasure in saying that I believe, up to the present time, I have succeeded in accomplishing the task imposed on me; for, in the trying and exciting times of the Lopez expedition, it required almost superhuman patience to submit to all their uncalled-for exactions.

I have the honor to remain, very respectfully, your obedient servant,

DAVID D. PORTER,
Lieutenant U. S. Navy.

Hon. J. P. KENNEDY,
Secretary of the Navy.

[Translation.]

HAVANA, *September* 4, 1852.

An individual named William Smith, who it appears is employed on board the steamship "Crescent City," has published, on his last voyage to New York, the most gross calumnies against the government of this island, and has taken advantage of the frank hospitality that is extended to all foreigners, to give the greater appearance of truth to his falsehoods.

This conduct, which the whole world will be able to qualify with its true colors, has attracted very seriously the attention of his excellency the Governor Captain General, whose elevated position places him so high above all such vile attacks against his administration, that he will not stoop for a moment to refute them; but he considers it a duty to make the author feel that the government will not permit such acts to be committed with impunity.

In consequence thereof he has given orders that, on the instant arrival of the Crescent City in this port, there will be placed on board an agent of the police, with the exclusive charge of Mr. Smith, to prevent him from leaving the ship; and the order of his excellency is transmitted to you, prohibiting in future the return of this individual in any of the company's ships, or any other person who will lend himself to abuse the frankness which the Spanish authorities offer in the ports of the island. The fact of such persons being on board will be sufficient to prevent the entrance of the vessel into the harbor—no matter how much the interests of the company may be affected or injured by the proceeding.

They have it in their power to prevent abuses by their subordinates; their honor and their interests should make them withdraw their confidence from persons who compromise them by their conduct.

M. GALLIANO.

New York, *September* 19, 1852.

Sir: I enclose you a communication I received from Messrs. Drake and company. I translate it from the original.

You will see that Mr. Smith is accused of writing injurious reports against the Spanish government. I assure you that Mr. Smith has never written a line against them; and the whole thing has originated in the correspondent of the "Diario de la Marina," a Spanish paper, in which Mr. Smith's name is put to the letter of somebody else.

I enclose you also my letter in reply to the communication and refusing to have a police officer on board to take charge of any of the company's officers.

They acted beyond their authority, aud they know it. They have once or twice attempted arbitrary measures with me, which I considered it best for the interests of the company to prevent by a firm and decided refusal to submit; and I never had cause to regret the course I pursued, as I have felt the benefit of it in not being subjected to petty annoyances which have been put upon other ships. Never having had any instructions from the company on the subject I acted as my reason dictated.

Very respectfully, &c.,

DAVID D. PORTER,
Lieutenant U. S. Navy.

M. O. Roberts, Esq.,
Agent U. S. Mail Steamship Company.

Office of the U. S. Mail Steamship Company,
New York, September 27, 1852.

Dear Sir: Your letter of the 19th inst., enclosing a communication from Messrs. Drake & Co., with a manifesto from the authorities of Havana, translated by yourself, and a copy of your replies thereto, was duly received.

Being satisfied that Mr. Smith, purser of the Crescent City, has done nothing which ought to subject him to censure, this company approves fully of your course in relation to the matter while at Havana, and of the tenor of your reply, through Messrs. Drake & Co., to the Cuban authorities.

Mr. Smith, so far as I can ascertain, has written nothing for any newspapers here or elsewhere, nor communicated anything at any time that ought to give offence to the Spanish authorities; and the allegation that he has done so I am satisfied is a mistake or a misrepresentation. He ought not to be held responsible for the newspaper publications, which are generally the repetitions of what the news collectors obtain from other sources, with such additions and comments as they choose to make, and which are entirely beyond the control of this company or of any of its agents or officers.

Mr. Smith is one of our most quiet, inoffensive, and faithful officers; and we ought not to consent to remove or discharge him when satisfied that he is innocent of any attempt to interfere with the Cuban government or to misrepresent it.

It has always been the policy of this company to avoid giving any offence by any interference in the affairs of other governments. They have uniformly so instructed all their commanders and officers of their ships, and I am happy to believe that such instructions have been most satisfactorily carried out.

Employed by the government of the United States in the transportation of its mails, it has been felt to be the duty of the company, and of the commanders of their ships, while they were careful to protect their agents and employés in their persons or property from undeserved suspicion, to impress upon them the necessity of avoiding any interference in the affairs of the government of Cuba or the authorities of Havana, or of affording any ground of complaint on their part. This I take the occasion to repeat for the government of your own course and for that of the officers and those under your command.

Very respectfully, yours, &c.,

M. O. ROBERTS.

Captain D. D. PORTER,
Commanding Steamship Crescent City.

UNITED STATES OF AMERICA, *Southern District of New York.* } *ss.*

I, William Smith, purser of the United States mail steamship Crescent City, being duly sworn, depose and say that the allegation contained in a certain order or manifesto, signed "M. Galliano," an officer of the government of the island of Cuba, and dated at Havana, the 4th day of September, 1852, and repeated in the official paper at Havana, that I had "published the most gross calumnies against the government of said island," and the further allegation, which I understand has been made unofficially to the government of the United States, that I had held communication with disaffected persons in the port of Havana, in the island of Cuba, and had been the bearer of letters or messages to and from such persons, are all utterly without foundation. I have never written or published anything against the government of the said island of Cuba; nor have I ever carried letters or messages to and from disaffected persons in said island, or had any communication with such persons, or in any manner interfered with the affairs of the said island, or the proceedings of its authorities. I have confined myself strictly to the discharge of the duties of purser of the ship, and have demeaned myself accordingly. Furthermore, it has been the express command of Capt. Porter, and of the Mail Steamship Company, that no officer or person employed on the ships should be allowed to carry letters outside of the mail, other than those belonging to the ship's business; and when letters have been sent on the steamer after the mails have been closed and received on board, they have been placed in the charge of the purser, and in all cases delivered to the postmaster in Havana. I also further depose and say, that I have never been in any manner connected with any association or expedition for hostile purposes, in relation to the island of Cuba, or for annoying, assisting, or interfering with its authorities.

WILLIAM SMITH.

Sworn to the 21st day of October, 1852, before me.

JOSEPH BRIDGHAM,
U. S. Commissioner Southern Dist. of New York.

NEW YORK, *October* 27, 1852.

SIR: I have the honor to enclose to you the communication from Mr. Galliano, the letter I received from the company on my last trip to Havana, and a copy of an affidavit (the original is sent to the Hon. Secretary of State) made by Mr. Smith, denying every species of charge brought against him. I also enclose you two articles cut from the Herald, which are the only articles relating to Cuba to be found in the papers at that time. They are evidently the articles alluded to by the correspondent of the government paper, and it will be seen at once that one is an editorial notice, and the other a letter from some one in the Havana.

I have the honor to remain, very respectfully, &c.,

DAVID D. PORTER,
Lieut. U. S. Navy.

Hon. J. P. KENNEDY,
Secretary of the Navy.

Mr. Calderon to Mr. Everett.

[Translation.]

WASHINGTON, *November* 17, 1852.

The undersigned has had the honor to receive the communication addressed to him by the Secretary of State under date the 15th inst., accompanied by a copy of the deposition, under oath, of Purser William Smith; and will transmit a copy of both documents to the Captain General of Cuba by the next opportunity, that of the steamer Ysabel, which will start from Charleston on the 22d instant.

The undersigned begs the honorable Edward Everett to accept the assurances of his most distinguished consideration.

A. CALDERON DE LA BARCA.

Hon. EDWARD EVERETT, &c., &c., &c.

Mr. Sharkey to Mr. Everett.

[No. 20.] CONSULATE OF THE UNITED STATES, HAVANA, *November* 17, 1852.

SIR: Since my dispatch No. 19, of the 8th inst., I have to inform you that the steamer Crescent City, from New Orleans, arrived in this port yesterday. Notwithstanding the previous determination of the authorities here that she should hold no communication with the shore, the order was again suspended, and free communication was allowed her. The captain of the port, however, informed Capt. Davenport that she would positively be excluded on her return from New York, if Purser Smith should be on board. In addition to this, the Captain General has made a written communication to the same effect to the house of Drake & Co., the consignees, a translated copy of which I herewith forward. A copy of that communication was also handed to Capt. Davenport, as I understand. I must presume this order will be enforced. It is hoped that prompt attention will be given to this matter; and, if I may be allowed to make a suggestion, it seems to me that the most decisive policy is required with this people, if we wish to avoid like difficulties hereafter. There is no abatement in the excitement which prevails here since my last dispatch. On the contrary, late events seem to have increased it. The condition of things is quite unsettled, and commerce much depressed in consequence of it. I am yet without advices from the government; and it is proper for me to say, that I have made no efforts to induce the Captain General to recede from his position in regard to the Crescent City, as I saw nothing that could justly call for such intercession on my part.

I have the honor to be, with great respect, your obedient servant,

WM. L. SHARKEY.

Hon. EDWARD EVERETT,
Secretary of State of the United States.

[Translation.]

POLITICAL SECRETARY'S OFFICE, 1ST SECTION.
Havana, November 16, 1852.

Notwithstanding that there remains in full force and vigor the order of his excellency the Governor Captain General, which I communicated to you on the 4th day of September last, to the effect that the return to this island of Mr. William Smith, an employé of the American steamer Crescent City, and the entrance of this vessel in the port, should she convey him, was forbidden, as a doubtful interpretation might be given to the special concession that his excellency has made on the last voyage of said vessel to New Orleans, and on that of her return to this port, which she has to-day effected—a concession founded on special reasons, of which his excellency the minister plenipotentiary of her Majesty in Washington has knowledge—his excellency instructs me to say to you that, in future, the order aforesaid will be enforced; to the end that, being informed, as you now are, of this particular, you make it known to whom it may concern, and avoid that, in consequence of a bad understanding, third persons be injured.

God preserve you many years.

MARTIN GALLIANO.

Messrs. DRAKE & Co.,
Consignees of the American Steamer Crescent City.

Mr. Sharkey to the Secretary of State.

[*By* telegraph.—Dated Havana, Nov. 17, 1852; received at Washington Nov. 27, 1852.]

To Honorable Secretary of State:

The steamer Crescent City was permitted to have free intercourse with the shore, but will be positively excluded on her return from New York. An order to that effect has been given to Captain Davenport by the captain of the port; and also a written notice to the consignees from the Captain General.

W. L. SHARKEY,
Consul United States.

Mr. Everett to Mr. Sharkey.

[No. 18.]

DEPARTMENT OF STATE,
Washington, November 30, 1852.

SIR: Your several dispatches to No. 20 have been duly received. You will have derived from public sources of information a knowledge of passing events.

It has been a matter of extreme regret to the President that the commercial intercourse between the island of Cuba and the United States should be interrupted by a misunderstanding like that which at present exists. The President does not question the right of the Captain General to prohibit the entrance into the island of any person whose presence he may think dangerous. That right, of course, ought to be exercised on reasonable grounds. In the present case the Governor General seems to have acted on misinformation; the purser of the "Crescent City" having made affidavit that he is entirely innocent of the matters laid to his charge. I placed a copy of this affidavit in the hands of Mr. Calderon, the Spanish minister here, and it was forwarded by him to the Captain General by the Isabel steamer, which sailed on the 20th.

If it is true, as we have been informed, that the Governor General has offered to revoke his order of the 4th of September relative to Purser Smith, provided he would disclaim the authorship of the calumnious articles laid to his charge, this affidavit would seem entirely to fulfil that condition. Mr. Calderon shares this opinion; and I cannot but think, that in furnishing the Governor General with a copy of the affidavit alluded to, this government has afforded to him ample ground for rescinding the above-mentioned order without discredit; in fact, that justice requires him to do so.

With respect to the refusal to permit passengers or the mail to be landed from any vessel having Purser Smith on board, or even to permit it to enter the harbor, the President considers that the Captain General has gone far beyond any necessity of the case, and has consequently taken a step of which this government has a right to complain. It wears the aspect of a purely vindictive measure, inflicting an injury on parties in no degree implicated in the supposed offence. The Governor General would be authorized by the law of nations to forbid the landing of the passengers and the mails from the United States if he thought them dangerous to the public safety of the island; but that he entertains no such apprehension is sufficiently apparent from the fact that this prohibition is extended to no other steamer, and has even been repeatedly relaxed in favor of the vessel having Purser Smith on board.

The President has accordingly felt it his duty to direct our minister at Madrid to address an earnest remonstrance to the government of her Catholic Majesty, on the subject of an interruption of the commercial intercourse between the island of Cuba and the United States, for a reason so entirely inadequate; and he entertains no doubt that due regard will be paid by the government of her Catholic Majesty to these representations.

The President strongly disapproves the course of the steamer company in persisting in sending a person in a mail steamer whose presence they are assured will prevent the mails from being received. He considers this course unwise in itself, and calculated only to embarrass the government in the discharge of its duties. An order has accordingly been given to the postmaster of New York not to furnish the mails to be carried by any steamer subject to this prohibition.

We are quite aware, of course, that no diplomatic relations exist between yourself and the Captain General. As you have, however, occasional opportunities of informal conference with him, you are at liberty to make any use of the information contained in this letter which you may think calculated to remove the existing inconveniences.

I am, sir, &c.,

EDWARD EVERETT.

Wm. L. Sharkey, Esq.
United States Consul, Havana.

Mr. Sharkey to Mr. Everett.

[Extract.]

CONSULATE OF THE UNITED STATES,
Havana, December 1, 1852.

SIR: Being without dispatches to reply to, I have only to inform you of events that have transpired since my dispatch of the 17th ultimo. The difficulty which heretofore existed in reference to the steamer Crescent City seems to be ended. The Captain General has issued an order, founded on dispatches received by him from the Spanish minister at Washington, that all obstacles in the way of her landing have been removed.

* * * * * * * * * * *

With great respect, your obedient servant,

W. L. SHARKEY.

Hon. EDWARD EVERETT,
Secretary of State.

Mr. Everett to Mr. Barringer.

[No. 66.] DEPARTMENT OF STATE,
Washington, December 4, 1852.

SIR: I transmit herewith a copy of a note addressed by me, a short time since, to the Spanish minister here, enclosing a copy of the affidavit of Purser Smith. I also transmit, for your information, a copy of a letter to Mr. Sharkey, consul of the United States at Havana.

I have the satisfaction to inform you that telegraphic messages were received last evening, from Baltimore and New York, conveying the information that the affidavit of Purser Smith had been deemed satisfactory by the Captain General of Cuba, and that he had withdrawn the order prohibiting passengers and the mail to be landed from any vessel having him on board.

The President recognises with pleasure this proof of the desire of the Captain General to relieve the commercial intercourse between Cuba and the United States from the embarrassment growing out of this unfortunate affair.

While the President does full justice to the conciliatory temper manifested by the Captain General in withdrawing the prohibition, and is also duly sensible to the liberal treatment extended generally by the Captain General to the mail steamers of the United States, he remains of the opinion originally expressed in the dispatch of Mr. Secretary Conrad of the 28th of October, that the course at first pursued by the Captain General in this unpleasant affair was matter of just complaint on the part of this government.

In your communications with the government of her Catholic Majesty, you will not fail to impress them with a due sense of the firmness and good faith with which the President has resisted the spirit of unlawful adventure against the island of Cuba. As a striking proof of this, I enclose you a copy of a private letter recently addressed by him to the collector of New York. I send it, for convenience, in a printed form.

I am, sir, respectfully, your obedient servant,

EDWARD EVERETT.

D. M. Barringer, Esq., *&c.*, *&c.*,
Madrid.

Washington, *November* 12, 1852.

Your note of yesterday came to hand this morning, in which you state a conversation you have had with Mr. George Law, from which you learned that the "Crescent City will go to Cuba and enter the port of Havana in defiance of the Spanish authority; and, if fired upon, she will be surrendered, and that then he and others will immediately commence hostilities against the island." You say, also, that "he desires to know whether he is right in persisting in the pursuit of his lawful business; and that if the government shall tell him he must not go, he will not go. If, however, the government says nothing against his going, he will infer he has a right to go." You say, also, that "he professes to be friendly to me and my administration." Of the sincerity of this latter profession, one can best judge by reading his letter of the 9th, published in the New York *Herald* of the 10th instant.

But, in regard to the chief matters of your letter, permit me to say, that, in the first place, I do not admit the right of Mr. Law, or any other citizen, to threaten a war on his own account, for the purpose of seeking redress for real or imaginary injuries, and then to call upon the government to say whether it approves or disapproves of such conduct, and assume its approbation unless the act is forbidden. The Constitution of the United States has vested in Congress *alone* the power of declaring war, and neither the Executive branch of the government nor Mr. Law has any right to usurp that power by commencing a war without its authority; and if he shall attempt it, it will be my duty, as it is my determination, to exert all the power confided to the Executive government by the Constitution and laws to prevent it. I am resolved, at every hazard, to maintain our rights in this controversy as against Spain, and I am equally resolved that no act of our own citizens shall be permitted to place this government in the wrong.

Mr. Law has an undoubted right to pursue his lawful business; but when a question is raised between this goveanment and a foreign nation as to whether the business which he pursues is lawful, or pursued in a lawful manner, the decision of that question belongs to the two governments, and not to him. If the object be to assert his right to enter the port of Havana with such persons as he may choose to select, in defiance of the laws and government of Spain, he has certainly done enough to present that question for the decision of the governments of Spain and the United States; and the negotiation has already commenced, and our rights, as we understand them, have been asserted, and as I said before will be maintained. But the act of this government cannot be controlled by the interference of any individual, and it is entirely unnecessary that Mr. Law should repeat these attempts for the purpose of settling this controversy; and if he wilfully does so, and in so doing violates the laws of a foreign nation within its own jurisdiction, and thereby loses or forfeits his vessel, he can expect no indemnity for such an act of folly from this government.

We regulate the terms and conditions upon which all foreign vessels shall enter our ports, and we fix the penalties for a violation of our laws, and the right to do so we shall never suffer to be questioned by foreigners, and we do not question theirs to do the same thing. He must wait the result of the negotiations between the two governments. This is a question not to be settled between him and Cuba, nor even between the United States and Cuba, but between the United States and Spain, which alone is responsible for the conduct of the Governor of Cuba.

I write in some haste, as the mail is closing; but you are at liberty to make known the contents of this letter to Mr. Law, and to inform him that as a good citizen I presume he will not attempt any violation of our neutrality laws by attacking Cuba.

I am truly yours,

MILLARD FILLMORE.

Hon. HUGH MAXWELL, *New York city.*

Mr. Calderon to Mr. Everett.

[Translation.]

LEGATION OF SPAIN, WASHINGTON,
December 10, 1852.

The undersigned transmitted to his excellency the Captain General of Cuba a copy of the communication which, under date of the 15th ultimo, the honorable Secretary of State did him the honor of addressing to him when he enclosed to him the affidavit or sworn declaration of Mr. William Smith, of which he also sent a copy to his excellency. General Cañedo, in his reply of the 30th of the same month, which the undersigned received the day before yesterday, says to him, in substance, that although, on his part, no step was taken to obtain this declaration from Mr. Smith, nevertheless, in view of the explicit terms in which it is couched, and in deferential consideration of the authority imparted to it by the fact of its having been communicated to the undersigned by the Hon. Edward Everett, he cheerfully accepts this necessary satisfaction, and deems it sufficient to enable him to direct, as he did the same day direct, that the Crescent City should be allowed to enter the port of Havana, and that the consequent permission to land should be given to Mr. Smith.

The Captain General, in requesting the undersigned to convey this information to the government of the United States, which he now does, adds that he congratulates himself on the circumstance, that thus will be contradicted the insulting calumnies and false statements which some persons, availing themselves of in the name of Mr. Smith, have spread with the perverse design of blackening his character, and at the same time fomenting tumult and discord. His excellency trusts, above all, that not only the government of the United States, but all others, will be persuaded that, although he is firmly resolved to discharge the sacred and imperative duty of preserving at every cost the tranquillity nnd integrity of the territory intrusted to his care, and of maintaining intact the national honor, he is also ever animated by a lively wish to cherish the best relations with all the neighboring States with which her Catholic Majesty is at peace, and to manifest all the deference due to their governments.

The undersigned avails himself of the occasion to renew to the honorable Edward Everett the assurance of his very distinguished consideration.

A. CALDERON DE LA BARCA.

Mr. Barringer to Mr. Everett.

[No. 116.] LEGATION OF THE UNITED STATES, MADRID, *December* 14, 1852.

SIR: Immediately after the receipt of dispatch No. 64, of the 28th October ultimo, from the Department of State, concerning the affair of the Crescent City, I brought the subject of its contents to the attention of her Majesty's government in an official communication. Believing that the gravity of the demand made, and the tenor of the instructions given, required such a course, this communication was an exact copy of that dispatch, with the necessary change of address, and the omission of the references to dispatches and other documents mentioned in the first part of the dispatch. It was also accompanied by a copy of the affidavit of Mr. Smith, purser of the Crescent City, denying in the fullest manner every charge against him by the authorities at Havana. Having failed for several days to receive an answer, although urged in personal interviews, both with the Minister of Foreign Affairs and Under Secretary of State, I deemed it my duty to address a note to the former under date of the 7th instant, a copy of which is herewith enclosed. The important political events referred to in my dispatch No. 115, which have since resulted in a dissolution of the ministry, combined with the proverbial disposition of the Spanish government to procrastinate the dispatch of public business, doubtless contributed to this delay. Allowance was also duly made for the delicacy and probable difficulty of the subject with her Majesty's government. On the 11th instant I received the answer, under date of the 8th, to the demand of the United States, and on the 12th I communicated my reply to the same. Copies of these notes are herewith transmitted.

It will be seen, I deeply regret to say, that the just satisfaction demanded by the government of the United States from that of her Catholic Majesty has been refused by the latter, and, instead of the "prompt and decided disapprobation" anticipated by the President from her Majesty's government, the latter has deliberately and emphatically approved the conduct of the Captain General of Cuba, and it is manifest that, for the present at least, it is their purpose to persist in the same line of policy, whatever may be the consequences. I believe the subject has been fully and maturely considered by her Majesty's government, and that instructions have been forwarded to the Captain General of Cuba not to change the system pursued by him in reference to intercourse with the United States. The policy of the Spanish government, as far as the same can be carried out without an actual interruption of peaceful relations, will be that of non-intercourse between our people and the island of Cuba.

This purpose, if not frustrated, will be gradually but surely adopted, or all commercial and social intercourse will be only tolerated on such conditions as we cannot honorably accede or submit to. The difficulty of adjusting all commercial questions with a people and government so wedded to antiquated and obsolete ideas may well be inferred from the recent correspondence of this legation and her Majesty's government on the subject of the refusal of the latter to assimilate the flags of the two nations under the royal decree of January last, and thereby place American shipping in the peninsula and adjacent islands on a footing with that of other nations. The tone assumed, and the policy pursued towards the United States by her Majesty's government in reference to the affair of the Crescent City, and other questions between the two countries, I think may be fairly attributed, not only to their devotion to ancient prejudices and notions of government, and their want of a true knowledge of our people and institutions, but to expectations of foreign aid for the security of the island of Cuba to the Spanish crown in the event of a rupture with the United States.

I have heretofore referred to this subject, of such interest to the government and people of the United States, as must necessarily be everything connected with the ultimate destiny of that island. They rely with much hope, and even confidence, on the assistance of both England and France, especially the latter, in such a contingency, to preserve and secure that island to their dominion. On this subject I have no official and authentic information to give the department; but, judging from that derived from various sources, in conversation with persons likely to be informed on such a subject, I state it as my conviction that, in regard to England, matters remain as heretofore represented by me, to wit: that instructions are given to the British naval forces in the Gulf of Mexico to assist the Cuban authorities whenever they may request such aid in preventing, by force if necessary, the landing of any armed and illegal expedition, such as that of Lopez, against the island, and that such instructions do not embrace any other contingency. Indeed, I believe the relations between Spain and England are not so intimate and cordial as they were a year since, but that French influence is now at this court in the ascendant. Spain has long been the theatre of diplomatic rivalry, and the contested ground of ambition for political ascendancy between England and France.

It is undoubtedly true that at present the government of her Majesty is on the best and most intimate terms with that of the emperor of the French; and it is now said that the latter has not only given assurances of aid, if required, similar to those I have referred to in the case of England, but that secret guarantees have been made to Spain for the security of her West India possessions in every contingency, and by the employment of the land and naval forces of his imperial Majesty, if necessary. I feel it my duty to give these rumors only for what they are worth, and for the purpose of drawing the attention of our government to the subject.

I may be allowed to state in this connexion that there is at present an increase of the naval forces both of England and France in the Gulf of Mexico, and that reinforcements, both naval and military, have recently been sent from Spain to the island of Cuba.

The Spanish government undoubtedly have serious apprehensions for the fate of the island, either from internal disaffection, foreign invasion, or a rupture with the United States, or all combined; and every effort to the last extent of their power will be made to preserve to their dominion this most cherished treasure of their once immense possessions in the New World. It is said that, as a last resort, to prevent its falling into the power of the United States, or becoming a free and independent State by revolution, secret orders have been issued to emancipate the slaves and place arms in their hands, for the conquest and maintenance of their own rule and authority in the island, and that is the true reason of the recent increase of the slave trade in that island in violation of public treaties.

It is repeated as a motto in the public press of Spain that Cuba must always be either "*Spanish* or *African*." What the future may bring forth it is impossible to foresee, but this is certainly the prevalent state of feeling and determination in Spain in reference to the aspect of affairs, and the final destiny of the island of Cuba.

I have referred to these considerations in connexion with the subject of this dispatch, not because I do not trust and believe that the affair of the Crescent City may still by some means be amicably and satisfactorily adjusted, but because I feel bound to say that if the course now complained of and the policy now pursued by Spain towards the United States, and so much deprecated by the latter, in reference to their intercourse and commerce with the island of Cuba, be persisted in by the former, the present peaceful relations cannot, in all probability, be continued between the two nations, and that we should be prepared for any event.

I have the honor to acknowledge the receipt of your dispatch No. 65, of the 13th ultimo, with its enclosures, and beg to remain, with sentiments of the highest respect, sir, your obedient servant,

D. M. BARRINGER.

Hon. EDWARD EVERETT,
Secretary of State.

LEGATION OF THE UNITED STATES, MADRID,
December 7, 1852.

SIR: On the 24th ultimo I had the honor to address your excellency on the subject of the affair of the "Crescent City." The nature of that communication, made under express instructions from my government, was such as to require an early reply. I am fully aware that recent events of importance at this capital have necessarily claimed much of your excellency's attention, as a minister of the crown; but as so much time has now elapsed since the date of that communication, I find it my duty to call the attention of her Majesty's government to the same, and to express my earnest wishes for a reply at the earliest period.

I avail myself of this occasion to renew to your excellency the assurance of my most distinguished consideration.

Your obedient servant,

D. M. BARRINGER.

His Excellency Don MANUEL BERTRAN DE LIS,

Minister of State.

[Translation.]

FIRST DEPARTMENT OF THE OFFICE OF STATE,

Palace, December 8, 1852.

SIR: I have received your excellency's note of the 24th November last, in which, by order of the President of the United States, you complain that the entrance to the port of Havana had been denied to the mail steamship Crescent City.

Your excellency will permit me to express the surprise which this reclamation has caused me, when, by communications from the minister of her Majesty at Washington, I had received information that the government of the United States had recognized the perfect right and sufficient motive with which the Governor Captain General of Cuba proceeded in this matter, and had taken measures, in consequence, that Lieutenant Porter, who had provoked that action by his imprudent conduct, should leave the command of the Crescent City.

But since my hope has been disappointed, and your excellency has thought it your duty to present this reclamation, I find myself compelled to answer it. Your excellency recognises, as you could not do less than recognise, the perfect right which every nation has of establishing the conditions which it may judge proper for the admission into its ports of foreign vessels, and, consequently, there is no need of discussion on this point. But your excellency says that these conditions ought not to be incompatible with received usages in commercial relations among the nations. I agree, without difficulty, that this is so, and so ought to be, in ordinary circumstances; but I regret to have to remind your excellency, that the actual situation of the island of Cuba, far from being able to be considered as a normal situation, is completely exceptional, (and not, certainly, by any fault of the Spanish government,) and that, in such a situation, the first duty of the authorities is to provide against dangers; and it would not be just to exact that its fulfilment should be subjected to the considerations which in more settled and quiet times, are wont to be observed among enlightened nations for the benefit of commerce.

The publication of [newspaper] articles injurious to a foreign government may not be, in ordinary times and circumstances, a sufficient motive for that government to exclude from its ports a vessel which shall have on board the author of those articles; but I invite the attention of your excellency to the circumstances in which the island of Cuba finds itself, and to those which accompanied the refusal of General Cañedo to receive the Crescent City.

The island of Cuba sees itself constantly menaced with invasion by bands of adventurers who collect in the United States, who there conspire, who there distribute arms and money, who there print incendiary libels, and who, united with some Cubans proscribed by the laws as traitors to the government of their country, exert themselves to light up in it the fire of sedition. Their audacity has arrived at the point of printing a revolutionary periodical in the very capital of the island, the authors of which have happily been discovered, thanks to the vigilance of the authorities.

This was the situation of things when the Crescent City presented herself at the Havana, carrying on board a man who, according to the information of those authorities, had fomented, by his writings, the conspiracies against the island. It ought not, therefore, to appear strange that the Governor General of the same should deem the presence of that man undesirable; and just as little that, in view of the Crescent City's not having respected the warning not to present herself again at the Havana with Smith on board, he should forbid the entrance to a vessel which thus ignored his authority and the weighty reasons for that measure. Your excellency cannot help knowing that the Crescent City, considered as a messenger of the enemy—for enemies of Spain declared are they who pretend to seize by force a part of her territory—might have been subjected, according to the laws of war, to measures still more severe than that of expulsion, to which the Captain General limited himself.

And this manner of proceeding is so much the more natural and justifiable, since, whatever may be the circumstances of the mail packets, and the contracts which the company may have with the government of the United States, it is undeniable that those vessels never can be considered as having a right to the privileges and attentions due to vessels-of-war, but as subject, like all commercial vessels, to the jurisdiction of the authorities of the port; and their condition is in nowise altered by the circumstance, purely accidental and dependent upon the interior regulations of the country, that those vessels are commanded by an officer of the war marine.

In taking the measure which has caused this reclamation from the government of the United States, it was in no way the intention of the Governor Captain General to offend that government; his only object was to adopt a measure which he deemed proper for the security and good order of the island.

In the same understanding, the government of her Majesty has also approved the conduct of General Cañedo, whilst it absolutely could not be its intention to do an injury to that of the United States, with which it desires to maintain good and amicable relations, and whose good will and wishes it appreciates.

I have no doubt that these explanations will be sufficient to satisfy in every point the government of the United States, but in view of what your excellency manifests in one of the paragraphs of the note to which I answer, your exellency will not be surprised at the declaration that the government of her majesty is resolved to adopt all the measures which it may think necessary, within the sphere of its attributes, as the government of an independent nation, to provide for the security of the territory of the same, and that from this firm determination it will not be driven by any menace or consideration, of whatsoever character it may be.

The government of her Majesty promises itself that this task will be the more easy for the good will with which it hopes that the government of the United States will co-operate to defeat the intentions of those unquiet and turbulent men who, in order to satisfy a criminal covetousness, neglect not the smallest pretext for exciting resentment between Spain and the United States; and the government of her Majesty, on its part, will neglect no means for destroying such projects, thus securing solidly the peace which now exists between the two nations.

I avail myself of this occasion to renew to your excellency the assurance of my distinguished consideration, &c., &c., &c.

MANUEL BERTRAN DE LIS.

To the MINISTER OF THE UNITED STATES.

LEGATION OF THE UNITED STATES, MADRID,
December 12, 1852.

SIR: I had the honor last evening to receive your excellency's note of the 8th instant, in reply to mine of the 24th ultimo, on the subject of the demand made by the government of the United States, in consequence of the refusal of the Captain General of the island of Cuba to permit the entry into the port of Havana of the mail steamer "Crescent City," or to allow her to deliver the mails or passengers destined for that island. The reasons for that demand, and the principles upon which it is based, are so fully and so explicitly stated in my former note, which indeed contained the exact instructions from my government, that it is not deemed necessary or becoming to enlarge upon them in this communication.

I cannot forbear, however, the expression of my sincere regret at the unsatisfactory nature of the answer of her Majesty's government as contained in your excellency's reply. The facts, as stated in my note, are uncontroverted, but the principles insisted upon by your excellency in behalf of her Majesty's government will, if persisted in, inevitably result in the most serious consequences, not only to all commercial intercourse between the United States and her Majesty's West India possessions, but necessarily, likewise, to the friendship and peaceful relations which ought to exist between both nations.

What is the pretence now made by the Captain General of Cuba—now sanctioned and authorized, according to the note of your excellency, by her Majesty's government? Why, that under an accusation, a mere suspicion indeed, that an individual has been the author of an offensive publication, or any other obnoxious act, in his own country, the Captain General may, at any time he may deem proper, without due notice, and without being in any way answerable for his conduct to the demand of a friendly nation, not only prevent such person from entering any port of the island, but also exclude the vessel, belonging to a friendly power, which has him on board, at whatever injury to commerce or inconvenience to other passengers, although such vessel may be commanded by a properly appointed officer of that friendly power, and chartered with the full knowledge and consent of the local authorities and the Spanish government, to deliver, at regular periods, the public mails of that nation at such port.

Under this extraordinary claim the Captain General of Cuba is not only made the censor and sole judge of what shall or shall not be published in a foreign press, to debar the author from all communication with the island; not only the exclusive arbiter to decide what are and what are not libels or "calumnies" against his government; but its practical assertion puts it entirely in his power to say who shall and who shall not be in the employment of owners of friendly vessels entering the ports, excluding or detaining all vessels, even the mail-ship, at his mere will and pleasure, for he alone is to judge of the exigency which requires the exercise of the power claimed by him. It is manifest that such arbitrary and unaccustomed requirements as are insisted upon by the Captain General of Cuba cannot be enforced without an interruption of all friendly intercourse.

Publications like that complained of are not within the control of the company owning the vessel, or its officers on board; they cannot know who are the authors. The most gross and violent abuses of authority must follow the claim to exercise such jurisdiction over foreign vessels for what may have been done in their own country. In the very case before us, even admitting the right of the Captain General to exclude Purser Smith on the ground stated, it appears that he was wholly in error, and that Mr. Smith was in no way guilty of the accusation against him. Besides the statement of Lieutenant Porter, and that of the company, testifying to his innocence as far as they believed or could ascertain, Mr. Smith himself, who is represented to be of inoffensive character and entirely worthy of credit, makes solemn oath that he "has never written or published anything against the government of the island of Cuba, nor ever carried letters or messages to and from disaffected persons in said island, or held any commúnicatiön with such persons, or in any manner interfered with the affairs of the said island or the proceedings of its authorities."

And, if the undersigned is not misinformed, in a similar and recent instance the mails on board an American merchant vessel were seized and examined, the passengers imprisoned and maltreated by the same authorities, when it appeared, on further examination, that the suspicions on which they had acted were groundless.

These facts are referred to merely to show how liable to abuse is the right claimed by the Captain General, admitting it to exist for certain purposes, on the ground of local police regulations for the general safety, and how harsh, inconsiderate, and injurious has been his conduct in the cases referred to. The important inquiry, however, is not whether Mr. Smith, or any other particular individual or class of persons obnoxious to the local authorities in her Majesty's government, can be excluded and held "incommunicado" with the island from any considerations of public security or order; but whether in this unusual, unadvised, and unfriendly manner, the Captain General can exclude, under existing treaties, and the acknowledged mercantile usages of the world, any American vessel from the ports of Cuba, because she may have one objectionable person on board, and thus interrupt commercial and social intercourse between the countries—more especially when that vessel partakes of a public character, by being employed by the government of the United States for the transportation and delivery of the public mail, and is commanded by an officer of the war marine for that purpose, with the consent and continued acquiescence of the local authorities of the island, as well as that of the Spanish government.

This claim is emphatically denied, and against such proceedings the government of the United States do solemnly protest. If persisted in, no American vessel can be exempt from liability to arbitrary seizure, detention, injury, and insult. Such a course is in gross violation of that international comity on which is founded almost all commercial intercourse. Besides the want of actual necessity, under the circumstances of the case, to justify such a proceeding on the part of the Captain General, it is believed to have been unwise and impolitic, and well calculated to defeat the very ends intended by its adoption. It is true, as I am happy to say, that in your excellency's note there is a distinct and full disavowal of all purpose on the part of the Captain General and of her Majesty's government, in approving his acts, to offend in any manner the government of the United States. But still his conduct is approved, and it is declared that a similar course of proceeding will be pursued in future, at every hazard. If such continue to be the assertion of her Majesty's government, it will be for that of the United States to take such measures as may be necessary to protect their own interests, and such as may be consistent with their own sense of dignity and justice, under all the circumstances of the case.

Your excellency is not ignorant, that while maintaining in their full extent the honor and interests of my own government and nation, it has always been my anxious wish and effort to do justice to Spain, and to preserve and confirm these ties of friendship between both nations. But I am free to declare, that perseverance in the policy which has been approved by her Majesty's government, and the continued exercise of the power claimed by the Captain General of Cuba, are not calculated to strengthen these ties, and maintain the peaceful relations which now happily exist.

Your excellency does injustice to my government and myself in supposing that in my former note the language of "menace" was employed. It is due, however, to the gravity of the subject itself, and the relations which subsist between both governments, that the true tendency of measures should be candidly and fully examined, and all the consequences fairly stated and looked in the face. Peace can be best maintained by cordial frankness and a perfect understanding of mutual views and purposes.

I deem it also proper to state, in reply to the surprise expressed by your excellency that this demand should have been made after the receipt of information from her Majesty's minister at Washington, that I have been furnished by my government with no such information as that referred to. On the contrary, the views of my government are to be found in the note which I had the honor to communicate on the 24th ultimo, and, so far from removing Lieutenant Porter from the command of the "Crescent City," in consequence of the government of the United States having recognized the perfect right and justice of the proceeding of General Cañedo in reference to that vessel, I have every reason to believe, in the absence of direct information from my government, that that officer was relieved and transferred to another vessel at his own request, to avoid any supposed irritation or complication of difficulties which might arise from his presence on the return of the steamer to Havana, in the regular performance of her contract with the government.

A copy of your excellency's note containing the answer of her Majesty's government to the demand made by that of the United States, shall be immediately forwarded to the latter for their further action on the subject.

I avail myself of this occasion to renew to your excellency the assurances of my distinguished consideration.

Your obedient servant,

D. M. BARRINGER.

His Excellency Don MANUEL BERTRAN DE LIS,
Minister, &c., &c.

Mr. Roberts to Mr. Everett.

OFFICE OF THE U. S. MAIL STEAMSHIP COMPANY,
New York, December 14, 1852.

SIR: On the 15th of November ultimo we were notified by the collector of this port, under instruction from the Department of State, by the direction of the President, that official information had been received at the department stating that "on occasion of the arrival of the Crescent City at Havana, on the 14th October last, she entered the port within the hours prohibited by a law or regulation of the island of Cuba, notwithstanding, as is alleged, she was hailed three times, and required to desist; that the sentinels whose particular duty it was to fire upon a vessel under these circumstances have been imprisoned for failing to perform their duty on the occasion; and that the Governor General of the island informed Mr. Conkling, the American minister to Mexico, on his visit to the island, that he had given peremptory orders, that should an attempt again be made by the commander of the Crescent City to enter the port of Havana at an irregular hour, she should be fired upon from the Moro."

When the above communication was received at this office, Lieut. D. D. Porter, who was in command of the Crescent City at the time referred to, was absent from this port. On his return I submitted the communication from the department to him, and received the reply enclosed herewith.

It has been the invariable course of this company to instruct the commanders and officers of its ships scrupulously to observe every regulation of the port of Havana, and I have no reason to doubt that such instructions have been complied with. I need not assure the department that no such regulation, so far as it may be known to exist, shall be infringed by the ships or the commanders of the company.

I have the honor to be, very respectfully, your obedient servant,

M. O. ROBERTS, *Agent.*

Hon. EDWARD EVERETT,
Secretary of State.

NEW YORK, *December* 6, 1852.

SIR: In answer to a communication from the Hon. Secretary of State, on which you ask information relating to the following charge brought against me while in command of the Crescent City, to wit: "On the arrival of the Crescent City on the 14th ult., she entered the harbor within the prohibition hours, notwithstanding, as is alleged, that she was hailed three times, and required to desist"—I beg to state that the statement is without foundation. I entered the port in broad day-light, and received no hail from the fort or guard-ship. There was not a single sentinel or other person visible on the Moro, and the telegraph house from which we are usually hailed was closed, and no one stirring, though it was the usual hour for telegraph. I know of no regulation prohibiting the entrance of vessels *into* the port of Havana, after night fall, though there is one prohibiting the exit of vessels without a pass. I have often entered the port at the same hour I did on the occasion alluded to; have sometimes been hailed, and sometimes not; and have, on two occasions entered after sunset, without having been accused of violating the port regulations. At the time I entered on the 14th, other vessels were also entering, and taking their departure from the harbor. I am firmly convinced that there is no port regulations prohibiting the entrance of vessels at any time; they are sometimes required to anchor at or near the guard-ship inside the harbor, but then only in case they are hailed, which was not done in the case of the Crescent City.

Very respectfully, your obedient servant,

D. D. PORTER.

M. O. ROBERTS, Esq.

Mr. Everett to Mr. Sharkey.

DEPARTMENT OF STATE,
Washington, December 30, 1852.

SIR: I transmit you, herewith, copies of correspondence between this department and the collector of New York and the agent of the United States Mail Steamship Company.

You will have the goodness, in a proper and discreet way, to ascertain the facts of the case, in reference to which there seems to be a direct disagreement between the statement received by us from an authentic source, and Lieutenant Porter. You will easily see that much delicacy may be necessary in pursuing the inquiry. You will also have the goodness to procure and forward to this department a copy of the port regulations of Havana.

I am, sir, &c.,

EDWARD EVERETT.

WM. L. SHARKEY, Esq.

United States Consul, Havana.

Mr. Roberts to Mr. Everett.

U. S. MAIL STEAMSHIP COMPANY,

New York, January 4, 1853.

SIR: On the 14th December I had the honor to enclose to you the statement of Lieutenant Porter, United States navy, in answer to the allegation made officially to the Department of State, that on the 14th October, he, as commander of the steamship Crescent City, had entered the port of Havana within the hours prohibited by a law or regulation of the island of Cuba, notwithstanding he was hailed three times and requested to desist; that representation of the fact had been made to Mr. Conklin, American minister to Mexico, on his late visit to Havana, and that the Governor General had given orders that should the attempt be again made to enter the port at an irregular hour, the ship should be fired upon from the Moro.

Lieutenant Porter denied the fact of being hailed by the sentinel, and stated that he knew of no law or regulation prescribing hours for *entering* the port.

It will be seen, by the enclosed official copy of the regulations of the port of Havana, that *no such prohibition exists*, so far as the regulations have been published and are known to the commanders of vessels engaged in commerce with the island.

I have the honor to be, very respectfully, your obedient servant,

M. O. ROBERTS,

Agent of the U. S. Mail Steamship Company.

Hon. EDWARD EVERETT,

Secretary of State.

Orders, that all masters of vessels entering this port observe the following regulations:

ARTICLE 1. Vessels entering port will be governed by the articles of these instructions: No vessel can be moved from one spot to another without first obtainining permission from the captain of the port; and such removal can take place only between sunset and nine o'clock of the succeeding morning; and any one contravening this regulation shall pay a fine of $12 for the first time, and of $24 in case of reiteration. No vessel shall pass across any of the shallows of the port, nor from one channel to another, without taking a pilot, although his captain knows them perfectly well, in conformity with trit. 5th, tit. VII, art. 36, of the royal naval ordinances; and he who shall contravene this regulation shall pay the pilotage just as if he had employed the pilot.

Art. 2. As soon as a vessel has anchored and her sails are furled, the captain shall moor on the east side of the channel, in order to leave it free. This must be done by all vessels alike, whether they have anchored outside the guard-ship or within. They will make fast to vessels near them until they reach their place of mooring. This rule is the more imperative if the vessel, on account of the lightness of the wind, has anchored in the narrowest part of the channel. In such case, the master must warp out of the channel immediately. If any master, after being required so to do, shall obstruct the channel, a boat with a pilot shall be sent, at his charge, to place his vessel in a proper position, and pay a fine of $12, besides the damages originated thereby.

The master, on coming ashore, must present himself at the office of the captain of the port; and if he has any colored man on board, his consignee must sign the bond before the twenty-four hours of his anchoring, according to the orders of the Captain General; and not doing it in the fixed time, will be taken ashore in deposite till the departure of the vessel in which he came.

Art. 3. If he has powder on board, he must report the quantity, in order to make the necessary dispositions for its deposite. If he conceals the whole or any part thereof, the master shall pay a penalty of $24, and of $48 in case the vessel should be moored at the wharf previous to said declaration; as it has been observed that some delay its deposite in order to gain time in hauling to the wharf, and others keep their powder on board while in the stream under pretext of it being but a small quantity. The discharge of cannon, or fire-arms of any description, in the harbor, is prohibited, under a penalty of $15, without permission from the admiral and giving notice at this office.

Art. 4. At sunset, fires on board of every vessel must be extinguished, whether in the wharf or in any other part of the port. The cabin light may continue till gun-fire, provided it is kept in a lantern in good condition. The master of any vessel who neglects to obey the above disposition will be liable to a fine of $25, if lying on the stream, and of $30 if he is fastened to the wharf.

Art. 5. No vessel can take ballast on board or discharge it without a written permission from the captain of the port, who will point out the place from which it must be taken, or where it must be discharged. Care must be taken to place tarpauling to prevent its falling in the water. In neglect of this, the master of such vessel will pay a fine of $2 for every twenty quintals, and of $4 being the vessel lying at the wharf in the harbor, or in any other place prejudicating the harbor. If for carelessness in taking in or out ballast, should fall any part of it into the water, the captain will pay the fine of $2 for every twenty quintals, and of $4 in case of reiteration, being the fine of one and a half dollars for a quantity less than twenty quintals in any of the preceding cases. Equal care must be taken in discharging bricks; and on no account must any straw, sand, or sweepings be thrown overboard, under a penalty of $6 for the first time, and in case of reiteration, of $24; for if there be any on board, the master, after putting it in his launch, may call at the captain of the port's in order to be told where to discharge it. Should there be violated by any step or act two or more of the above dispositions, the infractors will pay the value of the fines, as prescribed in every of said cases. To the same fines will be liable the captains or masters by disobeying the preceding regulations in any anchoring place on the coast, even not being there any authority of marine. It is likewise prohibited to heat tar or pitch on board, as this can be done only on shore, and at the place designated, it being understood that those who violate this article shall pay a penalty of $50.

Art. 6. All orders communicated to masters of vessels by pilots or port vigilants must be obeyed, since they emanate from the captain of the port.

Art. 7. In case of any vessel getting unmoored and being in danger of stranding or being lost by weather or other accident, it is the duty of all other vessels to render every possible assistance. If any one fails in this duty, he shall pay the damage resulting from his neglect.

Art. 8. Every master of a vessel, at the time of anchoring, must take care that his cables do not get foul of others, as he will be liable to make good any damage that may arise from his carelessness.

Art. 9. No vessel will be allowed to leave port before sunrise or after sunset, for they must be visited on going out.

Art. 10. In case a master wishes to caulk, repair, careen, heave down, or fumigate his vessel, he must first obtain permission from the captain of the port; but by no means will it be allowed at the wharf, under the fine of $12, as there are for this purpose several careening places, where it may be done without inconvenience or danger to the harbor, under the fine of $24 if done in any careening place without said permit; and any one smoking or breeming his vessel in any place of the harbor without said license will pay a fine of $100.

Art. 11. The master intending to haul his vessel to the wharf must first have a place assigned him by the collector of customs. He shall by no means lie behind those fastened to the wharf, under a penalty of $50 and a liability for all damage that may follow; particularly in case of gales or fire, when it would be necessary to haul a vessel from the wharf. He must also first brace the lower and topsail yards into port, cokbill his anchors, and in case it being a small vessel, the jib and flying jibboom must be taken in and the spanker boom unshipped, in order to avoid damaging other vessels. They must be distant from each other at least three feet by the beam, by which means they may haul from the wharf without difficulty. In hauling to the wharf or leaving it, or moving from one place to another, permission must first be had from the captain of the port: either one or the other can only be done from daylight until nine o'clock in the morning, or from sunset till dark; but by no means can they remain in the channel, or disturb the free ingress with lines or ropes, under penalty of $100 and payment of the damage they may occasion.

Art. 12. No vessel shall be moored in the channel but in the neighborhood of, or along the Casa Blanca shore, leaving a free space between the north end of Marty's wooden wharf and the northwest angle of the King's store, at Casa Blanca, for the free passage of boats to and from Cabaña; then along Aromy's wharf and the edge of the channel until the wharf of Lucas Padron, in which space they may moor with two anchors—the first ahead with forty fathoms chain, and the other on the stern thirty fathoms—bearing northwest during the months from October to March, and the rest of the year to the southeast, keeping themselves in a line to avoid doing any damage to one another; and from thence to the shallows on the east side can be moored with one anchor, with twenty-five fathoms of chain, during the season of light winds, and during the season of gale winds they may double the length of their chains as circumstances may require, keeping the same distance from one another, without obstructing the channel of quarantine or the pass of the English mail steamers, and also avoiding to anchor near vessels of war, from which they must be distant at least one cable's length. It will not be a pretext for not complying with the above rules that the vessel is going to or coming from the wharf, because, being in any of these cases, they must choose the proper time to moor in their appointed place the same day they move from another, being understood that those who shall not obey this disposition will be obliged to receive the saving launch or the pilot's boat, from the captain of the port, with its crews, to be properly moored, and all the charges will be paid by the neglecting masters of vessels according to the tariff, besides the fees of the pilot employed.

Art. 13. No vessel shall be fastened to the buoys which are placed to indicate the shoals in the channel, nor to those destined for the vessels of war; the master doing so shall pay a penalty of $12, and also the expense of all damage which may result from moving a buoy from its place. There are, for that purpose, seven buoys anchored on each side of the channel, at the entrance of the port, in which they can make fast their ropes to haul in the vessels, and are distinguished from the others by having an iron ring on the top, and those which indicate the shoals have only an iron point.

Art. 14. In case of fire breaking out on board of any vessel in harbor, it is strictly enjoined upon the master of every vessel in port to send immediately his boats to the scene of the fire, well manned, and provided with lines, buckets, swaps, and every other article necessary in such cases, as well as fire engines, if they have any on board, in order to extinguish the same as quick as possible. The captain of the port orders the most strict obedience to this article under the immediate responsibility of masters of vessels.

Art. 15. A master of a vessel who may require a launch is at liberty to make his selection, but he must give notice at the office of the captain of the port in order to have it examined, as prescribed by ordinance; and he who loads a launch without leaving the wales two inches out of water, shall be subjected to a penalty of $20.

Art. 16. In case of disturbances on board amongst the sailors, at late hours in the night, the master may call on board the guard-ship for assistance until the morning, when he may get a letter from his

5

consul to the captain of the port to lodge them iu jail. No master of a vessel shall discharge any seaman without permission from the consul of his nation.

ART. 17. The day before a vessel goes to sea the master may call at the office of the captain of the port for an order to take his powder on board, if he has any in deposite.

ART. 18. It is prohibited to pass backwards and forwards in the harbor in boats after evening gun-fire; all persons doing so are liable to be carried on board of the flag-ship, where they will remain at the disposition of the admiral.

ART. 19. 1st. As a safeguard against desertion, by preventing men from deserting or being stolen from the vessel to which they belong in order to ship in another, one licensed shipping-master has been appointed for the port, who alone is authorized to ship any man, or engage him to serve in any way on board any vessel in the harbor. This shipping-master is prohibited from shipping any sailor until he shall have ascertained that the sailor has been lawfully, and conformably in all respects to the regulations, discharged from the vessel which brought him to this port, with the knowledge and consent of the consul of the nation to which said vessel belongs. Captains are at liberty to make their own bargain with any man thus lawfully discharged, but no sailor shall, under any pretext whatsoever, be employed or received, nor shall he be allowed to remain on board of any vessel in this port until after he has been regularly shipped by the licensed shipping-master, and notice thereof has been given by him, and by the master of the vessel on board of which said shipment takes place, to the consul of the nation to which said vessel belongs.

2d. If one sailor should be employed or received on board of any vessel in violation of the foregoing prohibition, without the authorization of the commander of marine, (being Spanish subjects,) or without the same of the shipping-master, (being foreigners,) the master of such vessel shall pay a fine of $50 for every person; which fine shall be doubled in every case where a sailor shall unlawfully be on board of any vessel after said vessel shall have been cleared at the custom-house.

3d. It is the duty of the licensed shipping-master of the port, Mr. Daniel Warren, to comply punctually with this regulation, and to watch over all infractions thereof, that he may give immediate notice of the same to the captain of the port, who will impose and exact the penalty.

ART. 20. The carrying of deadly weapons about the person is prohibited by the laws of this country, which punish the offender with six years' imprisonment at hard labor. This being the penalty which awaits every man found on shore with a pointed knife, or a pistol, or any other instrument whereby death may be inflicted, about his person, shipmasters are strictly enjoined to caution their sailors on this point, and to take care that they do not, by wearing their sea-knives ashore, incur the penalty of the law. This penalty attaches to the mere fact of having such knife or other weapon about the person, and it is not necessary that the weapon be used.

ART. 21. All masters of merchant vessels are bound to hoist up their national flag every time the admiral ship does it fore and aft, being a holiday, or for any other cause; and the captain, on leaving the vessel, must take particular care to recommend the person, whoever may be in charge of the vessel, to comply with the said order; and not doing so, the captain will be responsible for the fault.

Art. 22. For the purpose that the vessels lying in this port (should the barometers indicate bad weather) might be able to moor properly in due time, there have been established the following signals, which will be hoisted for some hours on the flag-staff of the office of the captain of the port:

1st. Red triangular signal signifies that there are appearances of bad weather.

2d. Triangular signal, half blue and half yellow, horizontal, signifies that there are appearances of very bad weather; and every time that the aforesaid signals have a black ball at the top or above, this will signify that the bad weather is becoming clear.

Art. 23. On entering the port the first boarding officer will hand, gratis, these instructions to the master, who shall deliver them back to this office at the time of his clearance.

Art. 24. All steam-vessels are bound to shorten their speed, as much as possible, from the moment they are under the Moro coming in, until they reach the same place going out of the harbor; and the infractors, (not being their first visitation to this port,) besides the damages originated, will pay the fine as stated below; and in all cases, should they be proved that they have been instructed by the pilot of said order, $30.

Mr. Barringer to the Secretary of State.

[Extract.]

Legation of the United States, Madrid,
January 5, 1853.

I have the honor to transmit, herewith, copies of a note from her Majesty's Minister of State for Foreign Affairs, under date of the 28th ultimo, and of my reply to the same of the 30th ultimo, on the subject of the affair of the mail steamer "Crescent City." It will be seen from the former that her Majesty's government regarded the question in issue as finally adjusted, according to information in the Foreign Office, by the circumstance of the Captain General of Cuba having accepted, as sufficient and satisfactory to him, the affidavit of Purser Smith.

After the full and emphatic approval by her Majesty's government of the conduct of the Captain General in this matter, as contained in the note of her Majesty's Minister of State, dated the 8th ultimo, and in the face of their direct refusal to grant the satisfaction demanded by the government of the United States, I could not, acting on a just sense of what was due to my own government, concur in this view of the subject, especially in the absence of any similar information from the Department of State. It will be seen from the previous correspondence that the affidavit of Purser Smith was communicated by me to the Spanish government here, and that it was not regarded by this government as of the slightest importance; on the contrary, with that sworn declaration before them, the order of the Captain General was approved in all respects, and declared to be founded in just and sufficient reasons, notwithstanding the opinion of the President. Since the date of my said note of the 30th ultimo to the Spanish government, I have had the honor to receive your dispatch No. 65, of the 4th ultimo, with its enclosures, referring to this object. I do not feel authorized to infer from this dispatch that the President regards the question as finally adjusted, although informed of the gratifying circumstance that the Captain General had been pleased to abrogate the prohibitory order which has caused all the difficulty and embarrassment in this case. I am the more confirmed in this opinion, as your dispatch seems to contemplate further communicating with the Spanish government in reference to this unpleasant subject, for the satisfactory adjustment of which I now hope that the recent action of the Captain General, in rescinding the obnoxious order, has opened the way, if her Majesty's government are disposed to avail themselves of the same.

As to the assurances to be given to her Catholic Majesty's government of the firmness and good faith with which the President has resisted the spirit of unlawful adventure against the island of Caba, I have heretofore endeavored, on all proper occasions, to make them in the most solemn manner, and will continue to repeat them as often as may be necessary.

I regret to say, however, that, in my opinion, the government of her Majesty have never justly and fully appreciated the efforts of that of the United States in this respect, and have too often acted as if they entertained improper suspicions as to the real motives of our conduct. I have heretofore had occasion, in my correspondence with the department, to refer to the agencies which are too often employed to produce unfavorable impressions of our government and people in this peninsula.

* * * * * * * *

Hon. Edward Everett,
Secretary of State.

Madrid, *December* 30, 1852.

Sir: I have had the honor to receive your excellency's note of the 28th instant, announcing to me that, according to information received at the department of which your excellency has charge, the question concerning the order of the Captain General of the island of Cuba, refusing the entry of the American mail steamer "Crescent City" in the port of Havana, had been finally terminated, in consequence of the sworn declarations of Mr. Smith being considered by General Cañedo as "sufficient and satisfactory."

However rejoiced I should be to know that this unpleasant negotiation has been definitively adjusted on a basis satisfactory and honorable to both nations, I regret to say that I have, as yet, no such information from my government; and certainly no such inference can be made from anything that has yet occurred in the correspondence at this court, to which the question was referred by the United States. I fear, there-ore, that your excellency is under some misapprehension as to the much desired result of the final adjustment of this matter. I beg to say to your excellency that the demand now made is not an affair between General Cañedo and other subordinate officers of her Majesty's government and the steamship company to which the Crescent City belongs, or Mr. Smith, their purser. It is not a difficulty to be adjusted by an explanation to be given by Mr. Smith to the Captain General of Cuba, as if the latter were the author of a reclamation made for a wrong, real or supposed, done to his authority, and to the island of which he has the command only under a superior power. It is an affair between the government of her Catholic Majesty and that of the United States, who supposed they had a right to expect from the former the prompt and decided disapprobation of a course of proceedings on the part of their subordinate officer, the Captain General of Cuba, which was and still is regarded by the President, under all the circumstances, as unnecessary, unwise, harsh, and arbitrary towards a vessel of a friendly nation, upon what was then believed, and now proved to be, a groundless accusation against a single individual on board of the same.

The government of the United States conceived they had a just ground of complaint for what had been done by the Captain General of Cuba. This complaint they have made the subject of a remonstrance to the only responsible power, the government of her Catholic Majesty; and, in a spirit of friendship and earnest desire for an amicable and satisfactory result, have called on the latter to say if they approve the conduct of the Captain General in the matters which are made the foundation of the demand. Instead of the decided disapprobation which the President supposed he was justified in expecting, the government of her majesty have replied, according to the note of your excellency's predecessor in the office of foreign affairs, that they did approve of the proceedings of the Captain General, though in the course pursued by the Captain General and by her Majesty's government in approving the same no offence was intended by either to the United States.

This reply, which the undersigned deemed unsatisfactory, has been forwarded to the government at Washington, for their further advice and action. No answer has, or could yet have been received by me, to this communication. It will be awaited for with deep interest by the undersigned, and with an earnest hope that the question may yet be satisfactorily and honorably adjusted between the two governments, to whom it properly appertains. In the mean time, I had hoped, and still trust, that on a calm review of the whole case, her Majesty's government will admit that the grounds of complaint by the United States in the matters referred to were just, and that the conduct of the Captain General in this respect was indefensible. The act of the latter in accepting the voluntary affidavit of Mr. Smith as sufficient and satisfactory to him is duly and highly appreciated, as manifesting a conciliatory spirit, and as removing the embarrassments to commercial and social intercourse which had been caused by his previous conduct; but it does not atone for the wrong already done on two several occasions; it does not answer the demands made by the government of the United States, and has not, so far as I am advised, in any degree changed the opinion of the President as to the character of the proceedings of the Captain General. The principle involved is not thereby altered, and no guarantee is given that the same thing may not again be done by the local authorities of the island whenever they may think it proper or convenient. Indeed, the demand made is left in a state more unsatisfactory to the United States; for, if adjusted by the mere circumstances mentioned by your excellency, it would seem to imply, and may hereafter be quoted as a precedent to that effect, that the Captain General may justly exact from any officer he chooses to designate, on board an American vessel, of whatever character or description, a statement on oath that he is not, and never has been, engaged in any act whatever which the Captain General may, in his judgment or his caprice, deem obnoxious to the Cuban government, or any members thereof, as a condition precedent to the entry of such vessel in any part of the island. While the abstract right to exclude from the island Mr. Smith, or any other foreigner, for a specified reason, is freely admitted, it does not therefore follow that the vessels on which they are for the time being may also be excluded, and that it would be a friendly proceeding, in time of peace, to deny to the vessel of a friendly power the landing of the passengers and the delivery of the public mails on any such pretence as that made by the Captain General, and in regard to which he now admits, by accepting and adopting the statements of Mr. Smith, that he was entirely in error, and acted before on groundless suspicions.

It must be obvious to any one, and especially to one of your excellency's knowledge and experience in the commercial and other affairs of that island, that such a course of proceeding on the part of the Captain General as that now solemnly protested against, if recognised and allowed to be adopted as a precedent for future action, must sooner or later terminate in a complete interruption of all friendly communication, and an odious system of non-intercourse between the two nations, whose contiguity and mutual interests require a very different policy for the general welfare of both. I have too strong a conviction of the good wishes both of your excellency and of her Majesty's government towards the United States, and for the maintenance of peaceful and cordial relations with the same, to suppose that any such fatal result is desirable to either; and on the part of the government of the United States it is, I trust, unnecessary to remind your excellency of the friendly desires and kind offices which the President has on all occasions, and some of great responsibility, so firmly and faithfully shown towards the government of Spain, as an assurance that, under all circumstances, the American government will not fail to perform their whole duty towards a friendly power, and of their ardent desire to preserve perfect peace and harmony between both nations.

I avail myself of this occasion to renew to your excellency the assurance of my most distinguished consideration.

Your obedient servant, D. M. BARRINGER.

His Excellency the COUNT OF ALCOY,
President of the Council and Minister of State.

[Translation.]

FIRST DEPARTMENT OF THE OFFICE OF STATE,
Palace, December 28, 1852.

SIR: I had the honor to receive your excellency's note of the 12th instant, in which you reply to mine of the 8th relative to the question raised at the Havana with respect to the mail steamer "Crescent City."

I have now the satisfaction to announce to your excellency that, according to the information received in the department under my charge, this question is terminated by General Cañedo having considered the sworn declaration of Mr. Smith, of which your legation is already cognizant, as sufficient and satisfactory.

I believe it therefore unnecessary to pursue the discussion in reply to the above-mentioned note of your excellency; and I avail myself of this occasion to renew to your excellency the assurances of my most distinguished consideration, &c., &c.

The COUNT OF ALCOY.

The MINISTER PLENIPOTENTIARY
of the United States.

Mr. Everett to Mr. Barringer.

[No. 73.]

DEPARTMENT OF STATE,
Washington, February 4, 1853.

SIR: Your dispatches up to No. 121 have been duly received and submitted to the President. Your dispatch, No. 116, of the 14th of December, is accompanied by your correspondence with the Spanish government on the affair of the "Crescent City," and the President has directed me to express to you his approbation of the manner in which you have treated the subject.

Since the date of the letters which passed between you and Mr. Bertran de Lis, the message of the President at the opening of the session, and the paragraph relative to the affair of the "Crescent City," in my letter to the Count de Sartiges of the 1st of December, of which a copy was transmitted to you, will have shown to you, and to the Spanish government, in a still stronger light than it appeared before, the reasonableness of our complaints of the conduct of the Governor General in this affair, and the consequent justice of our demand that it should be disapproved.

The government of her Catholic Majesty appears to mistake the ground of our complaint. as it has mistaken, also, in the opinion of the President, the course which it should itself have adopted on this occasion. The United States have never denied the right of the Governor General of Cuba, under the unlimited powers with which he is clothed, to take any measures, however stringent, which he may deem necessary for the safety of the island committed to his government.

But this is a right to be exercised under a proper responsibility to all whose interests are involved in the measures adopted. It is to be exercised reasonably, and with due proportion of the means adopted to the end proposed—that is, the protection and security of the island. It ought also, as far as foreigners are concerned, to be exercised with the comity which one independent government owes to another. If it be said that the Captain General of Cuba, as a subordinate officer of Spain, could be under no responsibility and owe no comity to the United States, this consideration only shows that the responsibility of his acts devolves upon the government of Madrid, which, before it approves his conduct, is bound to show that the measure adopted by the Captain General towards Purser Smith, and the vessel having him on board, was necessary as a measure of protection and defence for the island, or at least well adapted to that purpose, and was resorted to, if not on sufficient evidence, at any rate on reasonable grounds of suspicion, and was promptly communicated to this government, with the reasons which led to its adoption.

It is scarcely necessary to say, that not one of these conditions was fulfilled. The exclusion of a single individual serving on board of the "Crescent City" in a subordinate capacity, and the prohibition of the landing of the mails and the passengers from any vessel having him on board, was certainly a measure indicating nothing but displeasure towards an individual, and not in the slightest degree tending to the safety of the island. Purser Smith's supposed offence has never, to this day, been specifically stated to this government, neither as to its nature nor the manner in which it was committed. It is supposed to have been that of furnishing the press of New York with accounts deemed calumnious of persons and things in Cuba. But considering the character which the Spanish minister ascribes to the company in whose employ Purser Smith sailed, it need scarcely be said that nothing was to be gained by excluding an individual whose place was sure to be taken by another equally dangerous, and that the only possible effect would be to induce a little more caution in the propagation of the calumnies complained of.

It is a striking commentary on the conduct of the Captain General of Cuba, in inflicting a blow upon the commercial intercourse of the two countries as a punishment for calumnious publications imputed, and that erroneously, to an individual, that in the journal "La España," transmitted with your No. 121, and stated by you to enjoy the countenance of some of the highest personages in Spain, the President of the United States is spoken of in terms equally unjust and disrespectful—a circumstance, however, which, instead of leading the government of the United States to desire to inflict any punishment on the culpable individuals or innocent third persons, is regarded by it with entire indifference. In countries where the liberty of the press prevails, it is found that these abuses furnish their own correction. They become important only by being made the subjects of coercive measures.

Again, what possible effect could the presence or absence of Smith have upon the passengers and the contents of the mail? Could they be innocent or dangerous, as he happened to be on board or not? And as this would be an absurd supposition, why confine the prohibition to the "Crescent City," when there were precisely the same reasons, as far as the safety of the island is concerned, to extend it to the other mail steamer, the "Empire City," in the employ of the same company? It is hardly possible to argue this question with gravity. The order was no doubt issued on the suggestion of some subordinate, in a moment of irritation; was not communicated to the American consulate for seventeen days, and then, without specification of the calumnies imputed to Smith, was persevered in after Smith had made affidavit of his innocence, and was adhered to for a considerable time upon the punctilio, afterwards abandoned, which required a personal disclaimer from Smith himself. To pronounce a course of measures like this, towards an individual in Purser Smith's position, necessary for the security and protection of an island garrisoned by twenty-five thousand troops and guarded by a powerful naval force, is an absurdity in terms.

It is quite evident that the Captain General, long before the date of Mr. Bertran de Lis's letter approving his conduct, had felt, himself, that he had taken a hasty step, and seized the first opportunity to retrace it; and, in the opinion of the President, her Catholic Majesty's government would have pursued a more friendly course, if, instead of expressing its approbation of a measure already rescinded in Cuba, it had at least offered to institute an inquiry into the circumstances of the case, of which I infer, from the contents of Mr. Bertran de Lis's letter, it was itself quite imperfectly informed.

In fact, this is perhaps the first time in the history of friendly States that an important branch of commercial intercourse has been suspended between two countries by a subordinate officer, without an offer, on the part of his superiors, of any explanation of the facts of the case, tending to show the necessity and reasonableness of the measure, or the evidence on which it was adopted.

The President has the greater cause to be dissatisfied with the manner with which the Spanish government has treated his complaint, inasmuch as he has uniformly, as is well known, exerted himself to the utmost of his constitutional powers, to prevent encroachment on the territorial rights of Spain. The tone of Mr. Bertran de Lis's letter would have been more appropriate if addressed to the mail steamer company which persisted in the attempt to force the admission of Purser Smith, in defiance of the order of the Captain General. The President knew the order to be an unreasonable and inappropriate one; but, recognising the *prima facie* right of the Captain General to issue it, he felt it his duty to discountenance the attempt to resist it at the risk of bloodshed. This circumstance alone should have led the Spanish government to treat his just reclamation with deference.

There are errors of fact and misconception of the existing state of things, which have inadvertently crept into the letter of the Spanish minister, on which I forbear to dwell. The immediate occasion has gone by. The course of the government of the United States, combining discretion with steadiness, averted a collision, and it is not worth while to engage in a protracted discussion of the past.

The President accepts the assurance of the Spanish minister that no offence was intended to this government by the sanction extended to the ill-advised course of General Cañedo; and he quite approves your conduct, in stating that it was no part of your purpose to intimate a menace to Spain. The last agent to be resorted to between independent States is the language of threat, and governments conscious of their strength and of the uprightness of their intentions, lose nothing by forbearance in the assertion of their rights. The President, however, directs you to state to the Spanish minister, with entire frankness, that his main ground for regretting the course pursued by her Catholic Majesty's government on this occasion, is, that it tends to weaken the hands of the government of the United States in performing the duties of an honest neutrality towards the possessions of her Catholic Majesty in this hemisphere.

The foregoing, with the exception of two paragraphs, was written before the receipt of your No. 121, with its accompanying correspondence, the contents of which do not vary the state of the controversy. You will communicate the substance of this letter to the Spanish government; but beyond this, unless something unforeseen occurs, the President does not think it worth while to continue the discussion. He has just directed me to propose to the Spanish minister here to obtain from his government authority to negotiate a commercial convention, the want of which is greatly felt; and he would be unwilling, by prolonging a fruitless controversy, to throw an obstacle in the way of such a negotiation.

I am, sir, &c.,

EDWARD EVERETT.

D. M. Barringer, Esq., *&c., &c., &c.*

Mr. Barringer to Mr. Marcy.

[No. 136.] Legation of the United States,

Madrid, April 7, 1854.

Finale of the Crescent City affair.

Sir: In pursuance of the instructions contained in dispatch No. 73, from the Department of State, I have communicated to the Spanish government the substance of that letter.

His excellency the President of the Council, who is also Minister of State for Foreign Affairs, expressed his regret that the course pursued by her Majesty's government in the affair of the "Crescent City" mail steamer had not been satisfactory to that of the United States, but he insisted that it ought not to have been expected that the government at Madrid should have disapproved of the course of the Captain General of Cuba. To this I answered, that I differed entirely, and throughout, from his excellency; that it was not my purpose or wish now to renew the discussion; that the ground taken by the United States was fully sustained by the facts and arguments of the case already presented; that the government of Spain ought promptly to have disapproved of the rash conduct of the Captain General, and at least to have instituted a full inquiry into the matter immediately upon the complaint of the United States, before expressing their entire approbation of his conduct; and that if this course had been pursued, my opinion was that her Majesty's government would have finally assented to the just demand of the United States; and the result would have been much more satisfactory than that which has actually followed the negotiation on this unpleasant subject.

It was evident, however, that the minister regarded the affair as now terminated; and that if I had ever been instructed to ask for a reversal of the former decision in the case it could not have been obtained under existing circumstances.

Having already communicated fully with the department in reference to this affair I forbear to add more, at present, than the expression of my regret and dissatisfaction with the course pursued by her Majesty's government, and my hope that a forbearance which, under peculiar circumstances, has been extended to a nation with which we are at peace, will not be shown again, after the full warning, under the aggravation of a similar outrage upon our citizens and flag.

I am happy to be informed that my correspondence on this subject has been approved by the government at Washington.

I have the honor to remain, with great respect, sir, your obedient servant,

D. M. BARRINGER.

Hon. W. L. Marcy,
Secretary of State.

CASES OF THE STEAMER OHIO AND SCHOONER MANCHESTER.

Mr. Marcy to Mr. Barringer.

[No. 77.]

Department of State,
Washington, April 19, 1853.

Sir: You will receive with this dispatch a copy of a communication made on the 20th ultimo to the President of the United States, by Mr. George Law, of New York, and a copy of a correspondence accompanying the same, presenting a case not only of annoyance, but of injury to our citizens and embarrassment to our commerce.

The documents now sent supply all the facts in the case which have come into the possession of the department. From them it appears that one of the United States mail steamships, the "Ohio," in the prosecution of her usual and lawful voyage, with a clean bill of health, (and, as was demonstrated in the sequel, without reasonable ground of suspicion that there existed on board of her any disease that ought to have subjected her to an hour's quarantine,) was forcibly and unnecessarily detained for two or three days at or near the port of Havana, deprived of intercourse with the shore, and her commander, Lieutenant Hartstene, an officer of the United States navy, denied even the privilege of communicating by letter with the American consul—all the circumstances set forth in the statement accompanying the correspondence, (which, but for an accident that is described, would have been signed by the whole ship's company and the passengers, upwards of 400 in number) exhibiting an apparently inexcusable exercise of power, disrespectful to our flag and oppressive towards our people.

The case thus presented was one which, in my judgment, called for the prompt interposition of our government. I consequently sought an interview with Señor Don Calderon de la Barca, the Spanish minister, and placed in his hands a copy of the papers above referred to. As he had no information on the subject, but was expecting intelligence in regard to it from the authorities of Cuba, I delayed communicating with you and directing you to call the attention of the home government to the matter until that information could be obtained.

A few days since Mr. Calderon furnished me with an extract of a letter to him from the Captain General of Cuba, which he regarded in some degree as private. Among the papers accompanying this dispatch you will find a copy of that extract. By examining it you will at once perceive that it does not in material points controvert the facts set forth in the complaint to this department, nor is it at all satisfactory to the President.

The two strong grounds of complaint and sources of injury are, first, that the "Ohio" was detained for two or three days on her trip from Aspinwall to New York, touching at Havana, under pretence of enforcing the quarantine laws against her, not only contrary to the uniform practice in regard to the mail steamers employed in this service, but after the "Ohio" had shown a clean bill of health, and without any evidence of contagious disease on board, or any inquiry into her condition as to the health of her passengers and crew. After a vexatious delay an examination into the condition of the "Ohio" was made, (which should have been done before her arrest,) and it was found that there was no cause for subjecting her to quarantine. The Captain General, even on his own statement of the affair, has, in my opinion, entirely failed to excuse the conduct of the authorities of Havana towards the "Ohio." Though I am unwilling to characterize their conduct as intentionally vexatious I cannot but regard it as unjustifiable; and, being so, I anticipate that the government of her Catholic Majesty will be willing and ready to repair the injury sustained by the owners of the steamer. You are instructed to demand reparation for the injury thus sustained.

It is stated in the Captain General's letter to Mr. Calderon that he has consented to allow our consul at Havana free access to his person. This avails nothing so long as our injured citizens are denied access to our consul in order to make him acquainted with their grievances.

In the papers submitted to Mr. Calderon it is distinctly stated that the officers of the "Ohio" were not permitted to have intercourse with the American consul. This allegation is not denied by the Captain General. There is no comment in his letter to Mr. Calderon upon this extraordinary fact, no denial of the allegation, and of course no attempted apology. Merely as an act of discourtesy it is a matter of grave complaint; and, as it aggravated the wrong by prolonging the unjustifiable detention of the "Ohio," you will press it upon the attention of the home government, not only as connected with the claim for indemnity, but as a proceeding calculated to disturb the existing friendly relations between Spain and the United States.

This case not only calls for prompt redress, but will furnish an occasion for urging upon Spain the wisdom of entering into some proper arrangement for preventing the too often recurring vexations which the United States experience in that quarter. She cannot but listen respectfully to any suggestions having for their object to disembarrass our commerce with one of her colonial possessions in such close proximity to the United States, and to guard against occurrences calculated to impair the amicable relations of the two nations.

You are directed, upon the receipt of this dispatch, to address a note upon the subject to the *Minister of Foreign Relations*, acquainting him with the sincere regret the President feels at being called upon, so soon after entering upon his duties as Chief Magistrate of the Union, to remonstrate against an occurrence which is, in some respects, not unlike the recent case of the "Crescent City."

You will urge, in as forcible language as official courtesy will authorize, upon the government of her Catholic Majesty, the claim for an indemnity for the damages sustained, and obtain from that government an assurance that the Captain General will be instructed to enforce upon the subordinate authorities in Cuba a course of conduct more in accordance with those rules which are essential to an unembarrassed commercial intercourse, and more regardful of the rights and property of American citizens.

Propositions have heretofore been submitted for some special regulations by treaty in regard to the commercial intercourse between the United States and Spain. A communication on this subject was made to Mr. Calderon, on the 5th of February last. I transmit herewith an extract from that communication, which will show you the objects of the proposed convention. It is desired to ascertain how far her Catholic majesty is disposed to entertain and to favor those propositions. It is confidently believed that proper treaty stipulations on that subject would go far to prevent the occurrence of difficulties, which hitherto have been too frequent, and of a character to disturb the peaceful relations of the two countries.

By the accompanying notices, cut from several American newspapers, you will see that some public excitement exists on the subject of another alleged "outrage" upon the American flag, in the case of the American schooner "Manchester," Captain Sterling, near the island of Cuba. The animadversions of the press you will perceive are very severe; but the department has no account of the circumstances beyond what you will find contained in the annexed copy of an extract of a letter from Mr. Sharkey, the consul of the United States at Havana, of the 7th instant, and of a letter to him from the captain and mate of the "Manchester," which was enclosed in the consul's communication. It will be your duty, however, to direct the minister's attention in a proper manner to this transaction, respecting which further instructions will be transmitted, if deemed necessary, after the receipt of any additional information in regard to it.

I am, sir, &c.,

W. L. MARCY.

D. M. Barringer, Esq., &c., &c., &c., *Madrid.*

U. S. Mail Steamship Company, New-York,
March 20, 1853.

Sir: I have the honor to transmit to you, herewith, the correspondence between Lieutenant Hartstene, United States navy, commanding United States mail steamship Ohio, and Judge Sharkey, United States consul at Havana. This correspondence furnishes the details of another outrage upon the flag and commerce of this country, committed by the authorities of Havana, and which I beg leave to bring to the attention of our government.

Repeated insults and aggressions, on previous occasions, against the commission of which the ships, persons, and property, of American citizens have as yet been afforded no protection or redress, are renewed at any moment that caprice or hostility may dictate, to the great detriment of our commerce with the island of Cuba, in violation of treaty stipulations, and in disregard of the rights and interests of American citizens.

In the present instance the Ohio was detained three days in the port or vicinity of Havana, in the most wanton manner, and under circumstances degrading to our national flag; surrounded by a guard, all communication with the shore interdicted, and Captain Hartstene refused permission to communicate with the American consul, without the slightest excuse for such an outrage, the vessel exhibiting a clean bill of health, and having no contagious or infectious disease on board, and only such sickness (the Panama fever, the intermittent or fever and ague of our own climate) as has never before been subject to quarantine or detention.

I need not assure you that with the United States California mails on board, two millions and a half of treasure, and a large number of passengers, all American citizens, or the property of American citizens, this unwarrantable detention was the source of the greatest uneasiness, inconvenience, and loss to the trade and business of shippers and the public generally. I enclose also, for the information of our government, a statement drawn up, at the request of the passengers on board the Ohio, by B. McAlpine, Esq., formerly a citizen of Alabama, of standing and respectability, and an acquaintance of the Hon. W. R. King, and which would have been signed by all the passengers, had not Mr. McAlpine been detained on the island beyond the sailing of the Ohio, whilst on a visit to Colonel King.

I have the honor to be, very respectfully, your obedient servant,
GEORGE LAW, *President.*

His Excellency Franklin Pierce,
President of the United States.

U. S. Mail Steamer "Ohio,"
In Quarantine, Havana Harbor, March 10, 1853.

Sir: I regret exceedingly that the unwarranted and unprecedented conduct of the authorities of this place, in quarantining this steamer, should make it necessary for me to protest against this outrage, and to ask your intercession; but, as I have on board a large and valuable amount of property, and the United States mails, I cannot do otherwise than to at least state facts, that they may reach the supreme ruler of the island.

This steamer left Aspinwall on the morning of the 5th instant, with four hundred and fifty-six passengers, about one hundred of whom were discharged railroad men, out of which number about twenty were sick with the Panama fever, (well known not to be contagious.) Since that time, to our anchorage this morning in this port, there has been no other case, and all the invalids are convalescing, with the exception of one very old man. I pledge my word, and that of the surgeon of the vessel, that there has been *no other disease* on board, and that there have been no *deaths*.

Every steamer that ever entered this port from Chagres or Aspinwall has had cases of the fever, and this is the first instance of quarantine for it. I must, therefore, most solemnly protest against the injustice of having United States mails and property delayed on so frivolous a pretext, and to demand, through you, that all the privileges and facilities guarantied, by treaty, to the vessels of the United States, be extended to this steamer. If continued in quarantine, we shall be detained here some four or five days, taking in sufficient coal to reach our destination, as we have only forty-five men that can be employed at that work.

Respectfully, &c.,
H. J. HARTSTENE,
Lieutenant U. S. Navy, commanding "Ohio."

Judge SHARKEY,
U. S. Consul for Havana.

P. S.—In continuance of the obstructions which this tyrannical and overbearing government have for sometime been opposing to steamers of this line, in charge of United States officers, and conveying her mails, we, after having been allowed to remain near our coal depot just long enough to commence work, and also some necessary repairs of machinery, are *now* ordered, at the expense of some ten tons of coal, and the partial loss of another day, to remove to the quarantine ground. Now, sir, as a lieutenant of the United States navy, acting under the orders of my government, I again most emphatically protest against all and each of the restrictions that have been imposed upon this vessel, that entered this port in distress, (short of coal,) with a *clean bill* of health, and having no *deaths*.

Respectfully, &c.,
H. J. HARTSTENE,
Lieutenant U. S. Navy, commanding "Ohio."

FRIDAY MORNING, *March* 11.

U. S. MAIL STEAMSHIP OHIO,
Havana, March 11, 2 *p. m.*

SIR: I herewith enclose you a communication of yesterday's date, which, up to the present time, I have been denied the privilege of forwarding; and I have now furthermore to state, that to the injuries which an unjust detention of this vessel has caused, have been offered insults of the grossest nature to myself and the surgeon of this steamer by the informal manner of relieving her from a quarantine imposed contrary to the usages of the port, in defiance of our assertions, and without any examination of the ship on their part, until, within the last hour, we were visited by a Spanish naval surgeon in a private manner, to whose kind intercession we are, I presume, indebted for the concession now made to us (after a detention of thirty-two hours) of the usual facilities of the port. Understanding that a report is in existence that I deceived the pilot, when entering the harbor, with regard to the state of this vessel, I unhesitatingly pronounce it a falsehood, as base as been our treatment since our arrival.

I have to ask that a copy of these communications may be sent to the Captain General, with a request that he will inform me why we have been thus abused.

Respectfully, &c.,
H. J. HARTSTENE,
Lieutenant U. S. Navy, commanding "Ohio."

Judge SHARKEY,
U. S. Consul for Havana.

CONSULATE OF THE UNITED STATES, HAVANA,
March 12, 1853.

DEAR SIR: I this morning received your communication, in which you complain of the unnecessary detention of your vessel, caused by placing her in quarantine, and desire that the Captain General may be informed of this, and, if possible, that an answer may be obtained from him. The matter will be duly attended to, but I must say that there can be but little hope of obtaining an answer. If, however, I should be disappointed, it shall be duly communicated.

I am, sir, with respect, yonr obedient servant,
W. L. SHARKEY.

Capt. H. J. HARTSTENE.

UNITED STATES MAIL STEAMER "OHIO,"
New York, March 18, 1853.

DEAR SIR: I regret exceedingly that this steamer, though performing well, has been frustrated in the due delivery of her mails by an unwarranted detention of two days in the port of Havana by the authorities, whom, you will perceive from their subsequent acts, did it to gratify their piques, and to further display what little respect or regard they have for a government that will countenance them as a civilized and honorable nation.

We left Aspinwall on the forenoon of the 5th instant, with the California mails, treasure, and 456 passengers, and at midnight of the 9th were off the Moro, awaiting daylight, agreeable to the regulations of the port. Shortly after mooring to the buoy near our coal depot, we were visited by the health officer; and, in defiance of a clean bill of health, and being distinctly informed by myself and surgeon that there were no contagious or infectious diseases on board, nor had there been any deaths; that we had but a few more than the usual proportion of cases of Panama fever, all which, with one exception, had improved during the passage; and that we had the United States mails on board, were ordered to remain where we were in quarantine, communicating with no one, and that we could have coal only by taking it from lighters with our own crew, which, in our crowded state, would have caused much delay. Mr. Johnson, with his usual promptitude and energy, after having exhausted all means of relieving us from this outrageous treatment, commenced supplying us; and when fairly under way with this, as well as some necessary work on the machinery, we were, in continuance of their overbearing persecutions, ordered to remove to the quarantine ground, nearly a mile distant, for which it was necessary to cease operations; and, when ready for starting, we were (after having been in the harbor thirty-two hours) suddenly and informally relieved from all restrictions. For this indulgence we are indebted to Doctor Don Jorge Ledo, of her Catholic Majesty's navy, who nobly, disinterestedly, and unofficially, examined the steamer at the risk of being sent from the island, should there be any contagion on board.

We were, you will perceive, quarantined without there being any measure taken to determine the correctness of the surgeon's and my own assertions, and then relieved on an impartial and private survey, in total disregard to all feelings of delicacy or respect for us or our flag.

Your obedient servant,

H. J. HARTSTENE.

M. O. Roberts, Esq.,
Agent U. S. M. S. S. Company, N. Y.

P. S.—We left Havana at half-past nine on the evening of the 12th instant, and arrived at Sandy Hook at 6 20 p. m. on the 17th, where, in consequence of a dense fog, we were compelled to anchor. I enclose you, herewith, copies of the correspondence between Judge Sharkey, United States consul at Havana, and myself, in relation to the detention of the "Ohio" by the authorities of that port.

Yours, respectfully,

H. J. H.

The following statement was drawn up by B. McAlpine, esq., formerly of Alabama, at the request of the passengers on board of the United States mail steamship Ohio, while detained by the unwarrantable conduct of the Cuban authorities; but when the steamer was permitted to come to her wharf Mr. McAlpine, having proceeded at once to visit Col. King, did not return in season to take the Ohio on her voyage to New York; otherwise, Mr. McAlpine gives the assurance, the statement would have been signed by every passenger, 456 in number.

BAY OF HAVANA, *March* 12, 1853.

The undersigned, passengers on board the mail steamship Ohio, bound for New York, deem it a duty we owe to the citizens of the United States and the authorities at Washington, to give a correct history of the conduct of the officers of this port on the arrival of the ship.

The ship arrived at the Moro castle early on the morning of the 10th instant, and was boarded by a pilot, who conducted her near to where she had to coal. After waiting some time the health and port officers came alongside, but did not enter the ship. They were met by the captain, Lieutenant Hartstene, United States navy, and the surgeon of the ship, and informed that there was no contagious disease on board the ship, and that there had been no death on the voyage. They were also informed that the ship had on board the United States mails, and that she required 400 tons of coal to enable her to proceed with the same. The port officer declared that the ship must land at the wharf on which her coal was deposited, and placed an armed guard to prevent the passengers from going on shore or having any communication therewith. The captain then requested that a letter should be conveyed to the American consul on shore, which was totally refused. All communication was entirely cut off from shore, and the authorities refused to allow any aid from the shore to coal the vessel, stating that the laborers on board must coal the vessel by lighters. The captain made several efforts, through the agency of a gentleman who came within speaking distance, to get the order rescinded, assuring the authorities through him that there was no disease on board, but received for answer that the ship must remain where she lay, and take her coal on board with her own laborers. The captain again requested to have communication with the American consul and the company's agent, informing the authorities that there were important documents on board for the Vice President of the United States of America, Mr. King, and the American consul. They were informed at the same time that there were about fifty passengers who desired to go to New Orleans; to all of which they paid no sort of respect.

Early on the morning of the 11th instant the port officers came within speaking distance and ordered the ship into quarantine, distant about two miles from where she then lay. At the time of this order the captain had two barges alongside with coal. He informed the writer of this that he intended to obey the order as soon as the coal was on board, the consequence of which would have detained the vessel two or three days longer, being compelled to coal by the tardy process of lighters. At 4 o'clock on the afternoon of the 11th, a physician, said to belong to the Spanish navy, seeing our situation, and having more of the milk of human kindness than many of his countrymen, volunteered to come on board, and promised the board of health of Havana that if there was contagion on board he would remain on the ship as passenger for New York. In a few moments after the physician came on board, the ship was set at liberty, and very soon after the passengers were permitted to go on shore by paying one dollar for a pass each. We have endeavored in the above to give a correct history of the proceedings of the officers of this port, and as American citizens we are compelled to condemn their actions from beginning to end. We are grieved to think that while our own government most scrupulously adheres to her treaty stipulations with all other powers, the government of Spain, through her officers, so far forget the obligations they owe to our government as to harass her citizens who happen to travel through their country, and prevent the free passage of the United States mails from point to point by such obstructions as we have above recited, and which were the more annoying and vexatious from the fact that no cause existed for them, and that no ship, so far as we can learn, has been quarantined under similar circumstances. Altogether the steamer was detained in the port of Havana three days.

[Extract.]

DEPARTMENT OF STATE,
Washington, February 5, 1853.

SIR: I have been directed by the President to bring to your consideration the subject of the commercial relations between the United States and Spain, with a view to their regulation by treaty. The treaty of 1795 is, what it purports to be, not a commercial treaty, but a treaty of "friendship, limits, and navigation." Such of its provisions as relate to commercial intercourse are few in number, and have, for the most part, specific reference to the state of things which then existed, and has since materially changed. It was, however, apparently the intention of the two governments to make their commercial interests the subject of negotiations at some future period; and in the 22d article it is provided, that "the two high contracting parties, hoping that the good correspondence which happily reigns between them will be further increased by this treaty, and that it will contribute to augment their prosperity and opulence, will in future give to their mutual commerce all the extension and favor which the advantage of both countries may require."

In fulfilment of this anticipation the commercial intercourse between Spain and her possessions in this hemisphere, on the one side, and the United States on the other, has greatly increased, but nothing has been done for its protection or regulation by conventional arrangements. The treaty of 1795, if applicable to the colonies of Spain, which is not admitted by the government of her Catholic Majesty, would by no means meet the exigencies of the commerce which has grown up since that time.

The United States government has never acquiesced in this limitation of the treaty of 1795; but so long as it is maintained by the government of her Catholic Majesty the main object of a treaty is lost, which is, by mutual agreement, to regulate the matters to which it relates. The commercial relations of the United States with the Spanish islands near the American continent are of great importance, and daily becoming more so, and interests of great moment are involved in them. There is, for instance, scarcely any foreign port where the consular office is so important as at Havana. Even if the treaty of 1795 extended to Cuba, the summary provision which it makes for the consular office would fall short of what is desirable in the existing state of things. It would be a matter of great mutual convenience to the local government of Cuba, to the government of the United States, and to all persons having occasion to resort to the island, if the consul were allowed to extend his functions to others than tradesmen and seamen, (to which they are now confined,) and to exercise some of the powers of a diplomatic agent. The almost vice-regal authority habitually confided to the Captain General of Cuba, removes the only obvious objection to such an arrangement. It would seem, in fact, that the right of treating with the representative of a foreign government was neccessary to the due exercse of the great discretionary powers with which the Captain General is clothed. To confine the consul to the ordinary duties of the consular office is to deprive the Captain General of one of the greatest facilities for carrying on his government. Recent events strikingly illustrate the justice of these remarks. Had the United States consul been authorized to treat with the Captain General, the late difficulties relative to the "Crescent City," which at one time assumed a formidable character, would not probably have arisen.

There are other subjects of much importance which require to be regulated by convention between the two governments: among these are the vexed question of discriminating tonnage duties, the rights of American citizens residing in the colonies under a "carta de domicilia," the administration of the estates of deceased Americans, the port charges on vessels engaged in trade with the Spanish islands, and postal communication. It is highly desirable that interests so important should be the subject of express stipulation, and not dependent on usage, which may be revoked at pleasure and the discretion of authorities frequently changed. The President, in proposing to negotiate a convention on these subjects has no motive but to obviate causes of dissension and to promote a good understanding between the two governments. Though the United States are remote from Spain, her colonies are our near neighbors, and every consideration that ought to influence the conduct of powerful States applies to our intercourse with them.

* * * * * * * * *

I avail myself of this opportunity to renew to you the assurance of my distinguished consideration.

EDWARD EVERETT.

Señor Don A. Calderon de la Barca, *&c.*, *&c.*, *&c.*

[Extract.]

[No 29.] Consulate of the United States, Havana, *April* 7, 1853.

Sir: * * * * * * * *

The reported search of the American schooner Manchester seems to be causing some excitement; and that the government may be placed in possession of all the evidence that this office can furnish, I enclose you a letter received by me from the captain and mate. This contains all the information I have on the subject; and you will perceive that it is very imperfect. The letter was delivered to me by a Spanish pilot, several days after its date, who demanded the sum of thirty dollars, which, of course, I did not pay. The vessel did not touch at this port.

* * * * * * * *

I have the honor to be, with great respect, your obedient servant,

W. L. SHARKEY.

Hon. Wm. L. Marcy,

Secretary of State.

Consulate of the United States of America, Havana.

On this seventh day of April, A. D. 1853, personally came and appeared James Otis, master of the ship Harriet, of Bath, (Maine,) and made the following statement, which he would have made the day the said ship was entered in the consulate of the United States, but he, said master, saw that the consul was busy investigating a case against some sailors, to wit: On the thirty-first day of March last, being about thirty miles to the westward of the Double-headed Shot Keys, early in the morning, I saw a steamer and a hermaphrodite brig about seven or eight miles to the northward of me; the steamer was running different courses, but after a short time she commenced to steer about the same course that I was; after an hour, or an hour and a half, I saw that she made sail; an hour after that she fired a shot, which I saw strike in the water, right in the range of us; I then ordered our colors set; but before the colors were up, she fired again; we then took in sail and hove to; after the steamer got to within about a mile of us, we saw that she had English colors flying; she then soon came up and hailed us, and asked where we were from and where bound; I told them we were from Savannah, bound to Havana; some officer on board then said he was going to send a boat on board of us; I told him I did not care what he sent; soon afterwards the boat came, with two officers in her; I was in my cabin; the mate came in and said the officers wanted to see me; I went out, and they said that they wanted to take a look around the vessel; I told them they had taken the liberty to stop me on my way, and I supposed they would do as they had a mind to; I asked them if anything new had taken place, that they were cruising, stopping a vessel on her lawful voyage; they said that they were cruising to see that their treaty was not infringed; after they had searched the vessel all round the house, forward, and looking down the hatches, they asked me for the ship's papers; I allowed them to see them, but observed that I did not know of any right they had to demand them; afterwards one of the officers went down between decks, and, lastly, went into their boats and left us; I was detained about one hour and a half.

JAMES OTIS.

Sworn to and subscribed before me by the said master.

W. L. SHARKEY,

Consul of the United States.

I, William L. Sharkey, consul of the United States of America for the city of Havana, and the dependencies thereof, do hereby certify that the copy of a sworn statement, written on this and the two preceding pages of this sheet of paper, is a true and correct copy of the original of record in this consulate.

In testimony whereof, I hereunto subscribe my name and affix the seal of my office, at Havana, this seventh day of April, A. D. 1853.

W. L. SHARKEY. [L. S.]

Mr. Barringer to Mr. Marcy.

[Extract.]

[No. 144.] GRANADA, *June* 10, 1853.

SIR: Your dispatch No. 77, of the 19th April last, reached the legation during my temporary absence from Madrid. I immediately caused a copy of the same to be forwarded to me at this city.

On the 6th instant I addressed to the Spanish government a note on so much of the same as relates to the affair of the United States steamship "Ohio." A copy of this note will hereafter be communicated to the Department of State, with a copy of the answer of her Catholic Majesty's Minister of State for Foreign Affairs, when received. Judging from my knowledge of the past and present policy of the Spanish government in reference to the affairs of the island of Cuba, and especially those connected with the commercial intercourse between that island and the United States, I regret to say that I anticipate no very satisfactory answer to this new demand for explanation and indemnity. It is the settled purpose of Spain to keep the island as independent as possible of all connexion with the United States. To this end the Captain General is intrusted with almost sovereign authority in the government of the island, and the government here are always disposed to sanction whatever he may do or cause to be done—or, rather, they seldom, if ever, disapprove any measure he may have adopted, and which, in his opinion or that of his subordinates, may be deemed necessary for the protection and security of the island.

On my return to Madrid, in the course of a few days, I will also call the attention of her Majesty's Minister of State to the case of the American schooner "Manchester," Captain Sterling, near the island of Cuba, referred to in your dispatch.

* * * * * * *

I have the honor to remain, with the highest respect, sir, your obedient servant,

D. M. BARRINGER.

Hon. W. L. MARCY,
Secretary of State.

Mr. Barringer to Mr. Marcy.

[Extract.]

[No. 147.] LEGATION OF THE UNITED STATES, MADRID,
July 8, 1853.

SIR: I have the honor to transmit, herewith, copies of my note of the 6th ultimo, of the answer of her Majesty's government of the 15th ultimo, and of my reply to the same of the 23d ultimo, on the subject of the affair of the detention of the United States steamship "Ohio" at the Havana, in the month of March last.

It will be seen that I have not regarded the answer of her Majesty's government as satisfactory, in reference to the demands of either for explanation or indemnity.

Nothing more has been received or heard from the Spanish government on this subject, except that, in a conference with the President of the Council, who is also Minister of Foreign Affairs, he expressed his regret at the repeated occurrence of similar difficulties and embarrassments with our steamships at the Havana, and the earnest desire of her Majesty's government to maintain the most friendly relations with the United States, but no change of opinion as to the case of the "Ohio."

* * * * *

HON. WM. L. MARCY,
Secretary of State.

LEGATION OF THE UNITED STATES, MADRID,
June 6, 1853.

SIR: I am directed to bring to the notice of her Majesty's government another unpleasant occurrence connected with the service of the United States mail steamers in the port of Havana— an occurrence presenting not only a case of annoyance, but of injury to our citizens, and embarrassment to our commerce.

It appears from the accompanying statement, which I have caused to be carefully prepared from authentic documents, that one of the United States mail steamships, the "Ohio," in the prosecution of her usual and lawful voyage, with a clean bill of health, (and, as was demonstrated in the sequel, without a reasonable ground of suspicion that there existed on board of her any disease that ought to have subjected her to an hour's quarantine) was forcibly and unreasonably detained for two or three days at or near the port of Havana, deprived of intercourse with the shore, and her commander, Lieutenant Hartstene, an officer of the United States navy, denied even the privilege of communicating, by letter, with the United States consul.

All the circumstances exhibit an apparently inexcusable exercise of power, disrespectful to our flag, and oppressive towards our people.

The vessel was thus detained under pretence of enforcing the quarantine laws against her, not only contrary to the uniform practice in regard to the mail steamers employed in this service, but after she had shown a clean bill of health, and without any evidence of cases of contagious disease on board, or any inquiry into her condition as to the health of her passengers and crew.

After a vexatious delay, an examination into the condition of the "Ohio" was made, (which should have been done before her arrest,) and it was found that there was no cause for subjecting her to quarantine. It further appears, that, although consent has been given for free access of the American consul to the person of the Captain General, this avails nothing so long as our injured citizens are denied access to our consul in order to make him acquainted with their grievances, and that in the case now under consideration the officers of the "Ohio" were not permitted to have intercourse with the American consul.

It was an act of discourtesy; furnishing matter of grave complaint and aggravated the wrong already committed by prolonging the unjustifiable detention of the vessel.

I am directed to express the sincere regret felt by the President at being called upon, so soon after entering upon his duties as Chief Magistrate of the Union, to remonstrate against an occurrence which is, in some respects, not unlike the recent case of the "Crescent City." Though unwilling to characterize the conduct of the authorities at the Havana as intentionally vexatious, the American government cannot but regard it as unjustifiable, and as calculated to disturb the existing friendly relations between Spain and the United States.

In presenting the facts of this case, I am instructed to demand from her Majesty's government indemnity for the damage sustained by the owners of the "Ohio" for her detention as herewith set forth, and to obtain from the same an assurance that the Captain General of Cuba will be instructed to enforce upon the subordinate authorities in Cuba a course of conduct more in accordance with those rules which are essential to an unembarrassed commercial intercourse, and more regardful of the rights and property of American citizens.

It is confidently anticipated that her Majesty's government, equally desirous with that of the United States of removing all grounds of just complaint between both nations, will be willing and ready to accede to these demands.

I avail myself of this occasion to renew the assurance, &c., &c.

D. M. BARRINGER.

His Excellency Don Francisco Sersundi,

President of Council and Minister of State.

Statement of facts concerning the unwarrantable detention of the United States mail steamship "Ohio" at the port of Havana, in April, 1853.

The United States mail steamship "Ohio," from Aspinwall for New York, arrived at the port of Havana on the night of the 9th April, and entered that port on the morning of the 10th, with the United States mails from California, two million five hundred thousand dollars of gold, and four hundred and fifty-six passengers on board.

Upon being visited by the health and port officers in their boat shortly after, those officers were met by the captain and surgeon of the ship, who furnished them with the ship's clean bill of health, and distinctly informed them that there were no contagious nor infectious diseases on board, and that there had been no deaths, and that, of the few cases of ordinary Panama fever (*terciava*) on board, all had improved on the voyage with the exception of one old man. They were also informed that the ship had the United States mails on board, and that she required coal to enable her to proceed with the same.

In spite of this information, the health officers, without making any further investigation of the condition of the ship, ordered the captain to remain where he was, not to approach the wharf where the coal for the ship was deposited, and not to communicate in any way with the shore. An armed guard was stationed to prevent the passengers from leaving the ship; and the captain, Lieutenant Hartstene, of the United States navy, upon his personal request to transmit a communication to the American consul at that port, was refused that privilege.

The authorities also refused to allow any aid from the shore to place coals on board the vessel, saying that the laborers on board must coal the ship by means of boats—a process involving unnecessary expense and great delay.

After some time, the captain of the ship, by means of a gentleman who came within speaking distance, requested again to be allowed to send a letter to the American consul, but no attention was paid to his request.

On the morning of the 11th of April, when the operation of getting the coal on board had already begun, the officers of the port came again within speaking distance of the vessel, and ordered her to remove to the ordinary quarantine ground, at some distance from where she then lay; to do which it was necessary to cease the operation of taking in coal, and to generate steam at great additional expense and delay. However, the captain of the steamer prepared to obey; but, to use his own words, "when ready for starting, we were suddenly and informally released from all restrictions." For this favor the ship's company were indebted to Doctor Don Jorge Ledo, surgeon of her Majesty's fleet at Havana, who, seeing the unusual and unjustifiable situation of the ship, "nobly and disinterestedly" volunteered to go on board and examine her, saying to the officers of the board of health, that if there should prove to be any contagion on board he would remain on the ship.

A few minutes after this gentleman had left her, at about 4 o'clock in the afternoon of the 11th April, the ship was set at liberty.

And Captain Hartstene concludes his narrative to the owners of the ship with these words: "We were, you will perceive, quarantined without there being any measures taken to determine the correctness of the surgeon's and my own assertions, and then relieved on an impartial and private survey, in total disregard to all feelings of delicacy or respect for us or our flag."

Altogether, the steamship was detained in the port of Havana, according to the statement of her owners, for three days.

[Translation.]

FIRST DEPARTMENT OF STATE,
Palace, June 15, 1853.

SIR: I have had the honor to receive your excellency's note, dated the 6th instant, which was accompanied by a relation of what is supposed to have occurred at the Havana, in connexion with the momentary delay in that port of the United States mail steamer "Ohio."

The government of the Queen, my lady, might reasonably hope that such an occurrence—so simple in itself, and subject in every point to the sanitary regulations which are observed scrupulously, and without exception, in all the ports of the island of Cuba, with the vessels of all nations—would not take an official character, and much less that of a reclamation by the government which your excellency represents.

Nevertheless, taking into consideration that the owners of the said steamer, who are also owners of the "Crescent City," to which your excellency alludes in your note, have manifested before now their decided purpose to excite embarrassments and difficulties between the two countries, the government of her Majesty thought proper to anticipate, and directed spontaneous and honorable explanations to Washington, through the Spanish representative in that capital, in order to avoid that the mind of the President of the United States should by any possibility be surprised by the relation, perhaps passionate and inexact, of the director of the Steamship Company.

The note of your excellency makes me suppose that these explanations did not arrive in time, and consequently I see myself obliged to reply to it.

In order to do this, I shall begin by refuting the principal statements contained in the narrative which your excellency encloses to me, which are very far from agreeing with the data and information which have been communicated to me by the proper authorities of the island of Cuba.

According to these data, (in this point agreeing with the narrative which your excellency transmits to me,) the detention of the "Ohio" was not three days, as is stated in your note, but thirty hours—the time necessary and indispensable in order to be assured whether or not the fever which existed on board the ship, and of which one of the passengers had died, had any malignant and contagious character which might put in peril the public health of the island.

On making the health visit to the "Ohio," it was known by the statement itself of the physician aboard that there were various passengers sick of the fever which prevails on the coasts of Chagres.

Nevertheless, the deputation of health, taking into account the provisions of the third article, chapter second, title second, of the general regulations of that service, determined that the vessel, which had no passenger for Havana (the which is worthy to be remarked) should remain simply isolated, passing to the quarantine station in order to provide herself there—with proper precautions—with the coal which she required.

But in view of the reasons which the consignees of the said steamer set forth, soliciting that she should be permitted to go alongside one of the wharves to take in the combustible, the superior board of health, assembled for that purpose, resolved that Don Jorge Ledo, auxiliary physician of the board, and first professor of the fleet, should be sent on board to inform himself of the state of health of the vessel, who made declaration that there existed, in effect, aboard of her an intermittent fever, of which one individual had died the same day of the examination, but that this fever had no malignant nor epidemic character.

By virtue of this, the board being desirous to conciliate, in whatsoever was possible, private interests with the very sacred and preferable interests of the public health, permitted from that moment free pratic to the "Ohio;" and in this connexion I cannot let pass unnoticed the unfounded statement set forth in the relation which your excellency encloses to me—that the vessel's having been left suddenly free from all restriction was owing to the efforts of Dr. George Ledo, surgeon of the fleet of the United States at the Havana, who lent himself disinterestedly to go on board and examine her, because it is exactly this same Ledo, health physician, who, by the express order of the superior board, went on board of the "Ohio" in order to make the report which must serve as a basis to the resolution which the said corporation should adopt.

This manner, so intentionally inexact, of presenting the fact, by the captain of the "Ohio," was, without doubt, with the purpose of taking away from the determination of the board that character of spontaneousness and of meditation which it really had, in order to cause it to be believed that suddenly, and without any formality, said vessel was admitted to free pratic, through the officious representations and the efforts of a surgeon of the fleet of the United States.

By this simple and unimpassioned relation of what happened with said steamer, your excellency will easily comprehend that the detention of the "Ohio" proceeded from the manifestations of her own physician; that it was well founded, seeing that there were sick on board, and even that the death of one individual had occurred; that she was considered suspicious only so long as there was no certainty had of the nature and class of the diseases, being placed voluntarily and without delay in free communication as soon as the report was received from the physician appointed for the inspection and examination of the sick on board; neither the deputation nor the superior board of health being able to dispense with such proceedings of prudence and precaution without infringing the clear and precise regulation which governs this matter.

In this connexion your excellency has thought proper to recall the case of the "Crescent City," considering it as in some respects like that now under discussion, in order to deduce conclusions concerning the conduct observed by the authorities of the Havana, which, as your excellency says, is calculated to disturb the amicable relations between Spain and the United States.

The only analogy which, for my part, I encounter between these two cases is, that in the case of the "Crescent City" the government of your excellency is recognised explicitly, as I flatter myself it will on this occasion, the right of the Captain General of the island of Cuba *to take, by virtue of the powers with which he is invested, whatsoever measure, however restrictive may be its character, which he may consider necessary for the preservation of the island whose government is given him in charge.*

Then, as in the present case, that which alone was sufficient, and is sufficient, for the conscience itself, and the justification of the government of her Majesty, is, to show that the measure adopted as means of protection and security, whether for the defence of the island, or to guard her from the ravages of a contagious disease which exists, or which it is suspected even may exist on board a vessel, are abundant motives for taking those reasonable measures of precaution dictated by the vigilance and the duty of the authorities of the island of Cuba.*

I do not perceive, in truth, what benefit can result to Spain and the United States from recalling events which were appreciated in their just value at their time, and which only signify the deliberate purpose of an individual to sow motives of dissension between two friendly governments.

But as your excellency has judged it opportune to invoke this remembrance as an argument against the authorities of the Havana, and in order to express fears that their conduct may appear calculated to disturb the friendly relations between the two countries, this supposition authorizes me to manifest to your excellency, in my turn, with all the frankness and faithfulness of an honest man, guided by the desire of dissipating unfavorable prejudices which might some day be converted into a motive of formal disagreement, that the director of the Steamship Company, Mr. Law, is he who is constantly, and without reason, provoking contentions and difficulties with the perverse intention of destroying the perpetual† intelligence which exists between the two governments; that whilst no reclamation is presented to the government of her Majesty by the commerce of any nation of the world—of the many which trade with Cuba, nor by the lines of English steamers, nor even by the private vessels of the United States—the line which Mr. Law directs is that which excites and originates every day such lamentable difficulties.

Necessary is it, therefore, that I should call the attention of your excellency seriously to the repeated complications which the presence of said steamers in the island of Cuba offers to the two governments; because, if this company is to be the apple of discord, the government of her Majesty may one day consider it preferable, for the preservation of her amicable relations with the United States, to withdraw the privileges which the steamers of the line of Mr. Law now enjoy, and subject them to precise and definite conditions, in the use of her imprescriptible rights of sovereignty.

With respect to the momentary detention of the "Ohio," after what I have manifested, in order to favor the entire lack of foundation for the complaint of the proprietor of this vessel, it would remain for me only

---

* The grammatical or rhetorical fault in this sentence, which makes the measures adopted to be "the abundant motives for taking those reasonable measures," &c., is faithfully translated as it exists in the original.

H. J. PERRY, *Translator.*

† The original is "perpetua," but there is every reason to suppose this is a clerical error, and should be *perfecta.* The translation would then be "*the perfect intelligence,*" &c.

to leave clearly written, in this note, the perfect right which Spain has, like every independent State, by the principles of the law of nations recognized by the publicists of all countries, including those of the United States, to establish the rules to which the vessels which arrive at her ports must be subject; this right being even more respectable when it has reference to the preservation of the public health; but the American government is too just, and too intelligent, to ignore on this occasion principles so generally accepted, and not to easily understand that the superior authority of the island of Cuba could not, in any case, interpose in a matter of the dispositions made by the board of health, subject to the regulations in force.

We do not pretend, nevertheless, that these are the most perfect; but such as our system is in this point, to it are submitted the Spanish commerce, and that of all the nations which trade with us; it not being possible to make an exception in favor of the United States, without the exceptions coming to be converted into the general rule; and however regretful it may be for Spain not to be able to be agreeable to the citizens of the Union, and what is more, even when these dispositions might exert an influence in the diminution of our commercial relations with the confederation, it would be necessary for us to submit ourselves to this inconvenience as a condition of the preservation of the public health.

For the rest, the government of her Majesty, constant in its purpose of facilitating commercial intercourse in the island of Cuba, will renew with pleasure to the Captain General the recommendation that foreign vessels are to be molested as little as possible in that island.

Very grateful it would be for me that the considerations which I have expressed should be of influence in the mind of the American government, so that it might listen in future with little confidence to the complaints and inexact representations of badly intentioned people; flattering myself that it will do justice to the sincere desires and intentions of Spain to cultivate intimate and friendly relations with the United States.

I renew to your excellency, on this occasion, the assurances of my most distinguished consideration, &c.,

FRANCISCO SERSUNDI.

To the MINISTER PLENIPOTENTIARY
of the United States.

LEGATION OF THE UNITED STATES, MADRID,
June 23, 1853.

SIR: I have the honor to acknowledge the receipt of your excellency's note of the 15th instant, (which, however, did not reach this legation till the 20th of the same,) in reply to mine of the 6th instant, on the subject of the detention of the United States steamship "Ohio," at the Havana, in the month of March last. The manifest and material differences in the statements of facts relative to this detention, as presented respectively to the governments at Madrid and Washington, together with the circumstance that the government of her Catholic Majesty, anticipating that difficulties and embarrassments might possibly grow out of this occurrence, had, previously to the receipt of my note, deemed it proper to address, in the language of your excellency, voluntary and favorable (leales) explanations to the government of the United States through the Spanish minister at Washington, render it, on my part, prudent, as well as respectful to both governments, that I should reserve for a future occasion, if necessary, observations which, but for these considerations, it would now be my duty to make. It is to be hoped that the circumstances of the affair may be more fully and exactly inquired into; and I shall be most happy if, from this examination of the character of the note already addressed to the government of the United States, (of whose contents, however, I regret I am not more particularly apprized than through the general terms applied by your excellency,) this negotiation shall result in a satisfactory and amicable termination, alike honorable to both nations. Justice and truth, however, require that I should not omit at present to say something in reply to remarks of your excellency, which must have proceeded from misapprehension on the part of your excellency, or incorrect information on the part of others. It is not true, as supposed by your excellency, that the statement of facts making the ground of this complaint originated with Mr. George Law, the owner, or one of the owners, of the line of steamships to which the "Ohio" belongs.

Whilst the government of the United States must be in all cases the sole judges, on their own responsibility, as to the authenticity of the sources of any knowledge on which they may act, I feel it due to the parties concerned to state, that the information on which they have acted in this case has been obtained from the officers and passengers aboard the vessel at the time of the occurrence. Mr. Law states no particular, except as to the length of time the vessel was detained, (and this is not of his own knowledge,) which he alleges to have been three days. In this, not being present, he may well have been mistaken by misapprehending the account given by Lieutenant Hartstene, of the United States navy, then in command, who states, that "the Ohio, at midnight of the 9th instant, (March,) was off the Moro," and that she left Havana "at half-past nine of the evening of the 12th instant;" thus making the entire detention at that port three days, less two and a half hours.

But this same officer states, (in this, as to the length of time only, nearly agreeing with the statements in your excellency's note,) that the actual time of detention caused by the unnecessary and unreasonable conduct of the local authorities was thirty-two hours.

But the length of time itself is not a material consideration, except as to the measure of injury sustained by the detention. If the vessel had been detained only one hour by frivolous pretexts, or by the unnecessary and vexatious, and groundless conduct of the authorities, the wrong would be as clear, though the injury might not be so great, as if she had been thus detained three days. In both cases the principle of objection would be the same.

The gist of the complaint here is, that the usual course of proceeding in such cases having been pursued by the authorities; with a clean bill of health from the port of departure; with the unequivocal declarations of the proper officers and surgeon of the ship, asserting solemnly and formally that there was not, and had not been, any disease of a contagious, epidemic, or malignant character on board, and no death on the voyage; that there existed only cases of the "Panama" or intermittent fever, usually if not always found on all the steamers from Chagres, and for which no vessel had ever heretofore been placed in quarantine or kept from communicating with the shore; and, furthermore, that without any examination whatever, but in defiance and in reckless denial of all these allegations, the ship was detained thirty-two hours, ordered to quarantine, and then, after a momentary inquiry and informal investigation of her condition, she was immediately discharged, in a most informal manner only, as the officers alleged and believe, through the voluntary and disinterested conduct of a surgeon of her Majesty's fleet at the Havana, who went on board, confirmed the statements made by her officers, and thus caused the authorities to do what they ought to have done, and what they could have done at first, and without this uncalled for delay, so annoying and inconvenient to the large number of passengers, and so detrimental to a vessel having on board the mails of the United States, and a very large amount of treasure destined for another and distant port. It was an aggravation of the complaint, and a discourtesy to our flag, that during all this time none of the officers of the ship were allowed to have even the slightest communication with the American consul.

In this connexion, I cannot forbear to refer to an error into which your excellency has, doubtless unintentionally, fallen, through the mistake of some subordinate—most probably the translator of the department over which your excellency presides—in supposing that the statement which accompanied my former note on this subject represented the surgeon who thus generously interfered for the release of the vessel as belonging to the fleet of the United States, instead of to that of her Catholic Majesty.

The statement was directly the contrary, as your excellency will perceive by referring to the same.

Having understood that this was an inadvertent mistake, I dismiss so much of your excellency's observations as relate to the same, and the "unfounded statement set forth" (*especie asendata*) and *intentional misrepresentation* so unjustly charged against the captain of the "Ohio," with the single suggestion that it is always safer to take a charitable view of fallible human nature than to indulge in constructions so disparaging to the character and good name of a person against whom nothing has been heretofore alleged, and who, as in the case before us, is believed to be worthy of every confidence and esteem.

Your excellency calls special attention to the circumstance that there was on board "no passenger *for the Havana;*" and it is thus left to be inferred that there was no necessity for personal communication with the shore, when the fact is that there were passengers, believed to be some fifty in number, bound for New Orleans, who had to land at the Havana on their voyage to the former city, and who did, in fact, thus land, with others on board the ship, by paying one dollar each to the local authorities for this permission.

Your excellency refers to the circumstance that there was a death on board; but if so, the Spanish surgeon himself states that it took place on the day of the examination made by him, and not before, or on the arrival of the vessel, when she was ordered to be detained by armed force from all communication with the shore. He further states that this individual died of *intermittent fever*, and that there was no contagious or malignant disease on board, thus promptly verifying the original statements of the surgeon and officers of the ship, which could have been as easily and effectually done at first as after this unnecessary detention.

Your excellency complains of Mr. George Law as being disposed to excite dissensions, and that he is constantly and unreasonably provoking contentions and difficulties between the two countries; and your excellency intimates that it may become the duty of her Catholic Majesty's government to withdraw the privileges extended to this line of United States mail steamships, and subject it to new conditions and restrictions.

If the embarrassments to which the line has heretofore been subjected are to continue, it may be that Mr. Law may deem it his duty and interest to anticipate the action of her Majesty's government, and voluntarily withdraw his ships therefrom, instead of availing himself longer of these *privileges*, provided he can be absolved from his contract with the United States, who are also deeply interested in the transportation of the public mails on board the vessels of this line, besides the general duty of giving just and ample protection to the citizens of the republic and their property, wherever to be found.

I do not suppose that the course pursued towards the vessels of this line by the local authorities is expressly so intended; but it certainly may have that effect in the end if allowed to be continued by the government at this court.

It is not my duty nor my purpose, in this correspondence, to become the defender of Mr. Law. He may have committed errors, as others have. I am here solely as the representative of the United States, to fulfil their instructions, and to take care, within the sphere of my duties, that the just rights of all their citizens, however humble or exalted, however rich or poor, are fully and fairly maintained and defended. But I cannot do less than say to your excellency that in the case of the "Crescent City," as well as in this of the "Ohio," the only two instances in which Mr. Law has appealed to his government on account of occurrences at the Havana, the justice of his requisition has been admitted by the United States, who believed that they had good ground of complaint in each case against the authorities of Cuba, and made corresponding demands for satisfaction and redress from the government at Madrid.

Your excellency seems to object that I should have referred in this connexion to the case of the "Crescent City." Believing, as the actual result demonstrated, that there was no well-founded ground for the action of the Cuban authorities in either case—in the case of the "Ohio" that there was no contagion or other cause to justify the detention and order to quarantine; and in the case of the "Crescent City" that Purser Smith did not write, transmit, or have any knowledge of, or agency in, the newspaper articles complained of; and that if he had, it was no reason why the *ship* should have been prohibited from entering the port of Havana to land her passengers and deliver her mails; and believing also that these proceedings were calculated, by their very nature, and their occurrence in quick succession, to disturb the friendly relations of the two countries—it was most natural and proper, in the opinion of the undersigned, that the analogy between them should be alluded to and commented upon in this correspondence. I must be allowed to remind your excellency, too, that the answer of her Majesty's government in the case of the "Crescent City" was not satisfactory to that of the United States, and was passed over at the time without further correspondence and negotiation, solely from the circumstance that the Captain General had revoked the order which had produced the difficulties; and in the further hope that her Majesty's government, seeing with regret, as do the United States, the occurrence of these embarrassments, might be disposed to enter upon some new and mutual arrangement by which the commercial interests and intercommunication between the Spanish colonies and the United States might be placed upon a better and safer basis for the continuance of harmony, and for the reciprocal advantage of both countries. I cannot forego the occasion also to remark, that while the government at Madrid were approving, and, as would seem from your excellency's note, still continue to approve, the conduct of the Captain General in the affair of the "Crescent City," and objected to by the United States, that officer himself had seen the error he had committed, repealed the order which had given so much trouble, and allowed the entry of the vessel with the "obnoxious Purser Smith on board;" thus voluntarily and substantially admitting the justice of the complaint of the United States, and that such an order was not necessary for the safety of the island, as at first alleged. Though his action was tardy, it was duly appreciated, and the subject was then permitted to drop.

The United States would be the last to question the right of Spain, as an independent nation, or that of the Captain General of Cuba, under authority from his government, to do whatever they may deem necessary for the protection and security of the island, as regards either the public health or safety. But then, this right must be exercised, and this authority executed, with due respect to the rights of others, and consistently with the usages and laws of civilized nations, who, of course, are equally competent to judge whether these laws have been violated and these usages improperly infringed or not. In the case before us, the government of the United States believe there was as little reason to detain the "Ohio," from any consideration or fear of danger to the public health of the island, as there was to exclude the "Crescent City," from any pretext of insecurity to the public safety.

The government of Spain may, if they think proper, interdict all communication, personal or commercial, with the United States,; yet, surely, such an act could only be regarded as anything but a friendly one, and would have to be done under all the responsibility for the consequences which might justly be expected to flow from such an inimical procedure. And whether such prohibition be effected directly by law, or indirectly by annoyances and embarrassments to such intercourse, on the part of the authorities of Cuba, and not disapproved of by the metropolitan government, the pernicious and fatal result would be the same to rhe interests and good will of the two nations.

Such a policy could but promptly end in the entire destruction of the peaceful relations of the two nations.

Believing that the government of Spain will be well disposed fairly to review the conduct of their subordinate authorities upon all occasions, when respectfully required to do so by a friendly power, the government of the Union will continue to appeal to them for redress, whenever they have reason to believe that such conduct has been unjust and injurious to their citizens and the property of those whom it is their highest duty to protect and defend against injustice and wrong.

When the facts of this case shall be fully and accurately ascertained, I think your excellency will discover that the government of the United States have not been "listening to inexact" and "passionate" statements of persons in whom "little confidence is to be placed," but that they have just ground of complaint against the authorities in Cuba, for which the government at Madrid ought to give prompt and plenary satisfaction and indemnity.

I avail myself of this occasion to renew to your excellency the assurance of my most distinguished consideration, &c., &c., &c.

D. M. BARRINGER.

His Excellency GENERAL SERSUNDI,
President of the Council and Minister of State.

Mr. Barringer to Mr. Marcy.

[Extract.]

[No. 148.] ROYAL SITE OF SAN ILDEFONSO,
July 16, 1853.

SIR: I have the honor to transmit, herewith, copies of my note to the Spanish government of the 25th ultimo; of their answer to the same of the 9th instant; and of my reply to this note under date of the 14th instant, on the subject of the detention and search of the American schooner "Manchester," near Cape San Antonio, in the month of March last.

* * * * *

Hon. WM. L. MARCY,
Secretary of State.

Mr. Barringer to General Sersundi.

LEGATION OF THE UNITED STATES, MADRID,
June 25, 1853.

SIR: I am directed to bring to your excellency's attention the circumstances of a transaction which occurred near the island of Cuba, in the month of March last. It appears that on the 14th of that month, the American schooner "Manchester," captain Sterling, of Baltimore, on her voyage from Jamaica, while off the island of Cuba, about twenty miles from Cape Antonio, being driven there by adverse winds, was boarded by a Spanish cruiser of twelve guns.

Twelve armed men were sent on board, who took possession of the vessel and carried her inside the reef, in spite of the remonstrances of the captain. They then demanded her papers and examined them; and although these were found to be correct in all respects, they broke open her hatches and took out about a third of her cargo, but not finding any guns or ammunition on board, put the cargo back again. They then threatened to take the vessel to the Havana; but after keeping her thus twenty-four hours under the guns of the cruiser, they decided to allow her to depart, getting out of the reef the best way she could. This, however, was not allowed until the captain had promised a pilot, for his services, the unjust demand of some thirty dollars, the cruiser being in company all the while.

It is sufficient, at present, to bring this affair to the notice of your excellency, that a prompt investigation may be had in reference to the same, that proper explanation may be given to the government of the United States, and a just satisfaction made to the injured parties. It affords another illustration of the necessity of some mutual arrangement between the two countries, by which their commercial intercourse may be placed upon a more definite and satisfactory basis; and also of the necessity of urgent and effectual instructions to the authorities in Cuba, to observe a course of conduct more in accordance with the recognised rules of commercial intercourse, and more regardful of the rights and property of American citizens.

I avail myself of this occasion to renew to your excellency the assurances of my most distinguished consideration.

Your excellency's obedient servant,

D. M. BARRINGER.

His Excellency GENERAL SERSUNDI,
President of the Council and Minister of State.

General Sersundi to Mr. Barringer.

[Translation.]

FIRST DEPARTMENT OF STATE,
San Ildefonso, July 9, 1853.

SIR: I have had the honor to receive your excellency's note relative to the detention near cape San Antonio, in the island of Cuba, of the

American schooner "Manchester," by a Spanish cruiser, which act took place, as your excellency states, of the 14th of March last.

The government of her Majesty has not received any intelligence concerning the occurrence to which your excellency refers; and in order to obtain such intelligence as precise as is necessary for forming a judgment in the case, I have addressed the Captain General of the island of Cuba, charging him to give information concerning the fact in question.

Meantime, and limiting myself solely to the act of detention, stripped of the circumstances which may have intervened in it, the which are as yet unknown to me, as I have had the honor to state to your excellency, I cannot do less than call your attention to the grave considerations which make excusable any excess of zeal in the exercise of their duties, if any shall have occurred, on the part of the cruisers, charged with watching the coasts of Cuba.

The especial situation of that part of the dominions of her Majesty, threatened by expeditions which already more than once have succeeded in touching the Cuban soil, exacts on the part of our vessels that no means nor efforts whatsoever should be omitted, within the limits of their jurisdiction, to keep off the danger of new incursions; and this, as your excellency knows, can only be attained by the examination and search of those vessels, national or foreign, which in passing those waters may excite suspicion for whatsoever reason. Without that, these suspicions once removed, the act of detention can be qualified as an offence, since it is authorized by the law of nations, by the duty of self-defence, and by a lamentable experience, that all the precautions are few for keeping at a distance the enemies of the public tranquility of the island of Cuba.

Also, the obligations contracted by virtue of international compacts with respect to the abolition of the traffic of negroes, impose upon the Spanish authorities in those dominions the duty of watching carefully, so that the disembarcation of slaves may not take place; and your excellency will easily comprehend that, if those who devote themselves to this so lucrative traffic could in any way elude the action of the cruisers, as would happen the moment in which fetters should be put upon the latter by establishing exceptions, the important object of the abolition of the negro traffic would come to be illusory and impossible.

Notwithstanding this, being desirous of avoiding every reasonable motive for reclamation on this point on the part of the United States, I have addressed to the Captain General of the island of Cuba the proper orders, so that the vigilance of the Spanish cruisers shall be exercised in such a way as to cause the least molestation possible to the vessels which may navigate the seas of the island of Cuba.

I avail myself of this occasion to renew to your excellency the assurances of my most distinguished consideration, &c.

FRANCISCO SERSUNDI.

To the MINISTER PLENIPOTENTIARY,
of the United States.

Mr. Barringer to General Sursundi.

SAN ILDEFONSO, *July* 14, 1853.

SIR: Your excellency's note of the 9th instant, on the subject of the detention of the American schooner "Manchester," by a Spanish cruiser, near Cape San Antonio, in the month of March last, has been received. Appreciating, in their fullest extent, the grave considerations urged by your excellency to show the necessity of constant vigilance along the Cuban coasts, for the purposes both of preventing hostile invasions and of suppressing the African slave-trade, and making all due allowance for the excess of zeal and want of discretion sometimes displayed by the Spanish authorities in performing these duties, I must still insist, as I think your excellency will more fully ascertain, npon an examination of the facts in the particular case before us, that there was no justification for the conduct of the officers of the cruiser, and that there was not the slightest ground of suspicion to authorize the seizure, vexatious search, and other annoying circumstances, which attended the detention of the said American schooner.

It is proper, however, to abstain from further remarks for the present, and until her Majesty's governmeut shall be more fully informed as to the facts of the case, upon the inquiry which, I am pleased to learn, your excellency has directed the Captain General of Cuba to cause to be made.

It is a source of much satisfaction, also, to learn that the necessary orders have been given to the same high officer, with a view to avoid, as far as possible, all improper interference with vessels navigating the waters of that island.

I avail myself of this occasion, &c., &c.

D. M. BARRINGER.

Mr. Barringer to Mr. Marcy.

[Extract.]

[No. 153.] SAN ILDEFONSO,
August 18, 1853.

SIR: I have the honor to transmit herewith, copies of a note from the Spanish government of the 10th instant, and of my reply to the same, of the 11th instant, being the final correspondence between the Spanish government and this legation on the subject of the detention of the United States steamship "Ohio," at the port of Havana, in the month of March last.

It will be seen, that in my final note relative to this affair, about which I have heretofore felt it my duty, under the instructions from the department, to remonstrate in strong terms against the conduct of the authorities in Cuba, I have acted on the information communicated to me from the Spanish Foreign Office, that it had been amicably arranged at Washington. I have no reason to doubt the correctness of this information, though I have no advice on the subject from the Department of State.

I trust my course in this negotiation will meet the approbation of the government at Washington.

* * * * * *

I have the honer to remain, with the highest respect, sir, your obedient servant,

D. M. BARRINGER.

Hon. Wm. L. Marcy,
Secretary of State.

[Translation.]

First Department of State,
San Ildefonso, August 10, 1853.

Sir: I have delayed answering the reply which your excellency was pleased to address me on the 23d of June last, upon the affair of the detention of the steamer "Ohio," in the port of Havana, because I was desirous to learn, beforehand, the estimation put upon this occurrence by the government of the confederation, in view of the explanations which Señor Calderon de la Barca was charged to make.

The situation of your excellency, as a mere executor of the orders of your government, obliged you to be persistent in the reclamation, however much your excellency might have comprehended that those orders had been dictated under the first impression caused by the complaints of the proprietors of the "Ohio;" but the government of her Majesty ought not to add warmth to a discussion for a motive so trivial and innocent, and on this account it addressed the explanations to the cabinet in Washington.

I have now the satisfaction to announce to your excellency that, according to information from the minister of the Queen in Washington, Mr. Marcy had been convinced, that in the momentary detention of the "Ohio" there was no motive for complaint on the part of the United States, having manifested to Señor Calderon de la Barca that "there was no occasion for saying anything more upon this subject."

I take especial satisfaction in considering as terminated a discussion so unnecessary, and in recognizing the good faith with which the government of the United States has done justice to the rectitude and impartiality of our intentions, and I avail myself of this opportunity to renew to your excellency the assurance of my most distinguished consideration, &c., &c., &c.

FRANCISCO SERSUNDI.

To the Minister Plenipotentiary,
of the United States.

Legation of the United States in Spain,
San Ildefonso, August 11, 1853.

Sir: Your excellency's note of yesterday has just been received. I have sincere pleasure in being informed thereby that the explanations which his excellency Mr. Calderon de la Barca had been instructed to make to the government at Washington, on the subject of the detention of the steamer "Ohio" in the port of the Havana, had proved entirely satisfactory.

I am rejoiced at this termination of a discussion in which I have been the mere organ of my government, to fulfil their express instructions; and I am sure I shall have the hearty concurrence of your excellency in wishing for a conclusion equally satisfactory to every subject of negotiation which may arise between the two governments.

I avail myself of this occasion to renew, &c., &c.

D. M. BARRINGER.

His Excellency GENERAL SERSUNDI,
President of the Council and Minister of State ad interim.

Mr. Soulé to Mr. Marcy.

[Extract.]

[No. 6.] LEGATION OF THE UNITED STATES, MADRID,
March 8, 1854.

SIR: I have the honor to transmit herewith the translations of two notes received from her Majesty's Minister of State, dated 15th November, 1853, and 14th February last, upon the subject of the detention and search of the American schooner "Manchester," near Cape St. Anthony, in Cuba, by a Spanish armed cruiser.

You will recollect that the original instructions of the department to my predecessor were not definite, nor did they authorize him to do anything more than to call the attention of her Majesty's government to the circumstances of the occurrence. Indeed, the facts of the case do not appear to have been at that time clearly known even to our government. They are now, however, sufficiently well ascertained, from the admissions contained in those two notes.

The "Manchester," it appears, was found stranded, and the cruiser, after getting her afloat, entertaining some suspicion of her errand on the coast, although her papers were probably in every respect correct, broke open her hatches and took out a part of her cargo, when, finding nothing to warrant suspicion, the same was returned to its place, the "Manchester" piloted out into the open sea, and put at liberty.

The Spanish government attempts to excuse this conduct by considerations connected with the peculiar condition of the island at that time, and in these last two notes seems to be desirous of diverting attention from the main features of the case to a transaction between the captain of the "Manchester" and the Spanish pilot, involving the payment of thirty dollars.

In my answer to these notes, dated the 3d instant, I have thought proper to bring the affair back again to its true signification and bearings, saving the two questions involved, viz: that of indemnity to the owners of the "Manchester," and that of the insult offered to our flag.

I have now the honor to refer the whole subject to you, for such further action, if any, as may appear proper to the government.

* * * * * * * * *

[Translation.]

FIRST DEPARTMENT OF STATE,
Palace, November 15, 1853.

SIR: The Captain General of the island of Cuba, from whom information had been sought concerning the circumstances of what took place in the detention of the American schooner "Manchester," by a Spanish cruiser, near the cape of San Antonio, in the said island, has transmitted to this first department copies of the communications which, on this subject, and at his instance, have been addressed to him by the Anglo-American consul at the Havana and the commanding general of that naval station.

According to what is remembered by the secretary of the consulate, with reference to the information which was given him at that time by his predecessor, Mr. Sharkey, and according to what appears from a dispatch which the latter addressed to his government, the consul of the United States has stated that, at the beginning of March of this year, a letter was received at that consulate, signed by the captain and mate of the "Manchester," in which they said that the schooner being swept by a strong current, and having stranded near the cape of St. Anthony, a Spanish war-schooner presented herself, which sent them men to assist them out of the difficult situation in which they were; that the officers of the Spanish vessel, on account of some suspicion which they entertained, caused the hatches to be opened and a part of the cargo to be removed, but not finding anything, they put the "Manchester" at liberty to continue her voyage.

The letter contained also a postscript, charging Mr. Sharkey not to pay to the pilot of the Spanish schooner thirty dollars, which he exacted for his services.

Mr. Sharkey, nevertheless, being of opinion that the captain of the "Manchester" was under the obligation of paying what had been claimed of him, (seeing that they had gotten him out of a perilous position,) caused the pilot to deliver him the account receipted, and sent it on for payment to the collector of the custom-house at New York. Afterwards, and in view of an article in a newspaper of that city, in which the captain of the "Manchester" gratuitously accused the crew of the Spanish schooner of various outrages which he supposed they had put upon him, Mr. Sharkey, in order to establish the truth of the facts, wrote to the minister of foreign affairs of the United States a narrative of what had occurred.

As your excellency will perceive, the result is, that, although a search of the "Manchester" did take place, it was only after having afforded her the protection and aid which were exacted by humanity and the difficult position in which she was, and in consequence of a suspicion sufficiently justified by the special circumstances of the island of Cuba, and the projects of invasion with which she has been more than once threatened. I ought nevertheless to say to your excellency that, in the communication of the commandant general of the naval station to the Captain General of the island, an explicit assurance is given that thirty dollars were not exacted from the captain of the "Machester" for having placed her at liberty, since, besides that the commanding officers of the Spanish cruiser had thus stated, such exactions are in open opposition to the regulations of the navy.

In view of the complete contradiction, as regards this point, which exists between the communications of the Anglo-American consul and the commandant general of that naval station, General Cañedo has sought from the latter new information, and a more detailed account of all which occurred.

I will hasten to transmit the same to your excellency as soon as it shall be received in this first department; although I am confident that, in attention to what is stated by the American consul, your excellency will have recognized the bad faith with which the captain of the "Manchester" has proceeded in accusing, without the slightest reason, the officers of the Spanish vessel-of-war, and of the little credit which, for this cause, his language merits.

I avail myself of this occasion, &c., &c., &c.

A. CALDERON DE LA BARCA.

To the MINISTER PLENIPOTENTIARY
of the United States.

[Translation.]

FIRST DEPARTMENT OF STATE,
Palace, February 14, 1854.

SIR: In accordance with what I had the honor to announce to your excellency in my note of November 10, of last year, the Captain General of the island of Cuba has transmitted to this first department the new information relative to the detention of the American schooner "Manchester" by a Spanish cruiser, which he had sought from tho commandant general of that naval station, with the object of verifying, if in fact any recompense was exacted from the captain of the American vessel for the services which were afforded him on that occasion.

The result of these last communications is, that the said schooner being put afloat, and after having been taken out from among the dangerous reefs where she was found, the captain asked the Spanish pilot what sum he should give him for having put him in the open sea; and having agreed that it should be thirty dollars, he stated that he could not pay it at that moment on account of being without money, but that he would give him a letter desiring the United States consul at the Havana to pay him that amount. Instead, therefore, of any violent exaction on the part of the pilot, there was, in this case, no more than the acceptance of the voluntary offering made by the American captain, who, at the same time, wrote in a contrary sense to the consul referred to, and afterwards published in a newspaper of the Union a false account of the occurrence, defaming the loyal deportment of the Spanish officers.

I ought, nevertheless, to say to your excellency that the commandant general of the naval station of the Havana has disapproved of the conduct of the pilot in having accepted a recompense which the regulations of the navy prohibit, imposing upon him also a punishment for not having made known the same, as he ought, to the captain of the vessel in which he served.

For this reason the proper communications have been addressed to the commercial agent of the United States at the Havana, to the end that he may not pay the indicated sum of thirty dollars, as often as the Spanish cruisers shall receive no recompense whatever for the extension of services of the same nature as those which have caused the unjust and unfounded complaint of the captain of the "Manchester."

I avail myself of this occasion, &c., &c.

A. CALDERON DE LA BARCA.

LEGATION OF THE UNITED STATES, MADRID,
March 3, 1854.

SIR: I have had the honor to receive your excellency's notes of the 15th November, 1853, and the 14th February last, referring to the case of the American schooner Manchester.

In reply, I beg leave to say that your excellency seems to have been laboring under a misapprehension in supposing that either this legation or the government of the United States had felt any considerable interest in the question of the payment of thirty dollars between the captain of the American schooner and the pilot of the Spanish armed vessel. Whether either or both of those individuals proceeded with good or bad faith in that transaction, is a matter of very little importance in this discussion.

The points to which, however, I feel it necessary to recall the attention of your excellency as important, are—

1st. The question of indemnity to the owners of the Manchester for the injury and losses which they may have sustained on account of the illegal detention and search of that vessel by a Spanish cruiser; and,

2d. The insult offered to the flag of the United States by the detention and search of a vessel under its colors, whether the same may have occurred in the waters of the island of Cuba or in any other of the waters which surround this earth. As regards the first, it may perhaps prove to be, in this instance, but a mere question of right, since the injuries sustained by the owners of the schooner may have been only nominal, and their losses more than compensated by the benefits received from the crew of the cruiser in aiding to get her out from among the reefs. But with regard to the second point I am not prepared to declare the explanations of your excellency as satisfactory to my government; yet, in view of the peculiar circumstances of this case, I will transmit the communications of your excellency to the Secretary of State of the United States, and will await his instructions before making any further communication on this subject.

I ought, however, to say to your excellency that, as regards the captain of the Manchester, no complaint has been preferred on his part to the government at Washington, or to any of its officers, so far as I am informed, either against the officers of the Spanish vessel-of-war or against any person connected with the occurrence which has been brought to the notice of her Majesty's government. The simple suspicion, only, that a vessel under the flag of the United States has been forcibly detained and searched by one of her Majesty's armed cruisers, in time of peace, will always be sufficient to excite the very serious attention of the government of the United States, and must necessarily, in every case, lead to a rigid investigation of the circumstances which may have conduced to the taking of so very delicate a step. Meantime, I take a sincere pleasure in assuring your excellency that no government is more sensible to the courtesy, nor more prompt in acknowledging the favors which its vessels or citizens in distress may receive at the friendly hands of the subjects of other powers, than is the government of the United States; and it would be for me a source of the highest satisfaction if I should hereafter be called upon to address your excellency in no other than cases purely of this last description.

I avail myself of this occasion to renew to your excellency the assurance of my most distinguished consideration.

Your obedient servant,

PIERRE SOULE.

His Excellency Don A. Calderon de la Barca,
Minister of State.

CASE OF JOHN S. THRASHER.

Mr. Webster to Mr. Sharkey.

[Extract.]

[No. 5.] Department of State,
Washington, January 7, 1852.

Sir:

* * * * * * * *

You will please obtain copies, if permitted by the Spanish authorities, from the records of the oaths and proceedings in the case of the domiciliation of Mr. Thrasher, and transmit the same to this department.

Your letter of the 24th ultimo has been received.

I am, sir, &c.,

DANIEL WEBSTER.

William L. Sharkey, Esq.,
U. S. Consul, Havana.

Mr. Barringer to Mr. Webster.

[Extract.]

[No. 75.] LEGATION OF THE UNITED STATES, MADRID,
January 14, 1852.

SIR: I have much satisfaction in informing you that Mr. *John S. Thrasher*, lately sentenced to eight years' *presidio* in Ceuta, Africa, by the Spanish authorities in Havana, was pardoned on the 11th instant, and will be immediately released.

The first notice I had of this sentence was on the 28th ultimo, in a private note from Mr. Thrasher himself of the 22d ultimo, announcing his arrival at Vigo as a prisoner on board the Spanish ship "Hispano Cubano," then in quarantine, and shortly to proceed to Cadiz on his route to Ceuta. Mr. Thrasher, without giving a detailed statement of his arrest and trial, referred me to the communications which he supposed I had received, or would soon receive, from Washington, whither he had directed the papers to be sent from Havana. Not having received any instructions from the Department of State on the subject, but still anxious to do all I could, under the circumstances, in behalf of the prisoner, on the 29th ultimo I addressed an unofficial note to the Minister of the Interior, (Gobernacion,) referring to his arrival, saying that I was ignorant of the charges against him, and did not know, therefore, whether his case was embraced in the recent pardon of the American prisoners, or not; that I desired copies of the proceedings and sentence against him; and, also, that Mr. Thrasher might be confined for the present at or near Cadiz, with liberty of the fortress or arsenal, as the case might be.

I stated to him frankly that I had no official instructions on the subject, and that all I asked was a personal favor. I subsequently had an informal interview with this minister on the subject, who manifested every disposition to do all in his power in answer to my request.

On the 5th instant I addressed a communication to the Minister of State and Foreign Affairs, a copy of which, marked A No. 1, is herewith enclosed. I also had several interviews with this minister and the under Secretary of State on this subject. It is not deemed essential to detail the conversations had on these different occasions.

It is sufficient to state that I maintained in substance, that, although ignorant of the specific charges against Mr. Thrasher, I regretted his detention in prison, especially since the recent satisfactory and honorable adjustment of differences between the two countries, and the general pardon and release of all the other American prisoners; that it would be most desirable to remove also this source of excitement; that it occurred to me this prisoner might well be embraced in the general amnesty or pardon, particularly as he had appealed from the decision in Havana to her Majesty the Queen, and inasmuch, as far as I understood the accusations against him, they had some connexion with the late expedition against Cubu; and that Mr. Thrasher complained of injustice done him on the trial, and that privileges had been denied him to which he was entitled as an American citizen.

It was replied that his trial and sentence stood on separate and independent grounds, though they might have some connexion with the invasion; that her Majesty's government felt the full force of the considerations urged, and had every disposition to remove every cause of difference between the two countries, whose friendly relations had been placed on so honorable a basis by the recent negotiations; that, as far as they were cognizant of the proceedings against the prisoner, he had no cause of complaint on account of the trial or sentence; but that the representations which I had made, added to their own knowledge on the subject, would be cheerfully and seriously considered, with every desire on their part to preserve in their full extent the most amicable feelings towards the American nation, and to grant my requests as far as was consistent with duty to their own government and people; but that, if Mr. Thrasher was an American citizen, he was still subject to the laws of Spain whilst resident in Cuba.

This latter proposition was admitted by me, with the proviso that if he was an American citizen—which I insisted and which they seemed to admit—he was entitled, under treaty, to some rights which might be denied to a subject of Spain.

These and similar views were urged upon the government here with all the force I could command, in the absence of instructions from Washington, or full details from Mr. Thrasher himself.

Having heard more at length from this latter gentleman at Cadiz on the 11th instant, I immediately had an interview with her Majesty's Minister of State on the same day, in which I repeated the views already stated, adding that I was now convinced that Mr. Thrasher was an American citizen and not a Spanish subject, though admitting that as a domiciliated resident he was amenable to Spanish laws and tribunals for any offence committed within Spanish territory, subject to his rights under treaty stipulations; that he had taken no oath of allegiance to make him a naturalized subject of her Majesty's government, or to deprive him of his rights under the treaty of 1795; but still it could not be denied that the Cuban tribunals had jurisdiction of the offence, as far as I was advised on the subject; and therefore I submitted, that the best course to adopt was the one which I had before suggested, and which seemed to receive the favorable consideration of the minister, viz: that he should be included in the general pardon granted by her Majesty to the American prisoners, and which was, as you will have perceived, limited to those who were "citizens of the United States."

On the 13th instant I received from her Majesty's Minister of State, the Marquis of Miraflores, a communication under date of the 11th instant, a copy of which, translated, is herewith transmitted, informing me of the pardon of Mr. Thrasher as heretofore stated. The prisoner has been detained at Cadiz until within a few days since, and treated with every consideration compatible with his situation. I fear, however, from a letter received from our consul at that city, that on the 10th or 11th instant he was embarked for his destination at Ceuta, under his sentence. I have taken the proper measures to cause the orders for his release to be immediately issued. Copies of the letter of Mr. Burton, and of all the important consular correspondence in reference to this case, are herewith transmitted, marked B.

It may be proper to mention, as connected with the history of the case here, that on the receipt of the letter of Mr. Burton of the 10th instant, feeling some surprise, after all that had occurred, that I had received no reply to mine of the 5th instant to the Minister of Foreign Affairs, I addressed, a note to that minister on the morning of the 13th, stating the information I had received from the consul at Cadiz, my surprise at the same, and recalling attention to my note, and urging early action on my requests. To this note I received an immediate answer from the under Secretary of State, in the absence of the minister, transmitting the minister's communication of the 11th instant, informing me that it had been already signed on that day; that he was in the act of sending it to me when my note was received, and requesting that inasmuch as the matter had been previously adjusted in a satisfactory manner, I would withdraw my note of that morning. To this request I readily and cheerfully assented.

It will be seen, from the correspondence and from this relation of facts, that I have not waited for instructions from the department in the case of Mr. Thrasher; that his release has been obtained on my personal application, and that I have considered that the exigency of the occasion required me to act on my own responsibility in the absence of instructions from the government.

The results I have just stated; and I trust my course will be approved by the government, as I have reason to believe it will be from the contents of your dispatch No. 51, of the 13th ultimo, delivered to me by the special bearer of dispatches, George H. Miles, esq., on the 13th instant, after the pardon of Mr. Thrasher had been granted and the negotiation concluded.

* * * * * * * *

With sentiments of the highest respect, I remain, sir, your obedient servant,

D. M. BARRINGER.

Hon. Daniel Webster,
Secretary of State.

A 1.

Legation of the United States, Madrid,
January 5, 1852.

Sir: Mr. John S. Thrasher has recently arrived at Vigo from the Havana, a prisoner on board the "Hispano Cubano," and is now supposed to be on his way to Cadiz to be sent to *presidio* in Ceuta, Africa.

I am ignorant of the accusations and sentence under which he is condemned, and am not certain whether this prisoner is embraced in the pardon recently granted by her Majesty to the Americans concerned in the late invasion of Cuba. I do not know, indeed, whether he has been tried and condemned as an *American citizen*, or not; but I am certain he claims to be such.

I have therefore to desire your excellency to furnish me, if in your excellency's power, with copies of the trial and sentence, and other judicial or military proceedings against Mr. Thrasher, and also to ask as a favor, that for the present, and until some investigation can be made into the nature of his case, he may be detained in the arsenal of the Caracca or other fortress near Cadiz, with liberty of the bounds of the fortification or arsenal in which he may be confined.

I avail myself of this occasion to renew to your excellency the assurances of my most distinguished consideration, and have the honor to be your excellency's obedient servant,

D. M. BARRINGER.

His Excellency the MARQUIS OF MIRAFLORES,
Minister of State, &c., &c., &c.

No. 2.

[Translation.]

FIRST DEPARTMENT OF THE OFFICE OF STATE,
Palace, January 11, 1852.

SIR: I have received the note which your excellency has been pleased to address to me, under date of the 5th instant, relative to the prisoner Mr. John S. Thrasher, from the Havana, desiring to verify whether this individual is or not comprehended in the pardon granted by her Majesty the Queen to the citizens of the United States who took a part in the last expedition of Bahia Honda.

I have the honor to inform your excellency, in answer to your said note, that the government of her Majesty, taking into account all the circumstances and antecedents which bear upon this matter, does regard Mr. John S. Thrasher as comprehended in the general pardon conceded by her Majesty the Queen, my august sovereign—considering that the process which has been instituted against him proceeds from the same occurrences which gave rise to the imprisonment of those who came before to the prisons of the peninsula, and have since been pardoned.

The government of her Majesty, in extending to Mr. Thrasher the benefits of the general pardon—in which it experiences a singular pleasure, by considering this resolution as highly agreeable and satisfactory to the government of the United States—does so with the positive condition that the said individual shall not return again hereafter to the Spanish provinces beyond sea; and that in case of his being found in any of them, he shall be subject to fulfil his sentence, as if he never had been comprehended in the pardon.

I avail myself of this occasion to renew to your excellency the assurances of my most distinguished consideration, &c., &c., &c.

THE MARQUIS OF MIRAFLORES.

The MINISTER PLENIPOTENTIARY
of the United States.

No. 3.

LEGATION OF THE UNITED STATES, MADRID,
January 13, 1852.

SIR: I have this moment had the honor to receive your excellency's note, under date of the 11th instant, informing me that Mr. John S. Thrasher is included in the general pardon of the American prisoners sent from the Havana, and connected with the late expedition against the island of Cuba.

Your excellency will readily infer, from the interviews which I have had the honor to have with your excellency in reference to the case of Mr. Thrasher, how much satisfaction I enjoyed from a knowledge of the fact that he has been pardoned and is to be set at liberty. This satisfaction is not lessened by the circumstance that his release has been obtained on my own personal application, and previous to any official advices from my government. I may, however, be allowed to anticipate the pleasure which I am sure the course of her Majesty's government on this subject will give to that of the United States.

Your excellency will excuse me for adding the expressions of my regret, that in the case of Mr. Thrasher there should have been any exception to the free and unconditional terms of pardon extended to the other American prisoners.

Having been informed, by a note received this morning from the American consul at Cadiz, that Mr. Thrasher was about to be embarked as a prisoner on board the steamer "Lepanto," bound for Ceuta, in Africa, I desire your excellency will cause the necessary orders for his release to be issued as soon as possible to the proper authorities, and that he be placed at the disposition and under the protection of the said consul at Cadiz.

With sentiments of the most distinguished consideration, &c., &c.

D. M. BARRINGER.

His Excellency the MARQUIS OF MIRAFLORES,
Minister of State, &c., &c.

B 1.

[Extract.]

LEGATION OF THE UNITED STATES, MADRID,
December 29, 1851.

SIR: At the request of Mr. J. S. Thrasher, who is a prisoner from Havana, on board the "Hispano Cubano," lately at Vigo, and soon expected at Cadiz, I enclose you a letter from him.

* * * * * * * * *

I am not yet informed of the charges against Mr. Thrasher, but learn, from the public papers of the United States, that he is a person of much respectability. I have now no official instructions to give you concerning him, but request that you will, if possible, see and confer with him as to his wishes, and extend to him all the alleviation in your power in his present situation.

* * * * * * * * *

D. M. BARRINGER.

A. BURTON, Esq., *Consul, Cadiz.*

No. 2.

[Extract.]

LEGATION OF THE UNITED STATES, HAVANA,
January 6, 1852.

SIR: I have this day received from Mr. Charles Tyng, of Havana, and herewith enclose to you, the second of a bill of exchange in favor of Mr. John S. Thrasher, for $1,000, on Don Angel Ma. de Castrisiones, of Cadiz, dated Havana, December 3, 1851. You will please immediately deliver the same to Mr. Thrasher, or place the proceeds to his credit, as he may direct. I have as yet received no instructions from the government of the United States as to the case of Mr. Thrasher. I have, however, applied to the government here for copies of the proceedings against him, and under which he is sentenced to *presidio;* and also that he may be detained at or near Cadiz, with liberty of the fortress or arsenal, until investigation can be made into the nature of his case. As the application for an order for this latter purpose was made some days since, I trust it may have been received by the authorities at Cadiz ere this reaches you, especially as I have not only written to the minister for the same, but have had two personal interviews with him on the subject.

* * * * * * * *

D. M. BARRINGER.

A. BURTON, Esq.,
Consul United States, Cadiz.

No. 3.

CONSULATE OF THE UNITED STATES, CADIZ,
January 10, 1852.

SIR: I have just learned at the governor's that the Cuban prisoners in the jail here are to be embarked to-day for Ceuta, on board of the government steamer "Lepanto," there to await such orders as may be given by the government, by whose direction this is done, and that Mr. Thrasher is to go with them.

This gentleman, whom I have just been with, requests me to inform you of the circumstance. He will be embarked with the same attention as he was landed, without guard, escorted only by me from this office, and a municipal officer in plain clothes.

In haste, I am, sir, your obedient servant,

A. BURTON.

Hon. D. M. BARRINGER, *Minister, &c.*

8

No. 4.

LEGATION OF THE UNITED STATES, MADRID,
January 14, 1852.

SIR: I have the satisfaction to inform you that Mr. John S. Thrasher has received the royal pardon, and is to be set at liberty immediately.

I have requested that he may be placed at your disposition and under your protection. You will of course consult Mr. Thrasher, when delivered to you, as to his wishes in reference to his return to the United States.

I remain, very respectfully, &c.,
D. M. BARRINGER.

ALEX. BURTON, Esq.,
Consul of the United States, Cadiz.

Mr. Barringer to Mr. Webster.

[No. 76.] LEGATION OF THE UNITED STATES, MADRID,
January 15, 1852.

SIR: After my dispatch No. 75, of yesterday, was mailed, I received a communication from her Majesty's Minister of Foreign Affairs, of the 14th instant, a copy of which, translated, is herewith enclosed, acknowledging mine of the previous day, and referring to the terms of the pardon of Mr. John S. Thrasher, as well as those of the other American citizens recently set at liberty.

You will perceive that Mr. Thrasher is recognised in this note as an American citizen. I fear, from a note just received from the United States consul at Cadiz, that Mr. Thrasher, who had been detained there for some time at my request, may have been sent to Ceuta before the orders for his liberation could have reached the authorities at Cadiz. This event, however, will only delay his release for a day or two, as you will observe from the note of the minister that orders for that purpose had already been issued by the Minister of the Interior, (Gobernacion.) In my dispatch of yesterday I omitted to mention that, in reply to my request for copies of the proceedings against Mr. Thrasher in Cuba, I was told that the government here had received no such copies. As these proceedings were under a military commission or tribunal, I doubt whether any record, as we understand the meaning of that term, was kept; and I believe that if any such copies could be obtained at all, which is extremely doubtful, they would consist simply of a brief statement of facts in the memory of some officer of the court, or an argument based upon such statement, like the one furnished to Señor Calderon de la Barca by the Captain General of Cuba, and presented to you by the former gentleman, and upon which your dispatch No. 51, to me, was founded. If exception were taken to the *form of trial* under this military commission, and that Mr. Thrasher had no opportunity of free and full defence, the certain reply (though it may well be doubted whether it would be a satisfactory answer) would be, that it was according to the "usual course of proceeding in such cases."

I have the honor, &c., &c.

D. M. BARRINGER.

Hon. DANIEL WEBSTER,
Secretary of State.

[Translation.]

FIRST DEPARTMENT OF THE OFFICE OF STATE,
Palace, January 14, 1852.

SIR: I have received the note which your excellency has done me the honor to address to me under date of yesterday, acknowledging the receipt of the communication from this department of the 11th instant, relating to the pardon granted to the American citizen, Mr. John S. Thrasher, condemned by the tribunals of the Havana.

I have the satisfaction to inform your excellency, that the orders belonging to the Department of the Interior (Gobernacion del Reino) have already been issued, with the object that Mr. Thrasher be put at liberty, and at the disposition of the consul of the United States in Cadiz, according to the desire of your excellency, as being comprehended in the general pardons; and, while I regret that your excellency should consider, as an unfavorable exception, the condition imposed explicitly upon Mr. Thrasher, of not returning again to the Spanish provinces beyond sea, and which was not expressed in the pardon of the other persons, I hope that the impression may disappear, upon my informing your excellency that the condition with which this pardon is accompanied is founded in the interest itself of Mr. Thrasher, who, being established at the Havana, might, perhaps, believe himself at liberty to return there again, the which could not be anticipated in the case of the other anglo-American prisoners, proceeding from the United States, and not from the island of Cuba.

The Captain General of that island has an order not to permit any one of the pardoned prisoners to enter it, and from this consideration arises the clause in the pardon of Mr. Thrasher, which is a warning profitable for the person interested, rather than a condition.

I avail myself, &c., &c.

THE MARQUIS OF MIRAFLORES.

LEGATION OF THE UNITED STATES,
at Madrid.

Mr. Sharkey to Mr. Webster.

[Extract.]

[No. 3.] CONSULATE OF THE UNITED STATES, HAVANA,
February 9, 1852.

* * * * * *

In obedience to your request that I should procure and transmit copies of the proceedings relating to the domiciliation of Mr. Thrasher,

I had the honor to address a note of the Captain General on the subject, a copy of which is herewith forwarded. My request was answered by the note, a translation of which I also forwarded, and with that the correspondence, of course, ended.

* * * * * *

CONSULATE OF THE UNITED STATES, HAVANA,
February 5, 1852.

MOST EXCELLENT SIR: I have the honor to inform your excellency that a dispatch has been received by me from the Honorable Daniel Webster, Secretary of State of the United States, by which I am instructed to ask copies, from the records of the government, of the oaths and proceedings in the case of the domiciliation of Mr. Thrasher, and to transmit the same to the Department of State. I, therefore, ask your excellency to grant the requisite order to enable me to examine the records, and to procure the requisite copies to be forwarded to my government.

I have the honor to be your excellency's obedient servant,

W. L. SHARKEY.

His Excellency Señor Don JOSE DE LA CONCHA,
Governor and Captain General.

[Translation.]

[L. S.] POLITICAL SECRETARY'S OFFICE.

I have received the polite communication that your lordship addressed to me, under date of yesterday, requesting me to furnish you copies of the precedents that exist in this superior government about Mr. Thrasher's domiciliatory letter, for the purpose of transmitting them to the Department of State, from which your lordship has received dispatches claiming them.

I regret that it is not possible for me to accede to this request, as this class of documents always remains on record, and it is not customary to furnish, even to the interested party, any other datum than the domiciliatory letter, which shows the motives there were for issuing it, and the obligations which the person obtaining it binds himself to.

However, if the Hon. Mr. Webster deems it of high importance to have said copy in his possession, he may address his excellency, the Minister of her Catholic Majesty, at Washington, to whom belongs, by his diplomatic character, to act upon this kind of demands.

God preserve your lordship many years. Havana, February 6, 1852.

JOSE DE LA CONCHA.

To the CONSUL GENERAL
of the United States.

Mr. Sharkey to Mr. Webster.

[No. 4.] CONSULATE OF THE UNITED STATES, HAVANA,
February 13, 1852.

SIR: The inhabitants of the island, who emigrated from the United States, are much concerned in reference to the question of their allegiance, and in obedience to their wish, as well as for the purpose of regulating my own conduct, I venture to make it the subject of a communication. They are living here under letters of domiciliation; but many of them assert that their letters were procured only to enable them to engage in business pursuits, without any intention of forfeiting their allegiance; and the impression seems to have prevailed, very generally, that no such consequence would result from the letter of domiciliation. They supposed, as they say, it was a mere license to them, as foreigners, to remain on the island for a given time, in their several business capacities, and they are still reluctant to believe that they have transferred their allegiance to the government of Spain. Being still attached to their own government, they indulge the hope that they may not be concluded by any opinion it may adopt, or action it may take, unless upon the most mature deliberation it shall be found that they are not entitled to its protection. It is proper to remark, that in many cases, as I am informed, no oath was taken; but that proper certificates, that the preliminaries had been complied with, were furnished by subordinate officers of the government, appointed for that purpose, on the payment of the customary fees, and on these certificates the carta domicilia issued.

I herewith forward a translation of the whole of the royal decree of 1817, and would remark, that it makes an evident distinction between temporary and perpetual settlers or between domiciled inhabitants and naturalized citizens; a distinction which seems to be recognized by the Spanish construction, as will be seen by reference to the letter of the Captain General, already before you. The decree provided that settlers in the island should profess the Catholic religion; that they should take an oath of fidelity and allegiance, offering to comply with the laws and general regulations of the island. This, although so called, is not an oath of allegiance, since it imposed no obligation that would not have existed without it. These requisites being complied with, and a record made, the party obtained his domiciliatory letter, which only conferred limited privileges for a limited time. It conferred, in fact, the rights and character of a domiciled inhabitant, as contradistinguished from the rights and character of a naturalized citizen, as will be seen from the letter itself. If, at the expiration of five years, the party wished to become naturalized, he could do so. The 24th section lays down the requisites to be observed.

The party was bound to apply to the government, to produce his *carta domicilia*, bind himself to remain perpetually on the island, and take the oath of naturalization, promising faithfulness to the Catholic religion, to the king, and to the laws, renouncing all rights, privileges, and protection as a foreigner, and offering not to maintain any dependence, connexion, or civil subjection, to his native country. This oath entitled him to letters of naturalization, which conferred full privileges and rights of citizenship, which of course were not possessed before.

Several circumstances conduce to show that, until this final step was taken, the domiciled inhabitant was still regarded as a foreigner. He had the unconditional right to leave the island any time during the five years; he was prohibited during that time from engaging in maritime commerce, and from keeping stores or shops, except in partnership with Spaniards.

In case of war with his native country, he was entitled to a special protection, necessary to foreigners, but unnecessary to naturalized citizens. The oath taken in procuring the letter of domicil only required a *profession* of the Catholic religion, and obedience to laws; the final oath required *fidelity* to the Catholic religion, to the king, and to the laws, and renounced foreign protection, and abjured allegiance to the native country.

It is certainly true that every one who goes into a foreign country, contracts, by his own free will, the obligation of obedience to the laws. It is also true, in one sense, that the domicil of the party will determine his national character; but this is true only in a mercantile sense. A *domicil* may be acquired by residence alone, without any declaratory act; and when so acquired, it will decide the mercantile character of the party, which, in times of war, will control his rights. In such questions as this, the *animus manendi* is presumed from the residence or domicil of the party; but allegiance is quite a different thing, and must be presumed still to exist, when nativity is once shown, until it is also shown that the party had, in the most solemn manner, fully and completely adopted a new allegiance. This must be true in those countries which hold that allegiance is perpetual. And, even in the United States, it was ultimately held that a citizen could not absolve himself from his native allegiance without a law giving the power to do so. Surely, presumption cannot destroy every thing so sacred.

If the foregoing remarks are well founded, it would seem to follow that the emigrants from the United States, residing here under the *carta domicilia*, are still citizens of the United States. And, while it is not pretended that this exempts them from liability to the laws of the island, yet, if there is any exemption or privilege to citizens of the United States, arising from treaty stipulations, they are entitled to claim them. It will readily strike you, that the 7th article of the treaty of 1795 contains important provisions in this respect. It guarantees to the citizens of the United States the right to be tried in criminal, as well as in civil matters, by the established law; and, even if it was not competent for Spain to change this law at pleasure, there is still one privilege, personal and special, that she could not take away without violating the treaty—I mean the right to employ and appear by counsel. The utility of this provision, and the reason for its adoption, are quite apparent. If American citizens were to be allowed advocates and counsel only, when they were allowed by law, then the treaty secured nothing. The law of nations would have done this without treaty.

I trust you will pardon the liberty I have taken in submitting these remarks, which are mere outlines. I have been induced to do so by the great solicition felt by our people here, and by a desire that your mind may again be drawn to this subject, and some general rule laid down for my government. It seems to me, too, that the friendly relations of the two governments, the continuance of which is so necessary to both, would be rendered more durable by some timely action in this and other interesting subjects.

I have the honor to be, with great respect, your obedient servant,

W. L. SHARKEY.

Hon. DANIEL WEBSTER,
Secretary of State.

Royal order of October 21st, 1817, for increasing the white population of the island of Cuba.

THE KING—GOVERNOR, CAPTAIN GENERAL OF THE ISLAND OF CUBA, AND INTENDENT OF THE ARMY AND ROYAL TREASURY:

In your letters of the 17th and 18th of June of this year, you recommended as very necessary for the welfare and preservation of that valuable island, a representation by you, accompanied of the city council, consulado, and economical society of Havana, wherein, making a succinct statement of the extent of the island, number and circumstances of the inhabitants, state or condition of its agriculture, and of its physical force, they show that one of the most important possessions of my royal crown is unpeopled and defenceless, and its fields without cultivation, which can yield fruits much desired by other nations; they state that after a most careful and mature consideration, upon an affair of such magnitude, they can discover no other means capable of conciliating and satisfying such various exigencies, but by the increase of the white population with Spaniards from the peninsula or Canary islands, and in default of these, with European Catholics from friendly countries; and for that purpose they petition me to extend to that island the privileges granted to that of Porto Rico, by my royal order of 10th August, 1815, with the explanations made by the authorities of that province, under the instructions and articles, which to that effect they had given, and are as follows:

"ART. 1. All foreigners from countries or nations at friendship with me, who are already settled, or may hereafter desire to settle, in the island of Cuba, must establish by the proper means, before the government thereof, that they profess the Roman Catholic religion, and without this indispensable circumstance they shall not be allowed to settle there; but my subjects from these dominions, or the Indies, shall not be obliged to do so, as there can exist no doubt in regard to their religious principles.

"2. From the foreigners that should be admitted, in conformity to the previous article, the governor shall receive the oath of fidelity and allegiance, offering to comply with the laws and general regulations of the island, to which Spaniards are subjected.

"3. After the foreign settlers have been residing five years on the island, and after binding themselves to remain there perpetually, they shall be granted all the rights and privileges of naturalization, and the same to the children, that they may have taken there with them, or that may be born on the island; that they be admitted to all public and military employments, according to the talent or capability of each.

"4. No tax per head, or personal tribute, shall ever be imposed upon white settlers; they shall only pay for their negro or mulatto slaves at the rate of one dollar per year for each slave, after ten years of having been residing on the island; this rate shall never be increased.

"5. Within the first five years the Spanish and foreign colonists shall be at liberty to return to their countries or former residences; and, in such cases, they shall be permitted to take away from the island all the moneys or property that they took there without paying export duties; but on the increase of property they must pay the per centum.

"6. I grant to the old and new colonists dying on the island without forcible heirs (*heredicos forsosos*) the privilege of leaving their property to their relations or friends, wheresoever they may be: and if their successors should desire to settle on the same, they shall enjoy the rights granted to the testator; but should they prefer to take away the inheritance, they may do so by paying upon the total fifteen per cent. for exportation duty, if it takes place after five years of the testator having been residing on the island; and if before the expiration of that time, they shall pay only ten per centum, in conformity to what is ordained in the preceding article. The parents, brothers, or relatives of settlers dying intestate shall inherit the whole of their property, even if they reside in foreign countries, on the condition of their coming to settle on the island, if they are Catholics; but if they cannot or will not settle there, then I permit them to dispose of their inheritance by sale or cession, according to the rules explained in the two preceding articles.

"7. I likewise grant to foreign colonists holding landed property on the island, that, in conformity to the Spanish laws, they may leave, by will or other disposition, the real property they may be possessed of, and not admitting of easy division, to one or more of their children, provided no injury is thereby caused to the rights of the others, or of the testator's widow.

"8. Any settler that, on account of law-suits or other urgent and just motives, should be in need of going to Spain, other provinces of my Indies, or to foreign dominions, shall ask permission of the governor, and may obtain it, provided it is not to unfriendly countries, or to carry away his property.

"9. Colonists, Spanish as well as foreign, shall be free for the term of fifteen years from the payment of tithes upon the products of their lands; and after the expiration of that time, (which must be reckoned from the date of the decree,) they shall pay only two and a half per cent., which is one-fourth of the tithe.

"10. They shall also be exempt from the payment of royal *alcabala* dues on the sales of their products and commercial effects for the term mentioned, and after the expiration of it, only two and a half per cent.; but everything shipped by them on Spanish vessels bound for these kingdoms shall be forever free of all export dues.

"11. As all the colonists must be armed, even in time of peace, to be respected by their slaves, and to resist any invasion or attack by pirates, I declare that this obligation must not be considered as binding them to serve in the regular army; that it will be sufficient for them to present their arms every two months at the review that the governor, or officer deputed for the purpose, must pass; but in time of war or mutiny of slaves they shall contribute to the defence of the island according to the measures that its chief may deem proper to take.

"12. Vessels of any size or build whatsoever belonging to old settlers must be taken to the island, and, after being registered, shall be considered as Spanish, and the same such as they may acquire in foreign countries by purchase or other legitimate title; they shall be exempt from duties as foreign vessels, or for being registered. Those settlers who may be desirous of building vessels on the island shall be permitted by the government to cut and use the necessary wood, except only such as may be destined for building vessels for my royal navy.

"13. Foreigners that may hereafter go to the island with the intention to settle on it must prove that they profess the Roman catholic religion, must make known to the government the trade or honest and useful profession to which they intend to apply themselves, and the property or moneys they import, which they shall be permitted to take away again free of duty, if within the first five years they should determine, to their countries or former residences.

"14. After the government has declared the colonist to be of admissible circumstances a record shall be kept of his name, country, family, profession, or trade, district or jurisdiction in which he intends to settle, and amount of money or property that the settler may state to be his; after which a domiciliary letter shall be issued in his favor, an oath of faithfulness and allegiance being first received, wherein he shall offer to comply with the laws and regulations that Spaniards are subjected to.

"15. A record shall be kept at the office of the royal treasury of the domiciliary letters, expressing in them the property or moneys stated by the settler, as a knowledge must be had for, in case of their being again exported, also by the council of the district, and by the commandant and justice thereof, without causing to the settler any expense for these proceedings, or charging him any fees whatsoever.

"16. The domiciliatory letters shall authorize colonists to be considered as residents of the island, and their persons and property shall enjoy the same inviolability as those of old residents. From the courts they shall receive good treatment and justice, and from the other residents all the aid and favor they should become deserving of for their qualities and good behaviour; they shall always have the liberty of applying to the government, and its protection secured to them, if any injury or detriment should be done to them.

"17. Foreign colonists, after obtaining the domiciliary letter, may acquire all descriptions of landed property on the island in town or country, with the same requisites and privileges as the Spanish residents. They shall be permitted to change their residences, or to remove from one district to others, with the knowledge of the respective territorial authorities. Those having useful trades or industry shall be allowed to settle and exercise it wherever it may suit their convenience, with the authorities.

"18. Foreign colonists cannot, during the first five years of residence, employ themselves personally in maritime commerce, nor have shops or stores, nor be owners of vessels. But they may be interested in company or co-partnership in the mercantile transactions of Spaniards; and the contracts made by them with these, verbally or in writing, shall have the same value and legal force as if they were between one Spaniard and another.

"19. The liberty of foreign colonists to return to their countries or former residences during the first five years is absolute, unlimited, and without conditions. They may take away their property or dispose of it as they think fit.

"20. In case of war with the country of which domiciliated foreigners are natives they shall not lose the rights and advantages of their residence on the island of Cuba. Even if the first five years have not elapsed their property shall not be subjected to embargo, sequestration, nor any of the ordinary or extraordinary measures of the state of war. Those who, notwithstanding the war, should desire to remain on the island to complete the five years, and become naturalized, shall be permitted freely to do so if known to be of good character and habits. Those preferring to leave the island shall be allowed sufficient time to commodiously arrange their affairs and dispose of their property, being permitted to take away, free of duty, such property, or the equivalent thereof, as they introduced into the island, and paying on the excess the ten per cent. stated in the 16th article.

"21. Domiciliated as well as naturalized colonists may dispose of their property by will, or in any other authentic form; in case of death their wills shall be religiously fulfilled; should they die without will or testament, their children or nearest relatives shall be their legitimate heirs, with the same rights the deceased had.

"22. It is declared that there never shall be put in practice on the island of Cuba the rights, usages, or customs, known in other nations under the name of *aubaine escheatage*, or others by which the government and treasury sequesters the property of foreigners at their death; which rights or customs, though they may be applied in cases of transient passengers, shall never be understood or applied to these that are domiciliated.

"23. Within the five years of domiciliation the colonists shall not be subjected to any contributions whatever, nor to the residence taxes established in the circular of 1st December, 1815, except only in the case of public calamities, dangers to the country, and defence of the coast against robbers or pirates; in which extraordinary events, or other similar ones, all must lend their aid and favor, according to the well-known principles of natural and international law."

Mr. Graham to Mr. Webster.

NAVY DEPARTMENT, *February* 21, 1852.

SIR: I have the honor to return herewith, after perusal, with my acknowledgments for the favor, the enclosed dispatch from the United

States consul for the port of Havana, of date February 9, 1852, and to inform you that instructions have been issued to Commodore Parker, commanding the home squadron, to be upon the alert upon the matter referred to.

I have the honor to be, sir, with high respect, your obedient servant,

WILLIAM A. GRAHAM.

Hon. DANIEL WEBSTER,
Secretary of State.

Mr. Thrasher to Mr. Webster.

MADRID, *March* 22, 1852.

SIR: In your dispatch of December 13 last, to the Hon. D. M. Barringer, United States minister to Spain, as published in the New York Herald, you are led into one or two errors, which I beg leave to correct.

You say, "it is much to be regretted that Mr. Thrasher has made no communication whatever to this department respecting the circumstances of his case, so as to enable us to see what are the precise grounds of his complaint."

I was arrested at Havana on the 16th day of October. For the first five days my arrest was merely an honorable detention; but no sooner had the semi-monthly steamers left for the United States, than I was thrown into a dungeon of the prison, and thence transferred to one in the Punta castle. For sixteen days, or until after the next semi-monthly departure of the steamers, I was kept in strict solitary confinement, with utter deprivation of all communication with the world. During this time it was impossible for me to transmit any information to the department.

When I was allowed to see my friends, Mr. Owen, the American consul, but lately appointed by the existing administration, came to see me, and assured me that he had laid my case fully before the Department of State at Washington. During the time intervening between this and my subsequent embarkation for Ceuta, Mr. Owen occasionally called at the fortress to see me, and continually expressed his great surprise that no communication had come from the Department of State in regard to my case; always assuring me that not only the communications I made to him, but several that had been made in my behalf by my friends, had all been transmitted to the government of the United States. Under these circumstances, I judged it superfluous to make a direct communication to the department, as I could add nothing to the information already before it.

You say, "if the official account of the Spanish authorities be correct, Mr. Thrasher appears to have *expatriated himself*, and to have become, at least for a time, a subject of the crown of Spain."

The authorities neglected to inform you, that on the 8th of September, 1850, in a communication to the Captain General of Cuba, I expressly and unequivocally refused to take out letters of naturalization, and thus become a subject of the crown of Spain.

I embrace the present opportunity to transmit you a copy of a letter addressed by me to General Concha upon the subject of domiciliation in Cuba, and the trial of American citizens by the permanent military commission of that country.

I submit to you, with much diffidence, the argument it contains, and not as my own views only, but as those of some of the first legal attainments in Spain. Whether you will find them of sufficient weight to induce you to modify any of the opinions expressed in your letter of 23d December last to the President, I know not; but it is to be hoped they may have some weight with the present rulers of Cuba.

The world now knows what an extorted and unwarranted interpretation was given by the Spanish government, both here and in Cuba, to the unfortunate wording of the presidential proclamations in regard to expeditions, and you are well aware of the extraordinary pretensions that have since been made by the Spanish ministers in relation to the right of capture on the high seas, (vide Contoy,) and in subsequent questions that have been suscitated between the two governments.

These facts, and the known disposition of the government of Cuba toward American citizens in general, lead me to anticipate the most disastrous consequences from the unwarrantable interpretation it may give to your letter.

If the government of Cuba was one administered in accordance with statute and justice; if the law were respected by its ministers; or even if the executive power there, absolute as it is, were guided in its action by any fixed principles, I am well aware there is nothing in that letter which would endanger the person or the property of a single American citizen. But while such is not the case; while not only existing laws are disregarded, but new ones are continually "decreed" by the arbitrary will of one man, as circumstances may seem to him to require; while the ministers of justice, and the administrators of executive power, seem animated solely by one idea, *that a war of races exists*, what interpretations and what actions therein may we not dread?

To prove to you that I do not speak from personal feeling alone, I will cite a well-known fact in the history of that same permanent executive military commission, which claims jurisdiction over all Americans in Cuba. I will only premise that, in 1778, torture was declared by Charles III. to be "barbarous and infamous," and was expressly prohibited in Spanish tribunals; and that when the inquisition fell before the decree of the famous Cortes of Cadiz, in 1812, that last relic of the barbarous ages disappeared even from the ecclesiastical tribunals of Spain.

In 1844–'45, in the trials during the execrated invention of a "black conspiracy," hundreds of negroes died under the lash, tied to ladders by order of the permanent executive military commission; and, in consequence of confessions thus extorted, hundreds of others were sent to the presidios and mines of Spain, (to the presidio of Seville alone were sent over 450;) large numbers were executed; and how many died in prison, or immediately after their liberation, can never be known. There were not wanting both American and English victims in this iniquitous affair. Many engineers and even proprietors were arrested, not a few of whom died during imprisonment, or in consequence of the sufferings they then experienced. The sequel is instructive. Pedro Salazar, the tool, fiscal of the military commission, followed his victims condemned to the presidio of Seville. Leopaldo O'Donnell, the master spirit, Captain General of Cuba, retired to Spain with something more than one million of dollars, the fruit of three years' loyal administration of the government. Shall we abandon our countrymen to the tender mercies of such a tribunal and such a government?

I have the honor to be your very humble servant,

J. S. THRASHER.

Hon. DANIEL WEBSTER,
Secretary of State, U. S.

Mr. Webster to Mr. Sharkey.

[No. 16.] DEPARTMENT OF STATE,
Washington, July 5, 1852.

SIR: Referring to the dispatch from this department, addressed to you under date of April 7, in which the receipt of your letter on the law of domicil, as understood in Havana, was acknowledged, I have now to inform you that the subject has received the full consideration which its importance demands.

The official dispatch to Mr. Barringer, on the 13th of December last, and the communication to the House of Representatives of the 23d of the same month, in respect to the case of Mr. John S. Thrasher, were particularly confined to the state of facts which, at that time, had been placed before the department. Upon the law and the facts, as they were then presented, it was considered doubtful whether Mr. Thrasher could rightfully claim the privileges secured to American citizens by the treaty of 1795. But it was carefully stated, in each of the communications above referred to, that no communication addressed to the department had been received from Mr. Thrasher himself, and that it was a matter of regret that the department had not before it his own statement of the case.

Since that time additional information has been obtained from your own dispatch, as well as from other sources, respecting the Spanish law of domiciliation, both in regard to its practical operation and the manner in which it has been construed by the Spanish authorities themselves, and by foreigners who have taken out letters of domiciliation.

It appears that the royal proclamation of October 21, 1817, by which provision was made for domiciliating foreigners, was issued at the request of the civil authorities of Havana, for the purpose of increasing the white population of the island of Cuba, by Spaniards from the peninsula and the Canary islands, and by emigrants from friendly European nations. The reasons assigned for its issue were, the small number of inhabitants in proportion to the extent of the island, the condition of its agriculture, and its limited physical resources; so that "one of the most important possessions of the royal crown was unpeopled and defenceless, and its fields without cultivation." Many privileges were granted to those who took advantage of the invitation thus extended to them—

such as exemption from taxation for fifteen years, perfect liberty to return to their native country at any time during the first five years, and free exportation of the property which they brought with them. As they were "strangers," they had permission to leave in case of war with their native country.

These and other parts of the proclamation exhibit very clearly its intent—that there was no disposition on the part of the Spanish authorities to exercise the power of forcibly domiciliating foreigners, even if such power were not contrary to all natural law. It is true that, on his arrival, the foreigner was required to take out a domiciliatory letter; but, according to the Spanish law, this "simply authorized a foreign subject to reside in the island more than three months, and to employ himself in commerce, or any other useful industry," and, it may be added, that any conditions or restrictions introduced into the domiciliatory oath inconsistent with the letter and spirit of the royal proclamation above referred to, or the provisions of Spanish law, must necessarily be null and void.

It does not appear that the foreigners who came to the island and took out letters of domiciliation considered that, by so doing, they forfeited their rights of citizenship in their respective countries, or assumed any obligations inconsistent therewith. This, too, appears to have been the general understanding of the Spanish authorities themselves. Throughout the whole Spanish law there is observed a wide distinction between domiciliation and naturalization. This is fully admitted in the communication of Mr. De la Concha to Mr. Calderon, of May 28, 1851, and also in the 14th and 24th articles of the above-mentioned proclamation. Thus it appears that, notwithstanding the terms of the oath of domiciliation are so strict, yet, taken in connexion with the provisions of the law above cited, the American residents in Cuba have never, in point of fact, regarded themselves as having changed their allegiance by taking out letters of domiciliation. They appear to have considered these letters as mere formal requisites to an undisturbed temporary residence for commercial or other business purposes. In point of fact, it is believed that these papers are usually procured by purchase—that no oath is taken, and no act done on the part of the American resident, except the payment of a small fee. Change of *domicil* is matter of intention, and notwithstanding residence in fact, there must be the *animus manendi*. Change of allegiance, which is manifested by the voluntary action, and usually by the oath of the party himself, ought always to be accomplished by proceedings which are understood, on all sides, to have that effect. It is certainly just that acts, which are to be regarded as changing the allegiance of American citizens, should be distinctly understood by those to whom they are applied as having that effect; that the practical as well as theoretical construction of such acts should be unequivocal and uniform; and that no acts should be deemed acts of expatriation, except such as are openly avowed and fully understood.

I am, sir, &c.,

DANIEL WEBSTER.

WM. L. SHARKEY, Esq.,
United States Consul, Havana.

Mr. Everett to Mr. Brooks.

DEPARTMENT OF STATE,
Washington, January 8, 1853.

SIR: In respect to the oath of domiciliation required to be taken by residents in Cuba, a copy of which you requested yesterday at the department, permit me to refer you to executive document No. 14, House of Representatives, 32d Congress, 1st session, and to the letter and accompanying papers of Mr. Owen, No. 32, which embrace all the forms you desire.

I regret that I cannot enclose a copy, as the department receives but five copies of Congressional documents, and there is no copy now remaining.

I have the honor, &c.,
EDWARD EVERETT.

Hon. JAMES BROOKS,
House of Representatives.

Mr. Hayes to the Secretary of State.

WASHINGTON, *March* 10, 1853.

SIR: I would respectfully call your attention to the accompanying letter of J. S. Thrasher.

I have the honor to be, sir, very respectfully, your ob't servant,
JOHN L. HAYES, *Counsellor at Law, Washington.*

Hon. SECRETARY OF STATE *of the United States.*

To the honorable Secretary of State for the United States of America.

John Sidney Thrasher, a native of the city of Portland, in the State of Maine, late a resident in the city of Havana, island of Cuba, would respectfully lay before the Department of State the following facts, and ask the intervention of the government of the United States of America in the prosecution of his claim against her Catholic Majesty the Queen of Spain.

In the month of August of the year 1850, the exponent became proprietor of a daily journal, published in Havana, styled the "Faro Industrial de la Habana;" and, confiding in the reciprocal rights usually accorded by friendly powers to citizens or subjects of any other power, and in the stipulations of existing treaties between the government of the United States of America and her Catholic Majesty, and in the existing rule by royal decree, in Spain, that rights not stipulated for foreign citizens or subjects by treaty shall be enjoyed by these in the dominions of Spain, in a like and reciprocal manner as may be enjoyed by Spanish subjects in the country to which such foreign citizens or subjects may owe allegiance, exponent desired to continue the publication of said journal in the city of Havana for his use and advantage. But on or about the 6th day of September of same year, 1850, Don Frederico Roncali, then Governor and Captain General, did arbitrarily issue a decree, directed to exponent, by the terms of which exponent was prohibited from publishing any newspaper in the island of Cuba, unless he should first take out letters of naturalization, and become a subject to the crown of Spain. This exponent refused to do, and made the same known to Don Frederico Roncali, Governor and Captain General of the island of Cuba, by a communication, bearing date on or about the 8th of September, 1850; and exponent was necessitated to abandon his undertaking, to his very great loss and detriment.

For the losses and damages thus caused to exponent he claims remuneration to him by the Spanish government in the sum of one hundred and fifty thousand dollars.

And exponent would further make manifest to the Department of State, that, on the 16th day of October, 1851, while residing in Havana, in the peaceful and lawful pursuit of his avocations, he was arrested by order of the government of the island of Cuba, without the manifestation of any charge against him; was thrown into a vile and loathsome dungeon in the common jail; was thence removed to one, more filthy and loathsome still, in the Punta fort; was deprived of all intercourse with his friends; was subjected during many days to a harsh, inquisitorial, and most severe interrogation, during which the government had the aid and assistance of the most profound legal knowledge and advice, while exponent was denied all counsel; was charged with the crime of constructive treason to a government to which he owed no allegiance; was arraigned before a military tribunal, with continued deprivation of legal advice; was put in the most imminent peril of his life, having been informed that the judges who sentenced him were three for sentence of death, and four for sentence to the galleys; was denied all legal defence; was sentenced to eight years labor in chains in Africa; was sent a prisoner to Spain; was thence transferred to the penal settlement of Ceuta, in Africa, where he was put in chains; and was finally liberated by a royal order of her Catholic Majesty, which expressly recognises his American citizenship, and prohibits his return to any colony of Spain.

For the injury done to exponent in the breaking up of all his plans and prospects in life by this arbitrary, unjust, and unwarranted procedure; for the moral and physical suffering which he was compelled to undergo; for the peril of limb and life to which he was subjected; for the moral stigma inflicted upon him, and for remuneration of the great losses and expenses to which he was thereby subjected, he claims from the Spanish government the sum of three hundred and fifty thousand dollars.

And exponent would respectfully solicit of the Department of State its interposition in his behalf, and its urgent prosecution, in every proper manner, of this his claim against her Catholic Majesty, as the only means whereby he can obtain justice.

And exponent would further solicit, that the Department of State recognize and assist A. H. Lawrence, esq., of Washington, exponent's duly constituted attorney in this matter, in his prosecution of this exponent's claim, and in the obtaining of justice.

And exponent has the honor to be, respectfully, &c., &c.

J. S. THRASHER.

Alexander H. Lawrence and John L. Hayes, of the city of Washington, counsellors at law, attorneys for J. S. Thrasher.

Mr. Marcy to Mr. Hayes.

DEPARTMENT OF STATE,
Washington, March 12, 1853.

SIR: In answer to your letter of the 10th instant, on the subject of the claim of Mr. J. S. Thrasher against the government of Spain, I have the honor to inform you, that a proposition has been recently made to Spain, and other powers, for the organization of a board for the mutual adjustment of all existing claims between the respective governments. Sufficient time has not elapsed to enable the department to learn whether Spain will accede to the proposition.

I am, sir, respectfully, your obedient servant,

W. L. MARCY.

JOHN L. HAYES,
Counsellor at Law, Washington.

Mr. Marcy to Mr. Lawrence.

DEPARTMENT OF STATE,
Washington, April 12, 1853.

SIR: In reply to your letter received this day, desiring a copy of such instructions as may have been issued to the United States consuls by this department, in relation to the citizenship of Americans residing in the Spanish islands, I beg leave to refer you to House documents No. 10 and No. 14, 1st session, 32d Congress, which contain the provisions of the Spanish laws on the subject of citizenship and domicil, with the construction that has heretofore been given to those provisions by this department.

I also inclose a copy of a letter addressed to the United States consul at Havana, on the 5th of July last, in which reference is made to the above-mentioned documents, explanatory of the rights enjoyed by citizens of the United States in Cuba.

I am, sir, &c.,

W. L. MARCY.

ALEXANDER H. LAWRENCE, Esq.,
Washington.

CASE OF THE STEAMER FALCON.

Mr. Owen to Mr. Webster.

COMMERCIAL AGENCY OF THE UNITED STATES,
Havana, August 17, 1851.

SIR: When I closed my letter on yesterday evening, it was supposed that the mail bag would then soon be sent to the steamer; as the bag will be open till 8 o'clock this morning, I am afforded an opportunity to state to you that Lieutenant Rogers, commanding the United States mail steamer Falcon, called at this office late yesterday evening, and complained of the conduct of a Spanish commander of a steamer, who boarded the Falcon off the Cabanas, about forty miles from this, on his way from Chagres to this port, with the mails, $1,500,000 in gold, and a large number of passengers.

He says he had previously been chased by another Spanish steamer, say for two hours. He says that the first steamer referred to in this communication fired over his stern and bow four or five times, and that upon being hailed, he stopped and demanded to know what was wanted. In answer, he was asked the name of his vessel; when he replied, "it is strange you do not know—it is the Falcon; a United States steamer, which has been here constantly for the past three years." He informed me that he spoke in an angry tone to the officer who boarded him, and said that he should not be detained by him, and that if he had any business it must be done quickly, as he was bound to Havana, and he should go on. Had it not been for the large amount of gold and large number of passengers, the commander of the Falcon thinks he would have fired into the Spanish steamer. He says that he has been informed by some of the passengers, that at the time he "came to," when hailed, the officers on the Spanish steamer took off hats or caps, and "hurraed," he now believes insultingly. He ended by saying, that at the time he was boarded he believed this port to be in a state of blockade, otherwise he would have resented the conduct of the Spaniards notwithstanding his cargo and passengers.

I called upon the Captain General, who expressed much regret at what had occurred between the Falcon and Spanish steamers, and said he would see that it should not be so in future; that there was a new vessel out here, and that it must have been the officer of her that had so acted. I told him that the officer had expressed a hope that he should not be blamed, as he acted under orders (perhaps) from the general of marine. The Captain General said it could not have been by the order of the general of marine.

I think Commander Rodgers said his flag was hoisted at the time of the occurrence.

The Captain General having enclosed his reply to me for the captain of the Albany, I said I had sent it to Captain P. He asked me if I had read it; said I had not, when (he) added, it would be entirely satisfactory. It is said that the hisses and curses that met the Albany and Vixen on coming in was not from the people generally, but from some excited persons.

I have the honor to be, with great respect, your obedient servant,

A. F. OWEN.

HON. DANIEL WEBSTER,
Secretary of State

UNITED STATES MAIL STEAMER FALCON,
Havana, August 17, 1851.

SIR: I desire to make to you the following statement, and through you to forward a copy of it to the Hon. Secretary of State: I have to complain that on the 16th instant, being on my regular voyage from Chagres to Havana, having on board the United States mails from California, with 211 passengers, and specie to the amount of a million and a half of dollars, when in sight of the port of Bahia Honda, and about fifteen miles from the land, I discovered a Spanish steamer-of-war in chase. I hoisted the United States ensign and pennant, and a blue flag at the fore, with "U. S. Mail" in large letters in its centre, and continued on my course for Havana, then distant about fifty miles.

I found the Spanish steamer to run very equally with us, and although not gaining, she continued in chase about four miles astern. At 9 o'clock I discovered another steamer coming out from under the land, apparently with the object of intercepting us. Approaching us at a large angle with our course, she commenced firing astern of us before she was in range, and upon her nearer approach I discovered her to be a steamer called the Almandares, recently, I believe, a packet between Matanzas and Havana; that she was armed with two guns, apparently 32-pounders, and with numerous soldiers and officers on board, the former drawn up on her deck in a threatening attitude.

She fired three shotted guns, apparently with the purpose of bringing us to, but I still kept my course. Being faster than the Falcon, she at length ranged alongside within hail, fired a musket, and hailed us to stop. I slowed the engines to enable them to communicate by hail more distinctly if they wished, but they still continued to call loudly to us to stop. After some deliberation, thinking that possibly the port of Havana might be blockaded, and unwilling to jeopard the lives of the passengers by resisting their force, I stopped, and they immediately sent an officer on board in a small boat. Upon demanding of him what he wanted, he said that he wished to know what ship it was. I told him the Falcon, and that it was strange that he did not know what ship, since she had been running to Havana every fortnight for the last three years. He asked me to go on board the Almandares, which I refused to do. He then asked me if there were any Spanish passengers on board, and I replied *no*. He then got into his boat, and told me to wait until he communicated with his superior; and I told him that I must hasten, for I could only wait long enough for him to reach his vessel, which in fact I did. The whole detention may have amounted to twenty minutes or half an hour.

When I asked the officer who came on board what their conduct in stopping the ship meant, he said that I must not blame him; he was only acting under orders.

The steam-frigate had, in the meantime, ranged up within shot; and after we again proceeded on our course, the Almandares was seen to communicate with her, and both of the Spanish vessels stood back again to the westward.

I had forgotton to say that it was remarked by the passengers of the Falcon, that upon our stopping, the officers on the deck of the Almandares waved their caps about their heads, and cheered—whether in exultation, or with what motive, I cannot tell.

All of the foregoing matter I conceive to be subject for protest; and I hereby declare, that for no other consideration but the lives of defenceless passengers on board, would I have refrained from using the force of the ship in resisting the indignity offered us.

Very respectfully,

HENRY RODGERS,

Lieut. U. S. N., commanding U. S. M. Steamer Falcon.

A. F. Owens, Esq.,

U. S. Commercial Agent, Havana.

Mr. Derrick, Acting Secretary, to Mr. Calderon.

Department of State,
Washington, September 13, 1851.

The undersigned, Acting Secretary of State of the United States, finds it his duty to place before Don A. Calderon de la Barca, envoy extraordinary and minister plenipotentiary of her Catholic Majesty, the enclosed copy of a formal communication, of the 17th ultimo, from Lieutenant Henry Rodgers, of the United States navy, commanding the United States mail steamer "Falcon," to Mr. Owen, the commercial agent of the United States at Havana, which contains a complaint and statement of facts relating to an insult offered to the flag of the United States by the "Almandares," one of her Catholic Majesty's war steamers, during a recent voyage of the "Falcon" from Chagres to Havana.

The undersigned is fully aware that occasions may arise in which the detention and search by a man-of-war, of a suspected vessel sailing under the flag of a friendly power, might be excusable; but this right of visitation is a belligerent right, and he cannot readily perceive what circumstances would justify the detention and visitation of a mail steamer like the "Falcon," a vessel which for a number of years has regularly visited Havana, and was, at the time of this occurrence, within some fifty miles of that port. The Spanish officer of the "Almandares," who came on board the "Falcon," seems to have been himself conscious of the gross impropriety of thus stopping a steamer in the service and under the flag of a friendly nation, since he apologized for the part which he had taken in this extrordinary visit, by stating that he was simply acting under orders.

The undersigned is not prepared to say what influence intelligence of the indignity offered on this occasion to the American flag may have had in exciting a part of the population of New Orleans to those deplorable acts of violence to which Mr. Calderon invites attention in his notes of the 26th and 29th ultimo, and of the 5th instant; but he may remind Mr. Calderon that the news of the "Falcon's" having been stopped and visited by one of her Catholic Majesty's war steamers, had reached New Orleans on the morning of the same day on which those unfortunate disturbances took place. It is not, however, with any view of extenuating the outrages of which Mr. Calderon complains in his notes above referred to, but in the expectation that her Catholic Majesty's minister may be able to furnish the government of the United States with a satisfactory explanation of the detention and visitation of the "Falcon," that the undersigned addresses this note to Mr. Calderon, and has the honor to request an early answer.

The undersigned avails himself of this occasion to renew to Mr. Calderon the assurances of his high consideration.

W. S. DERRICK,
Acting Secretary.

Señor Don A. CALDERON DE LA BARCA,
&c., &c., &c.

Mr. Calderon to Mr. Derrick.

[Translation.]

LEGATION OF SPAIN IN WASHINGTON,
September 29, 1851.

The undersigned has received the note which the Acting Secretary did him the honor of addressing on the 13th instant, enclosing a copy of a report presented to Mr. Owen, commercial agent of the United States at Havana, by Henry Rodgers, esq., captain of the Falcon, relative to the detention which he had been compelled to undergo by her Catholic Majesty's war steamer Almandares, on his way from Chagres to Havana, with the public mail on board. The Acting Secretary of State asks the undersigned to give him some explanation of this occurrence, begging him not delay sending an answer.

Although the undersigned, in consequence of his not being yet in possession of authentic details, knows very little more of this affair than what has been published in the newspapers of the United States, and the narrative of Captain Rodgers is an *ex parte* statement, he nevertheless thinks it not inappropriate to the occasion to submit, as he does, some reflections to the enlightened consideration of the Acting Secretary of State.

In the first place, although the Falcon carries the United States mail, she is a merchant vessel, and performs this service by contract. In this character, as a merchant vessel, she is clearly established by the additional fact that she receives pay for passage and for transportation of goods, not on account of the government of the United States, but for the benefit of the Steam Company, the agencies of which are established at various points throughout the United States. At the time when the Falcon made her appearance in the vicinity of Bahia Honda, a considerable number of American citizens had, a few days before, landed near that port, which they invaded by force of arms, perpetrating deeds of violence and of blood.

In order to repel this perfidious profanation of Spanish territory, it had been found necessary to assemble vessels of war and some of her Majesty's troops, which came in contact with the invaders, who had thus caused an unheard-of state of war to exist.

The invaders had been taken there by the American steamer Pampero, from New Orleans, whence they had sailed with the knowledge and consent of the authorities, whose duty it was to have prevented them. The Pampero had stopped at Key West, for the purpose of waiting for a favorable opportunity to cross the short distance which separates that point from the island of Cuba, in order to make sure of the bold stroke which they contemplated. She had, also, left Key West without impediment or hinderance, landing her infamous freight of passengers on the shores of Bahia Honda, and returned for reinforcements. She was every moment expected; and the Pampero had also been employed before in carrying the United States mail. Other steamers from various points of the United States, with ammunitions, arms, and men, were also expected; and the authorities of the island of Cuba, as well as the undersigned, had been informed that the schemers of these periodical piratical invasions had been in negotiation with the owners of the Falcon in order to purchase this very vessel from them, with a view of eluding vigilance and carrying out their infamous designs; treacherously hiding those designs under the folds of the American flag, and of her previous character as mail-carrier. But whether this accusation be correct or otherwise, the Falcon might have changed owners in Chagres, or have fallen into the hands of the pirates during her passage. Vattel, who certainly is not over-indulgent in the matter of detention and the right of search, expresses himself thus:

"The transportation of contraband goods cannot be prevented, if neutral vessels which are met with at sea are not visited. The right to visit them, therefore, exists. At this day, any neutral vessel which should refuse to submit to such visit, would be condemned, on that account alone, as a lawful prize."

A very modern author, (Richard Widman, chapter on the right of capture,) who has made a compilation of whatever has been considered, down to this day, as established and generally agreed upon in relation to this subject, speaks thus: "Every vessel is bound to submit to visitation and search, whether it be the vessel of a friend or of an ally, or even of a subject; and submission may be compelled, if necessary, by force of arms, without giving claim to any damages incurred thereby, if the vessel, upon visitation, should not be found liable to be detained. No circumstances can dispense with this obligation. A vessel is not excepted either by its build or by its flag; such circumstances furnish no proof of the national character of the vessel."

The same principles are asserted by Judge Kent, Wheaton, and by other public writers and eminent American jurisconsults, with whom the Acting Secretary of State is better acquainted than the undersigned.

If this, therefore, be the doctrine and the practice of civilized people, and if it be true that the Falcon is a merchant vessel, and that she was momentarily detained in the waters within the jurisdiction of the country to which the ship-of-war which detained her belonged, in sight of a port which had been invaded by armed Americans, who were still carrying on hostilities waged by them against a foreign territory, the undersigned, so far from seeing in the circumstance of that detention, caused for the purpose of ascertaining the character and destination of the Falcon, any cause of complaint on the part of Captain Rodgers, prefers, on the contrary, such complaint on the part of the nation the signals of whose ship-of-war said captain disregarded, especially as Captain Rodgers, who had been in New Orleans, could not be ignorant of the preparations which were going on there, publicly and without disguise, for an invading expedition against Cuba.

The aforesaid Captain Rodgers remarks that he has made various uninterrupted voyages to Havana. If he was never troubled before, he ought to have supposed that some imperative cause existed then to call for such a course.

Captain Rodgers remarks that the Spanish officer who boarded his vessel alleged, as an excuse for the act, the necessity he was under to obey the orders of his chief; and from this the inference is made that some irregularity had been committed. The undersigned is under the impression that Captain Rodgers did not clearly understand what the Spanish officer said.

Even in the cheers given by the crew of the Almandares, which may probably have been the usual salute exchanged between sailors when two vessels separate, or when they descry a friendly craft, Captain Rodgers desires to spy out an insult. In saying that on that occasion the Almandares was commanded in person by Don José Bostillo, commanding general of the Havana station, is to say more than enough, in order to put an end at once to so malicious an insinuation. A gentleman, and a Spanish admiral, would never have allowed a crew to indulge in any such vulgar and insulting demonstrations.

If, on the other side, the circumstance of the Falcon's detention should have contributed, unfortunately, another element of provocation, as the Acting Secretary believes, in creating the infamous disturbances which occurred in New Orleans, it is more natural to attribute the fact, not to the circumstance of the detention itself, which is so simple and so justifiable, but to the seditious and inflammatory manner in which that circumstance was alluded to in several of the newspapers.

The undersigned avails himself of this occasion to renew to the Acting Secretary of State the assurances of his high consideration.

A. CALDERON DE LA BARCA.

Hon. W. S. Derrick,
Acting Secretary of State of the United States.

CASE OF THE SCHOONER LAMARTINE.

Mr. Worrell to Mr. Marcy.

Consulate of the U. S. of America, Matanzas,
February 25, 1854.

Sir: I have the honor to enclose copies of a letter from Mr. Henry Harris, my agent at Cardenas, my letter to the senior United States naval officer at Havana, and my letter to the Captain General of Cuba, relative to an outrage committed on an American schooner in the Gulf of Mexico, on her passage from Mobile to a port in my consulate. I hope, sir, the time has now arrived when an explicit, full, and unequivocating demand will be made for redress upon this government.

These insults have been so frequent, their contempt so great, that we have become the object of ridicule to all about us. I hope, in the investigation, reference will be made to the false statements made by even the Captain General, as well as other officers of this government, in the case of the abduction from New Orleans, and let no equivocation screen the perpetrator of this gross outrage upon our flag. Let the demand be commensurate with the act, compel the redress to be equal to the outrage, and let Americans here be able to chime with that glorious sentiment uttered on the back porch of the Capitol, "That flag shall protect an American citizen wherever his foot shall be placed," and then, sir, Americans abroad will know they are safe.

I have the honor to be, &c., &c., &c.,

EDWARD WORRELL,
United States Consul.

Hon. W. L. Marcy,
Secretary of State, &c., &c.

P. S.—I have no doubt this is a part of a fleet crusing after "fillibusteroes," and they will make that an excuse. A copy of Mr. Harris's letter will be found in the one to the senior officer of the United States squadron, Havana, therefore unnecessary to add separately.

Consulate of the U. S. of America, Matanzas,
February 25, 1854.

Sir: I hasten to inform you of the contents of a letter received from my agent at Cardenas to-day, viz:

"The schooner Lamartine, of Camden, Geo. W. Thorndyke, master, arrived at this port on Wednesday, February 22d, and reports the following as an extract from his log-book:

"'Thursday sea-account, February 16, 1854.—A brig displayed Spanish colors to the American schooner Lamartine, from Mobile, bound to Cardenas, island of Cuba, at 4.30 p. m., latitude 27° 14', longitude 85° 25' west from Greenwich. A flag was discovered flying at the brig's main gaff end, which was promptly answered through courtesy, and whilst hoisting our flag we were fired at by the brig. The ball came within forty yards of the schooner, endangering the vessel and lives of those on board. This a solemn protest against an outrage perpetrated by a Spanish vessel on an American vessel, in American waters, pursuing a lawful trade.'

"The said brig was about three-fourths of a mile astern of the schooner, and after firing she stood on her course, and was in company with her two days after.

"Respectfully, &c., &c.,

"HENRY HARRIS,
"*United States Consular Agent.*

"Edward Worrell, Esq.,
"*United States Consul, Matanzas.*"

Above you have the history of a gross outrage committed on our flag, and I lay before you the history for your consideration, but I hope you will take immediate and prompt action in the matter. I would advise that the Fulton go to Cardenas and ascertain the full particulars, and then cruise after the insulter and force an apology or punish his insolence. I have written to the Captain General, and I shall send a copy of the letter to the Secretary of State.

Yours, respectfully,

EDWARD WORRELL,
United States Consul.

To the SENIOR OFFICER
United States Squadron, Havana.

CONSULATE OF THE U. S. OF AMERICA, MATANZAS,
February 25, 1854.

MOST EXCELLENT SIR: I enclose a copy of a letter I have this day received from my agent at Cardenas, which you will see describes an outrage upon the American flag by a Spanish war vessel. I cannot conceive what could have induced this high-handed measure by a national vessel of Spain, nor have I an opportunity of knowing what vessel it can be; but as Havana is the port from whence the fleet for the protection of the island sails, and the headquarters of the squadron on duty here, your excellency must know what vessels are at sea. Your excellency must be aware of the nature of this offence—at our very doors, upon the Gulf of Mexico, the very spot that Cuba commands as the key of the west and the southwest of the United States, the last spot upon the wide sea that such an act should have been committed, if it was expected to retain the friendly relations with the United States which so happily exist at the present time, and participated in by a large majority of the people. I cannot believe, your excellency, that my government will tamely submit to have a vessel of that government fired at by a foreign vessel-of-war whilst in the legitimate and peaceable pursuit of trade, and I therefore make this representation to your excellency that you may exercise your own good judgment in preventing a repetition, as well as to investigate the cause of this unauthorized and unsupported outrage upon the flag of a friendly power.

I shall immediately inform the Secretary of State of the facts above presented, as well as forward him a copy of this letter to your excellency. In the mean time I have addressed the senior officer of the United States navy in the harbor of Havana, and requested him to pursue such course as his judgment will dictate for the future protection of American vessels traversing the Gulf or the Atlantic between this and the United States.

With high consideration, I have the honor to be, your excellency's obedient servant,

EDWARD WORRELL, *U. S. Consul.*

His Excellency the MARQUIS PAZUDA,
Governor and Captain General, &c., of the Island of Cuba.

Mr. Worrell to Mr. Marcy.

[Extract.]

[No. 11.] CONSULATE OF THE U. S. OF AMERICA, MATANZAS,
March 4, 1854.

SIR: In my dispatch of the 25th February, numbered 10, I informed the department of the attack by a Spanish brig-of-war upon an American schooner on her passage from Mobile to Cardenas, and that I have communicated with the Captain General upon the subject. I now have the honor to enclose a translation of his reply, received at this office three days ago. I will in a few days transmit to the department the affidavits of the officers and a portion of the crew relative to the matter.

* * * * * * * *

I am, very respectfully, your obedient servant,
EDWARD WORRELL,
United States Consul.

Hon. W. L. MARCY.

GOVERNMENT AND CAPTAINCY GENERAL
OF THE ISLAND OF CUBA, *March* 1, 1854.

SIR: His excellency the Governor and Captain General has received your communication of the 25th ult., (February.) The deed does not appear probable. He will inform himself, and will give an account to our representative in Washington, for the intelligence of both governments.

Which, by order of his excellency, I say to you in reply; remaining
Your obedient servant,
JOSE ESTEVAN,
The Secretary of Government.

To the CHARGE (ENCARGADO)
of the Consulate of the United States in Matanzas.

Mr. Worrell to Mr. Marcy.

[No. 12.] CONSULATE OF THE U. S. A., MATANZAS,
March 9, 1854.

SIR: In my dispatch No. 11, under date of the 4th instant, I forwarded a copy of the Captain General's reply to my communication to him, complaining of the attack of a Spanish brig-of-war on an American schooner from Mobile to Cardenas, a full statement of which in my dispatch of February 25, No. 10, was forwarded to your department. I now have the honor to enclose a communication under oath of the captain, mate, and part of the crew, which shows a direct, wilful, and outrageous violation of treaty stipulations, as well as shameful insult to the flag of the United States, and hope it will receive the attention its importance deserves.

I am sir, very respectfully, your obedient servant,

EDWARD WORRELL,
United States Consul.

Hon. William L. Marcy,
Secretary of State, &c., &c.

Consulate of the U. S. of America, Matanzas.

Interrogatories and answers given by George W. Thorndyke, Henry L. McKee, mate, and Charles M. Smith, Wm. Harrison, seamen of, and belonging to the schooner Lamartine, of Camden, Maine, said vessel having been fired at by a Spanish brig of-war while on her passage from Mobile, Alabama, to Cardenas, Cuba, in lat. 27° 24′ north, long. 85° 25′ west.

1. How did the brig bear when first discovered?

Answer. The brig bore, when first discovered, nearly southwest by west, with her larboard tacks aboard and by the wind.

2. Did she run for the schooner; and if so, what were her actions on approaching her?

Answer. The brig was heading east-northeast nearly, and kept on her course by the wind until night set in. She did not change her course before or after she fired at the Lamartine, as we perceived.

3. Did those on board the schooner observe her all the time after her first discovery until she signalized the schooner?

Answer. We on board the Lamartine, captain, crew, (and one passenger, E. Dansville, who was much frightened,) saw the brig before we could see her signal, it being hid by her sails from our view, if set, but saw her signal nearly as soon as it could be seen in her position from the schooner.

4. How long after signal was raised was it before the schooner answered by her flag?

Answer. The time could not have been more than ten minutes after the brig's signal was discovered when the Lamartine's ensign was run up to her main peak; and when in the act of setting our flag in plain view of the brig, the Lamartine was fired at.

5. Was there any delay on the part of Captain Thorndyke after he saw the signal of the brig; and if so, what was the cause of that delay?

Answer. There was no delay in setting our signal after seeing the brig; we should be very sorry to depart from that common rule and courtesy practised generally.

6. How does the schooner carry her signal halliards—made fast to the end of his main boom or to his crosstrees?

Answer. The schooner carries her signal halliards at sea at her main peak, and made fast at the main boom.

7. What was the relative position of the vessels when the shot was fired?

Answer. The brig bore, when she fired the shot, about north from the schooner, and distant from one-half to three-fourths of a mile—the Lamartine was heading south, half west.

8. Where did the shot range—along his length, across his bows, or across his stern?

Answer. The shot ranged along the schooner's length, striking the water on our weather beam, scattering the spray for some distance; the ball struck about thirty yards from the schooner, a little forward of our beam, if anything.

9. What was his conduct when he again met the schooner two days afterwards?

Answer. We saw the brig the two following days, but not near enough to ascertain any particular movement of her, or the number of guns she mounted, or her name.

GEORGE W. THORNDYKE, *Captain*
HENRY L. McKEE, *Mate.*
CHARLES his ⋈ mark. M. SMITH.
WILLIAM his ⋈ mark. HARRISON.

UNITED STATES CONSULAR AGENCY, CARDENAS, CUBA.

Personally appeared before me, Henry Harris, United States Consular agent for the port of Matanzas, George W. Thorndyke, Henry L. McKee, Charles M. Smith, and William Harrison, signers of the foregoing document in writing, and made oath that it is their free act and deed.

In testimony whereof, I have hereunto set my hand and affixed the seal of the consulate of the United States, at Cardenas, aforesaid, this sixth day of March, in the year of our Lord one thousand eight hundred and fifty-four.

[L. S.]

HENRY HARRIS.

CONSULATE OF THE UNITED STATES, MATANSAS,
March 10, 1854.

I, Edward Worrell, consul of the United States at the port of Matanzas, do hereby certify that the annexed is a true and faithful copy of the original document now on file and of record in this consulate.

In testimony whereof I have hereunto set my hand, and affixed the seal of the consulate, this tenth day of March, one thousand eight hundred and fifty-four.

[L. S.]

EDWARD WORRELL,
United States Consul.

CASE OF REY, ALIAS GARCIA.

Mr. Barringer to Mr. Clayton.

[Extract.]

[No. 5.] LEGATION OF THE UNITED STATES, MADRID,
January 9, 1850.

SIR: * * * * * * * *
Much concern has been manifested, in private conversation, by influential persons connected with the government and ministry of Spain, on the subject of the arrest and expected trial of Don Carlos de España, their consul at New Orleans, for the alledged abduction of Rey. It is stated in the newspapers received at this legation by the last mail from the United States, that the grand jury, on the testimony of the principal witnesses for the prosecution, have refused to find a true bill against the defendant. The action of this body will, I presume, put a final end to the prosecution.

It might be important to me to have an official authority for any declaration, verbal or written, I may deem advisable to make on the subject to the authorities here. And if the prosecution is not terminated, but still proceeds, I think it important that I should be fully informed of all the steps taken in its course.

* * * * * * * *

CASE OF PEDRO RAICES.

Mr. Robertson to Mr. Marcy.

[Extract.]

[No. 64.] CONSULATE OF THE UNITED STATES, HAVANA,
November 7, 1853.

SIR: * * * * * * *
A serious case has just occurred within four or five days. Pedro Raices was taken from his bed at midnight; his papers were seized: among them was, as his wife assures me, his certificate of American citizenship, which, she says, he refused to let the officers have, but they took it by force from him. It is very likely that the certificate is merely one to the effect of his having signified an intention of becoming a citizen when allowed by law. The document was issued, I believe, in New Orleans. Mr. Raices is now confined in complete incommunication in the Moro castle. His mother and wife have presented themselves to me, informed me that he has several children entirely dependent on him for support, and begged me to extend to him the protection of this consulate. Several other arrests have been made within a few days; among them those of three Creoles, besides Raices, who have certificates obtained in the United States. I promised the mother and wife of Raices that, in my first interview with the Captain General, I would bring the subject to his attention; and so I did on Saturday, 5th instant, although I had no hope of affording them the least satisfaction. You

are fully aware that the government here deny the right, on the part of a consul, to meddle in any way in such matters. The Captain General informed me that he was aware, that among the arrested were four who had certificates of American citizenship, which he did not intend to acknowledge; that he knew them to be conspirators against his government, and bad men, whom he was going to put on trial; and if, after being tried, they were proved to be guilty, that he would have them severely punished.

* * * * * *

I have the honor to be, &c.,

WILLIAM H. ROBERTSON,
Acting Consul.

Mr. Robertson to Mr. Marcy.

[No. 76.] CONSULATE OF THE UNITED STATES, HAVANA,
December 1, 1853.

SIR: Referring to my dispatch No. 64, under date of the 7th ultimo, I beg leave to inform you that the wife of Pedro Raices (whose name is mentioned in my said dispatch) came to me this morning, and made known that her husband was yesterday allowed, for the first time since his arrest, to communicate with his family and friends; that she immediately went to the Moro castle, where he is confined, and saw him; that he told her he was accused of being an accomplice in the printing (he is a printer by trade) and publication of papers against the Spanish government and the authorities of this island. He declares the charges to be false; that he has never, in any manner, said or done anything against the government here. He also informed her that the only paper found in his possession, any way criminating him, was a copy of a letter written by him to a friend in New Orleans, at the time that the "Faro" newspaper was purchased by John S. Thrasher, which letter, among other things, expressed his satisfaction and pleasure that there was an American at the head of that paper. He was employed in his trade at the "Faro" office. Mrs. Raices also told me that her husband had assured her that he was a naturalized citizen of the United States, and had produced his certificate of citizenship at this office some months since, of which certificate a note has been taken at this office. On referring to the general record-book, I find the following entry:—"May 30, 1853, Pedro Raices, a native of the island of Cuba, this day appeared at the office of the consulate of the United States, and produced a certificate of American citizenship, by naturalization, in his favor, issued out of the fourth district court of New Orleans, on the 26th day of October, 1852, signed and sealed by Thomas Gilmore, clerk of said court, whose signature is duly authenticated by Mortimore M. Reynolds, judge of the court aforesaid, on the date before mentioned." This clearly shows that Raices is a citizen of the United States. Mrs. Raices tells me that she has been informed that the Captain General is enraged against her husband, and has said that he will have him severely punished. Both she and her husband have likewise been assured that the best result that he can expect will be his being sent to Spain, which would be a great misfortune, for he is a poor man, having, besides his wife and four children, and another soon to come into the world, his aged mother—all entirely dependent on his labor for support.

Although I fear that the Captain General will not give heed to any remonstrances I may make in favor of Raices, on the plea that consuls, and especially myself, who have no exequator, are mere commercial agents, having no right to intermeddle in such affairs, I will still, feeling, as I do, great interest in the fate of the unfortunate man and his family, who will be left entirely destitute, address his excellency on the subject, and exert myself (as long as I have charge of this office) as much as possible to obtain his release.

I beg to renew the request made in my communication before mentioned, for specific instructions in relation to this case, that may serve as a guide for other cases of the like nature that may occur in future.

I have the honor to be, sir, with great respect, your most obedient servant,

WM. H. ROBERTSON,
Acting Consul.

Hon. WILLIAM L. MARCY,
Secretary of State of the United States.

Mr. Robertson to Mr. Marcy.

[No. 15.] CONSULATE OF THE UNITED STATES, HAVANA,
January 11, 1854.

SIR: I beg leave to lay before you a copy of my communication to his excellency the Governor General, dated 7th instant, on behalf of Pedro Raices, of whom I treated in my dispatch No. 76, (old series.) I likewise enclose you a translation of the General's reply, through his political secretary, which reply supercedes all interference, on my part, for the relief of the prisoner; and yet his right to American citizenship is recorded in this consulate since the 30th of May last. This will clearly show how insufficient the consulate is to give protection to American citizens. So much has been said on this subject by every one that has been consul here, as appears by the records, that any comments from me seem unnecessary. I send you simply the facts of the case.

I received, last evening, from the Captain General, Mr. Clayton's exequator, as consul for Havana. It is in the usual form.

I have the honor to be, &c.,

WM. H. ROBERTSON,
Acting Consul.

CONSULATE OF THE UNITED STATES, HAVANA,
January 7, 1854.

MOST EXCELLENT SIR: I was this morning called to the military hospital by a Mr. Pedro Raices, who was born in this island, but became some time since a citizen of the United States. This fact appears in the records of this consulate, where an entry is found to the effect that he had, on the 30th day of May last, produced in this office a certificate of American citizenship, issued in his favor by the fourth district court of New Orleans, on the 25th of October, 1852.

He states that he was taken up on suspicion of doing something wrong against the government of this island—he knows not what—and that his papers have all been taken from him, even to his certificate of American citizenship. He assures me that he is entirely innocent of any culpability; that he has been confined in the Moro, in a dungeon, for a length of time, a great part of it incommunicated, and the rest, though allowed to be visited by his family, subjected to continual insult and abuse, until he became very ill, when he was transferred to the military hospital.

I am informed that Mr. Raices has a wife and several children, and that his wife is on the eve of confinement; and besides that, he has also his aged mother dependent upon him.

I beg leave to call your excellency's attention to this case. If the prisoner has been guilty of an intentional infringement or disregard of the laws of the country, he has made himself liable to the consequences of his acts; but, at the same time, I must observe, without any intention of going beyond what is conceded to the office I fill, that the government of the United States expects of me to see that the accused is fairly tried by a proper tribunal, and allowed all the facilities he may require for his defence, in conformity to the treaty existing between the United States of America and her Catholic Majesty; but if, on the contrary, the accused is innocent, that he be not subjected to unnecessary delays and inconveniences, but set at liberty. This is the more requisite in the present case, where a numerous family, destitute of resources, is entirely dependent on the accused for support. As Mr. Raices is undoubtedly an American citizen, it becomes my duty to report the facts to my government, and for this reason I would request your excellency to be so good as to inform me of the cause of imprisonment of Mr. Pedro Raices, and the state of his case. I would also desire to be informed if Mr. Raices will be allowed all facilities for his defence in case that it is deemed proper to bring him to trial.

Feeling confident in your excellency's desire to see that speedy justice is done in the present case,

I have the honor to remain your excellency's very obedient servant,

WM. H. ROBERTSON,

Vice Commercial Agent, in charge of the Consulate.

His Excellency the MARQUIS DE LA PAZUDA,

Governor, Captain General, &c., &c., &c., of the Island of Cuba.

HAVANA, *January* 10, 1854.

DEAR SIR: His excellency the Governor and Captain General has charged me to say to you, as I do, that he has received your official letter of the 7th of this month, relative to Mr. Pedro Raices; but that, as his excellency cannot enter into communications with that consulate upon these affairs, as he is so ordered, he gives all necessary information, in regard to this particular, to the minister of Spain in Washington.

On complying with his excellency's command, I repeat myself your attentive and true servant, that kisses your hand.

JOSE ESTEVAN,
Government Secretary.

The COMMERCIAL AGENT
in charge of the Consulate of the United States.

Mr. Marcy to Mr. Robertson.

DEPARTMENT OF STATE,
Washington, February 9, 1854.

SIR: I will thank you to inform the department, by the earliest opportunity, if the case of Pedro Raices, to which you have repeatedly adverted in your dispatches, has been decided.

You will transmit any further information that you may be able to obtain respecting it, so that the department may be prepared to act with a full knowledge of all the facts.

Your dispatches Nos. 21 and 22 have been received.

I am, sir, &c.,
W. L. MARCY.

W. H. ROBERTSON, Esq.,
Acting U. S. Consul, Havana.

Mr. Robertson to Mr. Marcy.

[Extract.]

[No. 29.] CONSULATE OF THE UNITED STATES, HAVANA,
February 20, 1854.

SIR: * * * * * * * *

In answer to the last, relative to the case of Pedro Raices, I have to inform you that his wife came to see me last week, and told me that the "fiscal" (prosecuting officer) had demanded against him "banishment to some interior place in Spain for three years," and that the military court were to render their decision on Saturday. Mrs. Raices has seen me again to-day, and notified me that her husband's case was brought before the court on that day, but she has not yet been able to ascertain what the decision has been; that she is trying to find out the result, and will, when she does learn it, without delay make the same known to me.

In my dispatch No. 15, (receipt of which you acknowledged on the 24th ultimo,) I enclosed a copy of my communication to the Captain General in behalf of Raices, and also a copy of the political secretary's letter in reply thereto, wherein he informed me that he had been instructed by the Captain General to acknowledge the receipt of my letter, and to tell me that, as his excellency could not correspond with this consulate on such subjects, as he had orders to that effect, all necessary information had been transmitted to the Spanish minister at Washington. I do not perceive that I can, after receiving such a peremptory answer, say anything further to the Captain General on the subject.

Should I be able to obtain more information of this case before the departure of the steamer Isabel, that conveys this to Charleston, I will avail myself of the opportunity to transmit it.

I have the honor to be, &c.,

WM. H. ROBERTSON,
Acting Consul.

Mr. Robertson to Mr. Marcy.

[Extract.]

[No. 36.] CONSULATE OF THE UNITED STATES, HAVANA,
March 5, 1854.

SIR: The wife of Pedro Raices came to see me yesterday, and reported that she has been informed that the military court which tried her husband's case did not grant the petition of the prosecuting officer, which was "banishment for three years to Spain," but condemned him to the chain-gang. The case has been referred to the superior court, (audiencia,) and Mrs. Raices has been assured that the chief justice has disapproved of the sentence, as many who were more culpable than he had been condemned to lesser punishment; and that he (the chief justice) is of opinion that a few months' imprisonment is a sufficient penalty.

I suppose the Spanish minister in Washington will, in conformity with what the Captain General wrote me, be placed in possession of all information on this subject, and will not hesitate to lay the same before you.

A Cuban named Isidore Richoux, a naturalized citizen of the United States, who has presented to me a passport signed by you, received, day before yesterday, an order from the Captain General to leave the island immediately. The officer that communicated to him the order made him understand that he was directed to conduct him (Richoux) to prison, if he asked for more than five days to effect his departure.

* * * * * * * *

I have the honor to be, sir, with very great respect, your obedient servant,

WM. H. ROBERTSON, *Acting Consul.*

Hon. WM. L. MARCY,
Secretary of State of the United States, Washington.

Mr. Marcy to Mr. Magallon.

DEPARTMENT OF STATE,
Washington, March 15, 1854.

SIR: I beg leave to call your attention to the accompanying extract of a dispatch from the acting consul of the United States at Havana, dated the 5th instant, and to request that you will do me the favor to communicate to this department the information referred to therein.

I avail myself of this occasion, sir, to offer you a renewed assurance of my high consideration.

W. L. MARCY.

DON JOSE MARIA MAGALLON, *&c., &c., &c.*

Mr. Magallon to Mr. Marcy.

[Translation.]

LEGATION OF SPAIN IN WASHINGTON,
March 18, 1854.

The undersigned, chargé d'affaires of Spain, has the honor to inform the honorable Secretary of State of the United States, that he has read the extract of the communication which the acting consul of the United States at Havana addressed to the Department of State, under date of the 5th instant, relative to the judgment pronounced in the suit which had been brought againt Pedro Raices.

In conformity with the wishes expressed by the honorable William L. Marcy, in his note of the 15th instant, the undersigned proceeds to state, that the notices which have reached his knowledge on the subject only come down to the 10th of January last, at which time Raices was subject to the process which had been instituted by the permanent military commission of that island, against several individuals, for having instituted and distributed about the streets of Havana, and forwarded to other parts of the island by mail, certain productions and other seditious documents.

The arrest of this individual, who, although born in Havana, alleges to have been naturalized a citizen of the United States in 1852, no doubt induced Mr. W. H. Robertson, consul *ad interim* of this country in that city, to write to the Captain General on the 7th of last January, in behalf of Raices. This communication was answered by the authority last mentioned on the 10th of the same month, through the medium of the political secretary, stating that he had furnished this legation with all the necessary information on the subject. This information referred then to the seizure of various suspicious papers in possession of Raices, together with a portion of printing materials, a gun, and a sabre; there being among the former a writing in English, which Raices sought to destroy by snatching it from the hands of the police officer. Mr. Robertson must have referred to this communication of the Captain General, in his aforesaid dispatch of the 5th instant.

The undersigned has received no official dates since, but he does not hesitate to assure the honorable Secretary of State of the United States, that while he does not believe that the president of the court of judicature (regente de la audiencia) had given his private opinion before trying the case in court, he is firmly persuaded that his decision will be in conformity with strict justice.

The undersigned avails himself of this opportunity to renew to the honorable William L. Marcy the assurances of his high consideration.

JOSE MA. MAGALLON.

Hon. Wm. L. Marcy,
Secretary of State of the United States.

Mr. Robertson to Mr. Marcy.

[Extract.]

[No. 45.] Consulate of the United States, Havana,
March 21, 1854.

Sir: * * * * * * *

The case of Pedro Raices has been brought to a termination: he has been sentenced to banishment for one year in the Isle of Pines, as his wife has just informed me; the Captain General has not yet approved or disapproved. Should the former be the case, as the Isle of Pines is an out of the way place, where no employment may be procured for a man of weak constitution like Raices, his numerous and indigent family will, unless something is promptly done in his behalf, suffer severely; and the said isle being the place where vagrants and confirmed drunkards are sent, the consignment of Raices to it appears to me to be intended to ruin his character and good reputation.

* * * * * * * * * * *

I have the honor to be, &c.,
WM. H. ROBERTSON,
Acting Consul.

CASE OF CHARLES PETER V. ESNARD.

Mr. Campbell to Mr. Clayton.

Consulate of the United States, Havana,
February 1, 1850.

Sir: I have the honor to enclose herewith a copy of a short correspondence with the Captain General, and of an affidavit of Mr. Esnard, whose arrest and imprisonment gave rise to the correspondence.

You will observe that my letter to the Captain General is a courteously expressed request to be informed of "the cause of arrest, and confinement in the royal prison, of the American citizen, C. P. V. Esnard." To this civil, proper, and in my opinion necessary request, I am informed by his excellency that Mr. Esnard is imprisoned, but the cause is not given; and his excellency concludes the letter by saying, "it being an affair of the government, it belongs exclusively to me." This letter of the Captain General appears to assume the principle that when an American citizen is arrested, with or without cause, by the Spanish authorities, neither the government of the United States nor its agents can claim to be informed of the circumstances which induce arrest and imprisonment.

My feelings and opinions prompted an immediate reply, contesting this position; but they yielded to a sense of duty which required me to obey instructions contained in your official communication of the 26th day of May, 1849, in which, while alluding to difficulties which I then thought might be impending over Americans in Cuba, you say: "Should the difficulties you seem to apprehend arise, you will immediately report the occurrence to the department, which will receive prompt attention." In obedience to which instructions, this communication is now made.

In Mr. Esnard's case it appears somewhat strange that the officer at the prison should, in the first instance, have denied to me having such a prisoner in custody; and it is equally strange that Mr. Esnard underwent no examination in Havana, although he had been informed by the governor of Alacranes, "that the Captain General wished to get information from him in relation to certain persons." Had the arrest been made solely to collect the fine of twenty-five dollars, the fine could have been collected where Mr. Esnard had funds and friends, and he would thereby have escaped the painful incarceration of more than nine days.

To secure Mr. Esnard from the despondence and alarm so apt to overwhelm the firmest when incarcerated in a Spanish dungeon, I had him repeatedly visited in prison.

I have the honor to be, &c.,

ROBERT B. CAMPBELL.

Hon. John M. Clayton,
Secretary of State, Washington City.

Consulate of the United States, Havana,
January 24, 1850.

Sir: At four o'clock yesterday afternoon I was called on by a lady, reporting herself as the wife of C. P. V. Esnard, an American citizen, who, she stated, had taken out a carte of domiciliation on the 29th of October last, had been arrested the day before at Nueva Paz, by order of the government, and brought to this city for imprisonment. The lady represents herself as knowing nothing of the cause of arrest, but states that her husband directed her to inform me, as the consul of his country, that he had been arrested, accompanied with a request that I would call at the royal prison to see him.

In conformity to that request I called at the prison, inquired for the alcalde, and was shown a person who I presume held that office; from him I learned that no such person was in prison.

About 6 p. m. I was informed, by the individual who I supposed to be the alcalde of the royal prison, that he had been mistaken in telling me that Mr. Esnard was not in confinement, as, upon examination, he discovered that he had arrived about 12 m., and that I could see him.

This morning I sent my clerk to the prison, who saw the prisoner in the galera de Santa Rosa, and learned from him that he was entirely ignorant of having committed any offence upon this island, or of the cause of his arrest. The alcalde, however, informed my clerk that the prisoner had been sent by the governor of Alacranes to be placed at the disposition of your excellency.

Failing in my efforts to obtain any definite knowledge of Mr. Esnard's offence, your excellency will excuse my asking of you the cause of arrest and confinement in the royal prison of the American citizen, C. P. V. Esnard.

An early reply to this communication will confer a favor.

I have the honor to be, with considerations of great respect, your excellency's most obedient servant,

ROBERT B. CAMPBELL.

His Excellency the GOVERNOR AND CAPTAIN GENERAL
of the Island of Cuba, &c., &c., &c.

[Translation.]

POLITICAL SECRETARY'S OFFICE.

The individual C. P. V. Esnard is, in fact, detained as subject to a judicial investigation, and I communicate to your lordship, for your information, although being an affair of the government, it belongs exclusively to me.

God preserve your lordship many years. Havana, 26th January, 1850.

EL CONDE DE ALCOY.

To the CONSUL *of the United States.*

CONSULATE OF THE UNITED STATES, HAVANA,
January 31, 1850.

Personally appeared C. P. V. Esnard, who declared that he was arrested on the 22d day of January, 1850, at his house in Vegas, department of Alacranes, and taken to the city of Nueva Paz, in presence of the lieutenant governor, by whom he was questioned: "Where he had resided during his stay on the island in July last?" He answered, "Upon his father's property." "What persons he had visited while there?" He answered, "Dr. Francisco Gonzalez, and no other." "When did he leave the island?" Answer, "The latter end of July." "Who had given him passport?" "Nobody." "What port had he sailed from?" "Havana, and that he had left without a passport, with the intention of returning to Havana with his family, which he did in October last; that upon his arrival at Havana he made application for a carte of domiciliation, which was given to him a few days afterwards; that the agent who got out the carte for him told him that his name was on a list, which he doubts not has been the cause of his (Esnard's) arrest; that the governor of Alacranes, at the time of the arrest, told him that the Captain General wished to get information from him in relation to certain persons, although no names were mentioned; that on the 23d instant he was sent, accompanied by the captain of the parish of Nueva Paz, to the prison of Havana, to be kept there at the disposition of the Captain General; that during his stay in the prison, which was to this date, in the department called Santa Rosa, with the thieves and cutthroats of the whole island, he was not questioned at all; that on the 31st January he was called by the jailor and taken in the presence of a respectable gentleman, who informed him that he would be set at liberty upon paying a fine of twenty-five dollars, and that if ever he made himself liable to suspicion he would be expelled from the island; that he answered that he had no money, as his wife had gone out to the country, but the gentleman told him that he could take his time for paying the money, and that the American consul having lent him the money he went and paid it; but what the fine was for he is entirely ignorant, except what is to be seen on the face of the receipt given for the money, viz: for having left the island without a passport.

CHARLES PETER V. ESNARD.

Sworn to before me, on the day of the date written on the first page.

ROBERT B. CAMPBELL.

CASE OF JOHN SALINERO.

Mr. Morland to Mr. Webster.

CONSULATE OF THE UNITED STATES, HAVANA,
April 7, 1851.

SIR: I have the honor to enclose to you herewith a translated copy of a communication which I sent to the Captain General, and of his excellency's reply thereto, in consequence of an American citizen having been taken up and imprisoned in a dungeon without being allowed any communication.

I beg leave to draw your attention to the Captain General's answer to my application, by which you will see that he does not allow consuls to interfere in such cases, stating (which is true) that their exequatur from Spain only allows them to exercise the functions of commercial agents. This has been stated before to General Campbell; and unless the government of Spain permits consuls to protect American citizens so far as to give them an open and fair trial, it may be very oppressive, and grow worse and worse. In the present case the Captain General did put the individuals in communication.

The United States steamship Saranac, with Commodore Parker on board, arrived here on the 19th ultimo, and sailed for Pensacola on the 3d instant.

Everything is quiet here; but there are reports, credited by the Captain General, that there are some eight or nine hundred men, embarking from Florida to invade this island. It is understood, however, that they sail unarmed, and for Yucatan first.

I have the honor to be, sir, with great respect, your obedient servant,

JOHN MORLAND,
Acting Consul.

Hon. DANIEL WEBSTER,
Secretary of State, Washington City.

[Translation.]

CONSULATE OF THE UNITED STATES, HAVANA,
March 27, 1851.

MOST EXCELLENT SIR: I have just been informed by the friends and relatives of Mr. John Salinero, a citizen of the United States and a resident of New York, where I understand he has a wife and family, that he has been arrested, on the 25th instant, by order of your excellency's government, and put in prison, in a state of incommunication, without his friends having any knowledge of the cause of his arrest. I therefore request, respectfully, of your excellency, to have the goodness to state to me the cause of the arrest of that individual, so as to have the opportunity of offering some explanations, or of making his defence, if he is accused of having committed any crime.

With the greatest respect, I have the honor to be, your excellency's very obedient servant,

JOHN MORLAND,
Acting Consul.

His Excellency Señor D. JOSE DE LA CONCHA,
Governor and Captain General of the Island of Cuba.

[Translation.]

OFFICE OF THE POLITICAL SECRETARY, HAVANA.
April 3, 1851.

Mr. John Salinero, of whom you treat in your communication of the 27th ultimo, is, in fact, imprisoned in this city, and subject to the court of the alcalde mayor, Señor Don Justo Sandoval, before whom proceedings are carried on against him, as he appears as an accomplice in a crime of falsehood. This being a mere affair of justice, to the courts of the territory that exercise it in her Majesty's name belong the prosecution and decision of the cause of the citizen to whom you refer, whose defence, by any means that he may think himself entitled to use, will be heard when the opportunity arrives. For this reason, I must remind you that the powers committed to foreign consuls in this island do not extend to their interfering in affairs of this nature, the regium exequatur annexed to the certificate of their appointment prescribing to them the merely commercial limits to which they must confine themselves in their powers.

God preserve you many years.

JOSÉ DE LA CONCHA.

To the COMMERCIAL AGENT *of the United States.*

CASE OF CAPTAIN LARRABEE, &c.

Mr. Trist to Mr. Forsyth.

[Extract.]

WASHINGTON, *September* 29, 1853.

SIR: Among other subjects, in regard to which, owing to the constant employment which my duties gave me, it proved absolutely impossible to find time for making the necessary communications to the department previously to my departure from Havana in August last, and the materials concerning which I therefore brought with me for that purpose, is the case of the master and two men of the brig Franklin, of Portland, to which the enclosed papers relate, and which would have been reported at an earlier day had I not been compelled to postpone doing so by the loss of time occasioned since my arrival in the United States by repeated indisposition, and by the exercise demanded by extreme debility from which I have suffered, whereby I have barely been enabled to give to my private affairs the attention they required.

The circumstances which led to my letter to the Captain General of Cuba, under date of May 28, 1835, (a copy whereof, A, is enclosed,) being therein detailed, it is needless to swell this communication by their repetition.

From the enclosed reply (B) of his excellency, under date May 29, it will be seen that my letter was referred to the Auditor of War, the officer to whom the cognizance of the subject, under the general power of supervision and correction vested in the Captain General as supreme judge, regularly belonged; and the course which the matter took appears in detail in the accompanying copy (C) of the "*expediente*" or paper book, made up of all the "*diligencias*" or proceedings which was communicated to me by the Captain General, with his letter of July 20th (D) herein enclosed.

I will state such particulars as may be necessary, to spare the trouble of reading the expediente, and afford a right understanding of the case.

Agreeably to the ordinary mode of proceeding of Spanish judicial functionaries, an accident of the kind which befel Captain Larrabee is always sufficient to seal the ruin of any man, unless he be protected by circumstances altogether foreign to the merits of his case. The first step is to throw every person, who can, by any pretext, be implicated in the matter, into a dungeon; from which he can hope for release only when it shall suit the will and pleasure of the interminable series of auditors, fiscals, assessors, notaries, &c., &c., whose action may be requisite in the case, to reach that stage in the proceedings at which an order can issue for his liberation. If he be altogether destitute of both money and friends, there is no motive for alacrity in disposing of his case, and it drags on most heavily, or lies neglected, and perhaps entirely forgotten. If he have, or be suspected of having, either money, or friends able to use it in his behalf, motives are not wanting to put his resources and their feelings to the strongest test; and nothing can be more easy, under a system where no officer engaged in the administration of the laws is ever expected to do any act as a matter of duty, and where the only responsibility or accountability attached to any office is to a court, at which nothing can be effected except by *empeñas* or money, and where there is nothing which may not be effected by their means.

In the present instance, everything was done in behalf of Captain Larrabee which could be accomplished by the joint influence of my official interference, addressed to the Captain General, (who is an honest man, and perhaps the only one holding office in the island, and the fear of whom does, to a greater or less degree, influence the conduct of them all) and the *private* exertions of Mr. George Knight, of the house of Mariatigué, Knight & Co., the consignees of the vessel; who, having long and extensive experience in all sorts of transactions with these gentry, took, in the most skilful way, every step that could be taken to hasten the case to a close. Nevertheless, although it was notorious to all, and acknowledged in the Captain General's answer to my first letter, that the death of the Spanish cooper was entirely "*casual*," Captain Larabee was, in the regular course of proceeding required by law, immediately brought to Havana at a time when the yellow fever was raging furiously, and thrown into a horrid dungeon, in the company of wretches of all shades of skin and crime, where, I am satisfied, a confinement of a few hours would have certainly caused my death, and whence it proved impracticable to obtain his release, even provisionally and under bond, until he had lain there a fortnight. As a great favor, granted at their peril and in violation of the law, by the *military* officers (whose general character is, from obvious causes, very different from that of the civil) of the guard, he was allowed, for some days previous to his release, to emerge from his dungeon for a few hours, to recover from the effects of its pestilential atmosphere.

I could not with any propriety interfere any further than I did, nor even know anything of the proceedings, until the result should be officially communicated by the Captain General. But I was kept privately apprized of them by Mr. Knight, as fast as he obtained any intelligence on the subject, and in that way I learned that, in pursuance of the "*dictamen*," or semijudicial opinion of the fiscal of the Auditor of War, (every officer, judicial or executive, has one or more of these fiscals or assessors, whose province it is to half judge or decide what his judgment or decision is to be) the case of Captain Larrabee and his imprisonment was to be protracted by sending the proceeding back to Bahia Honda, where they had begun, for new investigations, in regard not only to the occurrences which involved the death of the Spanish cooper, but *also to the previous ill-treatment of the crew of the brig Franklin, which had, in the course of the investigation, been alleged by the mutineers against the captain.* A point more utterly foreign to the death of the Spaniard, the only ground of the whole proceeding, and the only assignable pretext for the imprisonment of Captain Larrabee, could not be conceived, and the real object of this manœuvre to find a new subject for proceedings and extortion was but too evident. In this point of view, however, it could not be noticed by me, even if I could have avowed any knowledge of it. But, considering that, agreeably to every principle of international law, the cognizance of all questions between the masters and crews of our vessels, retrospectively founded upon alleged breaches of the shipping contract as to services required and food furnished, and having damages in view, properly belonged to the authorities of the United States; and convinced, if the right of those of Cuba to interfere in such matters were once generally established, there would be no end to the vexatious proceedings to which our ship-masters would become subject in every port of the island, as a mode of extorting money from them, my first impulse was, to address to the Captain General a remonstrance against any such pretension. The only difficulty was, that such a step would imply a knowledge that it had been advanced. This, however, I got over by founding my letter on the generally known facts, that the complaint of hard usage had been made, and that the proceedings had gone back to Bahia Honda, and the general presumption that such was the object. It was written and translated, but on further reflection I determined not to send it.

In the first place, by the terms of my exequator, (and all granted by the court of Spain are precisely alike,) which would be appealed to as the rule of their government, my right of interference in controversies between masters and seamen is expressly limited to the exercise of my "*arbitrio*," which, in one of its senses, and probably the sense in which it is intended by the Spanish government, (whose treaties and laws show the utmost jealously and circumspection on this point,) means my arbitration, and implies the previous voluntary submission of the parties thereto. On the other hand, the practices which have imperceptibly grown up at Havana, in relation to consuls, are very liberal, and leave foreign seamen at the absolute disposal of their consul, so that he is enabled to exercise a powerful control over their conduct in all respects; and where he cannot himself decide on their complaints, he may put them under the necessity of waiting until they can be brought before a court in the United States. For instance, as happens there among our shipping every week, and sometimes every day in a week, a seaman or two, or a whole crew, with or without cause, get the devil into them, refuse to do work, and come to the consul to demand payment of wages, damages, and their discharge. He examines into the case, and finds that, although they may, by our laws, be entitled to damages for the usage they have received, (which is but too frequently the case,) they are not entitled to their discharge. He tells them so, and that they must wait to be righted by a jury in their own country, and he requires them to return to duty. If they prove unmanageable, he gives to the master an order (in its terms a *request)* to the captain of the port for their arrest and confinement until the vessel be ready for sea, or they see fit to return to their duty, which they generally do very quickly. Except under circumstances which do not allow it to be waited for, a seaman is never arrested without this order from his consul, and, being founded on the fact of mutinous conduct, it is considered as bringing him under his exclusive custody. This mode of proceeding, together with the difficulty of communication with lawyers and magistrates, arising from the difference of language, proves a practical protection against our seamen having recourse to litigation there, which would never be attended with any other result than to strip them of any loose cash they might have or be entitled to, and subject the masters to extortion for the exclusive benefit of the judges, &c., for recourse would necessarily be had in every case, by the master or his consignee, to the only argument in which they can perceive any force, or by which a cause can be made to move; and the seamen would invariably be found, *prima facie*, in the right, but, on full investigation, in the wrong. The established custom being such as I have stated, I thought it dangerous to raise, in this case, a general question; the agitation of which, by awakening attention to a power so calculated to subserve their notorious rapacity as that of receiving complaints of seamen against their captains, might lead to general results of a permanent character, the most injurious to the interests of our shipping.

In the next place, I knew that, at the very quickest step known in the tactics of Spanish law officers, even with the fear of Tacon in their hearts, the various reports on which the official determination of such a question must depend, would, on the most favorable calculation, require from three to twelve months in their production; and that it would, to a certainty, be mixed up with the case of Captain Larrabee, so as to expose him to all the evils of such a delay.

Governed by these considerations, I confined myself to a simple demand made in my letter (E) of June 15, 1835, of the two seamen in question, as offenders against the laws of the United States, whom it was my duty to send home for trial. This demand did not require any reference to the inquiry which had been ordered with regard to the treatment of the crew by Captain Larrabee; and I entertained a hope that an order might forthwith issue from the Captain General, putting them at my immediate disposal, in which case I proposed to send them off by the first merchant vessel; and, by thus removing the chief if not the only complaints, to cut short a proceeding which might last, there was no conjecturing how long, and subject Captain Larrabee to new sufferings, and his owners to ruinous expenses and delays. This hope, however, was not realized. My letter was referred to the Auditor of War, whose fiscal, as appears from the expediente, decided, on the 2d of July, that he reserved his opinion upon it until the inquiry above referred to should be brought to a close.

To return to the circumstances immediately connected with the imprisonment of Captain Larrabee: The first decision of the auditor's fiscal, as was at the time privately learned, required that before any opinion on the merits of his case could be given, the widow of the deceased must make a notarial declaration, whether she renounced or adhered to her personal actions against Captain Larrabee, which comprised an action for a maintenance for herself and children. This renunciation being a *sine qua non* to his release from his dungeon, every hour's confinement in which endangered his life, it had to be bought; and the captain being very poor, and altogether unable to supply the means, the necessary sum had to be raised by subscription.

Fortunately, the widow proved to have some conscience, and made the renunciation at once, on receiving the assurance that something better than what could be wrung out of the prisoner's substance would be raised for her. Mr. Knight authorized me to subscribe six ounces ($102) for his house, as I did for myself, and the list thus commenced was carried to between one and two thousand dollars; not, however, without the necessity of a resort to other consuls and foreigners, that took place without my knowledge, and in violation of the heading of the list, and of my letter accompanying it, which were addressed, and confined the subscription, exclusively to American ship-masters and other citizens. As was very natural, the incarceration of Captain Larrabee caused a high excitement among the masters of our vessels, of whom there were upwards of ninety then in port, and, as was also not to be wondered at, from the ignorance and unreasonableness of the greater portion, this excitement was, in the minds of many, directed against *me*, for not procuring, by a wave of my consular sceptre, the *instant* liberation of this *American citizen*.

* * * * * * * *

The renunciation of the widow being obtained, and his consignees having given bonds for his appearance, Captain Larrabee was released from prison and permitted to go to Bahia Honda, whence, on completing the lading of his brig, he returned in her early in July. There being no assignable pretext for any further suspension of his case, he had every right to expect his immediate discharge, so as to enable him to put to sea as soon as his vessel should be cleared, which was but the work of a few hours. His disappointment in this just expectation caused me, after waiting several days in the hope that the necessity for my further interference would be obviated, to address to the Captain General my third letter, of July 9, (F,) which also was referred by his excellency to the Auditor of War, the decision of whose fiscal, approved by himself, was at length brought forth, under date of 15th July, and was instantly acted upon, in the final instance, by the Captain General.

In this decision, besides an acknowledgment that the death of the Spaniard was purely accidental, the allegation of ill-treatment of the crew is stated to have been entirely disproved; and the *latter circumstance* is made a *distinct ground* of the captain's acquittal and escape without *any penalty or punishment*, thereby implying their right to prosecute an American ship-master criminally, on the allegation of having required too much work of his crew, and given them bad fare.

It then proceeds (after a reservation of the principle that it belongs to the local authority of every country to punish those who offend against its laws, and that therefore the offences of the crew of the brig Franklin may and ought to be judged by "this superior government,") to consent that, without prejudice to his jurisdiction, and in the spirit of cultivating the harmony, &c., with the United States, the seamen may be delivered up to the consul, &c. This parade of the right to judge the local offences of the *crew*, which had never been called in question, and when the prosecution of *Captain Larrabee* had been the sole object of their whole proceeding, which was the only one they cared about or even contemplated, is a fair sample of the way in which these people always bring forward some common-place, as a means of shuffling out of view the real points of the case. The British consul has repeatedly told me that in his discussions with them he always receives some prolix compound of irrelevancies, in which the point in question is not so much as approached. And this is ascribable not only to their rooted habit of ill-faith in all transactions, but also to their indolence and ignorance, whence results an absolute incapacity to do justice to a subject, even when they may chance to be so disposed.

The decision winds up with strictures upon my interference, to this effect: first, the "*tribunal*" (that is to say, the auditor and his fiscals, in secret conclave in his bed-chamber, or bed, perhaps) had never decreed the detention of *the vessel;* and if this resulted from that of *the persons* proceeded against, it afforded no ground for my reclamation, inasmuch as those persons might have been replaced by others; secondly, the case having been conducted in the course established by the laws, there has been no delay in bringing it to a conclusion; and thirdly, that it is highly desirable that, confining itself to its functions of representing the individual interest of the subjects of its government on proper occasions, the consulate should not overstep the limits defined by the laws and reciprocal treaties, and should thus leave the authorities in the free exercise of their attributes.

The reason assigned under the first of these heads is specious; but, in such a case as this, it was, as they well knew, *practically* untrue; and the confinement and detention of Captain Larrabee (even independently of the *costs* of the proceeding, in the way of fees and douceurs, the latter of which always constitute by far the heaviest item) was unavoidably attended with serious pecuniary loss to all interested in the voyage. And knowing well that the most serious if not the only real responsibility which a Spanish officer could incur in such a case towards his government would be that of subjecting it to *claims for money*, I have never omitted to present every subject of the kind in a way calculated to awaken this idea in their minds as strongly as the circumstances of the case allowed.

With regard to the second head they would have said the same thing, and with just as much truth, had they made the case last twelve months or twelve years. God help the man who once gets the clutches of Spanish judges upon him, and has nothing to depend upon but "the course established by the laws!"

The third branch of these strictures manifests the vexation of the auditor and his first fiscal * * * * * at my interposition; and it is not to be wondered at, seeing that I can at any moment, and without an hour's delay, bring to this Captain General's knowledge any fact I see fit to ask his special attention to; whereas, in the course established by the laws, an appeal to him on the proceedings in a case, before it be regularly matured, must, of necessity, be always a matter of extreme and generally insurmountable difficulty. These objections offer an excellent opportunity for addressing a representation to the Captain General on the subject of consular powers, as I propose to do on my return, if, on a thorough examination of the subject, it should appear advisable to agitate it. Their treaty with us stipulates only for the footing of the most favored nations; and that with France, which, as they affirm, gives the general rule in relation to the powers of consuls, as it does, of course, to those of France, reduces them to mere cyphers. And if this proves to be the case, as it appeared to be on a close inspection of all the documents that I had the opportunity of obtaining any knowledge of, the less that is said about the matter the better. But if it prove to be otherwise, as the British consul informed me, just before I left Havana, would appear from the last treaty with Great Britain, it will be most important to come to such an understanding on the subject as will put the interests of our shipping beyond the reach of their villany.

Although the office of consul will, everywhere, even in the most civilized country, conduce to the *convenience* of commerce, and its security against the *petty* vexations to which, even if they be not brought upon them by any other course, mariners will subject themselves through ignorance and inadvertence; yet, in a truly civilized country, the necessity for a consul is of very secondary importance. But under such an atrocious system as that of Spain, which combines all the evils of the absence of all government, where no man is secure; and of the total extinction of individual liberty, where no man is allowed to defend himself—the case is very different. From what I know of the rapacity and irresponsibility of its functionaries, I had much rather risk my person and property in a tolerably armed merchantman at the anchorage of Quallah Battoo, than that they should be in a port of Cuba, unprotected by a consul, and subject to the various casualties which might put them at the mercy of the Spanish authorities, proceeding unchecked "in the course established by the laws." Even the unlimited power of supervision and correction vested in the Captain General, although exercised by a man so unique in their service as the present Governor, is a totally inadequate protection—it being utterly impracticable for one man, however vigilant, honest, and severe, to hold in check the universal rapacity which constitutes the sole spring of action in the whole administrative branch, from the constable to the highest judge. Hundreds of cases must occur every day, in relation to which he is under the necessity to adopt, without examination, in regard to both facts and law, the views of others; and it is only to those of a most flagrant nature that his own examination can be occasionally given, even when the difficulties of bringing them to his notice have been surmounted.

The two mutineers of the brig Franklin having, in the way stated, been put at my disposal, the only course left me was to pursue that with reference to which I had made the demand; although my chief motive in making it, and but for which I should have scarcely deemed it worth while to make it at all, no longer existed.

* * * * * * * * *

I deemed them, under the circumstances of the case, a sufficient ground for at least *bringing* against these men the charge of *revolt* or *piracy*, and going through the form of sending them home as prisoners, rather than that they should be turned loose without any show of prosecution; which, after all the trouble and excitement to which the case had given rise, and the sufferings which their misconduct had brought upon their captain, would have had a very bad effect upon our seamen in that quarter.

It is proper to add, in regard to my communications to the Captain General, that, except in cases of mere form, they were always sent in the *Spanish* language. Any communication addressed to him in any other, is subject to delays arising from its necessary reference to some government translator, who always takes his own time about it, and may, if he have any motive, carry the delay to a ruinous extent; and, what is worse, its meaning is ever liable to total perversion. I do not know of one of these translators who is capable of making a decent version of any paper in the English language; and if they were all ever so capable, there would be no security against intentional perversion. My only chance of conveying my real sentiments and views on any subject to the Captain General, or any other functionary, was, therefore, to send them in the Spanish language; my acquaintance with which, although very limited, is sufficient to enable me to judge if my meaning be exactly rendered. The certainty that it would always be wretchedly perverted by one of their official translators, besides being known to me from the general character of such of their productions as I have seen, was in every instance brought forcibly home to me, by the great difficulties encountered in getting a faithful version made under my own eye; although I employed the most capable man in that line at Havana, (whom I know the official translators have recourse to, in their straits) with the advantage, too, of explaining my meaning to him in French, when he did not seize it in English. The trouble and time required by every communication was thus at least quadrupled. But it was better not to write at all, on any subject requiring delicate treatment, (and this was more or less the nature of every subject, except mere matters of form, on which I had to make a communication,) than to expose my matter and manner to the certainty of perversion. This departure from the diplomatic rule of making all official communications in the language of the writer, being therefore a matter of absolute necessity, to secure the object I might have in view, I entertained no doubt of its propriety; only taking the utmost care, as I always did, that my precise meaning, and nothing else, was conveyed.

The perusal of this letter must, from its length, if no other cause, prove a very tedious job. But the necessity that I should convey some idea of the circumstances in which I was placed, in regard to the various aspects of the subject, will, I trust, be deemed a sufficient apology for the tiresome details into which I have entered.

I am, sir, very respectfully, your obedient servant,

N. P. TRIST.

Hon. John Forsyth,
Secretary of State.

Consulate of the United States.

I have just received from Messrs. Mariatigué, Knight & Company, consignees of the brig Franklin, of Portland, intelligence of a most unfortunate affair that occurred at Bahia Honda, on the 25th instant, in relation to which I beg leave to trouble your excellency with the following statement and request.

The said vessel, commanded by Captain Nehemiah Larrabee, a highly respectable man, left here on the 15th instant for Bahia Honda, to take in a cargo of molasses, having on board, for the necessary work to be done to the hogsheads, two coopers of this place, named Jacinto Munson and Andrez Fer.

On the morning of the 25th instant, when Captain Larrabee came upon deck, he perceived that his long-boat and two of his crew were missing. He immediately got into his small boat, with three of his seamen to row her, and accompanied by the two coopers above named, to assist him against his mariners should they all turn against him; and having done so, he proceeded to the mouth of the harbor, where he saw his launch pulling out to sea, and pursued her. Not having confidence in the fidelity of any of his crew, he had taken with him a gun, two pistols, and a sword. The sword and pistols he gave to the two coopers, keeping in his own hand the gun. When he had got near enough to the launch he hailed his two men, who were rowing her, and ordered them to stop, but they did not pay any regard to him. He then fired a shot at the boat, but this had no effect. He continued the pursuit, and, having approached still nearer, again ordered them to stop; but they still persisted rowing away from the harbor, when he fired another shot, which caused them to stop. When the small boat got up with the launch, Captain Larrabee jumped into the launch, and one of the two men showing a disposition to persevere in the mutiny, Captain Larrabee struck him with his gun, which, though at the half-cock, went off. The load, most unfortunately, entered the head of the cooper, Jacinto Munson, who was in the other boat, and caused his immediate death. Captain Larrabee immediately proceeded to the fort, and they were all taken into custody.

My object in troubling your excellency now is to state these facts, of the accuracy of which I have no doubt, and to ask, if it be consistent with your excellency's view of what is proper in the case, that Captain Larrabee may be permitted to take in his cargo without interruption, and bring his vessel round here; or, if your excellency should think it not proper to trust him at sea, that he be allowed to take in his cargo under any guard which may be thought necessary, and then be brought here in such way as your excellency may see fit to order.

The taking in a load of molasses is a work which requires constantly the eye of the master of the vessel; and if Captain Larrabee should experience a long confinement at Bahia Honda, or should be obliged to come here before his cargo is all taken in, the consequence will be a long detention, which will probably result in the ruin of a poor and honest mariner, who is already sufficiently afflicted with the calamity of having taken, however unintentionally and innocently, the life of a worthy man, who was in the act of rendering him service.

God preserve, &c. Havana, May 28, 1835.

N. P. TRIST.

Exemo. Sor. Don MIGUEL TACON, &c., &c.,
Captain General, &c., &c.

CONSULATE OF THE UNITED STATES.

William Marion and Ellis (*alias* Ezra) Buzzle, the two seamen belonging to the brig Franklin, of Portland, who committed the crime of putting to sea in the boat of said brig, and revolting against their captain when overtaken by him, which led to the fatal accident that occurred at Bahia Honda on the 25th of last month, have thereby offended against the laws of the United States in a degree which makes it my duty to send them home for trial and punishment. I have therefore to request that your excellency will give the necessary orders for putting them at my disposal, and securing against their release until I shall find an opportunity for sending them away.

God preserve, &c. Havana, June 15, 1835.

N. P. TRIST.

Excmo. Sor. Don MIGUEL TACON,
Captain General, &c., &c., &c.

CONSULATE OF THE UNITED STATES.

I beg leave to call your excellency's attention to the case of Captain Nehemiah Larrabee, of the brig Franklin, of Portland, whose misfortune in accidentally causing the death of a fellow-being has been not a little aggravated by the confinement experienced by him for some time in the callaboso de la fuerza, and by other harassing circumstances in the measures which it has been judged proper to pursue on the occasion.

After his release from the callaboso, Captain Larrabee returned to Bahia Honda, where he had been compelled to leave his vessel; and having completed her lading there, he brought her to this port, where she was cleared several days ago, and is now detained, to the serious injury of her cargo, (molasses) and of her owners in various other ways. Captain Larrabee having applied to me to know the cause of his detention, I am altogether unable to give him an explanation of it, except that the proceedings (*providencia*) in the case are not closed; but why they are not closed, it is out of my power so much as to imagine a reason. I am, therefore, under the necessity of asking the favor of your excellency to take the subject into consideration, and cause everything to be done which may properly be done to prevent the further detention of said Captain Larrabee in this port.

God preserve, &c. Havana, July 9, 1835.

N. P. TRIST.

Excmo. Sor. Don MIGUEL TACON,
Captain General, &c., &c., &c.

Mr. Robertson to Mr. Marcy.

CONSULATE OF THE UNITED STATES, HAVANA,
March 9, 1854.

SIR: I hasten to fulfil the promise I made in my dispatch No. 38. The judicial tribunals in the island of Cuba are as various as the modes of procedure that each one of them has adopted. The tribunals proceed according to their special regulations, in conformity to the divers and even contradictory Spanish laws, and also in conformity to the practice of the royal audiencias of the island. (There is one audiencia only at present, called the "Real Audiencia Pretorial de la Habana" that of Puerto Principe has lately been suppressed.)

The following named tribunals exist: The court of the royal exchequer, *tribunal de real hacienda.* The war or ordinary military court, *tribunal de guerra ó militar ordinario.* The permanent and executive military commission, *tribunal de la comision militar exsecutivo y permanente.* Special court of the navy or marine, *tribunal privativo de la real armada ó marina.* Special artillery court, *tribunal privativo de artilleria.* Special engineers' court, *tribunal privativo de injenieros.* Tribunal of commerce, *tribunal de comercio.* Tribunal of the church or ecclesiastical, *tribunal eclesiástico.* The ordinary or common courts, that judge all matters not coming within the jurisdiction of the various tribunals above mentioned.

As the island is divided into various governments, and lieutenancies of government, politico-military, each governor and lieutenant governor has jurisdiction as a judge of first instance (juez de primera instancia) upon all civil and military matters within his district.

There is another court, called "*Juzgado de Difuntos*," attached to the royal *audiencia*, that has jurisdiction upon all property belonging to residents dying intestate, when the heirs are abroad. The delays and expenses for the settlement of such estates, caused in said court, are not equalled in any other part of the world. Each court has the simple and mixed *imperium*—that is, each has power to render sentence and enforce or execute the same. However, the decisions of the *tribunal de real hacienda* are appealable to the *junta superior contenciosa.* Those of the ordinary military court, if one of the parties to the suit is an officer of militia, may be appealed against by petitioning that the cause be re-examined or revised: this revision is effected by the judge of the first *instancia*, (the Captain General,) with his *auditor de guerra*, and another lawyer appointed for the case. If no one of the parties is a militia officer, the appeal is admitted and carried before the supreme court of war and navy, *supremo tribunal de guerra y marina*, residing at Madrid, where the parties must appear personally, or appoint attorneys, to whom they are to furnish full instructions and the means to pay expenses. To the same superior court must go all suits appealed from the marine, artillery, and engineer courts.

Against the decisions of the ordinary or common civil and criminal courts, appeals may be carried to the *real audiencia pretorial*, which superior court resolves upon them in second and third instance, (en segunda y terciera instancia,) according to the amount or thing that is in dispute; and even these decisions may be appealed against and carried before the supreme court of justice in Madrid, whose first sentence may be revised. To make even a *brief* report of the various regulations of each one of these tribunals, would require many days, and to write some reams of paper. It is sufficient to know that in all of the tribunals, besides their special regulations and the laws of the Indies, the following Spanish codes are in use: *Fuero juzgo*, *Fuero real*, *Leyes del Estilo*, *Las siete Partidas Ordenamiento de Alcalá*, *Ordenamiento Real*, *Nueva Recopilacion de Castilla*, *Novissima Recopilacion*, *Ordenanzas Municipales*, *Ordenanzas de Intendentes de Nueva España*, *Código de Comercio*,

Sínodo Diocesana, Reglamento de Milicias, and other various codes which it is not necessary to enumerate; also all the royal ordinances and orders that, in a prodigiously large number, emanate from the sovereign of Spain. The most general practice in the proceedings of what is called a common civil suit, *juicio civil ordinario,* is the following:

In the first place, the plaintiff must appear before the court and desire that the defendant be summoned before the same for the *juicio de conciliacion;* in this act the judge endeavors to bring the parties to an amicable settlement. No suit at law can be carried on without having gone through that form, as all subsequent proceedings, no matter in what stage the suit may be, are illegal, and may be made null and void, if that prerequisite has not been complied with. If the parties come to no arrangement, the act is recorded. The plaintiff, if he desires to establish a suit at law, procures a certificate from said record, and then presents before the proper court his demand against defendant, *in writing,* upon stamped paper, accompanying the certificate before mentioned. The plaintiff's demand is ordered to be notified to defendant, and is called *contestacion:* of this notificaticn is given to the plaintiff, which is called REPLICA; then the defendant or accused is again notified under the name of DUPLICA. The cause is afterwards brought to proofs for the term that the judge may consider necessary, which term may be prorogued to eighty days, or even to six months, if the proofs or evidence are to be received abroad. When the term has elapsed, the evidence is made public, (to the parties,) and then the parties may challenge the witnesses. This proceeding lasts for a short time; and when decided upon, the *autos* (papers connected with the suit) are handed to the parties in the suit that they may plead, (alegar.) After the pleadings have been gone through, sentence is rendered. If the sentence or decision is not appealed from within five days after, the judge that issued it has it executed, and sometimes sixty days are allowed to argue against it as null. When the sentence is appealed against, the suit is carried before the *audiencia* as a superior court, where it is examined and decided upon. The first decision of the superior court may be approved or revoked on a revision.

In criminal cases, the same modes of procedure must be observed, according to existing laws; but the audiencias have restricted the proceedings and length of time formerly allowed for the defence. The present practice in criminal cases before the common courts is reduced to the following:

1. The summarial investigation of the criminal act; this is generally done by the commissaries of wards or captains of districts.

2. The charges are made known to the accused and his confessions taken.

3. Answers of the accused and his assertions against the charges received. To this precedes the appointment of counsel, whom the accused selects himself, if he is aged twenty-five years or upwards; and if a minor, he nominates a guardian, or curator, *ad litem.*

4. The proofs are received during the time that the judge may deem proper.

5. Sentence is rendered; which, whether it be appealed from or not,

is carried to the *audiencia,* who confirms, revokes, or amends the sentence, either in favor or against the prisoner.

The Governor and Captain General is an authority very difficult of defining; it is still more difficult to define what his attributes are. The all-powerful authority that he comes clothed with by secret royal orders, is the cause of the difficulty. He, the Captain General, may act agreeably to his own will, or according to circumstances; so that, although his powers are determined in the common laws that have been promulged, still there is a great difference in the practice. There are many facts to make evident that the Governor and Captain General has authority superior not only over all corporations and tribunals of Cuba, but even to that of the sovereign, as he revokes or amends the decisions of her tribunal and corporations, annuls or alters all regulations, and even leaves unfulfilled the sovereign's orders when he (the Captain General) deems it proper.

The Governor and Captain General is the chief of the island in all respects. He is the chief in civil, military, and naval affairs, as well as those appertaining to the royal treasury. And as the sovereign is the natural patron or protector of the church in the Spanish dominions, the Captain General is her vice-royal patron in Cuba. His legal powers are expressed in the laws of the Indies, and in a multitude of royal orders, all of which cannot be seen, some of them being secret.

Executive and permanent military commission.—This tribunal was established in Havana by order of the Governor and Captain General, on the fourth of March, 1825, to try all cases of conspiracy and treason, and robbery, murder, and other crimes committed on the highways or in the country, out of the jurisdiction of cities or towns. On the 16th October of the same year, (1825,) as such tribunals had been suppressed in the whole of Spain, the King ordered the suppression of that in Cuba. That royal mandate remained unfulfilled, because the Captain General deemed it proper that it should subsist. In the royal order of November 3, 1838, greater powers were given to this military commission, as the jurisdiction over causes before it cannot come in competition with that of any other tribunal in cases of doubt, be it of any class and nature whatsoever. There is no appeal or human recourse from its decisions, as will hereafter be seen, relative to the mode of executing its sentences. The tribunal is composed of a brigadier, who presides; four members of the rank of majors or colonels of the regiments that garrison the city, or attached to those regiments; four or more fiscales, (prosecuting officers,) of the rank of captains or majors, each with his respective secretary, who is also military, of the rank of lieutenants or sub-lieutenants. The mode of procedure of said commission or court is contrary to all Spanish legislation subsisting, and to all rational jurisprudence; as the mere denouncing that an individual is engaged in a conspiracy, or is suspected of holding treasonable ideas, whether the denouncer is present or absent, even in a foreign country, is sufficient. The military commission commences its proceedings by taking possession of the accused and *all* his papers; the person of the accused is secured in a bartolina, (dungeon,) and entirely incommunicated, that is, debarred from all communication with his family, friends, and the world, until the preventive proceeding called *sumario,* (the taking of his confessions, the informing him of the charges, and receiving the declarations of witnesses, &c., have been concluded. The melancholy and horrible spectacle has been very commonly seen of the accused dying in the prison during the incommunication. Very often the accused, after a long imprisonment of that nature, are set at liberty, because no evidence of guilt could by any possible means be established against them. This barbarous system destroys all social guarantees. Neither the subject of the country, nor the foreigner, the child or the old, nor any human being, is exempted from coming under this tremendous tribunal.

The proceedings in the causes before said court are diametrically opposed to the general laws of the kingdom, and contrary to reason or equity.

The following is the manner in which those causes are established, which always put in imminent danger the lives and fortunes of men, and the welfare and peace of families.

After one or more persons have been denounced, or the least suspicion entertained against him or them, their bodies are put in prison, &c., then the investigations that the fiscal thinks proper are commenced. That officer is entirely at liberty to form judgment upon the investigations he has made, and the result depends thereupon. All his proceedings are secret. When the summarial examination has been concluded, and the fiscal deems it proper, the confessions of the accused are received, and charges are preferred against him without informing him of the nature of the summarial investigations, or the names of the witnesses who have testified against him, and he is made to select a defender out of the ten or twelve officers whose names appear in a list made out by the fiscal, (the officer for the prosecution.) The officer named (who generally has no idea or knowledge of the laws, and in some cases, cannot even write his own name in a readable manner) makes out some sort of written defence, a mere form, because, being entirely ignorant of the laws, very little or nothing can he do in favor of the rights of his client. These defences are made within the peremptory and brief time allowed to the defender, and out of the memoranda of notes given to him, or that he extracts from the proceedings. A day is appointed when the cause is brought before the court, and the military judges decide upon it and issue their sentence. This sentence is reported to the Captain General, who refers the same to his *auditor de guerre*, and with the advice of this officer confirms or revokes the sentence, or amends the same, and the resolution of the Captain General is executed without appeal or recourse of any nature.

From the foregoing, the following conclusions are arrived at:

1. That the government of Spain has acknowledged and resolved that the tribunals of the military commission are not good; that it has suppressed them in the peninsula, and retained them in Cuba.

2. That the proceedings and modes of substantiating the causes over which such tribunals have jurisdiction, are contrary to the general laws of the realm.

3. That the military judges and defenders, who have no knowledge of the common law, judge according to their will and by military laws, which are not those established for the people.

4. That the inquisitorial system of secresy, in all proceedings,

destroys all social guarantees, and makes the lives, liberty, and fortunes of men depend upon the intrigues of a villain.

5. That as the accused is compelled to choose a defender from among the officers whose names are written down on a list, and limited in number to ten or twelve, he is deprived of a natural defence, and prevented from selecting the person that he may consider proper and capable for such a delicate trust.

6. That there being no appeal or recourse from the decision of the military court, and subsequently from that of the Captain General, the will of the said Captain General is the supreme law that disposes of the life and fate of every human being in Cuba.

The lawyers I have consulted advise me that, to avoid the confusion that the reading and studying of so many codes, regulations, and royal orders would produce, and to escape the many contradictions of the same, it is best to consult the work written by Don José Ma. Lamora, formerly chief justice (regente) of the audiencia of Havana, called *Biblioteca de Legislacion Ultramarina.* This work is considered to contain all that is important. It is now very scarce. The price, like that for every other book here, is extravagant; but I have the pleasure to be able to send you a copy of it. I had omitted to state that the audiencia has exclusive jurisdiction over causes for slave trade.

I have the honor to be, sir, with great respect, your obedient servant,

WM. H. ROBERTSON,
Acting Consul.

Hon. WILLIAM L. MARCY,
Secretary of State of the United States.

ANNULLING OF THE CUBAN DECREE OF OCTOBER 7, 1844.

Mr. Buchanan to Mr. Irving.

[No. 43.] DEPARTMENT OF STATE, WASHINGTON,
May 9, 1845.

SIR: On the 7th day of October last the supreme authorities of Cuba issued a decree, a copy of which, in translation, is herewith transmitted to you, authorizing the importation, duty free, of lumber and other articles necessary for building, and of corn, corn-flour, beans, Irish potatoes, and rice. This decree, by its terms, was to continue in force during six months from its date. It was dictated, as you will perceive, by a desire to relieve the distress of those who had suffered by the dreadful hurricane which the city and environs of Havana had then just experienced. No citizen of the United States could have supposed that the operation of a decree so humane and so politic would be arrested by the home government before the brief period had elapsed to which it was limited; and this more especially, after the confident conviction, expressed on the face of the decree itself, that her Majesty would give it her approbation.

On the faith of this decree our merchants, with a laudable promptitude, imported into Havana the materials for rebuilding the houses of the suffering people, and the flour, rice, &c., necessary for their subsistence. Whilst this trade was in full progress, the decree itself was annulled, without one moment's previous notice, on the 25th of Februry, 1845, by the promulgation of the fact that her Majesty had refused to give it her sanction, and that the former duties must henceforward be levied.

Many heavy shipments had been made in the United States of the articles embraced by the decree, under the confident belief that it would continue in force until the seventh day of April; and you may judge of the disappointment with which the information of its repeal must have been received by the masters of those vessels upon arriving at Havana after the 20th of February. Severe losses were the inevitable consequence; and these ought, in justice, to be borne by the Spanish government, which has received heavy duties on the articles that ought to have been admitted free.

It would be a vain labor to enlarge upon the injustice of annulling this decree without any previous notice, and its violation of the commercial usages prevailing among enlightened nations. In the opinion of the President, those of our fellow-citizens who imported any of the articles embraced by the decree into Havana between the 20th Febrnary and the 7th April, 1845, without any knowledge, at the time of their departure from the United States, that the decree had been annulled, are entitled to be indemnified by the Spanish government for the losses which they may have sustained. Without stating specifically what ought to be the measure of this indemnity, it would seem reasonable that, at the very least, the duties actually received upon the importation of these cargoes ought to be refunded by the Spanish government.

I transmit herewith a copy of a communication from Mr. Campbell, the consul of the United States at Havana, to the Count de Villanueva, intendente of Cuba, dated on the day the fact of the Queen's reversal of the decree was made public, solemnly protesting against the proceeding, and a copy of the reply which his excellency thought proper to make on the occasion. I transmit also a copy of a memorial from the Charleston Chamber of Commerce, and translation of the decree of 7th of October, with copies of other papers relating to the same subject.

With the motives and policy of her Majesty in reversing a decree dictated by humanity, and apparently by the best colonial interests of Spain, this government has nothing to do; but it has a deep concern in everything which affects the safety of the commercial intercourse between the two countries. And in submitting the facts here presented for the consideration of her Majesty's government, you are instructed to express to the Minister of Foreign Relations the confidence felt by your own government that prompt and effectual measures will be taken to repair the wrong which has been done to citizens of the United States.

Your dispatches No. 62, inclusive, have been received.

I am, sir, respectfully, your obedient servant,

JAMES BUCHANAN.

CONSULATE OF THE U. S. OF AMERICA, HAVANA,
October 14, 1844.

SIR: By the public journals forwarded by this consulate you will have seen that all duties for six months have been taken off the articles of rice, corn, corn meal, lumber, potatoes, &c. In this condition of things I would respectfully suggest that the discriminating tonnage duties between Spanish and American vessels in the ports of the United States, where the former are loading with free articles for this island, be removed for the space of time in which they are admitted free from duty. Such a modification would not injuriously affect our navigating interests, nor benefit that of Spain, for it is doubted if any Spanish vessel enters into the trade; the effect, however, might be beneficial, as evidencing, on the part of the United States, a disposition of reciprocity in the removal of commercial restrictions. Not that the authorities here, in the present instance, have been prompted in their action by aught but the necessities of the island. They are, however, disposed to lessen duties generally on American products, so far as the intendente and his council feel authorized.

In the article of flour, in which our western States are so vitally interested, I have endeavored, in conversation, to impress upon them the importance to the island of more moderate duties, and have discovered a favorable disposition. My suggestion in relation to the tonnage duty is made with a view to this great interest, the extent and importance of which needs no comment from me. I cannot, however, promise that the adoption of my recommendation will insure a modification of the present onerous duty upon flour, but am satisfied the effect would be to strengthen the parties interesting themselves about a reduction.

I have the honor, &c.,

R. B. CAMPBELL.

Hon. J. C. CALHOUN,
Secretary of State.

CONSULATE OF THE U. S. OF AMERICA, HAVANA,
February 26, 1845.

DEAR SIR: I have the honor to enclose to you a copy of an official communication addressed by me to the intendente, on the subject of the restoration of the duties on certain articles, which, by the decree of the 7th of October last, were admitted free. Accompanying this communication you will receive a translation of his reply thereto.

I have the honor, &c.,

ROBT. B. CAMPBELL.

Hon. JOHN C. CALHOUN,
Secretary of State, Washington.

CONSULATE OF THE UNITED STATES, HAVANA,
February 20, 1845.

SIR: I have been astonished to find in the Diario of this morning an official communication from your excellency to the effect that her Majesty has refused to sanction the measures adopted by the authorities of this island, and promulgated by the publication of a decree dated October 7, 1844, which authorizes, free of duty, the admission of certain articles for the period of six months from the date of that decree, provided the royal assent is given thereto; and in consequence of the royal disapprobation of the said decree, the duties are now restored. The citizens of the United States of America engaged in commercial transactions with this island had well-grounded reasons for supposing that the royal approbation would not be withheld. No fears were entertained that the duties would be restored until the expiration of the time stipulated, and on these views have their transactions been based. They presumed that the authorities of this island were well acquainted with the wants of the inhabitants, that they had reflected maturely on the steps they had taken, and had the best opportunities of knowing what would be the action of her Majesty. These considerations, and their confidence in the integrity and wisdom of your excellency and your advisers, induced large shipments from the United States, contributing to the comforts and relieving the necessities of her Majesty's subjects who were suffering from the effects of the disastrous gale that caused the remission of the duties. It is moreover understood that there has been an increased revenue from imports, and that your concessions to suffering humanity have not diminished the revenues, thereby giving additional force to the conviction that your order of 7th of October last would not be repealed. There is known to be in transitu from the different ports of the United States, predicated on your previous order, large quantities of rice, lumber, and all the various articles embraced in that order; and if the shippers are compelled by this sudden and unexpected edict to pay duties, they must sustain great and unjust losses; against all which, in their name, I solemnly protest, as no timely notice of the intention of this government had been given—a notice, in my opinion, good faith and common usage required. The observance of which faith and usage I must urge upon your excellency, so far as to suspend the execution of the decree for such a limited period as will protect the innocent and deceived shipper, and save others from the disastrous effects of this precipitate and unforeseen action.

I have the honor to be, &c., your excellency's, &c.,

ROBERT B. CAMPBELL.

HAVANA, *February* 26, 1845.

SIR: According to the royal instructions which govern this treasury in regard to foreign consuls of the island, the department does not deem itself competent to take cognizance of the subject referred to in your dispatch of the 20th inst., which I state to you as a reply, to be used in the manner you may judge most expedient.

God preserve your worship many years.

EL CONDE DE VILLANUEVA.

The Charleston Chamber of Commerce to Mr. Buchanan.

CHARLESTON, S. C., *April* 14, 1845.

The memorial of the Charleston Chamber of Commerce respectfully represents, that your memorialists, taking into view the late act of the Spanish government, would beg leave to bring to your notice the great injury done to the merchants engaged in the trade between the United States and the island of Cuba, and to request that the subject may be taken into consideration by you, and redress obtained if practicable.

The losses are heavy, and brought about entirely by the confidence in the integrity which all felt in the authorities of Cuba, and by which the merchants have been deceived into heavy shipments.

In the spring and summer of 1844 a severe and long-continued drought caused the loss of the grain and fruit crop in the island, and induced the intendente de real hacienda to issue a decree reducing the duty on breadstuffs and certain other articles one-half. The decree continued in force until the 6th of October last, when, owing to a severe hurricane by which a large portion of the island was devastated—ruining the crops, blowing down many houses, and destroying almost all their ground provisions—the intendente immediately, with a philanthropic spirit, seeing the immense sufferings of the people, issued a decree—a copy of which, translated, is annexed—admitting free of duty, for six months from the 6th October, rice, potatoes, and other vegetables, lumber, and all other building materials; thus fixing a definite period during which the above articles should be admitted free of duty.

This led to large shipments from this country to Cuba, nothing doubting that the government of Spain would continue to permit imports of the above articles for the above time—five or six weeks being still wanted to complete the same. Much, however, to the surprise, and greatly to the injury of the shippers, they were informed, by letters dated 20th February, that the duties were to be levied *instanter* in full, thus allowing no time to avoid heavy losses. The shippers certainly had no right to conclude or suppose that the time fixed by the decree might be shortened, and that at a period when it might be expected heavy shipments would be on the way. But if even, as it is affirmed, the home government at Madrid has refused to confirm the decree taking off the entire duty, the tariff which was established in the summer, of half the duties, might have been expected to take effect.

The injury done to the shippers has been very materially aggravated and increased by the manner in which the above order from Madrid was promulgated. The order, it is well known, was received in Havana prior to the 15th February, and was not promulgated until the 20th February. The regular packet, Hayne, sailed on the 16th February, and brought a large number of letters for this country. Most of the heavy shipments which are caught were made between the arrival of the Hayne and the 5th March, the time when the news of such order reached this place. Had the order been published at Havana on the receipt thereof, it would have been known here by the 20th February, and thus have prevented most of the shipments which were made, and have made a difference of several hundred thousand dollars to the merchants of this country. We are aware of heavy shipments of lumber from Maine, North Carolina, and Georgia, as well as from this State, besides other articles. From this State the loss on rice alone is heavy; the exports from Savannah and Charleston between the aforesaid periods being near 10,000 tierces, on which the duty will be $120,000.

Craving reference to the subjoined list of duties on the different articles as levied, and relying on your well-known regard for the interests of the commerce of this country, the subject is most respectfully submitted to you. And your memorialists will ever pray, &c.

Signed by order and in behalf of the Charleston Chamber of Commerce.

KER BOYCE,
President.

Attest: WILLIAM B. HERIOT, *Secretary.*

A list of duties on the different articles as levied.

Lumber per 1,000 feet, valued there at $20 per thousand, at 24¾ per cent.	$4 95
Add 2 per cent.	40
	5 35
Balanza duty 1 per cent.	5
Per thousand.	5 40
Rice per 100 pounds, valued there at $6 per 100 pounds, at 30¾ per cent., add 2 per cent.	1 97
Balanza duty.	2
Per 100 pounds rice.	1 99
Potatoes, valued at $2 50 per barrel, at 24¾ per cent.	62
Add 2 per cent.	5
	67
Beans, valued at $3 per barrel, at 30¾ per cent.	93
Add 2 per cent.	6
	99
Balanza.	1
Per barrel of beans.	1 00

Translation of Decree.

At an extraordinary meeting of the superior junta for direction of the royal revenues, the administrators general of the maritime and land rents, being present to take into consideration such measures as can be adopted by the (real hacienda) administrators of the royal revenues to alleviate the incalculable evils caused by the dreadful hurricane this city and its environs have just experienced, after taking into consideration, with the grief which should be felt, in view of the immeasurable calamities which are to be relieved, and the horrible distress which threatens all classes if such assistance as is within the control of the above authorities, who are charged with the well-being of all, be not promptly afforded—well assured that the magnanimous heart of her Majesty cannot but condole with us when she comes to the knowledge of such distress, and cannot but approve all that is done for the good of the inhabitants of this the preferred part of her monarchy—it was agreed:

1. To concede absolute liberty to the importation of lumber, slate, tiles, shingles, and all kinds of wood for the construction of buildings.

2. The same freedom from duties for six months, to count from to-morrow, to corn, corn-flour, beans, Irish potatoes, and rice, which, by resolution of the directive junta of 3d June last, do not pay but one-half; and that sweet potatoes, yams, and plantains continue to enjoy for the same term of six months that which was dispensed to them at that time, it being understood for this port, with reservation to extend to any other ports where necessity should require it for equally sad causes.

3. That the reduction of duties on the consumption of meat, granted by the aforesaid junta on the ninth of the month anterior, take effect from the fifteenth of the present month on the following terms: the larger classes of animals—such as oxen and cows—shall not pay more than three and a half dollars per head, in place of the four which have been designated, and which shall continue imposed upon calves. Hogs shall pay according to weight—from one to four arrobas, four rials per arroba; over four to eight arrobas, three rials; from eight and upwards, two and a half rials.

4. A subscription shall be immediately opened among the chiefs and those employed in the collection of the Queen's funds, (hacienda real,) the amount of which shall be placed for distribution under the orders of his excellency the Captain General.

5. That the loans of 300 dollars from the Mountains of Piety be applied, and the period of the payment of the loans be extended.

By all which measures, which shall be submitted for the sovereign approbation of her Majesty, and which they will announce to the public, the junta considered some of the effects of so terrible a calamity might be remedied without impeding any other measures which may be deemed necessary by his excellency the superintendent, in connexion with the other authorities of the island.

And his said excellency having determined upon the accomplishment of the foregoing, it is published by his order for general information.

JOAQUIN CAMPUZANO, *Secretary.*

HAVANA, *October* 7, 1844.

CONSULATE OF THE UNITED STATES, CARDENAS,
March 3, 1845.

SIR: I have the honor to enclose to the department a copy of a memorial signed by the American merchants of this place, which I send at their request.

I have also given notice of the same to the collector of this port.

Very respectfully, &c.,

FRANKLIN GAGE.

To the SECRETARY OF STATE *of the United States.*

CARDENAS, *February* 26, 1845.

SIR: The undersigned, citizens of the United States, engaged in commercial pursuits at this port, respectfully represent, that by an official order promulgated by the government of this island, under date of 20th February instant, certain articles which were declared free of duty on the 7th October last, for the six months then ensuing, are made to pay the same duties, with only a slight modification, as were levied previous to the issuing of that order; that this sudden re-imposition of duties, nearly two months previous to the expiration of the limited time, and without any notice whatsoever, most seriously will affect the interests not only of the undersigned, but more particularly of very many of their correspondents, in the United States, who, relying on the good faith of this government, and the representations of the merchants of this place, that these certain articles would be admitted free of duty until the 7th April next ensuing, the date limited in said order, have made, and are about making, large shipments of such property as will now be subject to duty, anticipating that they would be admitted free under the pledge given by this government and our representations; and that, in consequence, great and serious loss will accrue to all parties who may have availed or may yet avail, of the privilege given, particularly as we are advised of many adventures on foot and in course of shipment to afford the island extraordinary supplies, just previous to the expiration of the time named in said order of 7th October last; that these shipments, arriving here now in quick succession during the next six weeks, will all be subject to duty, under the new order, when it was anticipated they would be free, thus undoubtedly entailing great and certain loss to all concerned, aside from the breach of faith which the new order makes public.

The undersigned, therefore, in behalf of themselves, and more particularly of their friends in the United States, who are most likely to suffer under this state of things, consider it their duty to represent the same to you, as the constituted representative of the United States at this place, and to respectfully request you to remonstrate with the collector of this district and port of Cardenas, and, if necessary, to protest against this sudden and uncalled for change in the tariff; and further, to represent the matter to your government at home, for its information and action in the premises.

JOHN R. STANHOPE.
MATTHEWS & SAFFORD.
TAYLOR & THOMPSON.

FRANKLIN GAGE, Esq.,
U. S. Consul, Cardenas.

CONSULATE OF THE U. S. OF AMERICA, HAVANA,
March 17, 1845.

DEAR SIR: It appears from the public papers that a good deal of excitement exists in the United States on the subject of the restoration of duties on certain articles, which by the decree of the 7th of October last were to be admitted free of duty for the period of six months, provided that decree met the royal approbation. The Queen of Spain having refused to sanction the measures then adopted by the authorities of the island, an order was issued on the 20th of February last, by the intendente, for the immediate restoration of the duties. On the same day I addressed an official communication to him, protesting against this sudden and unexpected measure, without previous notice having been first given; a copy of which, and a translation of his reply, were forwarded to you by the ship Norma, that sailed from New York on the 5th inst. It is impossible for me to say whether the duties that have been paid since the 20th of February will be refunded or not. The intendente has given directions that a separate account be kept of all articles imported since the 20th of February embraced in said decree, and consequently since his order for the resumption of the duties with the names of the several vessels bringing these articles, and the amount of duties paid thereon; from which it is inferred that it is his impression that the excess of duties paid into the customs will be refunded by the Spanish government. On the faith of the decree of the 7th of October last, that the duties would not be exacted until the expiration of the time therein mentioned, (7th of April, 1845,) several cargoes of rice, lumber, potatoes, &c., have arrived from the United States, the shippers of which must, in case the duties are not refunded, sustain great and perhaps unjust losses. I am frequently called upon by parties interested for my opinion of the probability of these amounts being refunded, and have invariably found the querist dissatisfied with anything short of an affirmative assurance, which I am not able to give.

The course pursued by the intendente in ordering separate accounts of the duties collected on the articles that were temporarily free, would seem to indicate this opinion (as he has the wish,) that these amounts would be restored to the importer, and it is probable the interest of the parties thus situated may be advanced by the American minister at Madrid being instructed by his government to urge that restoration with all his official influence. It is true, the removal of the duties for six months was contingent on the royal approval, and the shippers knew this fact; but as the measures of this colony have generally been approved, no apprehension was entertained in this instance, although cases have previously occurred of the refusal of the Spanish government to sanction the changes made by the intendente and his advisers. You will perceive by my letter to the intendente, and his answer, (already forwarded,) that I did not communicate with the Captain General, the subject being one over which he could exercise no control, and belonging entirely to the department of the intendente, it would have been useless to address him.

It is understood that the course of the intendente, who is every way disposed to a liberal tariff, has made him unacceptable to the Spanish; his removal is deemed certain.

I have the honor to be, &c., &c.,

ROBERT B. CAMPBELL.

Hon. John C. Calhoun,
Secretary of State, Washington City.

Messrs. Henry A. Coit, Spofford, Tileston & Co., and Howland & Aspinwall, to Mr. Buchanan.

Sir: For ourselves, and in behalf of our fellow-citizens engaged in the trade with the island of Cuba, we take the liberty of soliciting your attention to a recent act of the Spanish government, affecting our interests.

It is, doubtless, known to you, that for the purpose of alleviating the distress occasioned by the hurricane and drought which have visited that island, a decree was promulgated by the authorities at Havana, several months since, liberating from the payment of duties certain articles of lumber, corn, corn meal, rice, beans, &c., upon their introduction into that and other ports in the island, for the term of six months, now about expiring.

In virtue of this decree, importations have been made to a very considerable extent into the island from this country, up to the latest dates which have reached us, all of which, subsequent to the date of a new decree, dated Havana, February 20th ult., reimposing duties on the articles referred to, in consequence (as therein stated) of orders received from Spain to that effect, have been subjected to the payment of duties, and have resulted in heavy losses.

We would, therefore, respectfully submit to your decision, whether, acting in the good faith of the original decree, and without a previous intimation of its reversal in season to prevent shipments which were in progress, or contracted for, from being made from this country, full redress, extending to the amount of duties thus levied, as well as to any damage which their interests may have sustained, is not due to us and our fellow-citizens who may have suffered in the manner described.

Very respectfully, &c., &c., &c.,

HENRY A. COIT.
SPOFFORD, TILESTON & CO.
HOWLAND & ASPINWALL.

Mr. Irving to Mr. Buchanan.

[Extract.]

[No. 67.] LEGATION OF THE UNITED STATES, MADRID,
June 25, 1845.

* * * * *

Dispatch No. 43 (accompanied by documents) relates to injuries, resulting to citizens of the United States from the annulling, by the Spanish government, of the decree of the supreme authorities of Cuba, authorizing the importation of certain articles into the island for six months free of duty. I passed a note to the Spanish government some days since in conformity with your instructions, but as yet have received no reply. The Belgian chargé d'affaires is making an urgent representation on the same subject, and it is vigorously advocated in the *Cronica*, a paper recently set up here, and devoted to colonial interests, especially those connected with the island of Cuba, and to which paper I occasionally furnish facts and intelligence.

It is extremely difficult, however, to get any questions of that kind attended to by this government at present. The disjointed state of the cabinet, part at Madrid and part at Barcelona, interrupts the regular course of business; while the complicated negotiations with the court of Rome; the perplexed question of the marriage of the Queen; the agitations and alarms caused by the recent abdication of Don Carlos, and the manifesto of his son; the reports of plots, conspiracies, internal and external, and the disastrous fluctuations of the funds, in which some persons high in place are supposed to be implicated—all these distract the attention and disturb the minds of ministers, and render them heedless of all affairs but such as are immediately important to their political existence.

I am, sir, very respectfully, your obedient servant,

WASHINGTON IRVING.

Mr. Irving to Mr. Buchanan.

[Extract.]

[No. 69.] LEGATION OF THE UNITED STATES, MADRID,
July 10, 1845.

SIR: * * * * * * *

I have received no reply as yet to my note to the Minister of State, claiming restitution of duties wrongfully imposed on American merchandise shipped to Cuba under the "duty free" decree. Indeed, the absence of part of the Cabinet with the Court at Barcelona interrupts the whole course of business. I have forborne to follow the Court to Barcelona this year, having received no instructions from government on the subject, and there being a probability that the royal sojourn in that city would be very short. Should the absence of the Court from the capital be prolonged, I may find it expedient to pay a brief visit to prevent being thought wanting in respect.

* * * * * * * * *

Hon. JAMES BUCHANAN,
Secretary of State, Washington.

Mr. Barringer to Mr. Marcy.

[Extract.]

[No. 152.] SAN ILDEFONSO, *August* 11, 1853.

SIR: On the 7th of October, 1844, the Captain General of Cuba issued a decree, suspending for a given period the usual import duties on *provisions,* with a view to induce a rapid supply of the scarcity under which the inhabitants were then suffering. Various vessels of the United States, England, France, Sweden, and others, on the faith of this decree, went with large cargoes of provisions; and although they reached Cuba within the period fixed in the same decree, and complied in all respects with its requisites, they were nevertheless compelled to pay the accustomed duties.

Reclamations have been made against Spain for the injury thus inflicted, and the claim of England especially is now being prosecuted with urgency. She has a demand for about $100,000. The loss sustained by vessels of the United States by this transaction is stated to be at least double that sum, or about $200,000. The subject was brought to the attention of the Spanish government shortly afterwards, under instructions from the department, but nothing was definitely done, and the matter has not been since considered. It was not until recently that I have obtained knowledge of the fact that other governments were prosecuting these claims, and I have not deemed it advisable, after so long a length of time, to renew the claims of our own citizens without fresh instructions from our government. Under all the circumstances, the subject is now brought again to the attention of the department, either for new instructions to my successor, or the adoption of such other course as may be deemed best by our government, respectfully adding my opinion that something ought to be done in reference to this claim.

* * * * * * * *

Hon. W. L. MARCY,
Secretary of State.

CASE OF MICHAEL D. HARANG.

Mr. Gallaher to Mr. Forsyth.

[Extract.]

CONSULATE OF THE U. S. OF AMERICA, PONCE, PORTO RICO.
March 2, 1839.

SIR: Since I had the honor to address you on the 23d November last, a demand of 15 per cent. on the property of Luis Alexander Harang, deceased, has been made and exacted by the intendant of Porto Rico.

On application of Michael D. Harang, one of the heirs, the other three of whom are residents of Parish Jefferson, State of Louisiana, I addressed a letter, of which the enclosed is a copy, to the intendente, and hoping to have heard from him, I have delayed writing you till now, but as yet no answer has been given, although our consul in the city has waited on him several times to know his determination.

In the mean time the exaction of near $11,000 has taken place, and the sole resource of the heirs of Luis Alexander Harang, who are citizens of the United States, remains in the view which will be taken by the government of the United States on this proceeding.

I remain, with great respect, your obedient servant,

J. C. GALLAHER.

Hon. JOHN FORSYTH,
Secretary of State, Washington.

P. S. I open my letter to enclose copy of protest made before me this day, by Michael Drausin Harang.

CONSULATE OF THE UNITED STATES OF AMERICA,
PONCE, PORTO RICO, *February* 4, 1839.

SIR: I have the honor to represent that Michael Drausin Harang, a native of New Orleans, in the United States of America, and for some time past a resident of the district of Ponce, has applied to me, claiming to be a citizen of the United States, and stating that the government of Porto Rico, in virtue of the real cedula of August 10, 1815, have demanded of him 15 per cent. for duty of extraction on the property left by his deceased father, Luis Alexander Harang, said Michael Drausin Harang believes (and I concur in opinion,) that said real cedula cannot apply to citizens of the United States without violating the 11th article of the treaty, made at San Lorenzo el Real, between the United States and Spain, on the 27th of October, 1795, which said treaty was confirmed in all and each one of its articles, excepting the 2d, 3d, 4th, 21st, and 2d clause of the 22d article, by another treaty made at Washington on the 22d February, 1819.

Under these circumstances, I beg leave respectfully to ask, that if any orders may have been given for the collection of said 15 per cent., that they may be suspended, until the understanding of the governments of the United States and of Spain may be had on this subject—said Michael Drausin Harang giving sufficient security in the mean time for the amount claimed.

I have the honor to be, &c.,

J. C. GALLAHER,
United States Consul.

Al Señor Don ANTONIO MARIA DEL VALLE,
Intendente de la Isla de Puerto Rico.

Know all men by these presents, that, on this second day of March, in the year one thousand eight hundred and thirty-nine, before me, James C. Gallaher, consul of the United States of America, at this port of Ponce, in the island of Porto Rico, personally came and appeared Michael Drausin Harang, a native of parish Jefferson, State of Louisiana, in the United States of America, who declared, that his father, Lewis Alexander Harang, died in the city of New York, in the United States of America, on the fifteenth day of September, in the year one thousand eight hundred and thirty-five, having left by will, to his four children, Lewis, Matilda, John Pascal, and the deponent, his property in the island of Porto Rico, which consisted of a sugar estate and some other property—of which said property deponent, by order of, and in pursuance of a power of attorney from the other heirs, made sale for the purpose of remitting the proceeds to the other heirs, residing in parish Jefferson, State of Louisiana, and all natives of said State. Deponent further states, that by order of the intendencia he has been forced to pay the sum of ten thousand nine hundred and seventy-eight dollars one real and sixteen maravedices, for the duty of extraction, contrary to the eleventh article of the treaty made between the United States and Spain, on the twenty-seventh of October, one thousand seven hundred and ninety-five, and confirmed by another treaty, made on the twenty-second day of February, one thousand eight hundred and nineteen.

And, therefore, the said Michael Drausin Harang doth solemnly protest against the order of the intendencia, as also against all and every other person or persons whom it shall or may concern, for all losses, damages, and detriments that have occurred, or may occur, to the estate of his father, Lewis Alexander Harang, deceased, in consequence of these proceedings, as well as for deponent's detention in this country, and doth appeal to the government of the United States of America, of which he is a citizen, for protection.

Of all which act I have hereunto affixed my hand, in Ponce, Porto Rico, this second day of March, in the year one thousand eight hundred and thirty-nine, as aforesaid.

M. D. HARANG.

Before me,

J. C. GALLAHER, *United States Consul.*

PONCE, PORTO RICO, *March* 2, 1839.

Mr. Forsyth to the Chevalier d'Argaiz.

DEPARTMENT OF STATE,
Washington, February 28, 1840.

SIR: A representation has been addressed to this department by Mr. M. D. Harang, a citizen of the United States, setting forth that the authorities of the island of Porto Rico had compelled him to pay, into their hands, a sum of money demanded of him as duty of extraction (*derecho de estraccion*) upon the proceeds of estates descended to him on the death of his father, Lewis Alexander Harang, also a citizen of the United States, who, some time before his death, had resided in said island. If the facts stated by Mr. Harang are such as he represents them, the demand referred to is so manifest an infraction of the eleventh article of the treaty of 1795, one of the articles confirmed by the treaty of 1819, that it must be supposed to have been occasioned by inadvertence or misconception on the part of the colonial authorities. No doubt is entertained that a proper application to her Majesty's government, at Madrid, would be followed by immediate orders for the repayment of the money thus wrongfully demanded of Mr. Harang; but as the delay necessarily attending such a step would greatly add to the injury already suffered by him, in consequence of the detention of his property, I request that you will use your influence with the authorities of the island to prevail upon them to re-examine the question with as little delay as possible, in order that justice, which is so clearly due under the treaty to which I have referred, may be done to the claimant.

I avail myself of the opportunity to convey to you renewed assurances of my distinguished consideration.

JOHN FORSYTH

The CHEVALIER D'ARGAIZ, &c., &c.,
Spain.

The Chevelier d'Argaiz to Mr. Forsyth.

[Translation.]

Washington, March 2, 1840.

MY DEAR SIR: I have received the letter which you were pleased to address me on the 28th February last, to inform me of the application which Mr. M. D. Harang, a citizen of these States, had addressed to the Department of State, setting forth that the authorities of the island of Porto Rico had exacted from him a certain amount of money for exportation duty upon the produce of property he inherited on the death of his father, who was for some time established in that island; and, inasmuch as this measure could not have been adopted, except through carelessness or misunderstanding on the part of the authorities of that island, of the eleventh article of the treaty of 1795, and that to apply to her Majesty's government at Madrid would involve new delays and injury to the party interested, you ask me to use my influence with the authorities of that island, recommending them to re-examine the question with all possible speed, in order that justice, so clearly due, according to the treaty you have quoted, may be rendered to the petitioner.

In reply, I must say to you, that herewith enclosed you will find a communication for her Majesty's intendant in the island of Puerto Rico, to whom, at the same time that I transmit a copy of your letter, I enclose a copy of the 11th article of the treaty of 1795, and recommend to him, as much as it is in my power to do, a favorable and prompt settlement of this business; and I have no doubt that, if it is in his power, he will hasten to give a new proof of the respect which her Majesty's government and its authorities have and observe for the stipulations of treaties which unite them with those powers that are her Majesty's allies and friends.

I avail myself of this occasion to renew to you the assurance of my distinguished consideration.

D'ARGAIZ.

Mr. Forsyth to Mr. Gallaher.

DEPARTMENT OF STATE,
Washington, March 4, 1840.

SIR: A letter has been addressed to this department by M. C. Harang, asking its interposition in obtaining from the authorities of Porto Rico restitution of a sum of money which he alleges to have been levied as a duty of extraction upon the proceeds of estates descended to him from his father.

So far as the circumstances of this transaction appear from Mr. Harang's letter and your several communications on the subject, the demand of the duty referred to cannot be viewed in any other light than a direct infraction of existing treaty stipulations between the United States and Spain, calling, very properly, for the representation interposed by you.

In support of the renewal of it, which you are hereby instructed to make, I have requested the minister of Spain near this government to use his influence with the proper authority in Porto Rico, recommending a just observance of the treaty; and the letter which, to that effect, he addresses to the intendant of the island is herein enclosed, to be forwarded by you.

Should the repayment of the money be longer resisted, you will state the fact to this department, and transmit to it all the information necessary to a full understanding of the merits of the question, with a view to a direct application for redress to the metropolitan government, if circumstances should be found to authorize it.

A letter from Mr. Harang to yourself is, likewise at his request, herewith transmitted to you.

I am, &c.,

JOHN FORSYTH.

J. C. GALLAHER, Esq.,
United States Consul, Ponce.

Mr. Gallaher to Mr. Forsyth.

[Extract.]

[No. 18.] CONSULATE OF THE U. S., PONCE, PORTO RICO,
April 11, 1840.

SIR: I have the honor to acknowledge the receipt of your communication of the 4th ultimo, enclosing a letter for the intendente, a letter from Harang, with power of attorney, and instructions with regard to my further proceedings in this business.

From the accidental mislaying of a paper, I was inadvertently led into an error in my communication to the department, No. 16, dated January 18, with regard to my never having received a communication from the intendente. On a careful re-examination of my papers, after receipt of your instructions of 4th ultimo, I discovered a communication which, according to my endorsement, had been received by me on the 19th March, 1839, (seventeen days after Harang's protest had been made,) but had been unaccountably mislaid and forgotten, in the press of other business. It however does not, in the least, affect the representations I have made to the department, as will be seen by the copy which I herewith enclose, attached to which I have put very nearly a literal translation in English. The true question, although attempted to be mystified by these gentlemen, is simply whether Mr. Harang is an American or not, and as an American is he entitled to the protection of the treaty. I have the honor to enclose you copies of the letters I have addressed to the Captain General and to the intendente, and will forward you copies of their replies the moment I receive them.

* * * * * * * *

CONSULATE OF THE U. S., PONCE, PORTO RICO,
April 6, 1840.

SIR: I have the honor to inform your excellency that I have received dispatches from the government of the United States approving of the representations made by me, as contained in my letter of February 4, 1839, to the Señor Intendente of the island of Porto Rico, of which I have the honor to enclose herewith a copy, as also of the protest made before me by Michel Drausin Harang, on the 2d of March, 1839, of which, on the same date, I forwarded a copy to the Señor Intendente.

I am instructed by the government which I have the honor to represent to state, that "the demand of the duty referred to cannot be viewed in any other light than a direct infraction of existiug treaty stipulations between the United States and Spain;" and I am further instructed respectfully to ask of your excellency to give the necessary orders for the repayment of the money exacted from said Harang by the authorities of Porto Rico, amounting to the sum of ten thousand nine hundred and seventy-eight dollars one real and sixteen maravedices; for the purpose of receiving which the power of attorney of said Michel Drausin Harang, sealed and certified by the chief judge of the circuit court of the United States, by the Secretary of State of the United States, and by the secretary of the Spanish legation at Washington, has been forwarded to me, under cover of the dispatches before mentioned, and can be examined by whomsoever your excellency thinks proper to name for that purpose.

I have the honor, &c.,

J. C. GALLAHER,
United States Consul.

His Excel'cy the GOVERNOR AND CAPTAIN GENERAL
of the Island of Porto Rico, and Superintendente of the same.

CONSULATE OF THE U. S., PONCE, PORTO RICO,
April 6, 1840.

SIR: I have the honor to inform you that, under cover of despatches from the government of the United States, I have received the enclosed letter, with directions to, and which I have now the honor to forward.

I have the honor to remain, with great respect, your ob't servant,

J. C. GALLAHER,
United States Consul.

To the INTENDENTE *of the Island of Porto Rico.*

I have received your communication of what Michel Drausin Harang has stated with regard to the 15 per cent. which is exacted as duties on the extraction of the property left by his deceased father, Luis Alexander Harang, and have passed it to the gentlemen, the fiscal of the royal custom-house and the assessor of this intendency, and, with dates of the 15th and 23d of the present month, they have answered me as follows:

"Sr. Intendente: The fiscal of the royal custom-house ought to state that, without doubt, Harang has purposed to confound and disnaturalize this business; that, if this minister does not recollect badly, Harang has made reclamations as a subject of the French government, after having placed himself before a tribunal; and, finally, that all these conducts are extemporaneous and captious, your excellency not being able to prescind manifesting it in this manner to the consul, indicating to him that Harang has suits pending before the tribunals, and in them is where he ought to represent without treating of surprising the consuls and authorities. Thus verified, this expediente ought to pass to the tribunals."

Sr. Intendente: I adhere to the opinion of the Sr. Fiscal, Dn. Miguel Harang being at liberty to use all the recourses which he may consider will assist him before the competent tribunals, being assured that that of the royal custom-house will observe religiously the existing laws, as well with respect and veneration for treaties which exist between Spain and the United States, without forgetting that Harang has made a representation to your excellency, through the French consul, not many days since. Your excellency may answer in this manner, or as you may judge more proper, being pleased to pass this answer to the tribunal, in order to give it the corresponding course. And in conformity with the foregoing opinions, I remit them to you for your information and as an answer. God preserve you many years. Porto Rico, 27th February, 1839.

ANTO. MA. DEL VALLE.

Sr. CONSUL *of the United States of America, Ponce.*

[Translation.]

OFFICE OF THE CAPTAIN GENERAL, AND OF THE SUPERIOR POLITICAL GOVERNMENT, SECTION 1.

Porto Rico, April 18, 1840.

By the official letter you have addressed me on the 6th instant, I learn what you state to me concerning the claim of Mr. Miguel Drausin Harang, relative to the reimbursement to him of the amount of ten thousand nine hundred and eighteen dollars one real and sixteen maravedis, which was exacted from him on account of 15 per cent. duty on the exportation of property which he inherited from his father, and which he conveyed to the United States; and, in replying to you on the subject, I must say, that the matter in question, of which until now I had no notice whatsoever, coming under the private cognizance of the intendente, to whom he has already submitted his claims by means of the document, a copy of which you enclosed to me; and the aforesaid intendente being in correspondence upon the same subject with the chargé d'affaires of Spain, near the government of the United States, he can settle the matter with the financial authority alluded to, in all that concerns the exaction of the duties which have occasioned his communication aforesaid. God preserve you a thousand years.

MIGUEL LOPEZ DE BAÑOS.

Mr. J. C. GALLAHER,
United States Consul at Ponce.

The Chevalier d'Argaiz to Mr. Forsyth.

[Translation.]

WASHINGTON, *December* 24, 1840.

SIR: You will remember that, in consequence of the note which you were pleased to address to me under date of the 28th of February last, I had the honor to enclose to you, with my reply of the 2d of March following, a dispatch to the most excellent intendant of the island of Porto Rico, in which I communicated to him your above-mentioned note, together with a copy of the eleventh article of the treaty of 1795. The intendant answered me, under date of the 30th of August, as follows:

"After a long delay I had the high honor to receive your excellency's official communication of the 2d of March last, containing, inserted, another from the Secretary of State at Washington, making various observations relative to the claim addressed to him by the citizen Mr. Miguel Drausin Harang, for the recovery of a certain sum of money which the royal treasury of this island extracted from the portion of the estate of his deceased father, Don Alejandro Harang, inherited by him, on carrying it to a foreign country, of which affair your excellency requested me to make an immediate examination, agreeable to the desires of the Secretary of State, based upon the literal expression of the eleventh article of the treaty of October 27, 1795, between the court of Madrid and the States of the Union.

"The absence of the legal counsellor, (ministro asesor) of this intendency, and the circumstance that the documents relative to the claim before the courts of justice are not to be found, prevent me from answering your excellency by satisfactory observations on a matter so complicated, and which really no longer remains within the limits of my authority, since the person, who is now regarded as a citizen of the United States, has subjected it to the course of law.

"I will state to you, with my characteristic frankness, agreeable to the suggestions made by the legal counsellor of this intendency, under my charge, that Mr. Miguel Drausin Harang has advanced several different pretensions with the view of freeing himself from the payment established by the royal cedula of colonization of August, 1815, upon all personal property *(capital)* acquired by persons naturalized in this island, after a certain number of years of residence, when it is to be taken to a foreign country, without any difference in regard to Spaniards or strangers. Harang pretended that his father should be considered as a Spaniard, from having been born at New Orleans when that place belonged to Spain; he then pretended that he should be considered as a Frenchman, because New Orleans was transferred to that nation by treaties; and, finally, he appears in the garb of a citizen of the United States of America. These observations will serve to convince your excellency that Harang's whole object has been to elude compliance with the laws governing this colony. No one will be conscientiously persuaded that his father could have been a Spaniard of New Orleans, a Frenchman of New Orleans, a colonist of Porto Rico, a naturalized Spaniard, and a citizen of the United States at one and the same time, with rights entirely contradictory.

"Don Alejandro Harang accepted the cedula of August 10, 1815, and all its consequences. The 14th article of that cedula, with which the Secretary of State of the Union is probably unacquainted, is in these exact words, which I have the honor of copying: "Art. 14. During the first five years of residence in this island, *Spanish* and *foreign* colonists shall have liberty to return to their countries, or former places of residence, and in that case they shall be permitted to take away from the island the money and effects which they brought thither; but of what they acquired, or added, they shall contribute ten per cent., it being well understood that the lands which may have been allotted to such colonists as leave the island voluntarily, shall revert to my royal patrimony, to be appropriated for the benefit of others, or as I may consider most advantageous." Your excellency will here observe, that in this article no distinction is made between Spaniards and foreigners, or rather that it comprehends both expressly, and consequently Harang can have no ground for complaint, and cannot cite in his behalf the eleventh article of the treaty of 1795, since that article requires a reciprocity which Spain never fails to observe, though it never can take place in the present question, as I shall in a few words demonstrate.

The 15th article on which the court of revenue [tribunal de rentas] relies in this case of Harang, says as follows: "I grant to the old and new colonists (Spaniards and foreigners, according to the 14th article) who may die in the island without regular heirs, the privilege of leaving their property to their relations or friends, wherever they may be; and if such heirs wish to establish themselves in the island they shall enjoy the privileges conceded to the person from whom they inherit; but if they prefer carrying away the property inherited they may do so on paying upon the whole fifteen per cent., as duty of extraction, in case the colonist from whom they inherit had been more than five years established, and only ten per cent. if he had been established only for a shorter period, agreeably to the terms of the preceding (14th) article. With regard to those who die intestate, their fathers, brothers, or relations, even though established in a foreign country, shall inherit fully, provided they establish themselves in the island, being Catholics; and, in case they cannot or do not wish to reside there, I allow them to dispose of their inheritance by sale or cession, according to the regulations prefixed in the two preceding articles."

Your excellency will easily understand that, by the articles which I have copied, Don Alejandro Harang, a colonist of the island of Porto Rico, whether considered as a North American, as is now solicited, or as a Frenchman, in which character he appeared at first, or as a Spaniard born in New Orleans, as pretended at another time, or even if born in Madrid, could, before the end of five years of residence in the island, himself or his heirs, take away his property to a foreign country, as he pleased, on paying ten per cent. as duty of extraction; and as Don Alejandro Harang did hold a letter of naturalization, and was converted into a Spaniard, which rights, according to the *cedula*, he could not have acquired until after having resided five years in the island, (where he indeed resided more than ten or fifteen years,) he was at liberty to dispose of his property by testament in favor of his children, who would inherit it *ab intestato*, or of his relations or friends, with the condition of paying fifteen per cent. upon the whole, as duty of extraction, if they wished to carry it away. Such is the case of Mr. Miguel Drausin Harang, in which he is not sustained by justice. His father, in soliciting the letter of naturalization rendering him a Spaniard, complied with the laws in force in the colony; and consequently, as the royal *cedula* of colonization bears date the 10th of August, 1815, twenty years posterior to the treaty alluded to, it cannot be cited in favor of Harang without straining its sense; and I do not understand how the Secretary of State at Washington can endeavor to support this claim, seeing that the same duty of extraction is levied upon subjects of Spain and foreigners.

Harang, indeed, cannot with any justice complain of the payment required from him in virtue of the above-mentioned *cedula*. The munificent character of that document may, perhaps, be unknown to the honorable Secretary of State at Washington. It has always merited the highest praise from subjects and foreigners, on account of the innumerable privileges and immunities accorded by it to the colonists. They thereby became freed for fifteen years from all duties on importation of articles of commerce from a Spanish country, and even from duties on exportation of the produce of the island. They were exempted from tithes, as also from *alcabala*, *alcabillila*, and every species of contribution or tax on consumption, transportation, or introduction. These colonists, whether Spanish or foreign, received grants of land according to their condition, sex, and family. At the end of five years of residence they entered, if they wished, into the enjoyment of the rights of Spanish citizens, by receiving letters of naturalization for the colonists and their children, without the slightest distinction. For so many favors, exemptions, and privileges some recompense, certainly trifling when compared with these great and abundant benefits, was demanded; and this shows the justice of the fourteenth and fifteenth articles of the above-mentioned *cedula.* The colonists accepted what was useful and profitable to themselves; and they also, at the same time, accepted all the consequences. The honorable Secretary of Foreign Affairs of the United States cannot certainly desire that the laws of other countries should be treated as jests and trifles. He certainly will not expect that the children of Don Alejandro Harang should be in a better condition than Spaniards themselves. He will not maintain that Alexander Harang, a Spaniard, who for so many years before his decease enjoyed the rights of a Spaniard, should at the same time have beeen, and have enjoyed the rights of, a citizen of the United States. This would be a play upon words, giving no rights and supporting no acts. And even though he should never have ceased to be a citizen of the United States, yet this plea would not avail in his favor; and still less would the treaty of 1795, and its eleventh article, since it only requires reciprocity. The *cedula* establishes that for Spaniards and foreigners.

Although I have no necessity to enter into another discussion, and with this treaty, which is invoked by the distinguished Minister of Foreign Affairs of North America, I will prove conclusively that not one of the articles meets the question. I regret that your excellency has not examined the 11th article, which is as clear as light. I shall abstain from inquiring into other details, which will not have escaped the penetration of your excellency, such as the origin and motives of this treaty of peace, amity, limits, and navigation, between the two powers. It will be sufficient for my purpose to analyze the 11th article, which is considered as the support of the extravagant pretension of Mr. Miguel Drausin Harang, the son of Don Alejandro Harang, a *Spaniard of the island of Porto Rico*, under the laws and in the faith and religion of which he died. That oft-mentioned article says: "The citizens and subjects of each party shall have the power to dispose of their personal goods, within the jurisdiction of the other, by testament, donation, or otherwise; and their representatives, being subjects or citizens of the other party, shall succeed to their said personal goods, whether by testament or *ab intestato*, and they may take possession thereof, either by themselves or others acting for them, and dispose of the same at their will, paying such dues only as the inhabitants of the country wherein the said goods are shall be subject to pay in like cases." Such is the first part of the said article—the only part which can be made to bear, even by a forced interpretation, on the question. Don Alejandro Harang was a naturalized Spaniard, and consequently he could not, at the same time, have been a citizen of the United States, and have appealed to a treaty which applies only to citizens of the Union who might be in Seville or Cadiz as foreigners.

If Don Alejandro died a Spaniard he could not have been considered as a citizen of the United States—that is evident; nor could his heirs lay claim to rights other than those of their father. Moreover, the same article says, in the last sentence of the part already quoted, that if their heirs be subjects or citizens of the other contracting party, they shall succeed to their goods by testament, or *ab intestato*. They may take possession by themselves, or by others, and dispose of them at their will, without paying higher duties than the inhabitants of the country where the property inherited is situated would pay in similar cases. Now, Mr. Miguel Drausin Harang, son of Don Alexander Harang, is the son of a Spaniard. Spaniards pay, as duty of extraction, after five years of residence, fifteen per cent. on the amount of the property inherited which is taken away, according to the 15th article of the above-mentioned *cedula*. Even though that *cedula* had not been posterior to the treaty of 1795, your excellency will see, that if it be carried into effect towards Spaniards, citizens of the United States cannot require any thing but reciprocity; and thusMr. Miguel Drausin Harang complains in vain, evidently most unjustly.

On my part, I would, if it were incumbent on me, request your excellency to interpose your good offices with the supreme government of the Union, for the purpose of having that treaty executed according to its terms, as laid down in itself, without interruption of its text, leaving to each authority the full and complete exercise of its own attributes. This affair belongs to the courts of justice, according to the laws of Spain, and according to the very treaty cited, as clearly proved by the second part of the eleventh article, the terms of which are so direct and evident that they admit no doubt. That this may appear fully, I will copy that second part at length: "And in case of the absence of the heirs, such care will be taken of the goods as would be taken of the goods of a native in like case, until the lawful owner may take measures for receiving them. And if questions shall arise among several claimants to the inheritance, they shall be determined finally agreeably to the laws, and by the judges of the land wherein the said goods are. And when on the death of any person holding real estate within the territories of one of the contracting parties, such real estate would, by the laws of the land, descend to a citizen or subject of the other party, who should, as a foreigner, be incapable of holding it, he shall be allowed a reasonable space of time to sell the same, and to collect the proceeds without molestation, and exempt from all right of detraction on the part of the government of the respective States." "If questions shall arise," says the article, "between different claimants to the property left, they shall be decided finally according to the laws, and by the judges of the country wherein the property lies. One of the claimants to the inheritance of Don Alejandro Harang is the treasury, which requires, according to law, the sum of fifteen per cent. upon all the exisiting property of Don Alejandro Harang; exceptions to this claim must be urged before the Spanish courts, and they are to be decided according to the Spanish laws, which will be justly administered. This has been actually done; and the affair in question is now by appeal before the supreme court of the island, which will decide on it with due attention to all the treaties and orders now in force with regard to the matter."

All which I transmit to you, Mr. Secretary of State, for your information and consideration, and I remain

Your most obedient servant,

PEDRO ALCANTARA D'ARGAIZ.

Mr. Vail to Mr. Webster.

[Extract.]

LEGATION OF THE UNITED STATES, MADRID,
May 2, 1841.

SIR: * * * * * * * *

Our consul at St. John's, Porto Rico, and Mr. Michael Drausin Harang, a citizen of the United States, have applied for my intervention to obtain from the government here an order for the return of a sum of money levied by the colonial authorities as duties of *detraction* upon the proceeds of the estate of Mr. Harang's father, who died possessed of property in that island. While I was in the Department of State, the case was brought by Mr. Harang, in person, to the notice of the Secretary, who deemed it entitled to his official intervention. The knowledge I then acquired of the circumstances of the case, has induced me to acquiesce in the request of the claimant, which I have done by addressing to the Minister of Foreign Affairs the note of which a copy is enclosed.

* * * * * * * *

I am, sir, respectfully, your obedient servant,

A. VAIL.

Hon. DANIEL WEBSTER.
Secretary of State of the United States, Washington.

Mr. Vail to Mr. De Ferrer.

LEGATION OF THE UNITED STATES, MADRID,
April 27, 1841.

The undersigned, chargé d'affaires of the United States of America, has the honor to transmit to his excellency Don Joaquin Maria de Ferrer, First Minister of State and of Foreign Affairs of her Catholic Majesty, a paper recently received from the American consul at St. John's, in the island of Puerto Rico. From this paper, and from letters accompanying it, it appears that the authorities of the island recognise the legality of a claim presented to them by Michael Drausin Harang, a citizen of the United States, for the return of a sum of money exacted of him, in contravention of existing treaties between the United States and Spain, as duties of detraction upon the proceeds of the estate of his father, likewise a citizen of the United States, who died possessed of property in said island. It appears, further, that their refusal to refund the money rests on the ground that there do not exist in the archives of the island copies of one of the treaties referred to, and of a certain royal order, mentioned in the enclosed paper; and in consequence of this—although the legality of the claim is admitted on all hands—it seems that the case has, with all the documents, been referred by the colonial authorities to her Majesty's government at home. The undersigned, impelled by a sense of the wrong inflicted upon the claimant by the long detention of his property, feels it his duty to recommend the subject to the early attention of Mr. de Ferrer, and to request that directions may, as speedily as possible, be given to the authorities of Puerto Rico no more to delay the repayment of the money so unjustly demanded in the first instance, and the restitution of which has now so long and so injuriously been withheld.

The undersigned avails himself of the opportunity to offer to his excellency the renewed assurance of his most distinguished consideration.

A. VAIL.

Mr. Vail to Mr. Webster.

[Extract.]

[No. 31.] LEGATION OF THE UNITED STATES, MADRID,
July 24, 1841.

SIR: * * * * * * *

I have received an answer to my interposition in behalf of the claim of Michael Drausin Harang, for the return of moneys demanded of him by the colonial government of Porto Rico, as duties of extraction upon the proceeds of property descended to him from his father, late a resident of that island. I communicate a copy of Mr. Gonzalez's note, but not of the enclosure, though itself constituting the answer, because that document—a letter from the intendant of the island to the Spanish minister at Washington—will doubtless, by the latter, have been laid before you. A motive alleged for not granting to Harang's property the exemption from duty claimed by him under the treaty is, that his father had become a Spanish subject by naturalization; and that, therefore, his estate was liable to the same charges as those of other Spanish subjects descending in the ordinary course of law. As the American citizenship of Harang, the father, was the only ground on which I rested my representation, and as I have no means of disproving or disputing the fact of his naturalization, I let the matter rest for the present, having informed the claimant of the state of the case, and of my intention to wait for further orders from your department.

* * * * * * * *

I am, sir, respectfully, your obedient servant,

A. VAIL.

Hon. DANIEL WEBSTER,
Secretary of State, Washington.

Mr. Webster to Mr. Vail.

[Extract.]

[No. 14.] DEPARTMENT OF STATE,
Washington, September 1, 1841.

* * * * * * * *

Enclosed you will find copy of a correspondence and of certain papers relating to the claim of Michael Drausin Harang and others, of Ponce, Porto Rico, upon the intendencia of that island, for "detraction" of a sum of money due upon the sale of his late father's estate, the payment of which was enforced against him and his co-heirs by the intendente, contrary, as the claimants allege, to existing treaties between the respective countries. Under the impression that the colonial decision was rash, and with a view to lose no time in obtaining reparation for an injury supposed to have been occasioned by inadvertence, a letter was addressed to the Spanish minister here, stating the circumstances, and asking his influence with the authorities of the island to prevail on them to re-examine the case, and to repair the alleged damage. After some delay, the Chevalier d'Argaiz replied, and enclosed the answer of the intendente on the subject of this claim. This answer has proved unsatisfactory to the parties, and you are now instructed, on the receipt of this dispatch, to bring the subject to the attention of her Majesty's government, which would have been done in the first instance, at the desire of the claimants, if the department had not believed that the course that was adopted would have resulted in speedier justice.

The facts are sufficiently explained in the accompanying papers to enable you to present the matter in a strong light at Madrid; and believing the case to have been one of manifest injustice, it is not doubted that the home governmant will hasten, not only to remedy the evil originally done by the authorities of the island, but to make reparation for so long a delay in rendering justice to the parties.

I enclose, for your further information, a statement of the case drawn up by Mr. M. D. Harang, who is now in Washington.

Mr. Vail to Mr. Webster.

[No. 48.] LEGATION OF THE UNITED STATES, MADRID,
November 2, 1841.

SIR: I have been led, by the directions in your dispatch No. 14, into a closer examination, and, by the documents accompanying it, I am enabled to arrive at a clearer understanding than before of the claim of Michael Drausin Harang upon the colonial treasury of Puerto Rico. The circumstances set forth by the papers, and the law and arguments adduced against the claim by the colonial authorities, have raised strong doubts in my mind of the practicability, with the means within my reach, of a successful interposition in behalf of the claim upon the principles hitherto invoked in support of it. The circumstances upon which the claim is founded appear to be these:

On the 10th of August, 1815, a royal cedula, or decree of colonization, was issued, to encourage immigration and promote the settlement of the colony. It offered to all persons, Spaniards or foreigners, gratuitous grants of land, and certain advantages to foster their cultivation; but it likewise imposed upon all settlers, Spanish and foreign equally, certain obligations, inherent to their character of colonists. Thus a continued residence of five years conferred upon the former the quality of Spanish subjects, and of course imposed upon them the corresponding obligations. It granted to all, without distinction of origin, who might die without heirs, the right of bequeathing their property to relatives and friends, who, if they chose to reside in the colony, were to enjoy the same privileges as the original grantees; otherwise the land itself was to revert to the crown, and the legatees were at liberty to withdraw from the colony such part of the inheritance as had been acquired by the grantee during his residence therein, but on payment of a duty of extraction, whether the grantee had been of Spanish or foreign origin, of ten per cent. if his residence had been of five years, and fifteen per cent. if over.

Now it appears from Mr. Michael Drausin Harang's own statement, that it was in consequence of the inducements held out by the cedula that his father removed to, and established himself in, the colony. If he thereby accepted the benefits of the law, he, as a matter of course, according to the argument of the Spanish authorities, which must be allowed to have great force, assumed likewise its obligations. Thus, after a five-years' residence he became a Spanish subject; and thus the property acquired by him became chargeable with the duty of extraction specifically provided; and all this in consequence of a voluntary and deliberate act of his—a species of agreement between him and the Spanish government.

If by this act Mr. Harang's father divested himself of his American citizenship, and placed his property beyond the pale of the protection of the United States, can the provisions of the treaty be invoked in the case? I am unable, without other information than that now in my possession, to arrive at any but a negative solution of that question, which, however, with all deference, I submit for your consideration.

In case the foregoing view of the subject should not prove the correct one, or if the claimant should be able to present his case in a light which would bring it clearly within the purview of the treaty, I would ask you to consider whether, under its provisions, exemption from the duty of detraction can be demanded for the proceeds of any other than real property.

As my dispatch No. 31, with the negative answer of the Spanish government to the application made in the case, will have reached your department since the date of your No. 14, I will, before I move further in the matter, await your ulterior directions on that and the present communication.

I am, sir, with great respect, your obedient servant,

A. VAIL.

Hon. DANIEL WEBSTER,

Secretary of State of the United States, Washington.

Mr. Webster to Mr. Vai

[Extract.]

[No. 16.] DEPARTMENT OF STATE,
Washington, January 31, 1842.

* * * * * *

A copy of that part of your dispatch, No. 48, which relates to Mr. Harang's claim, will be communicated to him; and anything further that the parties interested may have to offer will be transmitted to you. If the view taken by the intendente of Porto Rico be confirmed by the Spanish government, the claimants, unless able to set their case in a new light, will have to look to, and abide by, the decision of the tribunals of the island. Your No. 31 upon this subject has not yet reached the department.

Your dispatches Nos. 55 and 56 have been received.

I am, sir, respectfully, your obedient servant,
DANIEL WEBSTER.

AARON VAIL, Esq.,
Chargé d'Affaires of the United States, Madrid.

Mr. Webster to Mr. Irving.

[Extract.]

[No. 4.] DEPARTMENT OF STATE,
Washington, July 30, 1842.

SIR: Enclosed is a copy of a letter from M. D. Harang, dated at New Orleans on the 5th instant, the subject of which you will understand by referring to the correspondence on it in your legation, especially to dispatches, Nos. 14 and 16, to Mr. Vail, and to his dispatch, No. 48, to this department. As soon as convenient, after the receipt of this communication, you will address the Spanish government again upon the claim of Mr. Harang, and do all in your power to procure a favorable decision from it.

* * * * * *

WASHINGTON IRVING, Esq., *&c.*, *&c.*

Mr. Irving to Mr. Webster.

[Extract.]

[No. 4.] LEGATION OF THE UNITED STATES, MADRID,
October 8, 1842.

SIR: I had the honor to receive, on the 12th ultimo, dispatch No. 4 from the department, enclosing a copy of a confidential letter of the Captain General of the island of Cuba, and from Mr. M. D. Harang, dated at New Orleans, on the subject of his claim upon the Spanish government.

In relation to the latter I made an informal application to the Office of State for a copy of the royal decree under which the authorities of Porto Rico acted; and soon after I had procured it, I addressed, on the 24th September, a note to Count Almadora, Minister of State, of which the enclosed is a copy. To this I have, as yet, received no answer. After a careful examination of the treaty of '95, and the provisions of the decree above referred to, it appears to me very doubtful whether the case of Mr. Harang can be supported under the stipulations of the treaty; still, the reasons heretofore assigned by the Spanish government for their refusal to make restitution do not appear to have much force, and are mainly on the presumption that Harang, the father, was a naturalized subject of Spain; of which no proof is adduced, and which is totally denied by his heirs.

[Enclosure.]

LEGATION OF THE UNITED STATES, MADRID,
September 24, 1842.

The undersigned, envoy extraordinary and minister plenipotentiary of the United States, has the honor to call the attention of Count Almadora, First Minister of State and of Foreign Affairs of her Catholic Majesty, to the case of Mr. Michael Drausin Harang, an American citizen, which has already been the subject of correspondence with her Majesty's government.

It appears that Luis Alexander Harang, the father of the applicant, was a native of Louisiana, and citizen of the United States. In consequence of royal cedula, or decree, of 10th August, 1815, holding out inducements to foreigners as well as Spaniards to settle in the island of Porto Rico, by offers of gratuitous grants of land, and various privileges, he removed to that island, purchased land there with the funds which he had brought with him, cultivated, with his own means and industry, a sugar plantation; and, after having amassed considerable property, died at New York in 1815, bequeathing his property among his children.

After his death his son, Michael Drausin Harang, in his own behalf, and in virtue of a power of attorney from his co-heirs, sold the property lying and being in the island of Porto Rico, with the intention of conveying the proceeds out of the island, when the intendente interfered and exacted a *derecho de extraccion*, or duty of exportation of 15 per cent., upon the gross amount of the sales; the proceeds of which duty, amounting to near eleven thousand dollars, were gathered into the royal treasury.

Against this exaction Michael Drausin Harang protested; his father having been a citizen of the United States, and his property, bequeathed to his heirs, exempted from all *derechos de extraccion*, according to the eleventh article of the treaty of 1795.

The intendente maintained the justice of the exaction by alleging that Luis Alexander Harang, in accepting the royal cedula of August 10, 1815, and its benefits, subjected himself to its consequences, among which was this duty of extraccion of 15 per cent. on any property he might devise; and further, that in becoming a *naturalized subject of Spain* he forfeited the protection of the eleventh article of the treaty of 1795, which only extended to citizens of the United States.

At this point the matter rested when last brought before this government.

In reply, Michael Drausin Harang observes that his father, Luis Alexander Harang, when he migrated to the island of Porto Rico, never accepted the royal cedula—that is to say, the grants and benefits held out in it as a lure to colonists; and in not accepting these, he did not subject himself to "all the consequences" of that decree.

The most prominent inducement held out in that cedula was the gratuitous grant of land to any Spaniard or foreigner who would settle on the island and cultivate it; the said land to be assigned out in portions according to the number of colonists' families, and his slaves; and the assignment to be entered into the register of population, with the name of the colonist, the day of his admission, the number of the individuals of his family, &c. Luis Alexander Harang neither asked nor received any such grant of land. Had he done so, a record thereof would exist in the register of population, and an authenticated copy of it would no doubt have been produced by the intendente to support his assertion. But no such record exists. Mr. L. A. Harang purchased land with his own funds which he had brought with him; he cultivated and improved it at his own expense, and by his unassisted means and industry. So far, therefore, from being a beneficiary of the royal or colonial government, and, of course, subject to pay for the benefits received, he was, in this respect, a benefactor of the island.

Then, as to his being a naturalized subject of Spain: The article twelve of the royal cedula says: "The first five years of establishment of foreign colonists in the island being past, *and they then obliging themselves to remain permanently on it,* all the rights and privileges of naturalization will be conceded to them, as well as to the children they have brought with them, or which may have been born in the island, that they may consequently be admitted to the honorable employs of the republic and the militia," &c.

Now, Mr. Michael Drausin Harang declares that his father never, either at the time of his arrival at the island, or during his residence there, did or contemplate any act to divest himself of the character of a citizen of the United States, or to acquire the character and rights of a naturalized subject of Spain. This point, on which the intendente rests the main stress of his justification, ought to have been substantiated by documentary evidence. The mere evidence in the island for any number of years could not make him a Spanish subject, without some overt act or declaration on his part; nor could the royal offer of naturalization render its acceptance obligatory; a specific formality was necessary—*the declaration of an intention to remain permanently in the island.* If such declaration had been made for the purpose of obtaining naturalization, some record of it must exist, and ought to have been produced to maintain this vital ground of defence on the part of the intendente. No such proof is furnished, and Mr. Michael D. Harang declares that the archives of the secretaria of the island of Porto Rico have been diligently searched, but no evidences of his father's naturalization, or even domiciliation, can be found. In fact, he went to the island merely at the time when the decree of August 10, 1815, threw the door open to foreigners; he availed himself of the general license of the decree, without accepting its specific grants and benefits, and incurring the consequent obligations. He lived and died *a citizen of the United States;* and, as such, his heirs claim for the estate the right secured by the following paragraph of the eleventh article of the treaty of 1795: "And where, on the death of any person holding real estate within the territories of the one party, such real estate would by the laws descend on a citizen or subject of the other, were he not disqualified by alienage, such subject shall be allowed a reasonable time to sell the same, and to withdraw the proceeds without molestation, and exempt from all rights of *detraction* on the part of the government of the respective States."

The government of the United States, maturely examining the case, are of opinion that the duty of fifteen per cent. has been wrongfully exacted on the property of the deceased, Luis Alex. Harang, a citizen of the United States, and ought to be refunded, with damages for detention, to his heirs. They are convinced that her Majesty's government will concur with them in this opinion when they have investigated the case; and they have instructed the undersigned to use his utmost exertions in procuring a speedy adjustment of a claim where so much injury has been caused by delay.

The undersigned avails himself of this occasion to renew to Count de Almadora the assurances of his distinguished consideration.

WASHINGTON IRVING.

Mr. Irving to Mr. Webster.

[Extract.]

[No. 5.] LEGATION OF THE UNITED STATES, MADRID,
November 5, 1842.

* * * * * * * *

I enclose likewise a note from Count Almadora received in reply to my application in favor of the claim of Michael Drausin Harang; a reply which, according to the slow process of Spanish investigations, does not promise a speedy decision of the question.

* * * * * * * *

[Translation of a note from the Secretary of State of Spain.]

CHIEF DEPARTMENT OF STATE,
Palace, October 22, 1842.

SIR: It being shown to this department that a claim is now pending in the courts of Puerto Rico, advanced by Michael Drausin Harang for the restitution of $10,978, which were exacted from him as duties of extraction to a foreign country on the estate of his deceased father, L. Alexander Harang, to which your letter of the 24th of September refers, I have ordered that the necessary information should be obtained on the subject; and so soon as it has been received, I shall have the honor to reply to your above-mentioned note. I avail myself of this occasion to renew to you the assurances of my distinguished consideration.

COUNT DE ALMADORA.

Hon. WASHINGTON IRVING,
Envoy Extraordinary and Minister Plenipotentiary, &c.

Mr. Calhoun to Mr. Irving.

[No. 31.]

DEPARTMENT OF STATE,
Washington, April 30, 1844.

SIR: Since the receipt of your dispatches Nos. 4 and 5, no information has been received from your legation on the subject of the claim of M. D. Harang. You will, on the receipt of this dispatch, take an early occasion of renewing the subject, and endeavor to obtain a final decision, agreeably to the promise made by the Minister of Foreign Relations, in reply to your note renewing the claim under instructions from this department.

I am, sir, respectfully, your obedient servant,

J. C. CALHOUN.

WASHINGTON IRVING, Esq., *&c., &c., &c., Madrid.*

Mr. Calhoun to Mr. Irving.

[Extract.]

[No. 32.]

DEPARTMENT OF STATE,
Washington, May 29, 1844.

SIR: At the request of M. D. Harang, I enclose, herewith, certain papers respecting his claim upon the government of Spain, and refer you to my dispatch No. 31, dated on the 30th ultimo, for instructions on the subject.

* * * * * * * *

Mr. Irving to Mr. Calhoun.

[Extract.]

[No. 45.]

LEGATION OF THE UNITED STATES, MADRID,
June 24, 1844.

SIR: I have the honor to acknowledge receipt of dispatch No. 31, recalling my attention to the claim of Michael Drausin Harang. I have not lost sight of this claim since my correspondence with the Spanish Secretary of State on the subject in September, 1842, but have not been able to procure any other reply to my inquiries than that the government was waiting for information on the subject.

I have now addressed the Marques de Viluma, and hope the reply may be more explicit. It is difficult to give any view, however, of the delays and evasions to which all applications of the kind are at all times subjected in the Spanish offices, and more especially in the present agitated and revolutionary times. I believe, in general, I have fared better in my negotiations with the Spanish government than most of my colleagues, some of whom complain bitterly that their personal applications are unavailing and their letters unanswered.

*　*　*　*　*　*　*　*

Mr. Irving to Mr. Calhoun.

[Extract.]

[No. 48.] LEGATION OF THE UNITED STATES, BARCELONA,
July 14, 1844.

*　*　*　*　*　*　*　*

The documents which you forwarded relative to the claim of Michael Drausin Harang throw no new light on the case, which was discussed by me, to the best of my judgment, in a note passed to the Spanish government on the 24th of September, 1842, a copy of which was sent to your department. I was informed yesterday that I should soon receive a written answer on the subject.

Mr. Irving to Mr. Buchanan.

[Extract.]

[No. 71.] LEGATION OF THE UNITED STATES, MADRID,
August 23, 1845.

SIR: I have the honor to acknowledge the receipt of dispatch No. 47, with its enclosure.

I transmit herewith a copy of a note addressed to Mr. Martinez de la Rosa, concerning the long pending case of Michael Drausin Harang; also a note to Mr. Alexander Mon, Minister of Finance, relative to the nullification of the Cuba decree. The reply of Mr. Mon, herewith sent, states that the matter is undergoing investigation—a usual reply with the Spanish government when pecuniary indemnity is required.

*　*　*　*　*　*　*　*

Hon. JAMES BUCHANAN,
Secretary of State.

LEGATION OF THE UNITED STATES OF AMERICA, MADRID,
August 12, 1845.

SIR: It is with much regret that I find myself again obliged to urge the action of her Majesty's government in a case long since and repeatedly presented for its consideration. I allude to the case of Michael Drausin Harang, a citizen of the United States, claiming the restitution of several thousand dollars, wrongfully exacted by the intendente of the island of Porto Rico from the proceeds of the sale of the estate of Luis Harang, deceased, under the title of *derechos de extraccion*, and in contravention of treaties existing between the United States and Spain.

The claimant, who represents the heirs of the deceased, first attempted, many years since, to get redress from the tribunals of the island, but was put off with the declaration that the case, with all its documents, had been referred to her Majesty's government at Madrid. To her Majesty's government, therefore, he addressed himself, through my predecessor, Mr. Vail, but with no better success; so that, on my taking charge of this legation, I found the claim among the matters especially charged by my government upon my attention.

I accordingly addressed a note, on the 24th of September, 1842, to Count Almadora, then Minster of State and of Foreign Affairs, giving a full statement of the case, and complaining of the delay that had already occurred in its adjustment. Count Almadora, in reply, observed that, finding the claim pending before the tribunals of Porto Rico, he had inquiries made into the matter, the results of which he would communicate to me.

A *year* and *eight months* elapsed without my receiving any further communications from her Majesty's government on the subject. I therefore, on the 16th of June, 1844, addressed a note respecting it to his excellency the Marquis of Viluma, then Minister of State. He retired from office before he had time to reply. I made a verbal representation of the case to General Narvaez, who held the office *ad interim*. With his characteristic promptness, he wrote me a note, dated the 20th of July, informing me that on the same day the Minister of Finance had been written to with urgency, for information in the premises, and that as soon as he should receive such information he would send me an explicit answer. I was also assurred, about the same time, at the Department of State, that a reply was actually in the course of preparation. General Narvaez, however, ceased to have charge of the Department of State; and with his relinquishment of it apparently ceased all further attention to this case—the promised reply having never been provided to this legation, nor any other communication made on the subject by her Majesty's government.

Thus for nearly ten years has this claim been in a manner bandied backward and forward between the colonies and the mother country, and between tribunals and departments. Answers have been promised to this legation, but have never been sent; and there would seem to be a disposition to evade all definite action in the case, and tacitly consign it to oblivion.

The respect, however, which this legation owes to itself and to the government which it represents, will not permit it passively to acquiesce in such inattention to a matter which has so repeatedly been the subject of earnest communication; and I now most respectfully, but urgently, claim from her Majesty's government that explicit answer on the case which has so long been promised.

I have the honor to be, with high consideration, your excellency's obedient servant,

WASHINGTON IRVING.

His Excellency Mr. F. M. de la Rosa.

Legation of the U. S. of America, Madrid,
August 9, 1845.

Sir: Your excellency cannot but be fully aware of the serious losses sustained by citizens of the United States, who made heavy shipments to the island of Cuba in the course of last winter, on the faith of a decree of the supreme authorities of the island, admitting certain articles free of duty for the space of three months, but who found their merchandise, on its arrival, subjected to the old duties, in consequence of an act of her Majesty's government, carried into effect in the interim, and without due notification, annulling the aforesaid decree.

The government of the United States, keenly alive at all times to everything which may affect the rights of its citizens and disturb the harmonious relations of the two countries, could not but be deeply aggrieved by an irregular act, which took the confiding American merchant by surprise, and was calculated to impair that confidence and security in commercial intercourse, which it is the interest of both governments to sustain inviolate.

I received instructions from my government, therefore, to make urgent remonstrances against this irregular proceeding on the part of her Majesty's government, manifestly unjust in itself, and in contradiction to the commercial usages prevalent among enlightened nations. I was instructed, furthermore, to say that the government of the United States felt confident that prompt and efficacious measures would be taken by her Majesty's ministers to redress the wrongs thus occasioned, and I was instructed to intimate, that, in the opinion of the President of the United States, those citizens who had imported any of the articles embraced in the decree into the Havana between the 20th of February and the 7th of April, 1845, without knowledge, at the time of their departure from the United States, that the decree had been annulled, were entitled to be indemnified by the Spanish government for the losses they had sustained.

I accordingly, on the 15th June last, addressed a note to the foregoing purport, to his excellency Mr. Francisco M. de la Rosa, her Majesty's First Minister of State, and I trusted that the gravity of the case, the obvious justice of the claim presented, and the importance attached to it by the government of the United States, would have procured instant and satisfactory attention to my communication. It is with surprise and regret, therefore, that I find nearly two months suffered to elapse without the least notice being taken of my note, and without even the receipt of it being acknowledged.

To address a second note to the Minister of State appears to me, under present circumstances, useless. If he suffered the first to lie unregarded, when he was present in the capital, it is not likely he would pay more attention to a second, now that he is attending her Majesty in the distant provinces.

Under these circumstances, and knowing the earnestness with which my government looks for a speedy adjustment of this matter, I have deemed it expedient to press it upon the attention of your excellency. I will merely observe that it is a case in which nothing is gained by delay; on the contrary, it grows in importance under silence and neglect, so that an act which, if promptly remedied, might be palliated as the unintentional result of hurry or inadvertency, may be tacitly aggravated into a serious cause of offence.

I have the honor to be, with high consideration, your excellency's obedient servant,

WASHINGTON IRVING.

His Excellency ALEXANDER MON,
Minister of Finance.

[Translation.]

MADRID, *August* 13, 1845.

SIR: I have the honor to acknowledge the receipt of your note of the 9th instant, and, as the business to which it refers is actually undergoing investigation, (pendiente de instruccion,) the resolution which may be formed concerning it will be duly communicated to you through the regular channel of the Department of State, without more delay than is necessary. I have the honor to reiterate, &c., &c.,

A. MON.

Mr. Buchanan to Mr. Saunders.

[Extract.]

[No. 17.] DEPARTMENT OF STATE,
Washington, December 6, 1847.

* * * * * *

My present object is to call your special attention to the claim of M. D. Harang, respecting which ample instructions were transmitted to Mr. Vail in 1841, and to your predecessor, accompanied by documents and papers connected therewith. These will be found on file in your legation. You will discover that no reply has ever been given to a note of Mr. Irving, of the 12th August, 1845, representing the claim of Mr. Harang in very strong language, and urging upon the then Minister for Foreign Relations the necessity of a decision upon it. Since Mr. Irving quitted the mission, the subject does not appear to have received any attention.

* * * * * *

You will, as early as practicable after the receipt of this dispatch, remind the Spanish government that the letter of Mr. Irving, above referred to, remains unanswered, and will, at the same time, take occasion to urge a prompt and favorable decision upon the claim.

I have not, at present, leisure to look carefully into this case, and therefore express no opinion upon its merits, or the amount of indemnification that ought to be demanded. This examination will devolve upon you, with the advantage of all the evidence before you, furnished at various periods by the parties themselves, who will, doubtless, cheerfully supply you with any additional information or papers which they or yourself, after examination, may deem useful or necessary; and will correspond directly with you on the subject.

I am, sir, respectfully, your obedient servant,

JAMES BUCHANAN.

Mr. Saunders to Mr. Buchanan.

[No. 29.] LEGATION OF THE UNITED STATES, MADRID,
February 8, 1848.

SIR: I have the honor to acknowledge the receipt of your dispatch No. 17, with its enclosures, calling my "special attention" to the claim of M. D. Harang. As the counsel for the claimant seems to be laboring under some misapprehension as to the attention given to the claim by this legation, and to afford you some idea of the difficulties and delays which have to be encountered in all cases involving a pecuniary demand against this government, I take the liberty of giving you a brief recital of what has transpired in regard to this particular case.

The claim was first presented to the minister here by Mr. Vail, in April, 1841. In September, 1842, Mr. Irving renewed the application, giving, at the same time, a full and accurate statement of the facts involved in the case, with a reply to the grounds taken by the intendente of Porto Rico in support of his proceedings, in which he denied that Alexander Harang had ever been a naturalized citizen of Porto Rico, or that he had done anything to bring him within the operation of the royal decree of August, 1815. In June, 1844, he addressed a note to the minister, requesting to be furnished with certain information which, it appears, had been called for from the authorities at Porto Rico. Again, in August, 1845, Mr. Irving addressed a strong note to the minister, complaining of the delay, and urging, in the most pressing manner, the necessity of an early decision. Finally, in June, 1846, a few weeks before his departure, he again urged upon the minister, in the most earnest terms, that he should give some definite reply. In the dispatch to the department, No. 82, which followed, he states he had learned the case was then before the "royal council," for final adjudication. In this situation I found the claim when I succeeded to the business of the legation. I certainly did not feel myself called upon to do anything until such time should elapse as might be sufficient to enable a Spanish council to come to a conclusion. I had revived and pressed one or two other cases, with as little success as my predecessors. On inquiry, I find an answer had been received from the ministry of State, a short time before my return from France, which had been filed by the Secretary, and had escaped our attention until the receipt of your dispatch. But as the decision is not final, I presume nothing will be done by the authorities at Porto Rico before informing the parties interested. As the matter now stands, I do not see what further can be done here, unless I shall be furnished with some new matter, to ask for a reconsideration. That you may understand the grounds of the decision, so as to direct the attention of the council to the points on which it is made to rest, I herewith enclose a copy, and shall await your further directions.

I am, sir, yours, respectfully,

R. M. SAUNDERS.

JAMES BUCHANAN, Esq.,
Secretary of State.

[Translation.]

CHIEF DEPARTMENT OF STATE,
Palace, September 7, 1847.

SIR: With respect to the various communications made to this department by the legation of the United States, praying that Mr. Drausin Harang, a subject of that republic residing in Porto Rico, should be exempted from paying the duty of extraction on the property inherited by him from his deceased father, and that the sum of $10,978 exacted from him with that object should be repaid, I have the honor to inform you that a communication has been addressed to me by the Treasury Department, being a copy of the resolution (or order) on this subject given to the intendente of Porto Rico.

Agreeably to this resolution, (or order,) it appears clearly that, according to the testament and codicil of Mr. Harang, he was naturalized. In the treaty concluded in 1795 between Spain and the United States, it is established that the subjects of either power may freely dispose of the property possessed by them in the territory of the other, as well as their heirs, agreeably to a will or *ab intestato*, without paying other duties than those which the natives of the country would have to pay, declaring them free from the duty of *retention;* but as this latter duty is not now in question, the duty of *extraction* being that concerning which the present resolution is given, to the payment of which all persons who carry property out of Porto Rico are subject, even though they be Spaniards and colonists of the island, as well as their children and heirs, in virtue of the royal cedula of August 10, 1815, now in force, and confirmed by the treaty between Spain and the United States of October 27, 1819, the claim of Mr. Drausin Harang is not founded in justice. Accordingly, by agreement with the report of the assessor of the superintendency, and of the united sections of the State, grace and justice, treasury and the colonies, the acts and other documents annexed relating to this case are returned by the Treasury Department to the intendente of Porto Rico, in order that the superintendent, sub-delegate, and superior board of treasury of that Island may determine what they consider just, until the case be terminated.

I avail myself of this occasion, &c.

ANTONIO CABALLERO.

To the ACTING CHARGE D'AFFAIRES *of the United States at Madrid.*

Mr. Saunders to Mr. Clayton.

[Extract.]

[No. 50.] LEGATION OF THE UNITED STATES, MADRID,
July 7, 1849.

* * * * * * * *

I have received from Mr. Charles De Selding, the attorney for the heirs of Harang, sundry documents in support of their claim on the Spanish government, and as these proofs change, in some degree, the nature of the demand in favor of the claimants, I shall lose no time in taking the necessary steps for reviving the claim, and, as I trust, with more success.

* * * * *

Mr. Saunders to Mr. Clayton.

[Extract.]

[No. 51.] LEGATION OF THE UNITED STATES, MADRID.
September 25, 1849.

* * * * * * * *

I also submit copies of the correspondence relative to the claim of Michael Drausin Harang; from which you will see the matter has assumed a question of importance, not so much from the amount involved as from the construction given to the 11th article of the treaty of 1795, a construction which, as I humbly conceive, is not warranted either by the intent or letter of the treaty. As I considered it a matter of importance to have the question decided, and believed it not likely that the claimants would ever receive anything without some arrangement of the kind, I was induced to submit the proposition as contained in my note of the 26th of July. The claim of Mr. D. Harang stood rejected, without the smallest probability of its being reconsidered. The claim of Madame de Viar had been presented by my predecessor—had been again and again urged by him, and revived by myself, under special instructions from the department, to which no answer had ever been given. I considered it time to close the matter in some way. I was further induced to submit the proposition, from the belief that if acceded to by the government here, and approved of by the President, it might facilitate the appropriation by Congress for the settlement of the "Amistad case." This question, as you are aware, has already excited some feeling; and as the appropriation has been three times recommended by the President and refused by the House, it is likely to embarrass the legation here, unless the appropriation shall be made at the next session of Congress. It is a matter of importance, too, that those, who have made investments in real estate in the island of Cuba, which, as I understand, are considerable, and which have been made under the impression they were protected by the treaty, should know whether the interpretation of the royal council is to be sustained. The question is now altogether one of construction, as the facts are no longer in dispute. If the government has the right to levy this duty of 15 per cent., under the title of "derechos de extraccion," then one thing is certain—they are more likely to increase than to lessen it. But as I was unable to obtain any answer to my note, I felt constrained by a sense of self-respect to withdraw the proposition. Indeed, after my note of the 20th of August, I had no alternative but to adopt that course or to suffer the matter to rest, which I could not think of doing. The proposition had been made on my own responsibility, and, as I thought, I was entitled, as an act of common courtesy, to an answer. I know that Mr. Irving had addressed two very strong notes of remonstrance to the minister in this very case of Harang, and had been unable to command even an acknowledgment, and I considered it time to let them know that such gross inattention was not to be submitted to. Indeed, this very case of Harang strongly illustrates their manner of doing business, and what the foreign minister (it is not confined to one case alone) had to encounter in his intercourse with them. The case had been pending for ten years; notes of argument, of complaint, and of angry remonstrance had been repeatedly addressed to the different Ministers of Foreign Affairs, without receiving any other attention than the mere verbal answer that the matter was pending before the royal council; and after this long deliberation, they announce a decision which, if correct, should not have required twenty-four hours. Under these circumstances I felt fully justified in the steps I have taken. But as the minister has at length found time to answer, in which, as you will see, he declines the proposition, it will be for the President to decide what further is to be done in regard to the matter. Mr. Barringer will, of course, await your instructions on the subject.

* * * * * * * *

LEGATION OF THE UNITED STATES, MADRID,
July 10, 1849.

SIR: I have to call the attention of your excellency to the case of Michael Drausin Harang, and to the decision of the royal council, rejecting his claim, as notified by his excellency Don Antonio Cabellero, in his note to me of the 7th September, 1847. The claimant, when informed of this decision, complained of its injustice, as being in conflict with the treaty of 1795, but was unable until the present time to furnish the necessary documents to enable me to call the attention of your excellency to the subject, and to ask a reconsideration of the matter. These proofs I beg now to submit to the consideration of your excellency, from which it will be seen that the decision is clearly erroneous, and by which great injustice has been done to the claimant.

It appears that Luis Alexander Harang, the father of the present claimant, a citizen of the State of Louisiana, was induced to remove, about the year 1818, and to settle in the vicinity of Ponce, in the island of Porto Rico; that he there acquired real estate and other property of considerable value, where he continued to reside until the year 1835, when he returned to the city of New York, where he died in that year.

That before his death he had made his testament, by which he devised his estate in Porto Rico to Michael Drausin Harang and his other children, all at the time citizens of the United States; that the claimant having disposed of a part of the estate with the view of removing it to the United States, was forced to pay to the intendente of the island of Porto Rico the sum of near $11,000, as a tax or duty on export, which tax the claimant submits he was not liable to pay, and therefore claims to have refunded.

From the decision of the royal council, as communicated to me by his excellency Don Antonio Caballero in his note of the 7th September, 1847, it appears the royal council has treated it as a case of the removal of "personal goods" from the island; and being within the jurisdiction of her Majesty's dominions, the owner, though a foreigner, became liable to pay the same dues as the inhabitants of the country in like cases. This certainly would be so in the case of "personal goods," according to the 11th article of the treaty of 1795; but, as your excellency will see by adverting to the same article of the treaty, it is expressly provided in regard to *real estate*, that the devisee, when a citizen or subject of another country, shall be allowed a reasonable time to sell the same and to withdraw the proceeds without molestation, and exempt from all rights of *detraction* on the part of the government. It is for the violation of this provision of the treaty by the intendente of Porto Rico, in exacting the tax of which Michael Drausin Harang complains, and it is for the confounding real estate with that of "personal goods" by the royal council, in its decision, in which the error has been committed, and which the claimant now respectfully asks may be reconsidered, and that justice done him which has so long been withheld. Your excellency is too sound a lawyer to render it necessary for me to point out the marked distinction between real estate and personal goods, the sound policy on which that distinction rests, and which is so clearly recognised by the 11th article of the treaty of 1795; nor is it necessary for me to urge upon your excellency the importance of having this provision of the treaty observed between two countries who have hitherto respected its obligations with such good faith. I feel it only necessary for me to call your excellency's attention to the facts of the case, to signify my protest against the decision of the royal council, as in conflict with the treaty of 1795, and respectfully, but most earnestly, to solicit a reconsideration of the question, so that justice and right may be done.

I beg to renew to your excellency assurances of my distinguished consideration.

R. M. SAUNDERS.

His Excellency PEDRO JOSE PIDAL, *&c.*, *&c.*, *&c.*

[Translation.]

FIRST DEPARTMENT OF STATE,
At the Palace, July 14, 1849.

SIR: I have received your note of the 10th instant, in which you have been pleased to renew the demand for a return of the duties of detraction, levied in Puerto Rico, on the sale of the real estate of M. Drausin Harang, inherited by his sons, who are American citizens. You accompany that note with the proofs that Mr. Luis Alexander Harang was also an American citizen, although it appears at the same time that he was subsequently naturalized in Puerto Rico, and, moreover, that the papers of sale of the property which he possessed in that island were authorized by his son, Michael Drausin Harang, for himself, and in the name of his brothers, who had given him full powers for that object.

You assume that the royal council has confounded the regulations applicable to personal property with those relative to real estate; and you assert that, according to the 11th article of the treaty of 1795, personal property alone is subject to the duty of 15 per cent. of detraction, and that real estate is exempt from all duty.

Permit me to rectify the interpretation which you give to the article in question. In that article I do not find the distinction which you would establish between real and personal estate. When it is said that the subjects and citizens of both countries shall have power to dispose of their *personal* property, this word is not placed in contradistinction to real estate, for in that case the word would have been *moveable* property. In no form can it be admitted that *personal* property is synonymous with *moveable*. *Personal* property comprehends both real estate and *movable* property that may belong to the individual in question.

Respecting these descriptions of property in general, the article stipulates that the heirs, although they may be foreigners, shall succeed to the testator, without paying greater duties than those paid by the natives of the country in similar cases where the inheritance is established.

In the last paragraph of the article it is stipulated, that "if by the death of any person possessing real estate in the territory of one of the contracting parties, this real estate should pass, according to the laws of the country, to a subject or citizen of the other party, and if this subject or citizen, in his character of foreigner, should be disqualified from holding it, he shall have a suitable time for selling it and collecting the proceeds, without hinderance, and without being subject to any duty of *retention* on the part of the government of the respective States." But it is not to be inferred from this, that real estate is exempt from all duty; for you will agree that it would be absurd to subject *moveable* property to a duty, on its sale, as you suppose was done, and to leave free from all duty the sale of real estate, whose proceeds pass to foreign hands. The duty from which real estate is exempt is that of *retention*, and not that of *detraction*, amounting to 15 per cent., which is that paid by the heirs of Mr. Harang, and which was definitively established by the royal cedula of August 10, 1815, for the promotion of commerce, population, the arts and agriculture, of the island of Puerto Rico.

In this light the royal council regarded it, and it was thus presented to the United States legation by my predecessor, in his communication of September 7, 1847.

I trust that these explanations will convince you of the solid reasons for the resolution adopted in this matter, and that the duties exacted of the heirs of Mr. Harang were established by general regulations, for cases of this kind, which regulations are in no wise opposed to the treaties subsisting with the United States. These treaties the government of her majesty observes with the greater loyalty, as it secures the good relations subsisting between the two countries.

I avail myself of this occasion to renew to your excellency the assurances of my most distinguished consideration.

PEDRO J. PIDAL.

To the MINISTER PLENIPOTENTIARY
of the United States.

LEGATION OF THE UNITED STATES, SAN ILDEFONSO,
July 23, 1849.

SIR: I have had the honor to receive the answer of your excellency, under date of the 14th, to my note of the 10th instant, in regard to the claim of Michael Drausin Harang. The matter is thus made to appear a question of importance, not so much from the amount claimed as from the principle involved; as I do not hesitate to say the construction given to the 11th article of the treaty of 1795 by the decision of the royal council, as explained by your excellency in rejecting the claim of Mr. Harang, is not only in conflict with the understanding on the part of the United States, but, if sustained by her Majesty's government, will tend in a great degree to render this article of the treaty of little value.

As I understand the interpretation given to the article in question, when it is said in the first sentence of the article that the subjects or citizens of each party shall have power to dispose of their "*personal goods*," this phrase is not used in contradistinction to *real estate*, but the words "*bienes personales*" comprehend every description of property, whether moveable or immoveable, personal or real; and as this sentence gives the power to levy the same dues on the property of the foreigner as the subject, it justifies the intendente of Porto Rico in having collected 15 per cent. on the proceeds of the sale of the real estate of Alexander Harang, from his son, Michael Drausin Harang. That the last sentence in the article, which declares "that when on the death of any person holding real estate within the territories of the one party, such real estate would, by laws of the land, descend on a subject or citizen of the other, were he not disqualified by alienage, such subject shall be allowed a reasonable time to sell the same, and to withdraw the proceeds without molestation, and exempt from all rights of "*detraction*" on the part of the government of the respective States," does not exempt real estate or its proceeds, in the event of a sale for the purpose of withdrawing it from the country, from the payment of the same dues as personal effects. I certainly shall not undertake to question the superior knowledge of your excellency as to what may be the law of Spain; yet I feel equally clear in asserting that, by the laws of the United States, the words "personal goods" could never be interpreted as embracing "real estate." So we have the singular contradiction that, according to the Spanish version of the treaty, (both being equally obligatory,) we have one interpretation, and, according to the

English version, quite a different one—an anomaly which certainly calls for some explanation. But, as I respectfully submit, whilst the interpretation given by your excellency conflicts with the intent, if not with the letter of the treaty, that for which I contend accords alike with the plain intent as well as with the letter. The first sentence relates to the disposition of the personality, and the latter to that of the reality. There are several terms to be found in the first sentence whose technical and legal signification shows, beyond all question, that they could only be used as applicable to chattel estate, such as, subjects or citizens shall succeed to their personal goods, whether by testament or *ab intestato*, in case of the absence of the representative, such care shall be taken of the said *goods*. These and the like expressions appear to me too plain to admit of doubt that chattels alone were intended to be embraced, and not real estate. So in the latter sentence the language is equally clear in its technical sense, as having reference to real and not to personal estate. What sense are we to attach to the sentence, "such subject shall be allowed a reasonable time to sell the same, [*bienes raices*—landed property,] and to withdraw the proceeds without 'molestation,'" if the local authorities are to be allowed to exact a tax *ad libitum?*—for if a tax of 15 per centum may be exacted, so may that of any amount at discretion. Again, what meaning is to be affixed to the latter words in the sentence, "exempt from all rights of *detraction* on the part of the government of the respective States?" It may be that the word "detraction," in the English version of the treaty, has been improperly used, yet the word "retencion" is used in the Spanish version. I think it is quite apparent, taking the entire article together, that it was the intention of the contracting parties to give to the subjects or citizens of each power the right to settle within the dominions of the other, to acquire real estate, and at their death to dispose of the same, and to grant to the heir or devisee the right to sell and carry the proceeds to his own country without hindrance or molestation. Your excellency seems to think it would have been absurd to have rendered personal effects liable to a tax, and at the same time to have exempted the sale of real estate when its proceeds were to pass into the hands of a foreigner. I answer, however absurd this may seem to be, it would not be more so than the contradictory sense sought to be given to the Spanish and English versions of the article. But the policy which has prevailed with the governments of the New World to induce foreigners to emigrate and invest their capital in the lands of the country, may seem to explain what might otherwise appear as unreasonable. Such certainly has been the policy of the United States, and such seems to have been some of the inducements held out by the royal decree of August, 1815. In order to satisfy your excellency that the treaty has been thus understood and acted on in the United States, I give you an extract from a letter from the United States consul, resident at Porto Rico, who says: "Don Antonio Caballero, in his letter of September 7, 1847, to the minister of the United States at Madrid, says that the duty of retencion (in the English copy of the treaty it is called the right of detraction) is not in the question. I insist that it is this very duty of retencion which is in question, as regards the proceeds of the sale of this real estate of Alexander

Harang; when we separate this, the claim falls to the ground." It must have been so understood by my predecessor in presenting, as well as by my government in urging, the demand. For if the treaty is to receive the interpretation given it by the decision of the royal council, then the claim was too groundless to have raised a question, and the ten years' correspondence about it has been labor lost. Again, if the construction contended for by your excellency should prevail, there would be no equality in the privileges secured by the treaty, as a citizen of the United States, who may inherit real estate within her Majesty's dominions, is subject to a high duty in the sale and withdrawal of its proceeds; whereas a citizen of Spain is subject to no duty for the disposition of any real estate he may inherit in the States. I say this, as a female a few days since acknowledged before me, in Madrid, a deed conveying her real estate in Florida, which had been devised to her by a relative in that State, the proceeds of which she will, doubtless, receive without the payment of any tax whatever.

I submit, then, as worthy of the grave consideration of her Majesty's government, as the interpretation given to this article of the treaty by the decision of the royal council differs so widely from that which it has received in the United States, and operates so greatly to the prejudice of our citizens, the point should be settled so as to be understood alike in both countries for the future; and as to the past, common justice would seem to demand that due satisfaction should be made to the claimant.

I flatter myself her Majesty's government may be induced to take this just view of the question, and in order to the settlement of the present claim in a satisfactory way, as well as some others now pending, it is my purpose to submit a proposition for their adjustment, which I am induced to hope may receive the favorable concurrence of your excellency.

I avail myself of the occasion to renew to your excellency assurances of my distinguished consideration.

R. M. SAUNDERS.

His Excellency Don Pedro Jose Pidal, &c., &c., &c.

[Extract from Translation.]

First Department of State,
At the Palace, September 17, 1849.

* * * * * * * *

The claim of the heirs of Mr. Drausin Harang, you are aware, is positively denied by the Treasury Department, and I am very sensible that the reasons recently alleged by you have not changed my conviction upon this point. The last argument presented in your note of the 23d of July, is this: that you assert the English version of the 11th article of the treaty of 1795 has the words right of *detraction*, instead of right of *detention*, which occurs in the Spanish version. But in whichever mode this matter be considered, either in the English or the Spanish version, the result will always be, that in the first part of the

11th article, a perfect equality is established with the natives of the country, and nothing more, as to the right of acquiring and disposing of property in ther respective territories, "*without paying other or greater duties than those paid in like cases by the citizens of the country.*" Consequently, Mr. Drausin Harang could not dispose of his property on more favorable conditions than the other inhabitants of Puerto Rico.

The second part of the 11th article, in which the right of detraction appears to be abrogated, refers to the ancient right of advenia and detraction, which, at the time of negotiating the treaty, began to be abrogated in Europe. Thus it is seen that this abrogation is established where property fell to foreigners, "*who, in that capacity, were disqualified from holding it.*" This does not happen in the present case, since the son of Mr. Harang could hold the inheritance of his father without any legal impediment.

This interpretation of the second part of the 11th article I not only consider as logical and natural, but I also regard it as necessary; for, as it concedes to foreigners a privilege above the natives of the country, by exempting them from duties of detraction, which those pay, this part of the article would be in contradiction to the first, which establishes a complete equality upon this point between both.

I flatter myself that these considerations will satisfy your enlightened judgment, and that you will acknowledge my inability to give any other decision upon these claims, and to offer to you, before leaving this country, an evidence of my desire to please you.

I avail of this occasion to reiterate to you assurances of my distinguished consideration.

PEDRO DE PIDAL.

The MINISTER PLENIPOTENTIARY
of the United States.

Mr. Barringer to Mr. Webster.

[No. 111.] LEGATION OF THE UNITED STATES, MADRID,
November 8, 1852.

SIR: I have the honor to enclose, herewith, a communication addressed to Charles De Selding, esq., Washington city, agent for the heirs of Louis Alexander Harang, in the matter of their claim against the Spanish government. The communication is left unsealed, to be read by you, and then to be delivered to Mr. De Selding.

The amount claimed is considerable, and the principle involved is important, as the decision in this case asserts the right, under the 11th article of the treaty of 1795 with Spain, to demand and exact from American citizens in the United States, to whom inheritances in the Spanish possessions may have descended, a large per centage on the same as duties of export, ("right of detraction,") whether the said estates so descended may have been of real or personal property, situated and being in the said Spanish possessions.

The subject is respectfully submitted to your consideration.

I have to acknowledge the receipt of dispatches from the Department of State to No. 63, of the 14th August, inclusive.

I have the honor to remain, with the highest respect, sir, your obedient servant,

D. M. BARRINGER.

Hon. DANIEL WEBSTER,
Secretary of State.

Mr. Barringer to the Secretary of State.

[No. 127.] LEGATION OF THE UNITED STATES, MADRID,
February 23, 1853.

SIR: I have the honor to communicate the final decision of her Majesty's government, again rejecting the claim of the heirs and devisees of L. A. Harang, deceased, referred to in despatch No. 70 of the 3d ultimo, from the Department of State, and to transmit herewith copies of all the correspondence which has taken place between her Majesty's Minister of State and myself on the subject.

A full examination has induced me to believe that this claim is well founded and just, although so long subjected to the embarrassing delays and difficulties which are too often thrown in the way of the recovery of pecuniary demands from the Spanish government. I regret to say that, in my opinion, other and more stringent measures will be necessary if the government of the United States mean to enforce the payment of this demand. The future means of its final and satisfactory adjustment are now submitted to the government at Washington.

I have the honor to acknowledge the receipt of dispatches from the department to No. 72, (marked 71,) of the 26th ultimo, inclusive.

I have the honor to be, with the highest respect, sir, your obedient servant,

D. M. BARRINGER.

To the honorable SECRETARY OF STATE.

LEGATION OF THE UNITED STATES IN SPAIN,
Madrid, February 10, 1853.

SIR: I am instructed to present again to the attention of her Majesty's government the claim of the heirs and devisees of the late Louis Alexander Harang against the government of Spain, and to ask that it may have a prompt and favorable consideration and conclusion.

The case has been a long time pending between the two governments, and the department of which your excellency has charge is in possession of its history. My immediate predecessor brought it to the special notice of her Majesty's government in his notes to that department of the 16th and 23d July, 1839, and the reply which was then given by the Marquis of Pidal was deemed insufficient and unsatisfactory by the government of the United States. The claim is for $10,978 12½, and interest on the same, which was exacted in the year 1839, by the intendente of the island of Puerto Rico, as a tax of fifteen per cent. for the removal of the proceeds of the sale of the *real* estate owned in said island, and devised by the said Harang, a citizen of the United States, though resident for several years in the island, to his children, all of whom were born in, and at the time were resident citizens of, the United States. Against this exaction the said devisees and heirs protested at the time; and, under the auspices of the American government, soon afterward presented this claim for the repayment of the sum thus exacted. The government of the United States, looking at the clear distinction which is made in the treaty of 1795 between the proceeds of the real and personal estates of foreign residents in the island, have always insisted on the justice of this claim in the long correspondence which ensued, and a reference to which will more fully acquaint your excellency with all the facts and circumstances of its origin and prosecution. While it is clearly admitted that the personal goods of American residents in the island are liable to such dues or taxes to the government as are paid by Spanish subjects under similar circumstances, it is fully denied that the proceeds of *real* estate of American citizens are subject to any such exaction; but it is insisted that they may withdraw the same (in the language of the said treaty, article 11th) "without molestation, and exempt from all rights of detraction on the part of the government of Spain."

The consideration of this claim, as well as others which are still pending, has been postponed to other matters of more urgent importance, which have from time to time demanded my attention during the period (so important in the relation of our respective governments) of my residence at this court. I trust now, however, that it will receive the early attention of your excellency, and that a final and favorable conclusion may be given to the same.

I avail myself, &c., &c.

D. M. BARRINGER.

His Excellency COUNT OF ALCOY,
President of the Council and Minister of State.

[Translation.]

FIRST DEPARTMENT OF STATE,
Palace, February 17, 1853.

MY DEAR SIR: I have had the honor to receive your excellency's note of the 10th instant, relative to a claim of Mr. Luis Alexander Harang, for the reimbursement, by the Spanish government, of a sum of money which was exacted from him by the intendant of Porto Rico, as duty for exporting from the island certain property he possessed in it through the death of his father.

In support of the right, which your excellency says is on the side of the party interested, you cite the treaty of 1795, reproducing the argument to show that said treaty establishes a difference between personal property and real estate, by which the latter is declared exempt from the payment of 15 per cent. on exportation. This argument, as well as the other observations presented by your excellency's predecessors on taking charge of the matter, were duly answered in the note of the Marquis de Pidal, which you quote likewise, and to which I must now refer in everything. There had been previously addressed to that legation another note, dated 7th of September, 1847, communicating a decision which had been adopted conformably with the opinion of the royal council, disregarding the claim of Mr. Harang, on the grounds stated in the aforesaid note of September the 7th.

This decision, which was adopted after examining minutely all that had been alleged in favor of the claimant, all the proper formalities being observed, also put an end to the business; and it cannot be concealed from one of your excellency's enlightened mind that it is not in the power of her Majesty's government to set aside the decision aforesaid, provoking fresh discussions upon the subject which called it forth, much less to alter what is founded upon the opinion of the first consultative body of the State.

Nor are there any new arguments or facts alleged at present which could be a sufficient cause for resuscitating a question already settled. For this reason, and in view of the considerations I have set forth, I flatter myself that you will feel convinced that her Majesty's government has not acknowledged the claim of the American subject, Mr. Harang, because this would be in opposition to the rules of justice and the actual state of the matter.

I avail myself of this occasion to renew to you the assurances of my most distinguished consideration.

T. K. Y. H.

Your obedient servant,

THE COUNT DE ALCOY.

To the MINISTER PLENIPOTENTIARY
of the United States.

LEGATION OF THE UNITED STATES IN SPAIN,
Madrid, February 20, 1853.

SIR: I have had the honor to receive your excellency's note of the 16th instant, on the subject of the claim of the heirs and devisees of Luis Alexander Harang, deceased. The great length of time during which this claim has been pending, and the full examination which it has repeatedly received, as well as the declaration of your excellency that the decision heretofore made against it by her Majesty's government is reaffirmed, and now to be regarded as final and conclusive on their part, restrain me from observations which the merits of the demand might otherwise render necessary and proper.

Your excellency cannot, however, fail to perceive that there is a direct collision in the construction respectively given to the 11th article of the treaty of 1795 by the government of her Majesty and that of the United States. Under these different constructions Spanish subjects owning real estate in the latter country are enjoying advantages which are denied to the citizens of the United States in the dominions of her Catholic Majesty. This is manifest injustice. It seems to the undersigned that the distinction expressly made both in the Spanish and English text of the 11th article of that treaty between personal goods and real estate, "bienes personales y bienes raices," (a distinction between which is recognised in the legal code of every civilized nation,) is too clear to admit of a doubt, and especially when these two classes of property are contradistinguished, the one from the other, in the two paragraphs of that article, whose framers could not have employed plainer language to express their meaning. While the citizens and subjects of each party shall have power to dispose of their *personal* goods within the jurisdiction of each other, and may take possession of the same, paying such dues only as the inhabitants of the country wherein the said goods are shall be subject to pay in like cases, it is expressly declared that when, on the death of any person holding real estate within the territories of the one party, such real estate would, by the laws of the land, descend on a citizen or subject of the other, were he not disqualified by being an alien, such subjects shall be allowed a reasonable time to sell the same, and to withdraw the proceeds without molestation, exempt from all rights of detraction (derechos de retencion) on the part of the government of the respective States. This latter provision of the article embraces the very case now in question. It is unnecessary to say to your excellency that if this be the true construction of the treaty, it is not in the power of her Majesty's government, by any royal order or cedula whatsoever, or by any decision of the royal council, to change its effect without the consent of the United States. The final decision now made by her Majesty's government will be communicated immediately to that of the United States for their further advice and action in the premises.

I avail myself, &c., &c.,

D. M. BARRINGER.

His Excellency the Count of Alcoy,
President of Council and Minister of State.

Mr. Barringer to Secretary of State.

[Extract.]

[No. 129.] Legation of the United States, Madrid,
March 8, 1853.

Sir: I have the honor to transmit herewith copies of an additional note from his excellency the Spanish Minister of State, of the [25th] ultimo, and of my reply to the same, under date of the [4th] instant, on the subject of the long pending claim of the heirs of Louis Alexander Harang, deceased.

This claim originated in the year 1839. Michael D. Harang, for himself, and as attorney and agent for his brothers and sisters, having made his protest before the American consul at Ponce, in the island of Puerto Rico, on the second of March of that year, against the unlawful exaction of fifteen per cent. on the proceeds of the sale of the real estate of his father, the said L. A. Harang, by order of the intendente of that island, amounting to the sum thus taken of $10,978, 1 real and 16 maravedices.

After pending for some time in the tribunals of that island, to which Mr. Harang was directed for redress, the claim was presented to the government at Madrid, by a note from this legation, on the 27th of April, 1841. Since that time it has been the subject of much correspondence on the part of this legation, and of great and vexatious delays on the part of her Majesty's government—delays frequently and strongly complained of by my predecessor in office. In the year 1847, after taking the opinion of the royal council, the claim was rejected, and upon an application for reconsideration, was again rejected in the year 1849, and then referred by my immediate predecessor to the government at Washington for new instructions. Under these renewed instructions, received only during the present year, I deemed it my duty to present the subject at once to her Majesty's government, and, under all the circumstances of the case, to urge its immediate and favorable decision. In my dispatch, No. 127, of the 28th ultimo, I had the honor to communicate the correspondence then had by me with the Spanish government on this subject. It will be seen from that now transmitted, that the grounds of opposition to this claim, if not changed in fact, are added to by new arguments, involving most important principles in the construction of the treaty of 1795.

While the claim was originally resisted on the ground that the father and testator was a naturalized subject of Spain, (a circumstance which was not true, but which, if true, would not make the slightest difference in my opinion;) then, that in accepting the benefits of the royal cedula of 1815, he subjected himself to its consequences, one of which was the liability of this duty of "extraction" or export, on withdrawing the estate from the island; then, that there was no distinction between *personal* and *real* estate in the eleventh article of the treaty of 1795; then, that the tax exacted was not of the class referred to in that article; then, that the case was finally terminated by the decision of the royal council, with which her Majesty's government could not interfere; and by other similar objections, all of which have been successively, and, as I think, successfully answered; the Spanish government have now assumed the high ground that the stipulations of the treaty were never applicable in any manner or sense to the *colonies* of Spain; and that, even if they were, the case in question is not within the provision made in the last clause of the eleventh article of that treaty; for the heirs of Harang, the father, were not "disqualified," ("inhabiles,") as aliens, from possessing the real estate which was sold, and on the proceeds of which the tax was levied. How I have attempted to reply to these new arguments, the last of which, I freely admit, is the most plausible yet presented, will be seen by the correspondence now communicated to the department.

I am also free to say that I anticipate no favorable conclusion to this and other American claims now pending, unless other measures are adopted than those of mere official correspondence.

* * * * * * * *

I have the honor to remain sir, &c.,

D. M. BARRINGER.

Hon. SECRETARY OF STATE.

LEGATION OF THE UNITED STATES, MADRID,
March 4, 1853.

SIR: I have had the honor to receive your excellency's note of the 25th ultimo, in reference to the claim of the heirs and devisees of Alexander Harang, deceased, and will at the earliest period transmit a copy of the same to the government at Washington, to which the case has been referred for further advice and action. I cannot forbear, however, to remark briefly on the new arguments which have been adduced by your excellency in support of the decision taken by her Majesty's government on this subject.

In the first place, it is now insisted that the provisions of the treaty of 1795 do not extend to the colonies of her Majesty's government, but are confined in their operation to the peninsula; and that, inasmuch as there never has been any prohibition against foreigners holding real estate in the peninsula, the last clause of the eleventh article can only be considered as applicable to cases arising in the United States, where such prohibition does exist.

To this it is sufficient to answer, that there is no exception of the colonies of Spain in the terms of the treaty; on the contrary, its language is as comprehensive as possible, embracing within its operation the "dominions," "territories," "jurisdictions," "citizens and subjects," of both the high contracting parties, "*without exception of persons or places.*"

The territory of Louisiana itself, to which reference is made in the treaty, was then a *colony* of Spain. That its stipulations extended to the Spanish colonial possessions has never been denied, as far as I am aware, by either power, from its date in 1795, to the present time. Such has been the understanding ever since. Commerce has been conducted; claims presented and adjusted; judicial proceedings, both criminal and civil, instituted and terminated, not only without objection on this account, but for the very reason that such subjects, although arising in the colonies of Spain, are embraced by the treaty. Indeed the provisions of this treaty furnish the chief guarantee for the security of the rights of person and property in every part and jurisdiction of the two nations. What would be the condition of American citizens in the island of Cuba or Puerto Rico, without the stipulations of the seventh, twentieth, and other articles of that treaty? It is too late to say that it does not extend to the colonies of her Catholic Majesty, and against the conclusion of your excellency I do most earnestly protest, as contradicted by the words of the treaty itself, by the general understanding and practice under it ever since, and as jeoparding the highest and most important interests of American citizens, having commercial or other transactions with these colonies.

As to the construction of the particular clause in question, its very language manifestly shows that it was not intended to be confined in its operation to cases arising *in the United States only*. The expressions used are reciprocal and mutual, referring to the "citizens and subjects" of either government, and declaring that, in the case provided for, the proceeds of the property sold may be withdrawn by the heir without molestation, and exempt from all rights of "detraction" on the part of the governments of the "*respective States,*" ("sin obstaculo exerto de todo derecho de retencion de parte del gobierno de los estados respectivos.") If, then, this provision could not extend, as your excellency says, to the peninsula, because no such prohibition to hold real estate by a foreigner ever existed here, it must necessarily embrace the other and colonial territories of her Catholic Majesty, for certainly the territories of *both States* respetively are referred to and embraced in this clause of the treaty. But I contend, and respectfully submit to your excellency, that this provision of the treaty extends to *all* the possessions of her Catholic Majesty, *peninsula and colonial;* for although a prohibition to hold real estate, (bienes raices,) on the part of a foreigner has not yet existed in the peninsula, it does not follow that such prohibition may not hereafter be created by law, to take effect not only here, but in the colonies of Spain. In fact, we find that in the year 1815 it was deemed wise and necessary to provide by royal cedula of that year for the possession and occupation of real estate by foreigners as colonists, in the island of Puerto Rico.

And this brings me to the other principal argument of your excellency, to wit: That, admitting the stipulations of the treaty to extend to the colonies of Spain, this claim is not well founded, because not within the case provided for by the last clause of the 11th article of the treaty, for Mr. Harang was compelled to pay the duties of the products of the sale, not because the heirs of his father *could* not, but because they *would* not, possess the estate thus sold. In answer to this objection, I ask, how could the heirs have taken possession of this property except under the royal cedula of 1815, which cannot contradict or vary the terms of the treaty, and which could only apply to colonists from Spain or other countries, except the United States, for whose citizens, to whom the real estate might descend in case of the death of the first owner, provision was already made by the treaty? But this circumstance does not alter or weaken the argument, that when the case provided for by the treaty arises, whether under or independent of this royal order or any other law, the foreign heir is entitled to all the benefits of such provision, free from all condition, "*obstacle*," burden, or *tax* not therein stipulated. Spain could not make a law to impair or vary the full effect of the treaty in any respect, without the consent of the United States, so far as concerns the rights and privileges of the citizens of the latter under the same. In the case provided for by the 11th article, the person who would be the heir of the citizen or subject of either country, native or naturalized, holding real estate in the same, were he not disqualified by being an alien from possessing the same, shall be allowed a reasonable time to sell and collect the proceeds of the property, and to withdraw the same to his own country, without hinderance, or tax, or *condition* of any kind inconsistent with his residence or other privilege in his own nation. It is sufficient to bring such person within the provision of this article, that by the laws of the land such real estate would *descend* on him were he not an alien, (estos raices llegasen á pasar este por su calidad de estrangero fues inhabil para poscerlos.) Notwithstanding the apparent difference in the Spanish and English text of the treaty, this I take to be the substantial purport and meaning of the article. No change of residence is required on the part of the heir; no new conditions are allowed, other than such as are in conformity with the treaty itself. What is the case under the royal cedula of 1815? This royal order was intended to aid the colonization of the Spanish possessions beyond sea—to people with whites the islands of Cuba, Poto Rico, and St. Domingo. The privileges granted were *personal* to the colonists, who were required to be residents and established in the islands, and could not leave it, after a residence of five years, to live in their former country. These colonists could, it is true, leave their property, if they died in the island without forced heirs, to their relations or friends, wherever they might reside; and their successors might enjoy the privileges conceded to their testators, or the original colonists, if they would *establish themselves* in the island. But if they preferred to withdraw the inheritance, and did so after the testator had been established five years within the island, they must pay the 15 per cent., as improperly exacted from Mr. Harang. It is manifest that this is not the case provided for by the treaty, which simply required that the claimant should be the person to whom the inheritance would descend were he not an alien, and which exacted no change of residence from his own country to be entitled to its benefits. Whatsoever provisions existed in this or any other royal cedula, contrary to those of the treaty of 1795, were void and of no effect, with respect to the rights of the citizens of the United States, without the consent and concurrence of the latter; and it is not in the power of her Majesty's government to transfer a claim properly arising under the treaty, to other and different and contradictory provisions of the royal cedula of 1815, which was made and declared for another and wholly separate purpose. For these and other reasons contained in the previous correspondence of this legation with her Majesty's government on this subject, I cannot concur in the conclusion to which your excellency has arrived against the validity of this claim.

I avail myself of this occasion, &c., &c., &c.,

D. M. BARRINGER.

His Excellency the COUNT OF ALCOY,
President of the Council and Minister of State.

Mr. Barringer to the Secretary of State.

[No. 133.] LEGATION OF THE UNITED STATES, MADRID,
March 26, 1853.

SIR: I have the honor to transmit herewith copies of a note from her Majesty's Minister of State of the 16th instant, and of my reply to the same, under date of the 19th instant, and of the final note of the former, dated 24th instant, on the subject of the claim of the heirs and devisees of L. A. Harang, deceased, referred to in my dispatches, No. 127, of 23d ultimo, and No. 129, of the 8th instant, to the Department of State.

As it is now useless to attempt here to reverse the decision of her Majesty's government in this case, it is referred to the government of the United States for their further action in the premises, if deemed necessary or proper.

This claim has now assumed a high degree of importance, not so much from its pecuniary amount, though this is not inconsiderable, as from the magnitude of the principles involved, and especially from the position recently but solemnly taken by her Majesty's government, that the *treaty of 27th October*, 1795, *is not, and never was, applicable to the Spanish colonies*—a position which, with all its serious consequences, is respectfully submitted to the prompt and grave consideration of the government of the United States.

I have the honor to be, with the highest respect, sir, your obedient servant,

D. M. BARRINGER.

The Hon. SECRETARY OF STATE.

The Count of Alcoy to Mr. Barringer.

[Translation.]

FIRST DEPARTMENT OF STATE,
Palace, March 16, 1853.

SIR: I have had the honor to receive the note of your excellency, dated the 4th instant, in reply to mine of the 25th ultimo, relative to the claim of the heirs of the American citizen, Mr. Harang.

Although in the actual state of this affair a prolonged discussion seems to be unnecessary, nevertheless, certain principles having been affirmed by your excellency in the course of your remarks, which I do not consider that the government of her Majesty can admit, it is indispensable for me to enter again into the discussion, proposing, in so doing, to follow the same order in which your excellency is pleased to present your arguments.

In the first place, your excellency, maintaining that the stipulations of the treaty of 1795 comprehended the Spanish colonies, in support of this opinion, limits yourself to citing the words of the treaty, according to which the exception affirmed in my note does not appear.

In order that your excellency should allow the erroneousness of this opinion, it will be sufficient to observe, that when the treaty under consideration was made, every kind of intercourse between our colonies and foreign subjects was absolutely prohibited by the laws of the Indies; and this so express prohibition, which, by no stipulation of the treaty, was declared revoked, made unnecessary all explanation upon the fact that the said treaty was only applicable to the territory of the peninsula; in proof of which it was sufficient to consider, that in order that its provisions might extend to the territory of Louisiana, then a Spanish colony, it was necessary that a declaration to that effect should intervene, otherwise that colony would have remained comprehended in the general exception which then existed with respect to all.

As to the surprise which it seems was caused to your excellency by the principle affirmed in my former note, that the treaties cannot refer to those dominions, your excellency will permit me to say, that I do not comprehend that surprise, seeing that your excellency might have observed the difference between the usages established for the peninsula and those which are in force beyond sea, as well in the manner in which foreign consuls exercise their functions, as with respect to shipwrecks, intestate successions by the subjects of other countries, and other matters comprehended in the general administration in those points in which the stipulations of the treaties exercise their influence. Such a difference demonstrates that the colonies are not within the common law; and this being so, it could hardly be said that the stipulations of the treaties are alike applicable in all the territory of the Spanish dominions.

Upon this same point your excellency solemnly protests, adding that it is already too late for the government of her Majesty to make the declaration that the treaties are not extensive to the colonies. Your excellency will permit me to express my judgment that the protest, rather than the declaration, may be regarded as inconsiderate, (or extemporaneous,) this being sufficiently proved by the declaration of the government at Washington itself, stated in a recent note addressed by Mr. Everett to Señor Calderon, dated the 5th of February last.

Says the Minister of Foreign Affairs of the Confederation: "The treaty of 1795, if applicable to the colonies of Spain, which is not admitted by the government of her Catholic Majesty."

Such language shows clearly that to the government at Washington the declaration against which your excellency protests was not new, seeing that upon this is based its proposition for a reform of the treaty of 1795.

Limiting myself now to the particular clause of article 11th of this treaty, upon which it is pretended to found the right of Mr. Harang, I cannot do less than insist upon what I had the honor to expose to your excellency, that said clause cannot refer in any way to the colonial dominions of her Majesty. That clause was necessarily made reciprocal, and justly so, in provision of the case that the alien should be prohibited from holding real estate in the peninsula; but never could it comprehend the colonies, because these were closed, as I have said, to all foreign intercourse at the time the treaty was made.

Although subsequently the royal letters patent of 1815 changed the condition of that part of the Spanish territory, it was not, on that account, comprehended in the stipulations of the treaty; and although these stipulations may have been applicable there, in so far as they refer to the general obligations which serve as a basis to the relations of friendship, they have not been applicable, nor can they be, in so far as they conflict with the provisions of the said royal letters patent. These letters, published by the Spanish government, in the use and free exercise of its power to administer the affairs of the colonies according as it might deem best, did not provoke any protest on the part of any nation, nor from the United States—an evident proof that all recognised, as could not be otherwise, the independence of Spain to legislate in her colonies without attention or subjection to anterior treaties.

In support of what I have just said, another consideration offers itself, which comes in to destroy the reflections contained in the last part of the note of your excellency, in which it is pretended that although the Spanish occupants of land, or those of other countries, might be subjected to the payment of the duties on the exportation of an inheritance, the Anglo-Americans, citizens of the Union, ought to be exempt from such duties.

In order to give to the clause of the treaty referred to the interpretation which your excellency indicates, it will be necessary to place the citizens of the United States in a better condition even than the Spanish subjects; and such a situation, contrary to the rules of equity and to the exactions of self-respect, would have no better foundation than a stipulation inapplicable to the colonies, and which, even if it were applicable, would not comprehend cases of the kind of this of Mr. Harang, because the treaty makes no reference to property acquired under the condition of colonist-settlers on the land. With respect to such property, as advantages were enjoyed for its acquisition not in general conceded, compensations were also imposed, which depend in a certain degree upon the will of the alien; since, whilst he has the power to hold the property, only in the case of withdrawing its proceeds by a spontaneous act, is he obliged to pay the compensation for the benefits received.

If the Spanish government could have believed that the Anglo-Americans were not subject to the payment of the duty on exportation, it would have from the first moment excluded them from the privileges conceded by the royal letters patent of 1815, because it would have been highly unjust, not to say absurd, that the benefits should be extended to them, and not at the same time the burdens.

I will conclude by manifesting to your excellency that I have not been able to see without regret the turn which has been given to this affair, already determined, and which was believed to be abandoned for many years, and that a discussion already exhausted is still persisted in, since it may perhaps reveal a disposition little friendly, and little in harmony with that moderation and forbearance which the government of her Majesty employs when it addresses itself to that of the United States, on subjects of greater importance, and infinitely more clear in their justice, than that which is the object of this correspondence.

I avail myself of this occasion to renew to your excellency the assurance of my most distinguished consideration, &c., &c., &c.,

THE COUNT OF ALCOY.

To the Minister Plenipotentiary,
of the United States.

Mr. Barringer to Count Alcoy.

Legation of the United States, Madrid,
March 19, 1853.

Sir: I have had the honor to receive your excellency's note of the 16th instant, in reply to mine of the 4th of same month, on the subject of the claim of the heirs of L. A. Harang, deceased. It is not my purpose, in this communication, to renew the discussion on the merits of the claim itself, both because, in the argument of your excellency, I find nothing new on a subject already exhausted, and more especially because I do not deem it either becoming or useful to enlarge on a question which your excellency has been pleased to repeat to me is now finally determined *("ya resuelto")* by her Majesty's government. Your excellency will pardon me for saying, however, that it is a great mistake on the part of your excellency to suppose that this claim has ever been "abandoned" at any time by the government of the United States, much less for "many years." On the contrary, it will be seen from one of the last notes addressed by my predecessor to the department in the worthy charge of your excellency, that it was still to be prosecuted. Neither can any inference of abandonment be drawn from the length of time it has been pending; for such an argument would be fatal to most of the claims of American citizens presented and now urged upon her Majesty's government for final adjudication and satisfaction. If this claim has been a long time undecided, a reference to the correspondence will show that it has not been for the want of urgency on the part of this legation or the government of the United States; though I am happy to be able to do your excellency the justice to say, that since it has been brought to the attention of your excellency, it has received the most prompt consideration, as well as other matters which it has been my duty to bring to the notice of her Majesty's government during the period of your excellency's administration. As to the course *("giro")* which this discussion has taken, I must be allowed to say, that, while I am conscious of nothing inconsistent with the most friendly sentiments towards her Majesty's government, and least of all towards your excellency, and of nothing incompatible with the calm and impassioned style of diplomatic correspondence, I must nevertheless always reserve to myself the right of judging what is due in such correspondence, not only to myself and the much more important interests of my countrymen, but also to a proper respect for my own as well as the government which it is my duty to address under a just sense of all these responsibilities.

As to the great principle now for the first time invoked in bar to this claim, and compared with which the claim itself, though important to the petitioners, is as nothing, viz: *that the treaty of 1795 was never applicable to the Spanish colonies*, I cannot do less than repeat my surprise at a proposition, which a review of all the diplomatic intercourse between Spain and the United States will disclose, is of the most recent origin; which is contrary to what has ever been the understanding of the latter; and which, in the opinion of the undersigned, is not sustained by any examination of the provisions of the treaty itself, nor by its contemporaneous or subsequent history or construction. It is not my intention to be led into a general, though incidental, discussion of so grave a question on this much less important claim; still, I cannot forbear to remark, that if this objection be well founded, it is at once clearly a full and ready answer to a demand which is solely and originally founded on the eleventh article of that very treaty. Yet in all the previous discussion, and among the many and various arguments which have been urged against the validity of this claim since the year 1839, both in the island of Porto Rico, where it was examined by the judicial tribunals, and at this court, where it has been the subject of so much correspondence, this objection, so obvious to your excellency, and which must have been so to others, if true, has never been once suggested till urged in the note of your excellency of the 25th ultimo.

In the full examination given to the case by the Marquis of Pidal, so generally known for his acuteness as a jurist and his ability as a statesman, this plain objection escaped his astute and profound research, and his arguments were based on the proposition, that while the eleventh article of the treaty was indeed (as well as others) applicable to the colonies, the claim of the heirs of Harang did not come within its provisions. It would be difficult to find a single admission on the part of the United States that the principle now contended for is correct; and equally difficult, I think, to meet with a similar declaration on the part of her Majesty's government, until within a very recent period. On the contrary, the correspondence between the two governments is full of admissions that the treaty is applicable to the Spanish *colonies* as well as the peninsula. It is not necessary to refer to these more specifically at this time. Such has hitherto been the understanding of both parties to the treaty. Under this construction American consuls have been admitted, shipwrecks provided for, inheritances allowed, judicial proceedings regulated, and commercial intercourse permitted and controlled between the United States and these colonies. No "law of the Indies," then existing or subsequently enacted, could avoid and make null the stipulations of the treaty as to the rights therein secured to the citizens of the United States. As to the contracting parties themselves, such a compact is the *supreme law*, not to be abrogated by the *separate* legislation of either, or without the consent of *both*. But I refrain from further observation on this grave subject, with the single remark, that if, indeed, this treaty be not applicable to the colonies of Spain, it is surely time, as indicated by Mr. Everett in the *portion* of a sentence which your excellency quotes in his note of the 5th ultimo, to the Spanish minister at Washington, that it should be "*reformed*," as well for the continuance of the friendship and sentiments of harmony which now animate both governments, as for the best interests of their respective citizens and subjects.

I avail myself of this occasion to renew to your excellency the assurance of my most distinguished consideration.

Your excellency's obedient servant,

D. M. BARRINGER.

To his Excellency the COUNT OF ALCOY,
President of the Council and Minister of State.

[Translation.]

FIRST DEPARTMENT OF STATE,
Palace, *March* 24, 1853.

MY DEAR SIR: I have had the honor to receive the note of your excellency of the 19th instant, relative to the claim of Mr. Harang, and there being no reasons alleged, nor arguments presented, which have not been answered in my previous notes in regard to said reclamation, I must confine myself to reasserting all that is set forth in them, in support of the justice with which her Majesty's government thinks it has proceeded in this matter.

I avail myself of this occasion to renew to you the assurances of my most distinguished consideration.

T. K. Y. H.

Your obedient servant,

THE COUNT ALCOY.

The MINISTER PLENIPOTENTIARY *of the United States.*

Mr. Gallaher to Mr. Forsyth.

[No. 11.] CONSULATE OF THE U. S., PONCE, PORTO RICO, *November* 23, 1838.

SIR: I beg leave respectfully to call your attention to a claim made by the government of this island of fifteen per cent. upon the property of all persons, citizens of other countries than of Spain, who may wish to leave the island, and to carry away their property with them. This claim, although founded on the "real cedula" of August 10, 1815, is considered by the Americans and Frenchmen resident here as very oppressive, and as not treating them with the privileges which citizens of Spain enjoy in the United States and France.

A demand of from $45,000 to $50,000, made by this government the past week on the property of five individuals, deposited in the hands of the French vice-consul in Ponce, to be paid within twenty-four hours, having been resisted by him, the decision of the legality of the demand has been referred to the action of the French and Spanish governments.

It has been thought by my countrymen here that the simultaneous action of the American government would have a highly beneficial effect on the interests of American citizens residing at Porto Rico.

I have the honor to be, with great respect, your obedient servant,

J. C. GALLAHER.

Hon. JOHN FORSYTH,
Secretary of State, Washington.

CASE OF THE SEAMEN BELONGING TO THE BRIG JASPER.

Mr. Robertson to Mr. Marcy.

[No. 36.] CONSULATE OF THE UNITED STATES, HAVANA, *July* 6, 1853.

SIR: I have the honor to enclose you herewith a copy of a correspondence concerning three American sailors, who are now imprisoned in Havana. The three men are undoubtedly Americans, and make the following statement: "We sailed from New York on the 12th of last December, in the American barque "Jasper," Captain Townsend, bound for Sierra Leone; had on board rum, sugar, and other merchandise of lawful trade, as we believed. We did not go to Sierra Leone, but into another port, called Elmina, in Africa, where part of the cargo was landed;

then we proceeded to Cape Coast, where another part of the cargo was landed, and some other cargo taken in; we then went to another port and landed what cargo we had on board, except some twenty or thirty casks of rum; we then sailed for another place, where we were told by Captain Townsend that he had sold his ship. To our astonishment, about five minutes after arrival, we saw boats coming towards us with negroes; we thought at first that they were coming to take the ship from us; afterwards thought that they might be coming for purposes of trade, as we had still on board some twenty or thirty casks of rum, which were placed upon other casks, which, when taken in at the former place, we had supposed to contain rum, but turned out to have nothing but water. We then discovered that we were in a ship engaged in the slave trade, and demanded to go ashore. Captain Townsend paid us three months' extra wages, saying that he had made a losing voyage; told us that he could no longer protect us, and advised us to go back in the vessel as passengers, as we should either be killed by the natives or starved to death if we went ashore. We then had no other recourse but to remain on the ship, on which we did duty as sailors, and were very badly treated. A cargo of nearly 300 negroes was put on board—part of the negroes were on board before Captain Townsend had left the vessel to go ashore. The vessel then sailed for Cuba; used no flag on the passage to Cuba, but a Spanish flag was made on the way; and when we went into a place, the name of which we cannot recollect, where the slaves were landed and taken charge of by other parties, the Spanish flag was hoisted. After the cargo was landed the vessel put off and got aground, but was taken off. She soon after grounded again; we suspect it was done purposely, but are not sure. We worked to get her off without success; she was then burnt. We all went ashore. When there, the mate, a Spaniard, told us that he could do nothing for us but give us the long-boat, and told us to try and find our way. There was an Englishman, Radcliffe, in the party, who said that he intended to lay his case before the admiralty. The captain and officers were Spaniards; there was one man that they used to call Loper, and another Dionisio, but we believe these were assumed names. We never heard the captain's name on board, but subsequently heard that it was José Cortés. We took the long-boat, intending to proceed to Key West, but afterwards determined to go to the nearest place where we could find an American consul. Being short of water and provisions, we put up at Cape Antonio; while there, some people went and advised some troops stationed a short distance off, who came and arrested us. This was on the 5th of May. We were conveyed in our boat, guarded by soldiers, and delivered to a Spanish schooner of war, which kept us in the stocks, after her commander had asked us several questions, several days, then sent us to Havana, where we were detained about eight days on board the ship that fires a gun every night at 8 o'clock. We were subsequently, that is, last Saturday, put into this jail. When we were taken on the schooner, knowing that the slave trade was contrary to law, being ignorant of the Spanish laws, and being afraid that if we were discovered to have been engaged in that trade we should be in trouble, we evaded all the questions by saying that we had come from Jamaica."

The above is an outline of their statement, collected through the bars of the prison, and there may be some errors and omissions, but I believe I have given a full statement. Their declarations will be important, so far as Captain Townsend and other parties in the United States are concerned. From my conversations with the seamen, I entertain no doubt of their innocence. At the same time I feel apprehensive that there will be great delay in granting my request, if granted at all. Should this prove to be the case, and as the men complain of most brutal treatment, and are confined in a room with some thirty or forty criminals, I must request the favor of specific instructions on this subject. In the mean time I shall urge the permission to take their declarations; and, if I find them innocent, and the declarations important, shall then urge their immediate delivery to me, to be sent to the authorities of the United States.

As the vessel that has been engaged in the slave trade is the barque "Jasper," which was detained here for a long time by Judge Sharkey, I beg leave to refer to his communication to the department of July 7, 1852, numbered 9.

I have the honor to be, with great respect, your obedient servant,

WM. H. ROBERTSON,
Vice-consul, in charge of the Consulate.

Hon. Wm. L. Marcy,
Secretary of State.

Sir: There are three of us, Americans, that were picked up at Cape Antonio on the 5th of May last, and since that time have been confined, and are now lying in the Havana prison. We ask of you, sir, if you would favor us with an interview. We wish to state to you our case as it was, which is very plain, and can be spoken in a few words.

Yours, respectfully,

WILLIAM FREEBURN,
WILLIAM ATKINS,
HARVEY PARKS.

Consulate of the United States, Havana,
July 5, 1853.

Most Excellent Sir: On the afternoon of the day before yesterday I received a communication from William Atkins, William Freeburn, and Harvey Parks, three American seamen now in the royal jail of this city, requesting me to call on them at the jail, and hear their statement of the circumstances under which they have been imprisoned, and also the circumstances that led to it. I have repaired to the prison at their request, and learned sufficient from them to make it important that I should take their declarations at the office of this consulate; and for this purpose I have to request the favor of your excellency to permit these three men to come to my office, to be examined by me.

This consulate has received two communications in regard to these men from his excellency the commander-in-chief of her Catholic Majesty's naval forces, &c., at Havana; one, dated 18th of May, informing my predecessor, Mr. Sharkey, of their arrest at Cape San Antonio, of their having been delivered to her Majesty's schooner "Habenera," of their statements on board of that vessel, and of his excellency's having given orders for their being brought to this port, which determination of his excellency, the consul, Mr. Sharkey, deemed the best and most proper course, and so wrote to his excellency, with some other remarks. The other communication is of the 27th of June last, transmitting to me a copy of what the commanding officer of the "Habanera" wrote to his excellency he had ascertained about these men; and his excellency further informed me in his communication that the men had under that date been placed at your excellency's disposal. When I received this communication, it was at first my intention to have written to your excellency upon the subject, but thought that it was proper to await your excellency's communication to me, as the men were accused, though vaguely, of having infringed the laws of Spain, and some time would be necessary to investigate the affair. Not having had the honor of receiving any notice on the subject from your excellency, and the men having assured me that they are innocent of any intention to infringe either the laws of the United States or Spain, I feel it a duty to obtain as soon as possible all the reliable aud trustworthy information that may lead to their being released, if innocent as they say they are, from their painful situation, which is made more so by being placed (as they are in the prison) in company with men whom they naturally dislike, and who from prejudices or other causes have contributed to make their life disagreeable.

I have the honor to be, with great respect, your excellency's most obedient servant,

WM. H. ROBERTSON.

Commercial Agent in charge of the Consulate of the United States.

His Excellency Sr. Don VALENTIN CAÑEDO,

Governor and Captain General of the Island of Cuba,

&c., &c., &c.

Mr. Robertson to Mr. Marcy.

[No. 41.] CONSULATE OF THE UNITED STATES, HAVANA,

July 11, 1853.

SIR: I beg leave to call your attention to the annexed copy of a communication that I received yesterday morning from the Captain General, in reply to mine of the 5th, in relation to the three American seamen now in prison, of whom I treated in my letter to you of the 6th instant, numbered 36.

You will perceive that the Captain General expresses a regret that he cannot accede to my wishes, as the affair being one concerning the landing on this island of negroes from Africa, in a vessel which was set fire to after having effected the landing, and the men in question having formed a part of her crew, the investigation of it belongs to the real audiencia pretorial (superior court of judicature,) and the Captain

General asserts that he has not the power to intermeddle in affairs of that nature. He also tells me that he has transmitted my communication to that court. In the mean time the men remain in prison, but the Captain General having stated that the affair is undergoing examination before the proper court, and as I am recognised as a mere commercial agent, I have no authority to push the matter, unless positive instructions reach me from the State Department. I again beg of you to transmit them as soon as possible.

I have the honor to be, sir, very respectfully, your obedient servant,

W. H. ROBERTSON,
Vice-consul, in charge of the consulate.

Hon. WM. L. MARCY,
Secretary of State, Washington.

[Translation.]

[L. S.]

ALWAYS FAITHFUL ISLAND OF CUBA.—CAPTAIN GENERAL AND GOVERNMENT'S OFFICE, POLITICAL DEPARTMENT, SECTION FIFTH.

I have received your communication of the 5th instant, and I regret that I cannot accede to your wishes, as it is not in my power to interfere with matters of which the royal pretorial audience has cognizance, and which belongs to its jurisdiction, in conformity with a very recent law concerning the suppression of the slave traffic, in regard to the legal proceedings which he understands to refer to the landing of negroes at Bailen, which have been imported from Africa in a vessel that was burnt, of the crew of which the sailors, William Atkins or Ackiam, William Freeburn or Firbourn, and Harvey Parks or Pencas, in whose behalf you are interesting yourself. Nevertheless, I have this day transmitted to said superior tribunal your communication aforesaid, to be disposed of as it may be thought proper, and this is the reply I have to make to you on the subject.

God preserve you a thousand years. Havana, July 8, 1853.

VALENTIN CAÑEDO.

To the COMMERCIAL AGENT
of the United States.

Mr. Robertson to Mr. Marcy.

CONSULATE OF THE UNITED STATES, HAVANA,
July 13, 1853.

SIR: This morning I received a visit from * * * who read me a letter, dated on the 9th inst., in which the writer says there are still six of the crew on the Cortés key, of the bark Jasper, (Americans.) The writer intimates that he has had a conversation with them, and that they are almost in a state of desperation, and apprehensive that they are destined to be assassinated, and were beseeching assistance to be relieved. * * * regretted that there were no men of war in port, or he would send one down, and as soon as one came in he would despatch her down there, and find them or their graves. On the receipt of this information I repaired to the prison, and found the three prisoners in the same den as before, and also ascertained that they had left on said key John William Leo, from Palmyra, New York, near Niagara Falls; George Hunt, a colored man, from the State of Maine; William Huzzy, or Huzzing, of Nantucket; Charles Robinson, who reported himself from Canada; John Radcliffe, an Englishman, who had recently been discharged from a man of war; and William Hersey, of Yarmouth, Nova Scotia. A Mr. John Brown went out as mate, but quarrelled with Captain Edward Townsend, and was discharged at Cape Coast. These, with the three prisoners, were all the crew that left New York. They tell me they were thirty-five days on board of the man of war schooner "Habanera," near Cape San Antonio; the day they came on board they requested permission to communicate with an American consul, but were denied the permission. They state, also, that they have recently been examined by the Spanish authorities, severely questioned and cross-questioned, and Atkins thinks they have put down in their declarations more than was related. They also say, that the Spanish captain, mate, supercargo, and one other, all went passengers in the Jasper from New York.

* * * * * likewise informed me, that he was aware that four different commissions have been sent down to the neighborhood where the Jasper landed her cargo, and that four different reports have been made that no such vessel has been on the coast; at the same time he * * * * is in possession of all the facts.

You will perceive the dilemma in which these three prisoners are placed under such official reports.

I have just been informed that the United States sloop of war Albany is coming into this port.

Since the above was written I have been on board the Albany, and informed Capt. Gerry of the condition of the three men in prison, and of the circumstances that led to their imprisonment, &c. Capt. Gerry has promised me that he will call at my office to morrow, examine the papers in relation to the subject, and then address the Captain General. I regret very much that I shall not have it in my power to communicate to you, by this mail, Captain Gerry's course, as the steamer Cherokee will sail to-morrow morning at 8 o'clock; but everything will be laid before you by the earliest opportunity.

I have the honor to be, sir, with great respect, your obedient servant,

WM. H. ROBERTSON.

Hon. Wm. L. Marcy,
Secretary of State.

Eight o'clock, P. M.

At the moment of enclosing this communication, I have received a letter from the British consul general.

Commander J. T. Gerry, U. S. N., to Mr. Dobbin.

U. S. Ship Albany, Havana,
July 15, 1853.

Sir: Upon my arrival at St. Juan de Nicaragua, May 30th, I addressed a hasty communication to the commander-in-chief of the home squadron, by the steamer Daniel Webster, then under way, but at my request remained until I had closed the letter-bag to be sent by her. Upon a further acquaintance with the authorities at Greytown, and agents of the transit company, all of whom made an early call upon me, I clearly saw the necessity of a mediator to bring the two parties to a mutual friendly intercourse, and better understanding of each other's rights and views of subjects in dispute, and expressed my readiness to intercede and bring about a better feeling, provided each party stated to me all grievances, and consented to be influenced by my advice and opinion. The result fully convinced me that both parties had acted under strongly excited feelings, and that the one was quite as much in fault as the other; the inhabitants of Greytown certainly being entitled to more consideration than the transit company had extended to them, by whose invitation, and inducements held out to them, many had made large investments for accommodating the passengers of this company when the latter were unable to do so, and depended solely upon the conveniences to be found in Greytown. I am happy to say that the results of my investigations were attended with the most favorable consequences.

On the 5th of May I sailed from St. Juan, leaving all parties apparently friends, and with a determination of settling every point of controversy between them in future by arbitration, and not by violence. Shortly after my arrival the mayor informed me, that if I desired, a marine who had deserted from the Cyane to be apprehended, he would order him in custody of an officer on board of my ship the following morning, which was promptly complied with as set forth. From St. Juan to a little past the meridian of Carthagena, eastward, I experienced very light airs, calms, strong counter currents, and off-shore squalls, by taking advantage of which we made this distance by the 17th, and then encountered the very strong winds which constantly blow along the whole extent of the coast between Santa Martha and Carthagena during this season of the year, amounting to perfect gales, and obliging vessels to carry a heavy press of canvass to hold their own, and gain to windward; I was six days making less than three degrees to the eastward, and unavoidably split five or six of my sails, the roping being found defective and actually rotten. We continued using every exertion to get to windward, but with very little success, until the 27th of May, when finding that we had only twenty-eight days of bread and board, and had no prospect of reaching La Guayra in less than three, and probably five weeks, I reluctantly gave up the idea, and proceeded directly to St. Jago de Cuba, the next port of my destination, where we arrived June 30th, my crew showing many indications of scurvy, and officers nearly worn down by the effects of this trying climate and deprivation of the requisite refreshments.

I ordered a supply of bread baked without delay, and fresh provisions for the crew, who also had a fine opportunity of supplying themselves with fruit, &c. On the evening of July 3d, I received on board sixteen hundred pounds of bread, and sailed at daylight on the 4th for this port. Only one case of scurvy made its appearance among my crew, which being quickly attended to was soon cured. I have been reducced very low in watch officers, having, after passed midshipman Seawell was detached by order of the commander-in-chief of the Home Squadron just before I sailed, only two watch lieutenants and the master; and, on one occasion, all three of my lieutenants, the surgeon and a midshipman, who had been keeping day watch in charge of the deck, upon the sick report. We arrived here on the 13th instant, saluted the national flag and admiral as usual, and yesterday paid all official visits prior to opening a correspondence with the Captain General relating to the confinement of three American seamen, the particulars of which I herewith enclose.

The order of June 9th, from Commodore Newton, was delivered to me by the vice consul—the consul being absent in the United States.

The former consul, before his successor relieved him, had transmitted to the State Department all the facts in relation to the "Schooner Manchester" which had come to his knowledge, but did not corroborate the statement made by her captain and mate, and put a different construction upon the whole matter. The consular records were submitted to my inspection, and from the perusal of all the correspondence upon this subject, and communications to the State Department, was satisfied that further investigation by me was unnecessary.

Very respectfully, I have the honor to be, sir, your obedient servant,

JAMES T. GERRY, *Commander*,
Commanding U. S. Ship Albany.

Hon. Jas. C. Dobbin,
Secretary of the Navy, Washington, D. C.

United States Ship Albany, Havana,
July 18, 1853.

Most excellent Sir: The commercial agent in charge of the consulate of the United States in this city has read to me the contents of the communication that your excellency addressed him on the 16th instant, in reply to my official letter to your excellency of the previous day. I regret very much that your excellency did not think proper to address your reply to me direct, and also that the request made by me has not been acceded to by your excellency.

I am aware that the said commercial agent has made the request of your excellency to be permitted to take the depositions of the American seamen, Harvey Parks, William Freeburn, and William Atkins, prisoners in the royal jail, under accusation of having infringed the laws of Spain, which request was refused by your excellency because they had been placed in the hands of the superior court for trial; still it becomes my duty to urge upon the consideration of your excellency the importance of that request being granted, to promote the ends of justice in my own country, which, by delay, may be defeated. I would also state, that I cannot perceive how the taking of such depositions can interfere with the proceedings of the superior court in the investigation of their case.

I have the honor to be, very respectfully, your excellency's obedient servant,

JAMES T. GERRY,
Commander U. S. Navy, commanding U. S. ship Albany.

His Excellency
The GOVERNOR AND CAPTAIN GENERAL *of Cuba, &c.*

UNITED STATES SHIP ALBANY, HARBOR OF HAVANA,
July 15, 1853.

MOST EXCELLENT SIR: The commercial agent in charge of the consulate of the United States for the port and city of Havana, has given me official information that three American seamen, named William Atkins, Harvey Parks, and William Freeburn, are now imprisoned in the public jail of this city, accused, though very vaguely, of having been a part of the crew of a vessel that imported and landed near Bailen, in this island, a cargo of negroes from Africa. Upon receipt of that information I called at the jail, saw the men, questioned and cross-questioned them in regard to their places of nativity, and made them relate to me all of the circumstances that led to their imprisonment. The result of my inquiries has been, that I have become perfectly convinced that they are native-born American citizens; that they are entirely innocent of any intention of infringing either the laws of the United States or of Spain; and that those who are in reality the guilty parties are somewhere else. For my part, I entertain no doubt that some of the parties who got up the expedition to go for the cargo of Africans, and who deceived the unfortunate men now imprisoned, making them believe that they were going upon a lawful voyage, are now in the United States.

It is therefore of the utmost importance that these parties be tried, convicted, and punished for their nefarious and disgraceful proceedings. To secure their conviction, it will be necessary to produce in court the witnesses that can, under oath, give clear and succinct statements of all the circumstances connected with the case.

The men now in the prison of Havana, and their shipmates, if to be found, are the very witnesses that would be required. I feel it a duty, therefore, to express to your excellency my opinion of the innocence of the seamen Atkins, Parks, and Freeburn, and to request that your excellency will order that they be delivered to me, for the purpose of placing them at the disposal of my government. I have also been informed by the above-mentioned men, and from other sources entitled to full credence, that the rest of the crew, six men, three of whom are said to be Americans, are still remaining upon Cayo Cortés, in the Enseneda de Cortés, on the south side of Cuba. As they are within the jurisdiction of her Catholic Majesty's dominions, it is expected, and I very respectfully request your excellency, that prompt measures be taken by your excellency's orders to insure their safety, for it is understood that they are in a perilous situation. An early reply to this communication is respectfully requested.

I have the honor to be, with much respect, your excellency's obedient servant,

JAMES T. GERRY,
Commander U. S. Navy, Commanding U. S. ship Albany.

His Excellency
The Governor and Captan General *of Cuba, &c.*

Consulate of the United States, Havana,
July 14, 1853.

Sir: I beg leave to inform you that there are, at this moment, confined in the royal prison in this city three American seamen—named William Freeburn, Wm. Atkins, and Harvey Parks—who shipped on board the barque Jasper, E. Townsend master, in December last, at New York, bound to Sierra Leone, for which place the vessel was cleared. These men state that they never went to Sierra Leone, but to a port in Africa called Elmira, where they discharged some cargo; thence to another port called Cape Coast, where the mate, whose name was John Brown, quarrelled with the captain and was discharged; from Cape Coast they went to another place, and thence to another, where, soon after they came to anchor, there appeared sundry boats filled with negroes, which they at first feared were coming to attack them, but soon after found they were slaves to be received on board, when Capt. Townsend called the crew and informed them that he had sold his vessel, and was about to deliver her over to the Spanish authorities; that he had made a losing voyage, but that he was willing to advance them three months' wages, as his part of the voyage was ended, and he advised them to return in the vessel; that if they went on shore they would either starve or be assassinated. They, therefore, had no other alternative left, and remained on board with the rest of the crew. John William Lee, of Palmyra, New York; George Hunt, a colored man, from the State of Maine; William Huzzy, of Nantucket; Charles Robinson, of Canada; John Radcliffe, of England, and Wm. Hersey, of Yarmouth, Nova Scotia—these formed the original crew from New York, and the same that brought her to the island.

Captain Townsend, they say, left the vessel after a part of the negroes had been taken on board. The Spanish captain, mate, supercargo, and one other, went as passengers in the Jasper from New York.

On their arrival on the coast of Cuba, the slaves were landed at a spot near Bailen, as I have ascertained from other sources; the barque got aground, or, as the men suspect, was put aground purposely, on the Punta de la Llana, or Illana, and there was burnt. The whole crew went ashore; the three men now in prison took a boat and endeavored, they state, to reach some point where they could find an American consul; but, being without water and provisions, they stopped at Cape San Antonio to procure them. Some of the inhabitants there reported them to the guard of soldiers stationed near there, who immediately arrested them, and from thence they were conveyed on board the Spanish war schooner "Habanera," on board of which they were put in the stocks, and kept thirty-five days; from thence they were transferred to this port on board the admiral's ship, where they were eight days, and afterwards sent to the royal prison, where they now remain confined with criminals, and they complain of having been frequently maltreated. On the first notice of their situation, and examining into it myself, I became satisfied that they were innocent, and that it was important for our government to have their depositions. Whereupon I addressed his excellency, the Captain General, asking permission to take the deposition of these men at my office, under the charge of an officer. To this application his excellency replies that he regrets that it is not in his power, as he has turned them over to the superior royal court as parties who have been engaged in the slave trade, contrary to the laws of Spain. Copies of my communication and his excellency's reply have been transmitted to the Departments of State for specific instructions on the subject. It seems, from information that I have received, that the government here have sent down to the neighborhood where the slaves were landed several commissions, and the reports returned are that no such vessel had been on the coast; thus, no doubt, contradicting the statements of these three men on their examination by the government officials. I have also information that the rest of the crew are now secreted on the Cortés key, in the "Ensenada de Cortés,"—three Americans and three Englishmen; that all are liable to be abandoned by the slave dealers and left to starve to death, or be made away with by assassination or some other way. They are very apprehensive of this, and by the last accounts were in a complete state of desperation. They were alive on the 6th instant.

You have now the subject before you; all the records of the office have been submitted to you, and will be open to you at all times whenever it is required. I again repeat, that it is important for our government to be in possession of the declarations of these three men under oath, and equally important that they be released from their painful situation. Also, that some steps be taken to rescue the other six men from the perilous situation in which they are placed.

I am, sir, very respectfully and truly, your most obedient servant,

WM. H. ROBERTSON,

Vice-Consul in charge of the Consulate of the United States at Havana.

To JAMES T. GERRY, Esq.,

Commanding United States ship "Albany," Harbor of Havana.

[Translation.]

[L. S.]

ALWAYS FAITHFUL ISLAND OF CUBA.—GOVERNMENT AND CAPTAIN GENERAL, POLITICAL SECRETARY'S OFFICE, SECTION FIFTH.

I have received your lordship's official letter of yesterday, with the letter which the commander of the United States sloop of war

"Albany" addresses me. I have noted the contents of both communications, and in consequence you will state to the said commander in answer that, as I said to your lordship on the 8th instant, it is absolutely impossible for me to interfere in this affair, for it has been submitted to the "real audiencia pretorial," (supreme court of judicature,) to whom appertains the investigation of the same, conformably to the penal law relative to the reprobated African trade, as the individuals, William Freeburn, William Atkins, and Harvey Parks, to whom the said commander of the Albany refers, belong to the crew of a slaver vessel that landed at Bailen the Bozal negroes that she conveyed, and was subsequently burnt in the Ensenada de Cortés. The cause is actively carried on by the said superior court, and immediately that it shall communicate to me its decision, I will transmit it to you, as well as that respecting the six individuals who are said to be at Cayo Cortés, for whose deliverance (extraction) from that place I have given the proper orders.

God preseve your lordship many years. Havana, July 16, 1853.

VALENTIN CAÑEDO.

To the COMMERCIAL AGENT
of the United States.

Mr. Marcy to Mr. O'Conor.

DEPARTMENT OF STATE, WASHINGTON,
July 19, 1853.

SIR: I transmit herewith a copy of two dispatches received from the late consul, and the present acting consul* of the United States at Havana, which tend to implicate one or more persons in New York in the fitting out of a vessel designed to engage in the slave trade, and which actually, after a real or nominal transfer to other parties, succeeded in landing a cargo of slaves on the island of Cuba. I will thank you to give the subject, embraced in the accompanying communications, your immediate attention, with a view to bring the guilty parties to justice. An effort will be made to procure the liberation from prison of the three American sailors referred to in Mr. Robertson's letter,† in which case they will be sent to New York, to be used as witnesses for the United States.

I am, sir, respectfully, your obedient servant,

W. L. MARCY.

CHARLES O'CONOR, Esq.,
U. S. District Attorney, New York.

---

* See Mr. Robertson's letter of July 13.

† The letter here referred to is Mr. Robertson's, dated July 6, 1852.

[No. 9.] CONSULATE OF THE UNITED STATES, HAVANA,
July 7, 1852.

SIR: The object of this communication is to lay before you a difficulty which has occurred at this consulate with regard to the barque "Jasper." This vessel obtained a register in New York, which was granted in the name of * * * *, as owner and master. She arrived in this port on the 17th of December, 1851, from the coast of Africa, with a partial lading of palm oil, ivory, &c. Much was then said and surmised as to the subject of her cruise on that coast. The crew, I believe, claimed extra wages in consequence of her having gone there to engage in the slave trade, though this is not so material to my present purpose. On the 9th of January last, * * * * left the vessel, first having appointed his mate to be master, and went to New York, and has not been at this port since. A Spaniard of this city, named * * * *, who is quite celebrated as having been long engaged in buying slaves from Africa, employed a workman to make extensive repairs on the vessel, he being the responsible party. He did not profess to act as agent for * * * *, nor was he consignee, but, as the workman says, (whose testimony I have taken,) seemed to be the sole owner. The repairs were made, the vessel completely coppered, &c., amounting to about four thousand dollars. In the mean time, * * * *, who had been appointed master by * * * *, also left the vessel, and no one seemed to have charge of her but the Spaniard. He employed another master, and also seamen, and superintended the repairs. The new master (whose testimony I have also taken) says he knew no other owner but * * * *, who acted in all respects as owner by paying out money for necessary purposes, and that even the consignee, * * * *, would pay nothing except on the order of * * * *. * * * * was in the habit of visiting the ship almost daily to superintend the repairs; that he purchased provisions for the crew; paid the seamen their wages, &c. In this way months passed and nothing was heard of Captain * * * * or his mate. Some time in May I received a letter from a Mr. * * * *, of New York, by which he informed me that he was * * * * surety in his bond given when the register was obtained, and as * * * * had ceased to be onwner, he desired me to retain the register. About the same time Captain * * * * himself wrote to a citizen of this place to the same effect, with a like request. The ship was by this time getting ready for sea, but I had intimated to the acting master that I was not satisfied as to the ownership. Freights, however, were being engaged by this same Spaniard for the coast of Africa. He put seventy or eighty barrels of beef on board, and a corresponding quantity of bread; and, finally, application was made to know whether I would give the ship her papers. I had become so well satisfied that she was Spanish property in reality, although nominally under an American owner, that I did not hesitate to refuse to give her the register. This brought up the Spaniard, * * * *, who seemed to be in great distress, and stated that he had made a contract for freights, and would lose greatly unless I would permit the vessel to go to sea. He came several times, and his great solicitude was really positive proof of his ownership. Finally, he produced the contract under which * * * * had been acting as owner, from which it appeared that the money to purchase the ship was furnished by a Spaniard, who probably was only a nominal party, * * * * being the real one. This instrument professed to be a mortgage, but it was so drawn as to look like something more than a mortgage, and to leave the impression that the Spaniard was the true owner, even before condition forfeited. The money was to have been paid by * * * * in September, 1850, or 1851. The time of payment had elapsed, and * * * * seemed to have abandoned the ship. I still refused to let the register go. * * * * said he could not get her under the Spanish flag as she was too small, the law requiring foreign built ships to be four hundred tons. In this dilemma * * * * started to New York to see * * * *, and, a few days ago, a * * * * presented himself with a bill of sale from * * * *, and demanded the ship's papers. He also brought letters from * * * * and * * * *, by which I was informed of the conveyance, and also that their bond had been cancelled. My reply was, that I had before refused to let the ship go because * * * * was not owner, and if this was so, he could of course make no title, and unless he could produce the mortgage extinguished, the ship could not be permitted to sail as an American vessel. I have given but a general outline of the evidence, which might be filled out by many other circumstances.

The propositions seem to be clear under the laws of the United States: First, that a vessel cannot be American if owned in whole or in part by a foreigner, either directly or in trust, often express or secret. Second, that an American built vessel, if she has ever been once owned by a foreigner, can never become American afterwards. I would respectfully refer you to the 1st, 2d, 7th, 16th, and 17th sections of the act of the 31st of December, 1792; the additional act of the 27th of June, 1797; and the act of 27th March, 1810. * * * * I believe has laid his grievances before the Secretary of the Treasury, and has applied for relief. I will also forward a copy of this dispatch to the Secretary of the Treasury. I should remark, also, that I have no doubt that * * * * is not the *bona fide* ower. The conveyance was made to him merely for the purpose of getting the ship out of the harbor. I must adhere to my determination, unless instructed to the contrary.

I have the honor to be, sir, your obedient servant,

W. L. SHARKEY.

Hon. DANIEL WEBSTER,
Secretary of State of the United States.

Mr. Marcy to Mr. Robertson.

DEPARTMENT OF STATE,
Washington, July 20, 1853.

SIR: Your several dispatches, from No. 34 to No. 41, inclusive, have been received.

In respect to the three American sailors, William Atkins, William

Freeburn, and Harvey Parks, now awaiting their trial in Havana, charged with having been engaged in the slave trade, you are informed that the department entirely approves the course which you have taken.

You will spare no judicious efforts to effect their liberation, and, should you not be successful in this, to secure them a fair trial.

You will perceive by the enclosed copy of a letter addressed by this department to the United States district attorney in New York, that he has been instructed to prosecute the parties alleged to have been interested in the fitting out of the "Jasper" for the purpose of engaging in the slave trade. It is considered very important that the three American sailors, now confined in Havana, should be sent to New York, to be used by the government as witnesses for the prosecution.

Although there is no doubt that these sailors were on board the "Jasper," yet it is far more important for the ends of justice to bring the principals engaged in this atrocious business to punishment, than those who acted only in a subordinate capacity, and who, it may reasonably be supposed, knew nothing of the intended object of the voyage until the choice was given them either to be left destitute on the African coast, exposed to the savage ferocity of the natives, or return to America as passengers in the slave ship.

You will make known to the Captain General the steps which have been taken by this government for the prosecution, in this country, of those concerned in the transaction, and it is not doubted that he will immediately perceive the expediency of using his influence with the judicial tribunals to effect the liberation of the imprisoned seamen for the object above-mentioned.

In which event you will place them on board of one of the steamers bound to New York, with orders that they be delivered to the marshal of the United States on their arrival in that city.

I am, sir, respectfully, your obedient servant,

W. L. MARCY.

W. H. Robertson, Esq.,
In charge of the U. S. Consulate at Havana, island of Cuba.

Mr. Robertson to Mr. Marcy.

[No. 44.] Consulate of the United States, Havana,
July 21, 1853.

Sir: I beg leave to lay before you a copy of an official letter received from the Governor and Captain General of Cuba, in reply to one addressed him by Commander Gerry, of the U. S. ship "Albany."

Commander Gerry, on being officially informed by me that the three American seamen, Harvey Parks, William Atkins, and William Freeburn, were imprisoned, called at this office, and examined all the papers relating to their case. Subsequently he called at the prison, questioned and cross-questioned the men, and, as the result of his examination, he formed the opinion that the men were American citizens, and that they were innocent of any intention of infringing either the laws of the United States or of Spain; that the guilty parties were somewhere else—some of them probably in the United States—and he thought that it would be important to have their testimony taken in the United States. He therefore respectfully informed the Captain General of his opinion in the matter, and suggested that the men should be delivered to him for the purpose of placing them at the disposal of the government of the United States. Captain Gerry also notified the Captain General that the shipmates of these men (six in number) were secreted on the Cortés key, and requested that prompt measures should be taken to relieve them from their painful situation.

You will perceive that the Captain General does not accede to the request of Captain Gerry for the delivery of the three men now here, and informs me that he had already given the proper orders for the others being taken off the Key Cortés. He likewise promises to communicate to me the decision of the court before which the case is pending, immediately that the court notify him of the same.

The six men who were on the Cortés were subsequently removed to another key, as I am informed; they were alive on the 7th instant, and provisions were conveyed to them in a canoe every two days. Their names are John Wm. Leo, of Palmyra, New York; George Hunt, a colored man, from Maine; Wm. Huzzy, of Nantucket; Charles Robinson, of Canada; John Radcliffe, of England; and Wm. Hersey, of Yarmouth, Nova Scotia.

Captain Gerry on the 18th instant addressed another letter to the Captain General, requesting permission for me to take the depositions of the men here. No reply has been received, and Captain Gerry sailed this morning, intending to cruise outside of the port for the benefit of the health of his crew, there being considerable sickness in the city at present.

I have received the circulars you sent me of changes in the lights on the coasts of Norway and Spain.

I have the honor to be, with great respect, your obedient servant,

WM. H. ROBERTSON,
Vice-consul in charge of the U. S. Consulate.

Hon. Wm. L. Marcy,
Secretary of State of the United States of America.

[Translation.]

[L. S.]

EVER FAITHFUL ISLAND OF CUBA.—GOVERNMENT AND CAPTAIN GENERAL'S OFFICE, POLITICAL DEPARTMENT, SECTION FIFTH.

I have received your communication of yesterday, together with the letter addressed to me by the commander of the U. S. ship "Albany." I have carefully perused both documents, and you will accordingly say to the commander aforesaid, in reply, that, as I told you on the 8th instant, it is utterly impossible for me to interfere in this matter, seeing that it is before the superior court of judicature, which has jurisdiction over it, according to the penal law relative to the prohibited African trade, since the individuals (William Freeburn, William Atkins, and Harvey Parks) to whom the commander of the "Albany" alludes, belong to the crew of a slaver which landed her cargo of negroes at Bailer's, and was afterwards burnt at Key Cortés.

The trial is progressing rapidly before said tribunal, and as soon as the latter shall have communicated its decision to me on the subject I will forward the same to you, together with the decision concerning the six individuals who are said to be at Key Cortés, whose removal from said point I have given proper orders for.

May God preserve you many years. Havana, July 16, 1853.

VALENTIN CAÑEDO.

The COMMERCIAL AGENT *of the United States.*

Mr. Robertson to Mr. Marcy.

[No. 45.] CONSULATE OF THE UNITED STATES, HAVANA,
July 21, 1853, 6 *o'clock p. m.*

SIR: As I was about enclosing my other communication of this date, No. 44, an orderly of the Captain General handed me a communication from that authority, enclosing a copy of a report sent to him by the chief justice of the superior court of judicature of the island. I hasten to transmit to you copies both of the Captain General's letter and the chief justice's report.

You will see that it is now entirely out of my power to do any more for the unfortunate men in whose favor the correspondence has taken place, until I am favored with specific instructions from you. I deeply regret that such is the case, for I really believe these men to be innocent.

I have the honor to be, with great respect, your most obedient servant,

WM. H. ROBERTSON,
Vice-consul, in charge of the consulate.

Hon. WM. L. MARCY,
Secretary of State, U. S.

[Translation.]

EVER FAITHFUL ISLAND OF CUBA.—GOVERNMENT AND CAPTAIN GENERAL'S OFFICE, POLITICAL DEPARTMENT, SECTION FIFTH.

I have received your communication of the 18th instant, enclosing another from the commander of the ship-of-war "Albany," both relating to the three sailors who are in prison in consequence of their having formed part of the crew of a vessel which brought and landed a cargo of negroes on the southern coast of this island, whose trial has been going on before the supreme court of judicature. In reply I enclose to you a copy of a communication which said supreme tribunal has addressed me on the subject, by which you will perceive that your object of taking the depositions of the individuals aforesaid is not attainable, which is perfectly in accordance with the regium exequator that is issued to consuls, according to which they cannot exercise any act of authority whatever.

Nor is it possible for me to enter directly into an understanding upon any official matters with the commandant of said ship "Albany," the laws of the kingdom being opposed to such a course; and you will say so to him, with the assurance that my consideration for him, personally, must not be understood as being lessened, in any respect, on this account.

With regard to the sum of money which you assert to have been deposited by the sailors aforesaid with the keeper of the prison, I will order the latter to deliver the above-mentioned sum into your hands, if agreeable to the sailors aforesaid; and should this sum not be sufficient for the purchase of the clothes which you desire to effect, this government will facilitate the obtaining of the necessary means as a special favor.

God preserve you many years. Havana, July 20, 1853.

VALENTIN CAÑEDO.

To the COMMERCIAL AGENT
in charge of the U. S. Consulate.

Copy of the communication addressed by the Chief Justice of the Supreme Court to the Captain General.

[Translation.]

SUPREME COURT OF HAVANA.

MOST EXCELLENT SIR: Having made the attorney general (fiscal) acquainted with your excellency's communication of the 9th instant, containing what was written to you by the commercial agent of the United States, who wishes to receive the depositions of the three Americans lately arrested, in consequence of the suit which has been instituted relative to the landing of a cargo of imported negroes (negros Bozales) at Bailen, his lordship represented, and the first chamber of this tribunal provided, as follows:

"MOST POWERFUL SIR: The fiscal says that the President has forwarded to your highness a communication which has been addressed to him by the United States consul, who wishes to receive the depositions of the three American sailors arrested at his consulate, in consequence of this suit, stating that the place where they have been confined is disagreeable to them on account of the people by whom they are surrounded. These sailors having been arrested and tried for having formed part of the crew of a vessel that brought and landed on this island a cargo of negroes, imported from the coast of Africa, in violation of treaties and of the penal law which has been promulgated for the suppression of that inhuman traffic, are subject to the authorities and to the laws of Spain, and must be judged and sentenced by the former, and in conformity with the latter. The request, therefore, of the United States consul to have these men taken to his house, for the purpose of receiving their depositions, does not appear reasonable. It is natural that the place where they have been confined should be disagreeable to them, as the consul remarks, because a prison cannot be a desirable residence for any one, either here or elsewhere; but the sailors aforesaid have been treated in the same manner as those of her Majesty's subjects who render themselves liable to imprisonment; that is to say, they have been confined in the public jail; and when they have once become amenable to the Spanish authorities and to the Spanish laws, no other mode of proceeding could be adopted in regard to them, nor have they a right to ask to be treated differently than her Majesty's subjects are treated under similar circumstances. Havana, July 17, 1853."

Agreeably to the representation of the fiscal, in the first part of his foregoing answer, let a reply be sent to the President enclosing said answer, and this decision.

Signature, first chamber, Messrs. Buelta, Mojanietta, Antonio Ma. del Rio.

And I transmit the same to your excellency, and for the subserviency of the proper object.

God preserve your excellency many years. July 19, 1853.

The Most Excellent Señor PEDRO PIZARRO.

The Most Excellent President GOVERNOR CAPTAIN GENERAL.

True copy:

LORENZO DE BUSTO.

Mr. Cowperthwait to Mr. Marcy.

PHILADELPHIA, *July* 21, 1853.

SIR: The unhappy parents of William Freeburn, one of the three unfortunate sailors now confined in prison at Havana, under suspicion of being engaged in the slave trade, have requested me to write a few lines to you in their behalf, bespeaking your friendly services in aid of their poor son. I willingly comply with this request, because I am sure that the vindication of the rights of an American citizen, however humble, will find no more able advocate than yourself, nor one more ready to defend them. I am satisfied, sir, from my knowledge of the antecedents of this young man, that the statements contained in the letter of himself and colleagues, addressed to you from the prison, under the date of July 8th inst., and published in the New York Herald of the 18th inst., may be fully relied upon. The parents are in very humble circumstances, but are honest and of good character, and have endeavored to bring up their children respectably. The father has for *twenty* years past been employed by the superintendent of our Fairmount water-works as a laborer, and the mother, who is more particularly known to me as one of the directors of the public schools, has had the care of one of our large school-houses for many years. Their unfortunate son, who learned the trade of house carpenter, left this city for New York in November last, in quest of work, which not readily finding, was induced to ship as a hand on board the "Jasper," bound, as he supposed, on a fair and legitimate voyage to Sierra Leone, as is fully detailed in the letter already referred to. I will not trespass on your valuable time by further details, but will earnestly entreat your effective aid on behalf of this unfortunate youth, which I am sure will not be extended in vain, and which will not fail to be gratefully acknowledged by his afflicted parents; and it would be a great source of satisfaction to myself, personally, to learn that there was a chance of his speedy restoration to his country and to his family.

I have the honor to be, with great respect, your obedient servant,

JOSEPH COWPERTHWAIT.

Hon. WILLIAM L. MARCY,
Secretary of State, Washington.

Mr. Marcy to Mr. Dobbin.

DEPARTMENT OF STATE,
Washington, July 22, 1853.

SIR: I have the honor to enclose herewith a copy of a letter received this morning from J. Cowperthwait, esq., of Philadelphia, and also several extracts from despatches received from W. H. Robertson, esq., the acting consul of the United States at Havana, in reference to certain American seamen, a part of whom appear to be in distress, though at liberty near the Cortés key, and others are in prison, charged with having been engaged in the slave trade.

I beg leave respectfully to suggest that the presence of a United States vessel would materially assist the acting consul in his efforts to effect the liberation of these unfortunate seamen.

I am, sir, respectfully, your obedient servant,

W. L. MARCY.

Hon. JAMES C. DOBBIN,
Secretary of the Navy.

Mr. Dobbin to Mr. Marcy.

NAVY DEPARTMENT,
July 25, 1853.

SIR: I have the honor to acknowledge the receipt of yours of the 22d instant, with its enclosures, in relation to the condition of certain American seamen, late of bark Jasper.

Agreeably to your suggestion, directions will be given to the commander-in-chief of the Home Squadron to send a man-of-war, to assist the acting consul at Havana in his efforts to effect the liberation of these seamen.

I am, very respectfully, your obedient servant,

J. C. DOBBIN.

Hon. WILLIAM L. MARCY,
Secretary of State.

Mr. Dobbin to Mr. Marcy.

NAVY DEPARTMENT,
July 28, 1853.

SIR: I have the honor to transmit herewith, for your perusal, a letter received at this department from Commander Gerry, commanding the United States sloop-of-war Albany, dated at Havana, July 15, 1853, by which it will be perceived that the instructions to the commanding officer of the Home Squadron, in relation to certain of the late crew of the bark Jasper, have been anticipated by the action of Commander Gerry.

I am, very respectfully, your obedient servant,

J. C. DOBBIN.

Hon. W. L. MARCY,
Secretary of State.

The Vice-consul in charge of the Consulate to Mr. Marcy.

[Extract.]

CONSULATE OF THE UNITED STATES, HAVANA,
July 28, 1853.

SIR: I have this morning received from the prison the enclosed communication from one of the three American seamen. I shall repair to the prison to examine into the facts. * * * *

Since the foregoing was written I have been to the prison, found Freeburn in the hospital, quite sick with fever; the other two in the situation which Atkins in his letter describes.

With great respect, &c.

The VICE CONSUL,
in charge of the Consulate of the United States.

Hon. W. L. MARCY,
Secretary of State of the United States, Washington.

HAVANA, *July* 26, 1853.

DEAR SIR: We should like very much to speak to you because we are very badly treated here, and hardly can stand it any longer without incurring the danger of losing our temper and committing some rash act, and thus bringing ourselves into still greater difficulties; they treat us in fact worse than dogs; we have to do nearly all the dirty work for the rest, and are robbed and insulted in every possible way. When we came here first we were asked to pay four dollars, or help to do the dirty work. Accordingly we wrote to the head jailor Don Pedro for the money, but he would not give it to us, and said that he had delivered it into the hands of the government; we were in consequence obliged to do the work; we never got any money until two days ago.

Freeburn is at present in the hospital very bad with fever. Parks was there last week, and feels very sick still, but he would not stay there because they were starving him; he felt so weak this morning that he was unable to do the work, and told them so when they wanted him to work; but instead of excusing him from the work, the man whom they call Cabo de Yambuja rushed at him, and struck him five or six times with the butt-end of a broom as hard as he could, and even drew a knife on him, which he dropped however. It is not permitted to have knives here, and we could complain of this to the head jailor, Don Pedro; but if we did they would certainly stab us during the night. But if you would speak to Don Pedro, there might, perhaps, be effected a change for the better; you might insist on our not working any longer like slaves.

Hoping to have soon the pleasure of seeing you, I remain, dear sir, your obedient servant,

WILLIAM ATKINS.

Mr. O'Conor to Mr. Marcy.

SOUTHERN DISTRICT OF NEW YORK,
U. S. District Attorney's Office, July 29, 1853.

SIR: Your communication, accompanying copies of two dispatches received from the late consul and the present acting consul at Havana, has been received.

The department seems not to be aware that the bark Jasper was seized at this port on the 19th October, 1852, charged with sailing under a false register, she belonging, as we supposed and asserted, basing our opinion upon information derived from * * to a Spaniard named * *, mentioned in Judge Sharkey's dispatch, while at the same time her papers bore the name of * *; the bark was detained in custody for some time, but was at length bonded in the sum of ten thousand dollars, and afterwards, as I am informed at the custom-house, departed secretly without any clearance or papers. I had intended bringing on the case for trial at the last term of the court, but was prevented as well by the press of criminal business as by the absence of * * and * *, who are absent on a voyage to California, but are soon expected to return. In the mean time, I have been diligently seeking the parties interested in fitting out the vessel, and getting such information as may be desirable and necessary. * * has, as I have reason to believe, recently been here. If he is still in the city, or can be found, I will endeavor to procure sufficient evidence to justify the commissioner in issuing a warrant, and will then cause his immediate arrest. I would further respectfully suggest the importance of procuring the release of the three sailors confined at Havana, at as early a day as possible.

I have the honor to be, your very obedient servant,

CHARLES O'CONOR,
United States Attorney.

Hon. WILLIAM L. MARCY,
Secretary of State, Washington.

Mr. Mann, Acting Secretary, to Mr. O'Conor.

DEPARTMENT OF STATE,
Washington, August 2, 1853.

SIR: I have to acknowledge the receipt of your letter of the 29th ultimo, and to inform you that a copy of it has been sent to the acting consul of the United States, at Havana, with renewed instructions to send immediately to New York, in the event of their liberation, the three American seamen, lately belonging to the bark "Jasper," to be used as witnesses on the trial there of the parties alleged to have been concerned in the slave trade.

I am, sir, &c.,
A. DUDLEY MANN,
Acting Secretary.

CHARLES O'CONOR, Esq.,
U. S. Attorney, New York.

Mr. Robertson to Mr. Marcy.

[Extract.]

[No. 51.] CONSULATE OF THE UNITED STATES, HAVANA,
August 3, 1853.

SIR: I had the honor to receive, on the 29th of July, yours of the 20th of said month, accompanying your instructions to the district attorney in New York; and although the Captain General had made known to me that he could not either permit me to take the depositions of the three seamen of the late bark Jasper, now in prison, or deliver them up, for the purpose of sending them to New York to be used there as witnesses for the prosecution of the parties that were concerned in the fitting out of the "Jasper" for the slave trade, I avail myself of the instructions contained in your dispatch to urge upon his excellency the expediency of their being delivered up, laying before him on the same day (29th July) your views and wishes on the subject. I have not yet been favored with a reply to my communication, but received a few minutes since an official letter from his excellency, dated on yesterday, a copy of which I enclose herewith. You will be able to form an opinion upon the contents of his excellency's letter, wherein I refer you to my communication of the 21st ultimo, No. 44, wherein I stated that the six men who had been on the Key "Cortés" had been removed to another key; the name of this other key I believe is "Cayo Felipe." I obtained this information from * *, who had it from the same party that first communicated to him the circumstances connected with the landing of slaves by the "Jasper," the burning of this vessel, and the fact of the six men being secreted at "Cayo Cortés." I have seen both the reports to the said * *.

The letter referred to by the Captain General as received from me, dated 15th July, merely enclosed a letter to him from Captain Gerry, of the Albany. It was this officer who notified the Captain General that the six men were secreted at "Cayo Cortés."

The latter part of the Captain General's communication of the 2d instant I do not understand, for the "alcalde," or chief jailor delivered to me yesterday the money belonging to the seamen Freeburn, Parks, and Atkins; the amount paid over were the same (with the difference of a dollars or so) as reported to me by the prisoners themselves. * *

I have the honor to be, sir, your most obedient servant,

WM. H. ROBERTSON,
Vice-consul in charge of the Consulate.

Hon. William L. Marcy,
Secretary of State.

[Translation.]

[L. S.]

EVER FAITHFUL ISLAND OF CUBA.—GOVERNMENT AND CAPTAIN GENERAL'S OFFICE, POLITICAL DEPARTMENT, SECTION FIFTH.

On the 2d instant, I informed you of what the three North American sailors confined in jail had said to the alcalde of the same, concerning the twelve ounces which the latter has in his possession belonging to said individuals, who are waiting for the result of their trial in the royal pretorial court, in consequence of their having formed part of the crew of a slaver which was burnt after having discharged her freight of negroes, which she had brought from Africa, at Bailen.

I accordingly make the same known to you, in reply to your communication of the 29th of July last, relative to the matter; reiterating to you, moreover, that I regret not being able to comply with the request with regard to the wishes expressed by the Secretary of State of your government, as mentioned by you in your communication aforesaid, that the three sailors in question might be sent on to New York, because I am not at liberty to meddle with any of the proceedings appertaining to the jurisdiction of the court aforesaid, before which I will, however, lay your letter for its decision, in order that I may, in due time, convey the same to you. May God preserve you many years. Havana, August 13, 1853.

VALENTIN CAÑEDO.

To the Commercial Agent
in charge of the Consulate of the United States.

Mr. A. Dudley Mann, acting Secretary of State, to Mr. Robertson.

[Extract.]

Department of State,
Washington, August 3, 1853.

* * * * * * * *

In the event of your being successful in effecting the liberation of the American sailors now confined in Havana, charged with having been concerned in the slave trade, you will be pleased to cause them to be conveyed to New York, and surrendered to the marshal, for the purpose indicated in the letter of Mr. O'Conor, United States attorney.

In case they should be brought to trial in Havana, you will urge upon the proper authorities the obvious propriety of using one or more of them as witnesses, chiefly for the purpose of showing that these men were ignorant of the object of the voyage of the "Jasper" to the coast of Africa till the transfer of the vessel took place; that their remaining on board was a matter of necessity; and, more especially, that the parties in Havana, alleged to have been principally instrumental in fitting out the "Jasper," may be brought to punishment.

If there is a sincere desire to convict the slave dealers, this reasonable request cannot be refused.

* * * * * * * *

I am, sir, respectfully, your obedient servant,

A. DUDLEY MANN,
Acting Secretary.

Mr. Robertson to Mr. Marcy.

[Extract.]

[No. 54.] CONSULATE OF THE UNITED STATES, HAVANA,
August 29, 1853.

SIR: * * * * * * *
In my dispatch of August 3, No. 51, (which is in your possession,) I stated that I had not been favored by the Captain General with a reply to my communication to his excellency of the 29th July. His reply, dated on the 13th of August, reached me on the 16th—a copy of it I now lay before you. He reiterates his former assertions, to the effect that he cannot interfere in the matter, and promises to lay my letter before the court, and to transmit to me the court's decision upon the same. Since then I have heard nothing from him.

I have the honor, &c.,

W. H. ROBERTSON,
Acting Consul.

Mr. Robertson to Mr. Marcy.

[No. 56.] CONSULATE OF THE UNITED STATES, HAVANA,
September 24, 1853.

SIR: Referring to my last communication, dated 13th instant, No. 55, I beg leave to inform you that, on the 15th, I received an official letter from the Governor and Captain General of the island, notifying me that I could take the depositions of the three American seamen, (who have been in the jail of this city since the 2d of July, and detained by the authorities of the island since May,) in the presence of one of the justices of the superior court, with the attendance of one of the government interpreters, on the 17th, at the hall of the said court. I therefore prepared beforehand a set of interrogatories to be propounded to the prisoners, and presented myself in the court-room at the appointed day and hour. Then, outside of the room, I found the prisoners under charge (as customary here) of two soldiers, with muskets and bayonets fixed. The justice and interpreter were present. There was some conversation between myself and the judge, who thought that *he* was to receive the depositions. I made known to him that, if they were taken by any one but myself, they would be of no use in the United States. He then allowed me to proceed to question the first prisoner brought in, and, before I had got through, the judge assured me that the communication he had received was worded in such a manner that he did not feel confident that his course in allowing *me* to take the depositions would be approved of by the Captain General; and he proposed that I should finish examining the first witness, and then stop, until he could see the Captain General in the evening, and ascertain if no objection would be made to my course. To this proposition I assented. That was on Saturday. On Monday following, the judge informed me that the Captain General had given his assent to my continuing to take the depositions, as he had no desire to throw obstacles that would delay the ends of justice in the United States. I therefore received the two other depositions on Tuesday and Wednesday.

I now have the honor to enclose you the whole proceedings. Many of the interrogatories (having been prepared beforehand) were necessarily superseded, and I fear the answers contain much irrelevant matter; but the subjects they were taken from being seamen, who are prone to give long stories, I was afraid that, if I omitted any part of their statements, something important might be accidentally left out.

I have furnished the judge of the superior court here, at his request, a translated copy of the interrogatories and depositions. He, at first, thought it might be proper that he should subscribe his name to the papers; but, at last, concluded, after consultation as I understand with his colleagues, that it was not necessary or important.

I do not know yet when these unfortunate men will be released.

Your obedient servant,

WM. H. ROBERTSON,

Acting Consul.

Hon. William L. Marcy,

Secretary of State, Washington D. C.

Questions or interrogatories to be propounded by William H. Robertson, acting consul of the United States of America at the city of Havana, to William Atkins, William Freeburn, and Harvey C. Parks, seamen reporting themselves as Americans, who are at present detained in Havana by the authorities of Havana, charged with having formed part of the crew of the bark Jasper, which, it is said, landed a cargo of negroes from Africa at or near a place called Baylen, on the south side of the island of Cuba, and that, after the landing was effected, the vessel was burnt.

1. What is your name, age, profession, or trade? Which is the place of your birth, and which of your residence? When were you last at the place of your residence? Give us the names of some respectable person or persons who know you, and can give information about your character and conduct, from his, her, or their own knowledge.

2. In what vessel did you come to the island of Cuba? Where and when did you join her, and in what capacity? In what street and house were you living in New York when you shipped on the Jasper? State the name or names of your landlord or landlords, landlady or landladies. State also the name or names of the shipping-master or shipping-masters that shipped you on the articles of the Jasper. Where did he or they live in New York? Did you yourself subscribe your name to the articles? Did you ascertain the conditions of your shipment, and what were they; that is, to what port or ports was the vessel going? Was she to come back to New York or any other part of the United States, or not? Was any part of Cuba one of the places at which the vessel had to touch? Was or were there any person or persons connected or concerned in the bark Jasper present at the time you entered your name on her articles? If yea, give his or their names. State also the name of the captain that was in command of the Jasper when she sailed out of New York. Say if you were acquainted with Captain Townsend before you went on board the Jasper. What were your wages per month, or for the voyage?

3. Did you, or did you not, when you were going on board, somewhere near the wharf, see one or more females in a carriage, who asked you certain question or questions? What were the questions, your answers, and what did she or they finally say to you? Did you see Captain Townsend speaking to the female or females aforesaid before you went on board? Do you know the name or names of the female or females referred to above?

4. Do you know Capt. Wade, who formerly commanded the Jasper?

5. Do you know a Spaniard by the name of Don José Mora? If you do, when did you see him last? Was he in any way, to your knowledge, connected with or concerned in the barque Jasper, or the object of her voyage? If he was, state how. Did he proceed from New York in the vessel?

6. Did Captain Townsend continue in command and exercise control over the bark Jasper to her arrival in Cuba, or not? Relate all the important circumstances connected with the voyage of the Jasper, from her sailing from New York to her arrival at Cuba. State the places where she touched; what operations were done at each place; what cargo she brought to Cuba; whether she landed her cargo or not—where and how; and what became of her afterwards. Say whether she was anywhere near Sierra Leone.

7. After Captain Townsend left you, or previous to his leaving, and you discovered that slaves were brought on board, and the Spanish captain had assumed command of the Jasper, did you demand your discharge from the vessel? Was the discharge offered to you, and by

whom? If a discharge was offered you, why did you not accept it and leave the vessel? Or, if you demanded it, and it was not granted, what reasons were given you, and by whom, for not granting it? Were you paid your wages? Where, by whom, for what time? And state all the circumstances connected with the payment thereof. If your wages were not paid, say, did you demand them, and why, if you know, were they not paid you?

8. What treatment did you receive on the Jasper previous to and after the Spanish captain had assumed command? State the names (if you know them) of the persons who, after Captain Townsend left her, seemed to have charge of the Jasper and her cargo. Were you or were you not forced to work for the vessel after she was under Spanish charge? Did you perform service? If yea, say if you were or not offered remuneration for your services. If yea, by whom? Did you or did you not accept the offer? If accepted by you, was it fulfilled by the other party, and where?

9. Was the American flag used by the Jasper after Captain Townsend made known to you that he had sold his ship? If not, what flag was used on the voyage to Cuba, and during the time she remained on the coast?

10. After the Jasper was burnt, what did the crew and persons on board do? State the name (if you know it) of the place where you landed. How long were you there? State all particulars connected with your stay on the key, the treatment you received, and how you came to be found in a boat at Cape San Antonio. How many of the original crew were with you on the key? What were their names, what their country? And give us all the information you know about them. Why did not the other men accompany you when you left the key, and how long after the burning of the Jasper was it that you left the key?

11. Where were you conveyed when taken up at Cape San Antonio? State all the circumstances of your capture. How long were you detained, from the moment of your capture at the Cape to the moment of arrival on board the Spanish war schooner Habanera? What questions were propounded to you on board that schooner? By whom? Was a good interpreter used, or did the officer who interrogated you do it in English? Are you acquainted with the Spanish language? What account did you then give of yourself? Was not your report a false one? If so, what induced you to make a false report? How long were you on board the schooner, and how were you treated? If not well treated, was it occasioned by bad or obstreperous conduct on your part? When did you leave that schooner, and how, and where were you taken to? How were you treated on board the man-of-war in the harbor of Havana, and till what time did you remain on board? When removed from the vessel, where were you conveyed? How long have you been in jail? How have you been treated whilst in jail? If well treated, or badly treated, by whom?

12. Have you ever demanded your release and liberty? Of whom, and what were the replies?

13. Have you been examined at Havana by the authorities of this government since your capture? How many times? Have you been

informed by the authorities of the object of your imprisonment? If you have been examined, have your declarations been the same as you have made in the present examination?

14. State any thing, or things, further connected with the Jasper or her cargo, or voyage, or yourself or shipmates, that, to your knowledge, has occurred, and you have not mentioned in answer to the preceding interrogatories.

[L. S.]

SIEMPRE FIEL ISLA DE CUBA.—GOBIERNO Y CAPITANIA GENERAL, SECRÉTARIA POLITICA, SECCION 5A.

Consecuente á los deseos manifestados por V. de que se le permitiese tomar declaracion á los tres marineros Americanos presos, pertenecientes á la tripulacion del negrero que alijó en Bailen, por conceptuarlo V. necesario para perseguir judicialmente en los Estados Unidos á los armadores de dicho negrero, he dispuesto como gracia especial por la causa que la motiva, y en vista de lo proveido de conformidad por la rl. sala 1a. de justicia de la audiencia pretorial, en virtud del oficio de V. de 29 del último Julio que le transmité, segun dije á V. en 13 del ppdo. Agosto, que el dia 17 del corriente, á las 12 de la mañana, sean examinados los tres marineros espresados ante el Sor. Oidor Dn. Leon Herques, con la asistencia de V. y de uno de los interpretes de gobo., en el referido tribunal.

Lo que digo á V. é fin de que ocurra á la real audiencia mencionada el dia y hora designado con el objeto esplicado.

Dios guarde á V. muchos años. Habana, 15 de Setiembre, 1853.

VALENTIN CAÑEDO.

Sor AGENTE COMERCIAL,
encargado del Consulado de los E. E. U. U.

CONSULATE OF THE U. S. OF AMERICA, HAVANA.

I, William H. Robertson, acting consul of the United States of America at Havana, in the Island of Cuba, do hereby certify that the copy of a communication, written on the reverse page, is a true and correct copy of an original communication by me received from the Governor and Captain General of this island, and signed by him, which original is on file in this consulate.

In testimony whereof I hereunto subscribe my name, and affix the seal of this consulate at Havana, this seventeenth day of September, A. D. one thousand eight hundred and fifty-three. [L. S.]

WM. H. ROBERTSON.

CONSULATE OF THE UNITED STATES, HAVANA.

Be it known, that the Governor and Captain General of the island of Cuba having, at my repeated requests, consented to allow me to receive the depositions of three men, who say that they are seamen and American citizens, (which their appearances and other circumstances seem to confirm,) and named William Atkins, William Freeburn, and Harvey C. Parks, who have been for some months, and are still, in the prison of Havana, charged with having formed part of the crew of a vessel named the Jasper, which landed negroes from Africa at or near a place called Baylen, on the south side of the island of Cuba, and with having, together with the rest of the crew, after effecting the landing of the negroes, burnt the vessel; I William H. Robertson, acting consul of the United States of America for the port and city of Havana, in the island of Cuba, availing myself of the permission aforesaid, (which will appear in a copy authenticated by me, and hereto accompanying, of a letter from said Governor and Captain General to me addressed,) have, on this seventeenth day of September, in the year of our Lord one thousand eighth hundred and fifty-three, at Havana, in the presence of Don Leon Herques, one of the justices of the superior court of the district, and of one of the interpreters of the government of the island, commenced to receive the depositions of the said William Atkins, William Freeburn, and Harvey C. Parks, severally, and under solemn oath to make true answers to the various interrogatories that will be propounded to each and every one of said men by me, which interrogatories are hereto accompanied, and written on six pages, marked 1 to 6, both inclusive.

William Freeburn being sworn, doth depose and say as follows:

1. To the first interrogatory he saith: My name is William Freeburn; 24 years old; carpenter by trade; born in Philadelphia; residence Philadelphia. I was in Philadelphia for the last time last December, about the first of said month. George Geddies, in Willie Grove, about 12 miles from Philadelphia.

2. To the second interrogatory he saith: I came to Cuba in the barque Jasper; I joined her in New York, on the 12th of December last, as a sailor before the mast; I was living, I think, in Oak street; my landlord was Winehold; I cannot say for certain who were the shipping masters that shipped me, but I think it was Clark and Dean. I did not go to the shipping office; I signed the articles of the Jasper; I understood that she was going to the coast of Africa, Sierra Leone being the first place, on a trading voyage for palm oil, and then come back to the United States. The vessel had not, to my knowledge, to touch at any part of Cuba; there was no one concerned or connected with the vessel present at the time I entered my name on the articles, but William Atkins and William Leo. The captain that was in command of the Jasper was named E. Townsend, which I saw written on a bag; I was not acquainted with Captain Townsend before I went on board. I was to receive 15 dollars per month.

3. To the third interrogatory he saith: I saw one female in a carriage. She asked if I and two or three others, that had shipped for the voyage and were there, were looking for the Jasper; she said the captain would be there in a few minutes. I saw Captain Townsend speak to the female when he was on board and passing by; he shook his handkerchief to her and bade her good-bye. I do not know the name of the female.

4. To the fourth interrogatory he saith: I do not know Captain Wade.

5. To the fifth interrogatory he saith: I do not know the person called Don Josè Mora.

6. To the sixth interrogatory he saith: Captain Townsend commanded and controlled the Jasper only to the time that slaves were received on board on the coast of Africa. When we reached the coast of Africa the mate told us we were not going within a thousand miles of Sierra Leone. The mate was asked the reason, and he answered that he thought the supercargo had changed his mind; the supercargo was a Spaniard. This is all I know of him, except that when Captain Townsend left the ship, he took command of the ship. There were four Spaniards on board when we left New York; they came on board at the wharf where I saw the female—two of them as passengers, one as supercargo and the other as his nephew. The Jasper touched first at Elmina, discharged some cargo there, and the supercargo, with his nephew, went on shore. We sailed from thence; the nephew of the supercargo came on board, the supercargo remaining on shore, and proceeded to Cape Coast; discharged some cargo there, and took on board 100 bales of tobacco and some elephant's teeth. The captain and mate, J. Brown, quarrelled at this place; the mate was discharged and went ashore. He was discharged for drinking liquor, and the captain subsequently said he considered his life was not safe as long as the mate was on board. From thence we went to Little Mina; we were there boarded by an English war-steamer; we were under American colors; we discharged there some pipes of rum, took in some ducks and hogs, and filled our water-pipes. We asked the reason why all the water-pipes were filled there, when our next place of destination was so near, being only eight days sail; we understood our next place would be Laguna. We were answered, that the water further down the coast was brackish, and not fit to drink. Some of my shipmates, after the British steamer had boarded us, asked the captain of the Jasper for some clothes. He answered, that we were to meet the steamer at Laguna, and there he would exchange rum for some stuff to make clothes with. In a short time after the steamer boarded us; we started, as we understood at the time, for Laguna; we did not go to Laguna; in three or four days we went into a place, the name of which I know not, though it sounded something like Wiggie-Waggie. It was just dark when we got into the place and let go the anchor; the next morning a white man, that was either an Englishman or American, as he spoke very good English, came aboard, shook hands with Captain Townsend, and went into the cabin; he came out in a few minutes, and in the same boat that he came out in, took fifty bales of the tobacco that we took in at Cape Coast; we discharged some pipes of rum into some canoes; the same man that came aboard first came back with a letter for Captain Townsend; he took the rest of the tobacco, and, as he went over the side, Captain Townsend told him to tell Mr. Hutton he did not want a receipt for that tobacco; we put the hatches on then, and did not discharge or take in anything more. In about half an hour, or an hour, we saw twenty or thirty canoes or more; we asked what the canoes were for, as we thought they were coming for rum; and Radcliffe, who was acting

second mate, went aft and asked if he was to take off the hatches; a Spaniard named Loper, who was afterwards second mate, said he did not know what they were for, but that he knew they were not coming for rum; he said that they wanted to trade for palm oil, but that the supercargo had engaged for more palm oil already than he wanted; the canoes went down the coast, and did not come to the ship; the men went about their work till dinner-time; after dinner Captain Townsend gave orders to get the ship under way; we dropped down about twenty or thirty miles, as near as I could judge, and we saw all these canoes which we thought must be the same as we saw in the morning; when we got to about opposite to where the canoes were, we let go the anchor; the Spaniard named Loper was standing on the deck; we asked him if they were not the same canoes, and what they were for? He said he did not know; the canoes were coming towards the ship, and all were standing on the forcastle looking at them; the boy, John William Leo, came running forward, and said, "By G—d! there must be something up;" he said he heard Captain Townsend speak to Mr. Hussy, who was the second mate before the chief mate was discharged, that his wages came to ninety-six dollars; we did not know what to think at the time; Radcliffe was next called into the cabin; Atkins and myself were called to carry some bags forward; we had carried but two or three, when we were called into the cabin, together with Charles Robinson; the captain (Townsend) was sitting at the table with a pile of money before him; he asked us if we knew what was up; we hardly knew what to answer him, for we saw slaves coming in at the time; Captain Townsend said, *I have sold my ship and am going to pay you off with three months' extra pay;* we asked him why he had not let us know it before; Captain Townsend said he did not know it till yesterday; that he had sold his ship yesterday afternoon; he said they were bound to take us home in the ship as passengers; he said he could not protect us at this place, as we were five hundred miles from either American or English consuls; we went out and told Harvey Parks, who was sick at the time in the forecastle; he would not believe us at first; we at last convinced him by showing him our money; we had been on board about two months and a half, and sixty-nine dollars were paid to us; a short time afterwards Parks came out of the cabin, and I asked him what he intended to do? He said, *go ashore, of course;* he went to the gangway and beckoned to a canoe that had discharged her negroes on board; the Spanish supercargo was standing at the brake of the poop at the time, and beckoned with his hand to the canoe not to come alongside; Captain Townsend was standing then in the waist, and said "damn it, men, don't act like children;" we did not see when Captain Townsend went ashore, but the boy saw him and told us. In the mean time the Spanish mate, and second mate, and a white man from the shore, were employed taking in negroes on board. After the slaves were all on board, the Spaniard who acted as second mate, generally called Loper, was employed in unshackling the chain; the supercargo said that he was now captain, and that, if we would work the ship he would give us fifty dollars a month; he also told us, if we went on shore in the bush, if we were not killed before morning, that we should be starved to death. We, therefore, were afraid to go on shore, and thought it best to work the ship. We went to work, got the ship under weigh, and one man was placed at each hatch, (there were three hatches,) and one on the forcastle on the look-out; one was at the masthead in the day time; the rest of the men were made to sleep on the poop, as they would not permit us to sleep in the forecastle. We were very badly treated, and kept at work all the time. Loper struck Harvey once with a pump, and then pulled out his knife and made a pass with it at him, when Harvey caught his wrist. In the mean time, the knife dropped; Harvey dragged him up on deck; the old second mate, Mr. Hussy, went up and took the wheel, and Radcliffe came forward and struck the Portuguese, whose name was Domingo, for giving the knife to Loper. The first mate came forward first, and then the captain; and the first mate caught hold of Harvey Parks's arm, so that he should not hit Loper; the captain went between the ones that were fighting, and told the first mate to go aft and get the pistols, and forced us to go to work. The second mate, at another time, also struck Atkins for not going to the wheel. We sailed in February for Cuba, where we arrived in the latter part of April. The cargo brought from Africa was landed at a place about seventy or eighty miles to the eastward of Cape Antonio. There were some high grounds near the place where we were. The slaves were landed in two boats of the ship, and several boats (three, I think) from the shore. One negro died on the passage. The Jasper was aground at the time; one day was spent in trying to get her off, and all the rum and water that was in her was stove to lighten her. A party of Spaniards from the shore came on board the next night to help the vessel off; we made every effort to get her off; we were in the boat towing the large boat that had the anchor; we were told to come on board, that they were going to fire the ship; we were told to put our things in the boat, and go with the second mate, (Loper.) We got all our things out into the boat, and were towed about twelve miles above the place where the slaves were landed.

7. To the seventh interrogatory he saith: I asked for my discharge, and the captain (Townsend) said he could not protect us; I was paid my wages by Captain Townsend.

8. To the eighth interrogatory he saith: I have explained the treatment we received on board; the captain was named José, the chief mate Dionisio, (but generally called Dennis,) and Loper; we were forced to work in the vessel after she was under Spanish charge; I did do duty; I was offered remuneration; I received seventy-eight dollars after the slaves were landed.

9. To the ninth interrogatory he saith: The American flag was not used; the Spanish flag was used.

10. To the tenth interrogatory he saith: After the Jasper was burnt the crew remained on shore, doing nothing; ten days after the captain came and paid us off, and said that a schooner would be there in five days to take us to Havana; we were not ill-treated while on shore. The following are the names of the original crew that were with me: William Hussy, Charles Robinson, Robert Radcliffe, William Hersey, William Atkins, Harvey C. Parks, John William Leo. On the 15th day after we were on the place, which was a key, no schooner came

for us; the Spanish first mate was close by the place; we asked him if nothing was coming to take us away; as far as we could understand, he said he had nothing to do with us, and we might go where we liked; that same night we took the long-boat, after the Spaniards were asleep, (the boat had been off the Jasper,) got a couple of boat's masts, a couple of sails, and two jars of water, and a saw, and the top-sail halliards of the ship; we put out to sea with the expectation of being picked up by a merchantman or a man-of-war; when out about two days, we put into the shore to get some provisions; when we landed, a man came to us, and asked what we wanted; we said we wanted to buy some provisions; he asked where we were from, and we answered, *from Jamaica*. Whilst getting the provisions, several soldiers came to the house. Radcliffe was an Englishman; Atkins is an American; Parks is an American; Hussy hailed from Nantucket; Hersey was a Nova Scotian; the cook, whose name I have omitted before, was named George Hunt, an American; Robinson was a French Canadian; and Leo was an American. The reason why the others did not come with us, was, that Radcliffe was very sick, and Robinson was his friend and would not leave him; Mr. Hussy and Hersey did not know of our plan; the rest, after agreeing to come with us, declined.

11th. To the eleventh interrogatory he saith: When the soldiers came to the house where we were taking the provisions, they asked us who we were, and where we were from. We told them we were Americans, from Jamaica; they said they would send us on board the Habanera schooner. We were a little more than two days on the way from the cape to the schooner. When on board, we were asked who we were, and where from; we said *from Jamaica*. We were asked if we belonged to a ship there. I said I left the Duke of Wellington. I do not know what was the office of the person that asked the questions; he appeared to be an officer, and spoke in pretty good English. My report was a false one. I was afraid that if I told the truth, perhaps they would not believe, or perhaps put me in prison, and I did not wish to be detained from making my statement to the authorities of my country. We were put in irons, but not otherwise ill-treated. I was on board the schooner about thirty-five days; from thence conveyed to Havana in a small merchant schooner, and put on board of a man-of-war in this harbor. We were not ill-treated. We were on board this man-of-war about eight days; then to the prison we have been till now, on shore. We have been in the prison since the 2d of July. We have not been ill-treated by the officers of the prisons, but have been by the other prisoners.

12th. To the twelfth interrogatory he saith: I have not asked, except of the consul of my country, now taking my deposition, for liberty, or my release or trial.

13th. To the thirteenth interrogatory he saith: I have been examined by the authorities of Havana once. I have not been informed by the authorities of the object of my imprisonment. I have made at the examination by the authorities here the same declarations that I have made now.

14th. To the fourteenth interrogatory he saith: At Cape Coast one of the men asked for his discharge, and it was refused him: he asked for his discharge on account of the victuals not being good. There were several means taken to deceive us before we got to the place where the slaves were taken in, Captain Townsend assuring us that we were to go back to the places we had been at to take palm oil.

Further this deponent saith not, and subscribes his name.

WILLIAM FREEBURN.

SEPTEMBER 20, 1853.

Harvey C. Parks, being sworn, did declare and depose as follows:

1. To the first interrogatory he saith: My name is Harvey C. Parks, aged twenty-three years; a seaman; born in Adams, Jefferson county, in the State of New York; residence in the town of Palmyra, New York, Wayne county. I was there about fourteen days before I embarked. Judson N. Pond, who lives in Marion Corners, a town adjoining Palmyra.

2. To the second interrogatory he saith: I came to Cuba in the bark Jasper; I joined her on the 12th December, in New York, in the capacity of sailor; I lived in 94 Roosevelt street, the house kept by William Cloudsley. I think my shipping-masters were Clark and Dean, who kept in South street, somewhere between Pine and Fulton streets, as I believe; I subscribed my name to the articles. I did ascertain the conditions of the voyage; I understood, for I was told, that the vessel was going to the coast of Africa on a trading voyage; but they told me in the office that they could not tell which would be the first port we were going to; I understood we were to come back to the United States; no part of Cuba was mentioned; the voyage was not to exceed six months; there were persons in the office, but none that I knew; the name of the captain that was in command was E. Townsend; I did not know the captain before I went on board; my wages were fifteen dollars a month.

3. To the third interrogatory he saith: I saw a female in a carriage, who asked a person that was with us, and afterwards proved to be our mate, if we were looking for the Jasper; he answered that he was, and she told him then to wait a minute and the captain would be there; we waited a few minutes, and the captain came round in a boat; he told us, *Men, put your things in the boat, and pull across the Atlantic dock*, where the Jasper laid; I saw Captain Townsend speaking to the female, but did not hear any conversation; I do not know the name of the female, but, from some conversation I overheard, I understood she was the captain's lady.

4. To the fourth interrogatory he saith: I do not know Captain Wade.

5. To the fifth interrogatory he saith: I know the Spaniard called Don José Mora; after the vessel was got out of the dock, a steamboat took hold of her; there was a man told the captain of the steamboat that he wanted to stop at the other dock a minute, which he did, and took in three or four trunks; and three Spaniards came on board, one of whom was said Don José Mora, as it afterwards proved; we were told that he was the supercargo of the vessel; nothing worthy of notice

occurred about him (we did not see him but once or twice the whole passage) till we got to Africa; the last time I saw José Mora was on the island of Cuba, to which he came as captain of the Jasper.

6. To the sixth interrogatory he saith: Captain Townsend did not command the Jasper to her arrival in Cuba. Nothing important occurred until our arrival in Africa. The first port we went into was Elmina; we put ashore some rum, a few boxes of sugar, and some cigars; received some elephant's teeth. The supercargo, with another of the Spaniards, who was called his nephew, went ashore. After lying there three or four days, the supercargo's nephew came on board, and we dropped down to Cape Coast, which is about four miles to the southward of Elmina; we put ashore some rum there, and sugar and cigars, and received some more elephant's teeth, and some hundred and eighty bundles of tobacco done up in hides, and one hogshead of tobacco. There the mate, John Brown, was discharged, and he went ashore. The captain made Robert Williams, who was sometimes called Radcliffe, act second mate; the former second mate was made first mate. There the supercargo came on board. We got under way and went down the coast to Little Mina; there we put ashore a good deal of rum and all the cigars remaining; there we filled all our water-casks. We asked why they were filling so many casks. One of the Spaniards, who was called Pepe, answered us, and said that the water down the coast was brackish; there were about ten casks filled; we did not know at the time that there were any more casks of water on board, but subsequently, after we left the coast, we discovered that there was a very large quantity of water. We received on board at Little Mina a large quantity of ducks, hogs, and fowls. An English war steamer boarded us here; I forget her name. We asked for some stuff to make light clothes; Captain Townsend said that he would procure us the stuff on the first opportunity. From thence we went to a little place called Ackie Wackie; we understood that we were going to Laguna, but did not go there. At Ackie Wackie, a gentleman, who was either American or English, came on board, to whom was delivered a quantity of tobacco; this man received all the tobacco; I heard Captain Townsend tell this man to inform some one that he wanted no receipt for the tobacco. The supercargo's nephew left us at Little Mina. A quantity of canoes, which we thought were coming down towards us, went down the coast. We laid there some two or three days, and put ashore also some casks of rum. We got under weigh soon after dinner; dropped along down the coast some twenty or twenty-five miles; Captain Townsend told the second mate to overhaul twenty-five fathoms of chain round the windlass and weatherbit it; we all inquired what that was for; Williams said he did not know. At this time we were dropping down coast, all sail loose, only the fore topsail hoisted up, and the jib; we all considered this very strange manœuvring. We then saw a large number of canoes lying near the beach, and a large number of negroes on the beach. As we approached, the canoes came towards us; we thought they were after rum; we let go the anchor shortly close to the beach, and let all sail hang; the captain called the second mate, who went aft; the boy, John Leo, was coming forward at the time; the boy said, "By G—d, there is

something up;" we asked him why, and he said he heard the captain paying Mr. Hussy off. In a few minutes, we were all called aft into the cabin. By this time the canoes were alongside filled with negroes. We went into the cabin, and the captain (Townsend) said, "*Men, I have sold my ship, and made a losing voyage of it; I am going to pay you off with three months' extra pay; you can go in the ship if you like; I cannot protect you here ashore.*" We asked him what he was going to do, and he said he was going right ashore. By this time the cabin was half full of negroes. We asked Captain Townsend if we could not go ashore. He said we could if we liked, but that he could not protect us, and that it was as much as he could do to protect himself; he said also, "*Be men, and go in the ship.*" We received our money and went on deck. The Spaniards and Williams, alias Radcliffe, were at work taking in the negroes. José Mora informed us that he was now captain of the vessel, and said also, "*Men will you go with me; if you will, I will give you fifty dollars per month each.*" We told him we did not know—that we wanted to think on it. We went forward and divided our money, as the whole had been paid together. All this time negroes were coming on board. I asked the other men what they thought about it, and told them I did not like to go. We went again to Townsend, who said, "*Men, don't be children, go with the captain and he will treat you well;*" saying, also, "*fifty dollars don't grow in every bush.*" The Spanish captain came up to us and asked us again if we were not going, and said that all would be right. We told him we could not tell yet; we wanted to wait a minute, and went forward and sat down again. In a few minutes he called us aft, and asked again if we were going, repeated his offer of fifty dollars a month, and promised that when we came out he would send us to the United States. Whilst he was talking I hailed a canoe, but the Spanish captain spoke something in Spanish, and the canoe did not come alongside. My intention was to go ashore in the canoe. We again went forward, and concluded that we would go to work; we saw that Williams, Hussy, and Robertson, had gone to work; we went to the gangway, and I asked the Spanish captain what his conditions were: he said he would give us fifty dollars a month; that we should not be misused; and after the negroes were landed we should all be sent to the States; we then went to work. That same night we left the place with from three hundred to three hundred and fifty negroes on board. Nothing important occurred until we got to the coast; here we landed the negroes on a small key on the south side of Cuba, in the morning. After they were landed, the carpenter and myself went ashore and asked the captain what was going to be done; he said, get the ship off (she was aground) and round the key, and I will pay you off and send you away; the captain was sick at the time; we went on board; nothing was done that day till the evening tide; the captain sent on board a pilot to take the vessel round the island; we got her off that night, and the Spanish mate wanted the pilot to take her round that night, which he undertook to do, but by some mismangement she was got aground again; there was nothing more done that night; the next day we were employed in lightening her. The same evening about a dozen Spaniards came on board to help us get her off; we did not succeed in getting her off; a boat went ashore and came back, saying that the captain had ordered her to be burnt; the mate told us to get our things into the boat and go ashore, which we did; and as we were going down the coast, about eight or nine miles from the vessel, we saw the smoke and light rise from the spot where the ship lay; the Spanish mate was with us in the boat, and said we were to stop there a few days; the place was a key, as we were told; we stopped there ten days.

7. To the seventh interrogatory he saith: I did not demand my discharge, because I supposed that I was discharged; I demanded to go ashore, but could not.

8. To the eighth interrogatory he saith: I received good treatment before getting to Africa, and very bad afterwards.

9. To the ninth interrogatory he saith: After we were informed that the Jasper was sold, the American flag was not used, but the Spanish.

10. To the tenth interrogatory he saith: I have already stated, in my answer to a preceding interrogatory. I do not know the name of the place; we stayed there fifteen days; I was well treated by the Spaniards; the captain, at the expiration of ten days, came and paid us, and promised that we should be taken off in three or four; five days after, finding the promise unfulfilled, myself, Atkins, and Freeburn took the ship's boat in the night, leaving the balance of the crew on the key; we went into Cape Antonio for provisions, and were taken up by the authorities and conveyed on board the man-of-war schooner Habanera; the names of my shipmates were, William Hussey, of Nantucket; John William Leo, of the western part of New York; George Hunt, a colored man, of Maine; John Radcliffe or Williams, an Englishman; Robinson, a French Canadian; Charles Hersey, of Nova Scotia; William Atkins, of New York; and William Freeburn, of Philadelphia.

11. To the eleventh interrogatory he saith: As stated to the tenth, I was sent on board the Habanera; I was asked where I came from, and where I was going; it was asked in very good English; I replied that we were from Jamaica, and were going to Key West; my report was a false one; I was induced to make a false report, fearing that if we told the truth they would not believe us; I was on board thirty-five days; I was well treated; from thence I was sent on board a man-of-war in Havana; I was there eight days; I was very well treated; from thence conveyed to the jail of Havana, where I have been since the 2d of July and have been well treated by the officers, but ill treated by the other prisoners.

12. To the twelfth interrogatory he saith: I demanded on the Habanera to be sent to the American consul.

13. To the thirteenth interrogatory he saith: I have been examined once; I have not been informed of the object of my imprisonment; my declarations to the Spanish authorities have been the same as I have made now.

14. To the fourteenth interrogatory he saith: I do not think of anything more; and further this deponent saith not, and subscribes his name.

HARVEY C. PARKS.

SEPTEMBER 21, 1853.

William Atkins being sworn, did depose and say as follows:

1. To the first interrogatory he saith: My name is Williams Atkins; 23 years of age; I am a seaman; I was born in the city of New York, in Roosevelt street; I have resided for the last eight years in Oak street, city of New York; my landlord was Winhold; Captain Skofield, of ship Joseph Badger, of Brunswick; Captain Sawyer, of Mystic, in Connecticut.

2. To the second interrogatory he saith: I came to Cuba in the bark Jasper; I joined her in New York, on the 12th December last, as a seaman; I was living at Winhold's, Oak street—I think No. 45; I am not sure who were the shipping-masters, but think it was Clark and Dean, who came and shipped me at Winhold's; I signed the shipping articles; was told we were going to Sierra Leone, and other ports on the coast of Africa, on a trading voyage, which we were informed would last about seven months; the vessel was to come back to New York; no part of Cuba was named; no one concerned in the Jasper was present; the captain's name was Townsend—his first name I think was Edward; I was not acquainted with Capt. Townsend before I went on board; my wages were fifteen dollars per month.

3. To the third interrogatory he saith: I saw a female in a carriage; she asked us if we were after the Jasper; we answered in the affirmative, and she told us to wait—that the captain was coming in a few minutes; I saw the captain speaking to her; I do not know her name.

4. To the fourth interrogatory he saith: I do not know Capt. Wade.

5. To the fifth interrogatory he saith: I do not know the person called José Mora.

6. To the sixth interrogatory he saith: Captain Townsend did not command and control the Jasper to her arrival in Cuba. When we were getting the vessel out of the dock, a boat came from the opposite side with a man, who proved to be a pilot; Captain Townsend exclaimed, *My game is up now.* Some chests were brought on board, and three or four men came on board; they were Spaniards. Nothing worthy of notice occurred till our arrival in Africa. We first went into Elmina; from thence to Cape Coast; our mate was discharged—his name was Brown; from thence we went to another place that I heard called Little Mina; we took water there, and fowls, pigs, &c.; an English man-of-war steamer visited us here; the captain, as the second mate told us, said to the officers of the steamer that we were going to Laguna; from thence we went to another place, the name of which I do not know; from thence to another place without houses. While busily employed on board, the second mate, the first thing we knew, had been paid off; then myself and others were called into the cabin. The captain said, *I am going to pay you off with three months' extra pay; I am going to leave the ship here, and I'll have nothing more to do with you.* He said that he was going ashore there—that he had made a losing voyage of it. I told him that I wanted to go ashore too. He said, you can't go ashore here—the negroes will kill you for what money you have got; and if they don't kill you, you won't get anything to eat, and will starve to death; he said, also, that he could not protect us, as there were no consuls nearer than 500 miles; he said, also, *You*

see what is up. I told him, why did you not tell us before? He answered that he had no knowledge till the day before—that he had sold his ship; negroes were coming on board at the time, and before we were paid off there were about a dozen of them in the cabin. When we were on deck, one of the passengers, who had been called supercargo, had then assumed command, and told us that he would give us fifty dollars a month to continue in the ship. I told him I did not want his money; but it seemed that we had no other alternative but to go in the ship. Captain Townsend advised us to go in the ship, saying, *You had better put money in your pocket—it is nonsense to go ashore here;* the rest of the crew went forward and consulted together. We were afraid to go ashore from what the captain had represented, and what we ourselves could see. After we were paid, the captain (Townsend) came to me, (I was standing on the waist,) and said, "*Well, Atkins, what do you think of it now?*" I answered, "*I do not know; you have done it so quick that we are taken all aback.*" *He then said,* "*let me alone for that; that is the way I do business—quick is the word.*" Then we went to work —took in a little over three hundred negroes, I think. I did not see when Captain Townsend went off, but he did go. About three hours after we were paid off, we got under way. There were a few disturbances on the passage; we were badly treated and kept separated as much as possible, and sometimes without sleep; we sailed on the 2d of March, and arrived on the coast of Cuba between the sixteenth and twentieth of April, on the south side; were not anywhere near Sierra Leone; we dropped anchor at two or three places on the coast of Cuba; at one of the points a boat came; the next day after arrival on this coast the vessel struck; the negroes were landed then; they were landed in the boats of the ship, and some two or three boats from the shore; that night, after some work, the vessel floated; a pilot came on board; she grounded again; we worked to get her off, without success; we were told to put our things in a boat and go ashore—that they were going to set fire to the ship; we put our things in a boat and were transported about 12 miles up the coast to the westward; we went ashore; ten days after, the captain came and paid us off; he told us that in a few days a schooner would come there and take us off; a schooner did come, but took no notice of us, The Spanish mate, (Dionisio,) who was with us, then said that he would not stop any longer, and that we might do what we best could. That night we waited till all were asleep, and myself, Freeburn, and Parks took the ship's boat and proceeded to sea, intending to go to Key West and inform where the rest of the crew were, if not picked up in the Gulf. Thirty-six hours after we put into Cape San Antonio, to procure water and provisions. There we were taken by the Spanish authorities, and sent on board the man-of-war schooner Habanera.

7. To the seventh interrogatory he saith; When I was paid my money I took it as a discharge, but did not avail myself of it, for reasons given in the preceding interrogatory.

8. To the eighth interrogatory he saith: I was well treated before Townsend left, but very badly after. The names of the persons in charge appeared to be all assumed. The captain's name I never heard. The first mate was called Dionisio; the second mate, Loper. I was

forced to work, but we were paid for our work on landing at the rate of fifty dollars a month.

9. To the ninth interrogatory he saith: The American flag was not used; the Spanish was used.

10. To the tenth interrogatory he saith: I have answered the greater part of this interrogatory before. The names of the rest of the crew were Mr. Hussy, (second mate,) William Radcliffe, George Hunt, (a black man,) Robinson, John William Leo, (a boy,) Charles Hersey, and the two that are now in prison with me. Radcliffe was sick, and pretty nearly dead; and Robinson, who was his friend, would not leave him. The cook, Hunt, agreed to come with us, but changed his mind: the rest were afraid. We left the place some fifteen days after the burning of the Jasper.

11. To the eleventh interrogatory he saith: I was conveyed to the schooner Habanera. I was there thirty-five days. I was asked where I was from, and what countryman I was? The officer that interrogated spoke some English. I said we had left a vessel called the Duke of Wellington at Jamaica, which was a false report. I was afraid if I told the truth something worse might happen to me. The other two men were put in irons, but I was not, as I had sore feet. We were otherwise well treated. Then we were placed in a small schooner, that conveyed us to Havana in thirteen days' passage, and we were placed on board the admiral's ship. In this ship we remained eight days, and were well treated; from thence to the jail of Havana, where we had the opportunity of communicating with the American consul. I have been in the jail two months and nineteen days. We have suffered a great deal from being confined with criminals, who have ill treated us and stolen our property; but the officers of the prison have treated us well.

12. To the twelfth interrogatory he saith: I have never demanded my release or liberty, except once on board the schooner, and once of the American consul here. I am not informed of any charge against me.

13. To the thirteenth interrogatory he saith: I have been examined by the authorities once; have not been informed why I am in prison. My declarations were the same as I am now making.

14. To the fourteenth interrogatory he saith: I believe I have stated everything. Further this deponent saith not, and subscribes his name.

WILLIAM ATKINS.

I, William H. Robertson, acting consul of the United States of America for the city of Havana, in the island of Cuba, do hereby certify that what appears written on thirty pages preceding this, numbered from 10 to 39, both inclusive, are the answers given under oath by William Freeburn, Harvey C. Parks, and William Atkins, and signed by them in my presence, to the interrogatories propounded to them by me, and appearing on pages 1 to 6, both inclusive.

In testimony whereof, I hereunto set my hand, and affix the seal of the consulate of the United States of America at Havana [L. S.] aforesaid, this twenty-third day of September, A. D. one thousand eight hundred and fifty-three.

WILLIAM H. ROBERTSON.

Mr. Mann to Mr. Robertson.

DEPARTMENT OF STATE,
Washington, September 30, 1853.

SIR: Referring to your dispatch No. 45, in which you make known to the department that it is now entirely out of your power to do anything more for the unfortunate American seamen now confined in prison at Havana, charged with having been engaged in the slave trade, I have now to inform you that a copy of the correspondence on the subject will be transmitted to the minister of the United States at Madrid, with an instruction to bring the subject to the attention of the Spanish government.

* * * * * * *

I am, sir, &c.,

A. DUDLEY MANN,
Acting Secretary.

W. H. ROBERTSON, Esq.,
In charge of the U. S. Consulate at Havana, Cuba.

Mr. Robertson to Mr. Marcy.

[Extract.]

[No. 60.] CONSULATE OF THE UNITED STATES, HAVANA,
October 20, 1853.

SIR: * * * * Information has just been brought to me that the three prisoners whose depositions have been sent to the department are about to be brought to trial, and that the fiscal (prosecuting attorney) has asked the court to condemn them to imprisonment for four years. Their final hearing will take place in a few days, and notice was sent to them to appoint a lawyer for their defence. * * It seems that they will be tried on the ground that they stated in their declaration, when first captured, that they had escaped from an English vessel, and therefore they deem the whole statement untrue; but still take that part of their declarations admitting that they had been on board the Jasper, and engaged in the slave trade, for which they must be punished. The same court, I am informed, has liberated, within a few days, all Spanish prisoners that have been imprisoned for the same cause, taken in the act.

I have the honor to be, sir, with great respect, your obedient servant,

W. H. ROBERTSON,
Acting Consul.

Hon. WILLIAM L. MARCY,
Secretary of State of the United States, Washington.

Mr. Robertson to Mr. Marcy.

[Extracts.]

[No. 61.] CONSULATE OF THE UNITED STATES, HAVANA,
October 26, 1853.

SIR: On the 20th instant (dispatch No. 60) I had the honor to inform you that the three American seamen in prison here were to be brought to trial in a few days. * * * * * There is not one particle of evidence against the accused, but their own testimony. * * * * The prosecuting attorney rests his demand upon the plea, *that they have not been able to prove that they were forced to remain on board* the Jasper after she ceased to be engaged in a lawful trade.

* * * * * * *

I am fearful that this affair will become more complicated, and more delay occasioned, by the fact that the six other men of the Jasper, of whom no information had been had for some time, are now in the hands of the authorities of the island. This fact was communicated to me on the 22d instant by the general of marines. A copy of his communication, and of my reply thereto, are herewith enclosed.

* * * * * * *

I have the honor to be, with great respect, sir, your obedient servant,

W. H. ROBERTSON,
Acting Consul.

Hon. W. L. MARCY,
Secretary of State of the United States, Washington.

[Translation.]

CONSULATE OF THE UNITED STATES, HAVANA,
October 22, 1853.

MOST EXCELLENT SIR: I have just received the communication that your excellency has done me the honor to address to me, accompanying the report which, under date of 19th instant, was addressed to your excellency by the commander of the war steamer Guadalquiver upon the occurrence at Cayo Jutias, and informing me at the same time that the six men to whom the commander makes reference, and calling themselves North Americans, belonging to the crew of the vessel they called Jasper, have been placed by your excellency at the disposal of his excellency the Governor and Captain General of the island, for the purpose that he may deem proper.

I doubt not that his excellency the Governor and Captain General will, at the proper time, officially communicate to this consulate what may be ascertained relative to said individuals. Be pleased, however, to receive my thanks for the information your excellency has in advance communicated, and to accept the assurances of respect and consideration with which

I am your excellency's very obedient servant,

W. H. ROBERTSON,

The Commercial Agent in charge of the Consulate.

His Excellency Sr. D. JOSE MA. DE BUSTILLO,

Commander General of Marine.

Mr. Robertson to Mr. Marcy.

[Extract.]

[No. 62.] CONSULATE OF THE UNITED STATES, HAVANA,

October 28, 1853.

SIR: * * * * * * *

I ascertained yesterday that the six men of the barque Jasper had arrived in the morning, and were on board the guard-ship. I immediately called on the captain of the port and requested permission to see them. He immediately granted it, and very courteously and kindly placed his own barge at my disposal to convey me to the guard-ship. I saw the men; their story is equal in all respects to that given by the other three at their examination before me. I suppose the Captain General will write to this consulate soon on this subject.

I expected Judge Clayton would arrive to-day in the Black Warrior, but he has not come. He may be here to-morrow in the Crescent City steamer from New Orleans.

Very respectfully, your obedient servant,

WM. H. ROBERTSON.

Hon. W. L. MARCY,

Secretary of State, &c.

Mr. Cowperthwaite to Mr. Marcy.

PHILADELPHIA, *November* 3, 1853.

SIR: Since my respects of the 27th ultimo, the parents of the unfortunate young American, William Freeburn, are plunged into the deepest distress on the receipt of the intelligence, brought by the last mail steamer from Havana, that their unhappy son and his two companions have been condemned by the Spanish authorities of Cuba and sentenced to an imprisonment of four years. At their earnest solicitation I again address you, sir, to know whether official information of this kind had reached Washington, and whether the needful steps for the reief of these young men had been taken on their behalf.

On the 25th of September the mother of young Freeburn addressed a letter to William H. Robertson, the acting consul at Havana, entreating his good offices on behalf of her son. His reply, under date of the 6th of October, is now before me, in which he says, "I hasten to relieve a mother's feelings, as the steamer goes in the morning, to say, I have just sent the deposition of your son and his two companions to the government at Washington, which deposition purges them of all guilt."

I hope this document has safely reached Washington, and that measures have been taken to vindicate the rights of these unfortunate young Americans.

The consul seems to have done all in his power to alleviate their miseries, and expresses the strongest conviction of their entire innocency, and the confident expectation of their speedy release.

If the deposition forwarded by consul Robertson has reached Washington, it would be a consolation to the parents to be furnished with a copy of it, as it would vindicate the integrity of their son. May I ask to have a copy sent to me, and for a reply to this communication as early as the pressure of your important duties will permit.

I have the honor to be, with great respect, your obedient servant,

J. COWPERTHWAITE.

Hon. W. L. MARCY,
Secretary of State, Washington.

Mr. Graff to Mr. Marcy.

PHILADELPHIA, *November* 5, 1853.

DEAR SIR: I take the liberty of addressing you with the object of giving some testimony to the good character of one of the unfortunate sailors who shipped under mistaken impressions in the "barque Jasper," and are now imprisoned in Havana; hoping that what knowledge I may communicate of such good character may be useful in establishing an impression in your mind as to his innocence of any voluntary connexion with the nefarious trade, as is now alleged against him.

The young man referred to, William Freeburn, I have had in my employ several times, and have had considerable knowledge of him for a period of at least eight years, and known him to have been a remarkably upright, amiable, truthful, and perfectly sober young man; and from the numerous opportunities I have had of judging of his disposition, I feel perfectly confident of his entire innocence of the charges now brought against him; and that his assertions, that he was induced to ship upon the bark on account of false statements as to her business and destination, are all entirely true. He is poor, and, of course, has but few to interest themselves for him, even in his own city. In his letters from Havana he speaks in the highest terms of the United States consul there, whom he thinks has done all in his power for him and his unfortunate companions, of which of course, you are already aware.

The government, through you, will, I know, take all the proper steps in this matter, and I merely write these few lines with the hope that what testimony I can give as to his character, and the reliance I have in the statements made by him, may assist you in forming some conclusion as to the innocence of the charge upon which he is imprisoned. Hoping that you will receive my anxiety for the young man (in whom I am much interested) as sufficient excuse for the liberty I take in intruding these few lines upon you,

I remain, very respectfully, your obedient servant,

FRED. GRAFF,
Civil Engineer, Sup. Fairmount Waterworks.

Hon. WM. L. MARCY,
Secretary of State.

Further testimony can be obtained if you should consider it necessary or desirable.

Mr. Robertson to Mr. Marcy.

[No. 64.] CONSULATE OF THE UNITED STATES, HAVANA,
November 7, 1853.

SIR: I had the honor to receive on the 3d instant a dispatch from the State Department of the 30th September last, signed by Mr. Dudley Mann, as acting secretary. I feel gratified to learn that the department takes an interest in the fate of the three seamen (our unfortunate countrymen) now lying in prison here.

* * * * * *

The defence of the three American seamen has been presented to court. I understand that it is an able document, and regret that I cannot forward by this opportunity a translated copy of it. The next steamer will convey it.

I have the honor to be, sir, with great respect, your obedient servant,

WM. H. ROBERTSON,
Acting Consul.

Hon. WM. L. MARCY,
Secretary of State.

Mr. Marcy to Mr. Clayton, United States Consul, Havana.

DEPARTMENT OF STATE,
Washington, November 8, 1853.

SIR: Your special attention is directed, immediately on your arrival at your post, to the condition of the American sailors now imprisoned in Havana, and awaiting their trial, charged with a violation of the laws of Spain in regard to the slave trade. The facts, so far as they are known to the department, from the dispatches of Mr. Robertson, (who has discharged the duties of United States consul at Havana since the departure of Judge Sharkey in June last,) and from gentlemen in the United States, are chiefly these: The barque "Jasper" was seized in New York on the 19th of October, 1852, charged with sailing under a false register, and belonging, as was supposed, to a Spaniard named * * * * * , though her papers bore the name of * * * * * * * . The barque having been detained in custody for some time, was at length bonded in the sum of ten thousand dollars, and on or about the 12th of December sailed secretly from the port without any clearance or papers, under the command of Captain Townsend, for the African coast. After touching at two or three places on the cape coast, and landing nearly the whole carge, Captain Townsend sailed for another point, where, immediately on his arrival, he informed his crew that he had sold his vessel. She was at once filled with a cargo of three hundred negroes, a part of whom were put on board before Captain Townsend left the ship. Having paid his crew three months' extra wages, and saying he could no longer protect them, he advised them to go back in the vessel as passengers, as they would either be killed by the natives or starve to death if they went on shore. Having no other alternative, they remained on board the vessel, doing duty as sailors, and subjected to much hard treatment. The barque then sailed under the command of Spanish officers, and with a Spanish flag, for Cuba, where, having landed her cargo, the vessel was run aground and burnt. The Americans who composed the original crew of the vessel, having been told by the Spanish mate that he could do nothing for them, took to the long-boat, and tried to make their way to some place where they could obtain assistance. On the 5th of May the three sailors above referred to, and believed to be citizens of the United States, while seeking water and provisions near Cape Antonio, were arrested by some Spanish soldiers and sent to Havana, where they are now awaiting their trial, which the department is informed in Mr. Robertson's No. 61, under date of October 26th, will shortly take place.

The department regrets that the representations which Mr. Robertson has repeatedly been instructed to make to the Captain General have been disregarded, viz: that these unfortunate sailors were, most likely, ignorant of the intended object of the voyage when they shipped on board the "Jasper" at New York, and are at least entitled to the benefit of the doubt; that they had, in fact, no other way left, when on the African coast, but to return to America in the vessel; and they were thus unwillingly compelled, contrary to their inclinations, to participate in the odium, the danger, and the criminal offence, (though without criminal intent, and innocent in point of fact;) that the ends of justice would be best subserved by yielding to the urgent request of the United States district attorney at New York, a copy of whose letter on the subject is on the files of the consulate, to permit them to be sent, under the care of a United States officer, to that place, for the purpose of using their evidence to convict parties in that city supposed to have been concerned in fitting out the "Jasper" and engaging in the slave trade.

It was suggested also to Mr. Robertson, in the case of refusal, to request that they might be allowed to be witnesses in suits which might properly be brought against persons in Havana, whose names are well known, and who were the chief instigators of the offence with which these unfortunate men now stand charged.

The department has been given to understand that the Spaniards who were arrested and imprisoned for the same offence have all recently been set at liberty, without the form of a trial, by the very court which has been asked by the fiscal to condemn to imprisonment for four years the American sailors. A proceeding so partial and so contrary to justice, if true, needs but to be stated to receive universal condemnation; while, at the same time, it must tend still further to excite in this country, and among a portion of the Cuban population, a spirit of increased hostility to the existing institutions of the island. If a part of those alleged to be guilty of the same criminal offence may be discharged without trial by the Spanish court, there would seem to be no reason why the same indulgence should not be extended towards those who, by their own account, which yet remains uncontradicted, were entrapped into the apparent commission of a high crime. Even if the court should be unwilling to assume this responsibility, it is understood that the Captain General is invested with ample power for the purpose.

The Spanish authorities seem now determined to press the case of these seamen to a trial, and you are instructed to take care that all the provisions of the seventh article of the treaty between the United States and Spain, of 1795, are complied with. That article declares that "in all cases of seizure, detention, or arrest for debts contracted or offences committed by any citizen or subject of the one party within the jurisdiction of the other, the same shall be made and prosecuted by order and authority of law only, and according to the regular course of proceedings usual in such cases. The citizens and subjects of both parties shall be allowed to employ such advocates, solicitors, notaries, agents, and factors as they may judge proper, in all their affairs and in all their trials at law in which they may be concerned before the tribunals of the other party; and such agents shall have free access to be present at the proceedings in such cases, and at the taking of all examinations and evidence which may be exhibited in the said trials."

It is deemed of the highest importance that the prisoners shall be allowed the advice and assistance of counsel in all the examinations of witnesses in the case, and in every step of the proceedings.

If the seamen desire it you will be present as the natural defender of their rights, and, by virtue of the treaty stipulations, as their counsel and advocate. Should there be any disregard of these stipulations you will at once enter your protest against it and report the fact to this department.

In view of the circumstances of the case you are authorized to employ other counsel, and to charge the expense of the same in your account—it being understood that this is not to be considered a precedent for the employment of counsel, except under special authority from the department.

I am, sir, &c.,

W. L. MARCY.

ALEXANDER M. CLAYTON, Esq.,
United States Consul, Havana.

Mr. Marcy to Mr. Cowperthwaite.

DEPARTMENT OF STATE,
Washington, November 10, 1853.

SIR: I have to acknowledge the receipt of your communication in respect to William Freeburn, one of three American seamen now imprisoned in Havana, and awaiting his trial, charged with having been engaged in the slave trade.

In reply I have to inform you that the department has taken a deep interest in the fate of these unfortunate men from the moment it received information of their arrest and imprisonment. Mr. Robertson has been acting throughout under the instructions of this department; and Mr. Clayton, the newly-appointed consul at Havana, has been informed of all the circumstances of the case, and additional instructions sent to him since the receipt of your letter.

The deposition of William Freeborn, to which you refer, has been transmitted to Mr. O'Conor, the United States district attorney in New York, for the purpose of being used in an important trial in that city.

I transmit herewith an extract from Mr. Robertson's dispatch, dated October 26th, which is the latest information in respect to these seamen which has been received at this department.

I am sir, &c.,

W. L. MARCY.

J. COWPERTHWAITE, Esq.,
Philadelphia, Pa.

Mr. Robertson to Mr. Marcy.

[No. 65.] CONSULATE OF THE UNITED STATES, HAVANA,
November 14, 1853.

SIR: In my dispatch, No. 61, dated 26th of October, I had the honor to inform you that the six men, shipmates of the three belonging to the bark Jasper, and that have been so long in prison, had been captured, and that the general of marines had informed me of their capture, and of his having placed them at the Captain General's disposal. With that dispatch I forwarded to you a copy of the General's letter and my reply thereto.

On the evening of the 7th I received a communication from the Captain General, dated the 5th, on the subject. I send you a copy (translated) of it, and my reply. You will see my object in the reply was to save the six men from a long imprisonment, if possible, and at the same time to prevent more delay in the case of the other three. I am sorry to say that I was unsuccessful, for the Captain General on the 9th informs me, officially, that the six men belonged to the Jasper, and that he had put them at the disposal of the royal audiencia. Copies of his excellency's communication and of my reply are also herewith enclosed, together with a translation of the defence sent to court by the lawyer of Parks, Atkins and Freeburn. Sentence has not yet been decreed by the court.

* * * * * *

I have the honor to be, sir, with great respect, your obedient servant,

WILLIAM H. ROBERTSON,
Acting Consul.

Hon. WM. L. MARCY,
Secretary of State, &c.

[Translation.]

EVER FAITHFUL ISLAND OF CUBA.—GOVERNMENT AND CAPTAINCY GENERAL, POLITICAL SECRETARY'S OFFICE, SECTION SEVENTH.

There are detained on board the guard-ship Villavicencio six individuals who say that they are shipwrecked men, and that they belonged to the American bark Jasper, lost on the Colorado reefs.

Therefore, I hope that your lorship will be pleased to inform me as early as possible all that you may know in regard to said bark's place of sailing and her loss, and whether the said individuals detained belonged to her, so as to resolve what may be proper.

God preserve your lordship many years. Havana, Nov. 5, 1853.

VALENTIN CAÑEDO.

To the AGENT
in charge of the Consulate of the United States.

CONSULATE OF THE UNITED STATES, HAVANA,
November 8, 1853.

MOST EXCELLENT SIR: I had the honor to receive, on the evening of yesterday, your excellency's official communication of the 5th instant, wherein I am informed of the detention on board the ponton Villavicencio of six individuals who belonged to an American vessel and were wrecked on the Colorado reefs. I presume that these individuals are the same about whom his excellency the general of marines courteously wrote to me on the 22d of October last, as having been sent to his excellency by the commanding officer of her Catholic Majesty's steamer Guadalquiver from Cayo Justias, and as having been placed by his excellancy at your excellency's disposal.

Your excellency desires me to inform you, as soon as possible, all I may know in regard to these men, and the circumstances of their shipwreck. I have no further reliable information on the subject but that which has been communicated to me by your excellency, and by his excellency the general of marines. I have therefore no good reason to suppose that they are anything but what they state themselves to be.

It is my duty, in obedience to one of the standing instructions of my government, to aid and succor all distressed American seamen that may be found within the jurisdiction of this consulate, and if no employment may be obtained for them, to send them to the United States at the expense of the government. It is also my duty, of course, to ascertain by their papers that they are Americans; but in many cases of shipwrecks, seamen lose their papers, and the consul must in such cases abide by their word and general appearance. It is very probable that the seamen referred to may be in the latter condition, and I am ready to receive them and take charge of them, if your excellency will be so good as to order that they be placed at my disposal.

I have the honor to be, with great respect, your excellency's obedient servant,

WILLIAM H. ROBERTSON,
Com. Agent in charge of Consulate.

His Excellency Señor Don VALENTIN CAÑEDO,
Governor and Captain General of the Island of Cuba.

[Translation.]

[SEAL.]

I have received your official letter of yesterday, in answer to mine of the 5th instant, about the six seamen who are on board the ponton Villavicencio, and were found at Cayo Justias, and who were sent by the commanding officer of her Majesty's steamer Guadalquiver; which seamen having turned out to be the same whom you referred to in your communication of 15th July last, stating that they were on the Cayo Cortes, and who, from information obtained, it was supposed had embarked on a molasses vessel bound to this port, I have put them, under this date, at the disposal of the real *audiencia pretorial*, (superior court,) as they belong to the crew of the corvette or bark "Jasper," that landed the cargo of bozal negroes she brought from Africa, at the place called Baylen, or Cortes Cove, where she was burnt after the landing, to the end that the said superior court may determine what is proper on the subject, as said court is still investigating and proceeding in the cause instituted in consequenee of the act mentioned. Which I say to you for your information.

God preserve you many years. Havana, November 9, 1853.

VALENTIN CAÑEDO.

To the Señor COMMERCIAL AGENT
in charge of the Consulate of the United States.

CONSULATE OF THE UNITED STATES, HAVANA,
November 11, 1853.

MOST EXCELLENT SIR: I had the honor to receive, last evening, your excellency's communication of the 9th instant, in regard to the six sailors on board the ponton Villavicencio. I am sorry to learn that these men belonged to the Jasper, that landed negroes at Baylen; though I feel gratified that their personal safety is secured. They have no doubt undergone great anxiety and trouble, and their being now subjected to the delays consequent to a judicial investigation will make them feel very uneasy, even in the case of their being eventually acquitted, as I hope they will be, for I am well convinced that they, as well as the other three who have been so long in prison, and at present undergoing trial, were deceived by the parties interested in the vessel, and that they were innocent of all intention to infringe the laws of their country or of Spain.

I trust that the proceedings in regard to these six men will not cause more delay to prevent the case of the other three from being brought to an immediate termination. I will respectfully solicit of your excellency to use your powerful influence to bring their trials to a prompt conclusion.

I have the honor to be, very respectfully, your excellency's obedient servant,

WM. H. ROBERTSON,
Commercial Agent in charge of the Consulate.

His Excellency Señor Don Valentin Cañedo,
Governor and Captain General of the Island of Cuba.

Most Powerful Lord: Don José Gregorio Ibarrola, an attorney of this royal superior court, and guardian (curador) appointed by the court, of the seamen, William Atkins, William Freeburn, and Harvey C. Parks, in the proceedings carried on before this superior court, about the landing of two hundred and eighty bozal negroes at a place called Baylen, in the manner most conformable to law, says: that the parties whom I defend have been informed of the charge made by the fiscal (prosecuting attorney) asking that the penalty of four years' imprisonment be decreed against them, unless they prove, they having confessed that they formed a part of the crew of the Jasper, that when they embarked at New York, they did so in the understanding that that vessel was going to Africa after goods of lawful trade; not on account of the necessity in which every judicial defender is, of exhausting every means for the saving of his client, but because, sincerely speaking, the opinion of the learned and zealous representative of public vengeance (vindicta publica) appears exaggerated, that I will try to demonstrate that the unfortunate minors, victims and not criminals, in the affair of the Jasper, ought to be absolved from all culpability and penalty, declaring, at the same time, their right to be in force, that they may exercise it against whom it may concern. The attorney for the prosecution, to whose strenuous efforts is due the discovery of such facts as the finding of the hull of the vessel that was burnt, and of another fact not mentioned in the process, has shown, in his severe style, the profound aversion with which he looks upon the filthy traffic in slaves, seconding the noble conduct of the president of this court, Don Valentin Cañedo, and has acknowledged, with the immense pain with which honest men in Cuba must confess it, that there are many parties interested in the traffic that make the investigation of the facts impossible. Well, if opinion is to be considered in these cases, allow me also to allege the opinion of the country of the accused. Were they natives of the southern States, there might exist a presumption against them; but they are all, most powerful lord, natives of the northern States, where a hatred to the institution of slavery grows in the midst of attempts of future and serious disturbances to the American Union. The first reason appearing to establish their innocence, is their birth. But it will be said that they have confessed the crime, or the infringement of the Spanish law. The assertion is not entirely exact. The confession that law requires is not that of a fact, but that of *an intention*. The fact always exists; it is one and invariable; it is sign of matter, but not of the spirit or of the will. The accused might stand convicted, but not confessed (confesos.) In the proceedings there is not one single datum besides the declarations of the prisoners, and not one of their letters says that they went to Africa to bring slaves. Even if an explicit confession existed, the true meaning of the law of partida would not justify the punishment of the supposed criminals, because the mere confession is not a sufficient foundation, according to the Spanish law. As long as the voluntary infringement of the penal law is not proved, there is no *crime;* for the same reason that the punishment is possible, just, and necessary, is the proof possible, necessary, and just. Presumption is as moral for the judge, as inefficient for punishment. The confession upon which the report I am answering is based, does not exist in its judicial form, as the only thing the accused have said is, that they belonged to the crew of a vessel that sailed from New York, bound to the coast of Africa; there exists nothing more than their declarations upon the subject. In this manner is their existence in the said vessel explained:

The accused were captured or arrested at the Cape San Antonio by two matriculated of the Spanish mercantile marine, and when they were first examined they had no discrepancy in their statements as to the circumstances that brought them to this country. They stated that they were arrested on a morning of May last, when they had disembarked at Cape San Antonio to provide themselves with water and provisions; that they had arrived at that place from some sixty miles to the eastward of the southern coast, and that the boat which conveyed them belonged to the American bark Jasper, of which they had formed part of the crew, and which had come to these waters from the coast of Africa with a cargo of bozal negroes, numbering about three hundred, that had been landed on the said southern coast, where the vessel was burnt without their knowing by whose order; they said that the negroes had been landed in the boats of the bark and in three other boats that came from the shore; they are ignorant who were the parties interested in the cargo. The vessel did not sail from any point of the island of Cuba, but from New York, to make a voyage to Sierra Leone, for the purpose of bringing goods of lawful trade, and no insinuation was made to them about negroes, neither did they know of such negroes until they saw them in the vessel. The narrative that has just been read has all verisimilitude imaginable. Those who fitted out or purchased the vessel were in no necessity of revealing the object of the voyage to the sailors, who were instruments and not agents in the business. It suited the interest of the purchasers that the American flag should protect their crime, because, as the vessel could not be visited, she went safely to the coast of Africa itself; but the American officers, who were engaged to that place to deliver the vessel to the purchasers, would not continue their services any further after they learned the object of the voyage. The captain remained on shore at the place they touched at off the coast, and the mate had previously left, and the command was taken as captain, and the capacity of first and second mates, by the Spaniards mentioned in the declarations. The unfortunate seamen, deceived and taken by surprise, had no other resource but to yield to the law of necessity; neither could they appeal to force, had rebellion occurred to their minds as a resource, as it may be seen in the declarations that the Spaniards and Portuguese exceeded the sailors in authority and numbers. It was necessary to resign themselves to the imperious necessity that oppressed them, till the moment of their arrival and separation in the boat. Even then they were warned to be silent, to continue oppressing their minds, and threatening them with serious troubles if they made known what had taken place, which they are now verifying in a prison to their misfortune.

In regard to the truthfulness of the declarations, other data appear in the proceedings that destroy the suspicion that they are mere excuses. The consul general of England, on participating to the government the imprisonment of the three sailors, about whom governmental communications had already taken place, states the facts as repeated by the accused, and these coincide with those opinions—not only the official communication of the consul or commercial agent of the United States, but also that of the commanding officer of the United States sloop-of-war Albany, in which he affirms by a *perfect conviction* that the American citizens imprisoned have not intended to infringe the laws of Spain nor of the United States, and that therefore they were deceived by the parties interested in the expedition; that it was necessary that these latter should be punished for their nefarious and iniquitous conduct; that, considering the sailors innocent, he claimed them, and requested of the Spanish government to have arrested the six individuals remaining, who, he understood, were on Salt Key. These statements of three foreign functionaries in favor of the intention of my clients give credit to their assertion. Were not the presumption of innocence sufficient, unless a criminal intention shall be proved? and were it for the sameness of the declarations, which appear as if they had been copied from each other?

In the act of taking their declarations, the accused were reproved on their defending themselves from cupability, without any other foundation than the fact of their not having presented themselves to the authorities when they found themselves free from coaction, to prosecute the authors of the evils they had undergone. The censure will become of no force when it is observed—1st. That they were ignorant who were the parties interested in the vessel. 2d. That they were made to believe that if they confessed what had taken place they would fare badly. 3d. That in their country they had the right to make claims against those who had deceived them there, by means more expeditious and in accordance with their habits, customs, and laws.

Had they believed themselves to be guilty, they would not have landed in a country where everything was strange to them, and where the first suspicion they were going to create was by their use of the English language, which was the cause of their being observed and detained, as one of the captors has said. They believed themselves to be at the worst in the case of deserted seamen, who, by an article of the treaty in force, are to be mutually delivered up; but they forgot that, there not existing a role d'equipage, (crew list,) the delivery could not be effected, and now they are undergoing the rigors of a jail.

Your highness is well aware that in criminal cases it is dangerous to give estimation to presumptions not corroborated by full proofs. History presents us examples that are now weighing upon the public conscience of nations like grave-stones. It is vain that memories have been honored and posterity satisfied, if the evil has been unavoidable. This case itself presents serious suspicions against a Spanish high functionary and all his subordinates at New Filipinas. It has been proved that the cargo was landed in that territory, and that the vessel was burnt in a bay; and, what is still more scandalous, an accusation by the English consul about the delivery of money to pay for those infringements has been confirmed; and still the facts are explained, and your highness has discontinued all proceedings in regard to those individuals. The most dishonorable part of the affair—that of the participation of a price for consenting to the landing—I have heard the friends of Ayllon explain in the most satisfactory manner.

The lieutenant governor had for enemies those whom he prevented from committing misdemeanors, and these enemies either calumniated him, or supposed that the money that had been remitted without mystery, there being no motive for concealment from the public eye, was the price of the crime.

The facts have not been blotted out; the suspicions could not be completely removed; and the doctrines of the fiscal (attorney for the prosecution) I adopt as positive. As long as there is no proof, presumptions may exist in vain. My clients have not confessed a crime; they have made known one fact, which *is made apparent* ONLY in their declarations. Their situation cannot be made more painful than it has been till now. Were it fully established that the three sailors belonged of their own will to the crew of the bark Jasper, the penalty demanded by the fiscal against them would still be excessive. The law makes no mention of the case in point. It was very difficult to be foreseen, as it was very difficult to conceive of the frank statement made by the three foreigners who are the subjects of the present proceedings.

The law has considered that the capture may be made by cruisers of a vessel with bozal negroes on board, or already without them; for the two cases it has indicated different penalties to the captain and others of the crew.

What penalty does the law impose against a seaman who is captured taking provisions to return to his country, and by no means on board of a vessel?

What penalty does the law indicate against him who acknowledges that he was an involuntary seaman of a vessel that has disappeared?

If the law, in the case of the vessel being captured without negroes, has diminished the penalty one half, and even more, how is it that four years of imprisonment are demanded, when the law imposes no penalty in the strange case now in question? If any penalty is to be imposed, it should be that of the fourth article of the law of 1845, or, what is the same, that of one year's imprisonment, as it is the minimum between the various cases. It is not, however, applicable to the present question, because no proof exists, no vessel has been captured, no negroes have been found, nor have the local authorities been punished for the infringement or negligence. Nothing exists but the statements of the accused, which have already been analyzed. In short, there exists only one fact demonstrated, which is, that three American seamen have revealed and given the means to investigate that they have been by violence brought in a slaver vessel that disembarked her cargo in Cuba; that in virtue of the eighth article of the treaty between Spain and the United States of 27th October, 1795, they believed themselves authorized on account of the greater penalty suffered, *urgent necessity*, to come ashore for provisions; that, resting on the personal provisions of the international law of their country, they believe themselves to have the right of prosecuting their deceivers, and did not presume that they would be subjected to suffering for their forcible permanency on board of the slave ship; that by virtue of their condition as sailors, they supposed, in conformity to the thirteenth article of the treaty of 22d February, 1819, that they would be delivered up to their consul, as they had been looked upon as deserters, about which they subsequently changed their purpose, but not their condition.

On making these suggestions, it is my mind to demonstrate that, on the part of my clients, no law of the country has been infringed; that they were not voluntary slavers, nor have they exercised rights which they had not when captured. It is true, that by reporting themselves deserters they did not tell the truth, but they have not failed against truth in any solemn act. Therefore, I petition of your highness to be pleased to decree and ordain in conformity to what I have solicited at the commencement, and dispose, in consequence, that the three prisoners be delivered to the American consul, as has been asked by the commander of the Albany, that they may be transmitted to New York, there to make the investigations already indicated, so that the accused may be allowed the damages they have suffered.

Mr. Marcy to Mr. O'Conor.

DEPARTMENT OF STATE,
Washington, November 16, 1853.

SIR: Information has been received at this department, that the Spanish captain of the barque "Jasper" is now staying with his wife, under the assumed name of * * * * * *, either at the New York or St. Nicholas Hotel, and that he is engaged in fitting out another expedition to the coast of Africa. This intelligence is deemed of sufficient importance to be communicated to you without delay.

I am, sir, &c.,

W. L. MARCY.

CHARLES O'CONOR, Esq.,
U. S. District Attorney, New York.

Mr. Clayton, United States Consul, to Mr. Marcy.

[Extract.]

CONSULATE OF THE UNITED STATES, HAVANA,
December, 5, 1853.

DEAR SIR: * * * * * *

In your dispatch of the 9th ultimo, relative to the American seamen imprisoned here, you refer to the 7th article of the treaty of 1795. I learn from various sources, among others from a letter of the late consul Sharkey to your department, of date the 15th of January, 1853, No. 23, that the authorities of this island do not regard that treaty as having any force or effect here. Whether this view be correct or not, is of little practical import so long as they adhere to it. It furnishes reason for an effort to form a new treaty, or to get this recognized, expressly, as extending to all the Spanish islands and dependencies.

* * * * * * * *

I have the honor to be, &c.,

ALEX. M. CLAYTON,
U. S. Consul, Havana.

Hon. W. L. MARCY,
Secretary of State.

Mr. Robertson to Mr. Marcy.

[Extract.]

CONSULATE OF THE UNITED STATES, HAVANA,
December 21, 1853.

SIR: I received last evening notes from several of the prisoners, begging me to come and see them; that their condition was becoming every day more desperate. I went, and took them some money and other articles necessary for their comfort. The three prisoners that were first captured had some money of their own, which they placed in my hands, and I have been giving it to them in small sums since. The other six had not a cent when they were brought; they had been robbed, and spent every dollar they had. I have advanced to the second mate, for the benefit of the six, $17, and have directed the secretary to charge it to me, until I was authorized by the department to charge it to the government, which I hope may be allowed, in consideration of the circumstances. * * * * * * * * * *

The fiscal (prosecuting officer) has asked that the six be condemned to four years' imprisoment also, on the extraordinary grounds that their testimony agrees with that of the other three.

The prisoners informed me that there had been many men confined in the same room with them, who had been placed there at different times, having been taken in the act of landing negroes, all of whom had been released, as they were required for other slavers fitting out; and that there was a large crew there with them waiting for a vessel fitting out in the harbor, to sail in a week, when they would go on board.

I am not disposed to think that these men will be condemned. I cannot think that this government will commit such an act.

Mr. Clayton wrote to the Captain General on the 7th in behalf of these men, but this office has not yet been favored with a reply. I enclose a copy of Mr. Clayton's communication.

I have the honor to be, sir, your most obedient servant,

WM. H. ROBERTSON,
Acting Consul.

Hon. WM L. MARCY,
Secretary of State, &c.

CONSULATE OF THE UNITED STATES, HAVANA,
December 7, 1853.

MOST EXCELLENT SIR: I have been instructed by the government of the United States to solicit the attention of your excellency to the case of nine American seamen who have been imprisoned in Havana for some time past, charged with a violation of the laws of Spain in regard to the slave trade. I understand that three of the nine have had a trial, but that no judgment will be rendered in the matter until the other six have been likewise tried.

In their depositions they have declared that they shipped upon the vessel without knowing the purpose of the voyage, and that from necessity, and not from choice, they were against their will compelled to do duty on the return voyage as sailors. There is no testimony opposed to their statement. It would seem, then, from these facts, that they acted without criminal intent, and are innocent in point of fact.

The government of the United States has been given to understand that certain subjects of Spain who were arrested and imprisoned for the same offence had been set at liberty without trial. It would tend very much to promote the harmony and good feeling which now subsist between the two governments if the same course were pursued in reference to the American seamen. This act of courtesy in the commencement of your excellency's administration would be properly appreciated by the American government, and would no doubt meet with a suitable reciprocity if occasion should offer.

I am directed, also, to state to your excellency that if this request should be granted, and the prisoners delivered to an American officer, they will be carried to the city of New York for the purpose of giving evidence there against the parties supposed to be concerned in fitting out the vessel on which they shipped, so that the really guilty may be punished.

A reply to this communication at as early a day as may be compatible with the convenience of your excellency will be regarded as an especial kindness.

I have the honor to be, &c.,

ALEX. M. CLAYTON.

His Excellency the MARQUIS DE LA PEZUELA,
Governor and Captain General of the Island of Cuba, &c., &c.

Mr. Robertson to Mr. Marcy.

[No. 12.] CONSULATE OF THE UNITED STATES, HAVANA,
January 5, 1854.

SIR: On the 31st ult. I received from the Captain General a reply to Mr. Clayton's communication of the 7th, (of which I sent you a copy on the 21st ultimo,) requesting the release of the American seamen, the crew of the bark Jasper. Accompanying this I send a copy of the answer, by which you will perceive that the Captain General took umbrage at certain expressions in Mr. Clayton's letter, and that he has declined to accede to the request. I have replied, on the 3d instant, to his excellency's letter, and now forward you a copy of mine, hoping that the contents thereof will meet your approbation.

I entertain very little doubt that the seamen will be liberated, and I am inclined to think my letter may hasten that result. If such is to be the case, I sincerely hope it may be before Judge Clayton's successor arrives, as I should regret extremely that any other should have the gratification of leading them forth to liberty from the unjust imprisonment, and sending them home to their families. If success is obtained by me, I shall consider myself amply compensated for many days of toil in their behalf.

I have the honor to be, sir, with great respect, your most obedient servant,

WILLIAM H. ROBERTSON,
Acting Consul.

Hon. WILLIAM L. MARCY,
Secretary of State of the United States, Washington.

[Translation.]

[L. S.]

EVER FAITHFUL ISLAND OF CUBA.—GOVERNMENT AND CAPTAIN GENERALCY, OFFICE OF THE POLITICAL SECRETARY, SECTION FIFTH.

Having transmitted to the royal "audiencia pretorial" (superior court) your lordship's official communication of the 7th instant, in reference to several seamen of your nation belonging to the American bark Jasper, that discharged 280 bozal negroes in the Bight of Cortes, jurisdiction of Pinar del Rio, upon which occurrence a criminal proceeding is pending in the first chamber of justice of said superior court, to which they are subjected, and they are imprisoned in the royal jail, the court have informed me, under date of the 23d, that the course of the proceedings, which are in conformity to our judicial forms, had not to that day suffered but the requisite delays on which the fate itself of said sailors is concerned, the same having passed to the lawyer of three of the last six to answer to the charges of the "fiscal," (prosecuting officer,) conformable to the penal law of the matter. In such understanding, and they being considered in the same light as Spanish subjects, and with the same guarantees in the process, of which you are aware, as you have been on the look-out, and have even furnished them for their defence one of the distinguished lawyers of this capital for his ability and zeal in the exercise of his profession, it is to me very strange that it should have been given to understand to your government that some Spanish subjects, initiated and imprisoned for the same offence, had obtained from the tribunal a release from jail, *without being tried.*

This odious difference, and the want of zeal for the right administration of justice that such a precedent involves, causes a serious offence to the well-known uprightness of the royal audiencia, and I therefore repel it.

Consequently, and there not existing good motives for the release that your lordship claims, and less for your government to make depend, from the result of your lordship's exertions in this affair, the promotion of the harmony and good relations that subsist between it and that of my august sovereign, I regret that I cannot accede to the favor that your lordship solicts in your said communication that I am now answering.

God preserve you many years. Havana, December 31, 1853.

The MARQUIS DE LA PEZUELA.

The Commercial Agent
in charge of the Consulate of the United States.

Consulate of the United States, Havana,
January 3, 1854.

Most Excellent Sir: I had the honor to receive, on the evening of the 31st ultimo, your excellency's official communication of that date, in reply to one from this consulate of the 7th of the same month, written by order of the government of the United States, and containing a request that the nine American seamen who had the misfortune to come to this island in the bark Jasper, should be set at liberty.

These seamen have undergone long imprisonment and suffering. As no evidence has been presented to contradict their statements, in which they all have declared their innocence of any intent to infringe the laws of Spain, my government came to the conclusion that they were innocent in point of fact.

It has never been intended by the government or by this consulate to assert that the judicial forms of the country have not been complied with in the case. I am aware that, so far as regards the prisoners, those forms have been observed. Still, my government deems it very strange that the Spanish subjects, and others who belonged to the Jasper, and who were really the guilty parties, have escaped and that only the American part of the crew have been made to suffer for the act of landing the slaves.

Your excellency feels indignant at the information given to my government that several Spanish subjects, arrested and imprisoned for the same crime, had been released without being tried, as it involves a a serious offence against the well-known uprightness of the royal audiencia. I beg to assure your excellency that no offence was intended by Mr. Clayton when he made the statement in his letter. He desired to convey to your excellency the fact that the government of the United States having been given to understand that such releases had taken place. The government continually receives information from this island that, notwithstanding all the vigilance and energy of the Spanish authorities and naval forces, as well as the efforts of the British cruisers, many cargoes of slaves are landed upon the island, and very few captures are made, and the parties concerned and engaged in such importations are not discovered.

This leads the government of the United States to apprehend that distinctions are made to the prejudice of those men because they are Americans, or call themselves such.

It is the wish and intention of the President of the United States to preserve and promote the harmony and good relations that have so long subsisted between his government and that of her Catholic Majesty; but, at the same time, he stands pledged before the country, and the world, to extend his protection to the citizens of the United States abroad, when such citizens find themselves in difficulty not brought on by an intentional disregard or contempt of the laws of other countries. He cannot make distinctions between individuals—it makes no difference if they are sailors or senators; all are equally entitled to the watchful care and protection of the government.

From the nature of the last dispatch received at this office from the State Department, I am led to believe that my government considers that all the exertions made by this consulate to obtain the release of those seamen have been unnecessarily and coldly diregarded. I therefore deeply regret that your excellency should have come to the determination not to accede to the last request; that determination will be transmitted to my government. I sincerely hope that it may not produce a weakening effect upon the relations between the two governments.

I have the honor to be, with great respect, your excellency's very obedient servant,

WM. H. ROBERTSON,
Vice Commercial Agent in charge of Consulate.

His Excellency the MARQUIS DE LA PEZUELA,
Governor, Captain General, &c., &c., &c., of the Island of Cuba.

Mr. Robertson to Mr. Marcy.

[No. 18.] CONSULATE OF THE UNITED STATES, HAVANA,
January 12, 1854.

SIR: I called yesterday at the jail for the purpose of taking some money and necessaries to the unfortunate American seamen. One of them handed me the inclosed note, by which you will perceive that all but two of the Spanish prisoners that were there for being engaged in the slave trade have been released. Our seamen told me that those parties had stated that they were about to embark for the coast immediately. They likewise informed me that they had lately passed two entire days without food of any kind. They exhibited to me their dinner of that day, which consisted of about two ounces of bad meat, and a quarter of a plate of dirty-looking rice. Their complaints are very strong. I have no answer to the communication I wrote to the Captain General on the subject of these men, and presume he is waiting for the action of the superior court.

I have the honor to be, sir, with great respect, your obedient servant,

WM. H. ROBERTSON,
Acting Consul.

Hon. Wm. L. Marcy,
Secretary of State of the United States, Washington.

Havana, *January* 10, 1854.

Dear Sir: I wish to inform you that they set all the slaves at liberty on Monday, but two. On Sunday morning the prisoners had a row about their rations, and sent for the governor, and told him that there was not enough there for everybody; there was wanting thirty men's rations, so we had no breakfast that morning. The meat was so stinking that we could not bear the smell of it; the same rice was sent up for dinner; there was not enough for everybody, and, being strangers, of course had to go without; so all we had was about two ounces of bread. We hardly get enough any day to cover the bottom of our plates—say about five or six mouthfuls. There was a man stabbed here on Monday night; he was carried to the hospital.

On Tuesday morning there was a man beat nearly to death; he struck the man that was serving out the coffee, because he would not give him any; he now lies in the hospital in a very precarious state; if he lives, he will never be of any use to himself; he is completely ruined for life. You would oblige me if you would let me have seventeen dollars, and two or three papers, if you have them to spare; they will keep us from worrying so much. Hoping to have the pleasure of seeing you soon,

I remain, yours respectfully,

WILLIAM ATKINS.

Mr. Robertson's certificate.

Consulate of the United States, Havana.

On the day of the date hereof, I, William H. Robertson, acting consul of the United States of America for Havana, at about 9 o'clock a. m., called at the royal jail of said city, where the American seamen, William Freeburn, William Atkins, and Harvey C. Parks, are imprisoned, and asked them for the sheet of paper hereto annexed, containing one interrogatory on each page of the same, which I had left with them some days since, requiring them to write their answers in continuation. They handed me the said sheet; and being by me sworn, through the grates of their cell, they, said seamen, solemnly and sincerely declared that the answers they have appended to my interrogatories are, to the best of their knowledge and belief, true and correct.

In testimony whereof, I hereunto set my hand, and affix the seal of [L. S.] my office at Havana, this sixteenth day of January, Anno Domino, eighteen hundred and fifty-four.

WM. H. ROBERTSON.

Interrogatories propounded by William H. Robertson, acting consul of the United States at Havana, to William Atkins, William Freeburn, and Harvey C. Parks, seamen now in the public jail of Havana, and to be answered by said seamen.

1. How many individuals, Spanish or other nations, (as near as you can judge,) have been in the jail since your confinement in it, for being concerned or engaged in the slave trade? If any have been, and you know the names and other circumstances of them, or of any part of them, state the same.

In answer to the above, to our knowledge, there have been thirty-two prisoners, not including ourselves, all Spanish but four Manilla men; all have brought slaves from the coast except eight that were captured by an English man-of-war, when they were about proceeding to the coast; they are captain and seven others, sailors, all Spanish; their names we do not know. There has been a crew of twenty confined in the same apartment that we are in: they were captured on the south coast of this island. Previous to their capture they landed two hundred and fifty slaves that they brought from the coast of Africa, and set fire to the vessel, a schooner; we do not know the full names of any of them; four of them are Manilla men—the rest are all Spanish. They landed their slaves about one month after the Jasper's slaves were landed; there were also two for assisting to land slaves. There is a Spanish mate belonging to the ship Ellen Parks, sailed 13th December, 1852, from New York to Mozambique, back to the island of Cuba, with eleven hundred negroes; none of the crew were arrested that belonged to the ship.

2. How many of said individuals do you believe (from information received by you, and that you may consider entitled to credence) have been tried by the courts? If you know the names of all, or part of those tried, state them.

The crew of twenty that belonged to the schooner has been tried by the court; four were liberated on the plea that they were passengers from the coast. We cannot give their names, because we do not know them; one of the four that were liberated as passengers, spoke pretty good English; from him we gained our information. We don't know that there has been any more tried by the court, except it be the Spanish mate, whom they wish to serve six months in one of their men-of-war, but to which he says he will not give his consent.

3. Have any such individuals left the prison? In what way did they leave it? In what number at any one time?

The captain and seven sailors that were arrested by the English man-of-war have left the prison, but in what way we do not know; they were not in the same apartment with us.

Four of the twenty were liberated as before mentioned; the remaining sixteen were liberated about two weeks since.

The two men for assisting to land slaves have also left the prison, as we understand—have been liberated.

4. State, as near as you can, their history, and conversations relating to the cause of their imprisonment, and other things connected with it and their release, during the time that such persons were confined in the jail.

The crew of the schooner that brought two hundred and fifty negroes state, in their conversations, that they left the south side of this island, having previously shipped for the slave trade in Havana, proceeded to the coast of Africa, there shipped four more men that had been engaged in the traffic on shore; took two hundred and fifty negroes on board, and came to this island and landed them, and set fire to the schooner close to the place where the Jasper was burnt; they told us that it was through us that they were arrested; they said that the officers that were in search of the remainder of our crew happened to come across them, and took them in custody; however, they said it did not make much difference to them—they were getting the same pay that they got all the voyage, and good board found them from outside the prison, which we know to be the fact; they said that when they were asked where they were from, they did not deny coming from the coast of Africa, but said they brought no negroes; this they told to the authorities. The four that got clear at first, as passengers, were no more passengers than the rest; they got the same wages, which was forty-five dollars a month and a negro each; so they told us in their conversation.

WILLIAM FREEBURN.
WILLIAM ATKINS.
HARVEY C. PARKS.

Mr. Marcy to Mr. Robertson.

[Extract.]

DEPARTMENT OF STATE,
Washington, January 18, 1854.

SIR: * * * * * * *

Your letter to the Marquis de la Pezuela, in reply to his communication of the 31st of December, in respect to the American sailors forming a part of the crew of the "Jasper," and now confined in Havana, receives the entire approval of the department.

The answer, however, which the Captain General has given to the letter addressed to him by the late consul, is not fully satisfactory to the President.

It will be remembered that some of these men have been imprisoned more than eight months, awaiting a decision in their case by the Spanish authorities; that their condition is one of great hardship and extreme suffering, confined as they have been in a tropical climate, through a sickly season, in a Cuban prison. No wonder they declare that "their condition is becoming every day more desperate!" Had it not been for your own friendly and zealous services, and the pecuniary relief which, as the department has learned, you have extended to them, their fate would have been wretched indeed.

The protracted delay attending the official proceedings in their case has excited sympathy in their behalf in this country, where the right is not questioned of requiring a strict account from the executive government of all circumstances that appear to be an infringement by foreign governments of the rights of American citizens.

As you well remark in your letter of the 3d of January, it is the wish and intention of the President to preserve and promote the harmony and good relations that have so long subsisted between this government and that of her Catholic Majesty; but, at the same time, he stands pledged before the country and the world to extend his protection to citizens of the United States abroad, when such citizens find themselves in difficulties not brought on by any intentional disregard or contempt of the laws of other countries. He cannot make distinctions between individuals—all are equally entitled to the watchful care and protection of the government.

Trusting in the rectitude of the Cuban authorities, and their desire to administer impartial justice in the judicial tribunals of the island, the President has refrained in this case, hitherto, from adopting any course that might place the Cuban authorities in an unfavorable light before the American people, or disturb the harmony now subsisting between the United States and Spain; but forbearance towards a foreign power may be carried to an extent which is inconsistent with the duty which the President owes to his own countrymen. He still trusts that such may not be the case in relation to these men; but the warm interest taken in their fate by persons of high standing and influence in this country, as well as a regard for right and justice, demand, as the President believes, more attention on the part of the Cuban authorities to this case, and a speedy and just settlement of it, if they desire to preserve friendly feelings between the two countries.

You will request from the proper authorities, unless the trial be very shortly terminated, authenticated copies of the charges against these American citizens, and the proofs by which it is supposed they can be sustained, for transmission to this department, to be laid before the President.

Your especial attention is likewise called to the instructions given to the late consul, Mr. Clayton, on the 8th of November last, in relation to the strict observance of the 7th article of the treaty of 1795, relative to the rights of persons prosecuted for alleged offences.

* * * * * * * *

I am, sir, &c,, &c.,

W. L. MARCY.

W. H. Robertson, Esq.,
Acting United States Consul, Havana, Cuba.

Mr. Robertson to Mr. Marcy.

[Extract.]

[No. 20.] CONSULATE OF THE UNITED STATES, HAVANA,
January 21, 1854.

SIR: * * * * * * *
I have received no reply to my last letter to the Captain General in behalf of the imprisoned seamen. I am informed that the court, on the 17th instant, decreed that they should be allowed fifteen days to produce their proofs to the judge commissioner. This seems to be an endless affair. The unfortunate men were all alive yesterday, but several of them are in a feeble state of health.

* * * * *

I have the honor to be, sir, with great respect, your obedient servant,

W. H. ROBERTSON,
Acting Consul.

Hon. WM. L. MARCY,
Secretary of State.

Mr. Marcy to Mr. Florence.

DEPARTMENT OF STATE,
Washington, February 3, 1854.

SIR: In reply to the inquiry made by Mr. J. Cowperthwaite, of Philadelphia, in regard to the present condition of the American sailors now confined in Havana, charged with having been engaged in the slave trade, I transmit, herewith, extracts from two recent dispatches of Mr. Robertson, the acting United States consul, which contain the latest information on the subject in possession of the department.

I am, sir, &c.,

W. L. MARCY.

Hon. T. B. FLORENCE,
House of Representatives.

Mr. Robertson to Mr. Marcy.

[Extract.]

[No. 24.] CONSULATE OF THE UNITED STATES, HAVANA,
February 7, 1854.

SIR: * * * * * * *
Allow me, sir, to express to you the great satisfaction I have experienced at the contents of your dispatch of the 18th January, as it conveys to me your approbation of my conduct in regard to the unfortunate seamen who have been so long suffering under a most unjust imprison-

ment. Be so good as to accept my sincere thanks for your kindness. Since the receipt of your instructions, I have not addressed the Captain General. The trial of the prisoners has been consummated. I received * * * information that they are to be arraigned before the superior court at the close of this or the beginning of next week, to receive sentence. It is not known what the sentence will be.

* * * * * * * *

Should I discover any more delay, I will then lay before the Captain General the views of the department, that he may know what the consequences of the policy of his government will be. Whether the men are condemned or not, I shall demand an authenticated copy of the proceedings against them, to forward to the department.

* * * * * * * * *

There is not one particle of evidence against the seamen but their own depositions. I have very strong doubts that the copy of these proceedings will be furnished, but I shall, of course, demand it.

The Captain General has not yet been pleased to reply to my letter, which you have done me the honor to commend.

I have the honor to be, sir, with great respect, your obedient servant,

WM. H. ROBERTSON,
Acting Consul.

Hon. Wm. L. Marcy,
Secretary of State of the United States, Washington.

Mr. Robertson to Mr. Marcy.

[Extract.]

[No. 27.] Consulate of the United States, Havana,
February 14, 1854.

Sir: I have the honor, in my dispatch No. 24, dated 7th instant, and forwarded per steamer Isabel to Charleston, to acknowledge the receipt of yonr dispatches of the 18th and 24th ultimo. I stated to you that if I discovered any more delay in the case of the imprisoned American seamen, I would lay your views, in regard to their case, before the Captain General. Finding, on the evening of last Saturday, that no decision had been come to by the authorities, I addressed a communication, a copy of which I now have the honor to enclose herewith, hoping that it may also meet your approbation.

I cannot withhold from you, sir, my feelings of indignation at the extraordinary delays and sufferings that these American citizens have been made to experience in being confined in cells with upwards of one hundred and fifty criminals, charged with the highest to the lowest grades of crime. I have repeatedly remonstrated, to the Captain General, against this treatment of men who were not yet declared guilty, but very little, or rather no notice, has been taken of my remonstrances, except once, when General Cañedo candidly replied that the jail was the usual place where criminals, and those that were believed to be such, were confined, and that their situation could not be changed. In this manner the accused are made to undergo severe punishment for a long time before their cases are decided. As for the food allowed the prisoners, I have seen it once or twice, and I assure you that it was not only insufficient in quantity, but of the very worst quality.

It will probably be in my power to send you shortly a detailed account of the whole of this affair, from the time of the Jasper's arrival on the coast of Cuba, with the names of the owners and the other parties concerned in the cargo.

* * * * * * * *

I have the honor to be sir, with great respect, your very obedient servant,

WILLIAM H. ROBERTSON,
Acting Consul.

Hon. William L. Marcy,
Secretary of State of the United States, Washington.

Consulate of the United States, Havana,
February 11, 1854.

Most Excellent Sir: It is now upwards of one month since I had the honor of addressing your excellency on the subject of the unfortunate American seamen composing the crew of the bark Jasper, confined in the jail—some of them for more than eight months past—without any charge against them other than their own declarations, which clearly prove their innocence. Copies of your excellency's official letter, in answer to that of the consul, Mr. Clayton, and of mine to your excellency, of the 3d of January ultimo, on that subject, were, at the propei time, transmitted to my government; and, a few days since, I received a dispatch from the honorable the Secretary of State, wherein, among other things, I was informed that my communication to your excellency of the 3d of January "has received the entire approbation of the department," and that the contents of your excellency's letter of the 31st December "is not fully satisfactory to the President."

Although my communication before mentioned has received, so far as I know, no notice from your excellency, I have refrained from making any further observations, in the hope that my unfortunate countrymen would, ere this, have been placed at my disposal; but finding that week after week has passed without a satisfactory result, but that, on the contrary, these men are still imprisoned, associated with criminals charged with the highest to the lowest of crimes; that they are undergoing such punishment as criminals justly condemned only should be made to undergo; and that their sufferings are daily increasing—for even their food has been reduced to such a small quantity, and of such bad quality, that they would starve to death, were it not for the pecuniary relief afforded them by this consulate—I cnnnot, after hearing their just complaints, remain silent any longer. I deem it to be my bounden duty to communicate to your excellency the views of my government in regard to this matter.

The honorable the Secretary of State, under date of 18th of January ultimo, said to me as follows: "It will be remembered that some of these men have been imprisoned more than *eight months*, awaiting a decision in their case by the Spanish authorities; that their condition is one of great hardship and extreme suffering, confined, as they have been, in a tropical climate, through a sickly season, in a Cuban prison. No wonder they declare that *their condition is becoming every day more desperate.* Had it not been for your friendly and zealous services, and the pecuniary relief which, as the department has learned, you have extended to them, their fate would have been wretched indeed.

"The protracted delay attending the official proceedings in their case has excited sympathy in their behalf in this country, where the right is not questioned of requiring a strict account from the executive government of all circumstances that appear to be an infringement by foreign governments of the rights of American citizens.

"As you well remark in your letter of the 3d of January, it is the wish and intention of the President to preserve and promote the harmony and good relations that have so long subsisted between this government and that of her Catholic Majesty; but, at the same time, he stands pledged before the country and the world to extend his protection to citizens of the United States abroad, when such citizens find themselves in difficulties not brought on by an intentional disregard or contempt of the laws of other countries. He cannot make distinctions between individuals; all are equally entitled to the watchful care and protection of the government."

Your excellency will perceive that the foregoing last paragraph contains almost the very words used in my letter above referred to; it will show that they were not used at random, but expressive of the spirit of my country's institutions, and of the policy of the administration in whose hands the destinies of the nation have been placed by the suffrages of the people.

The Secretary of State continues: "Trusting in the rectitude of the Cuban authorities, and their desire to administer impartial justice in the judicial tribunals of the island, the President has refrained in this case, hitherto, from adopting any course that might place the Cuban authorities in an unfavorable light before the American people, or disturb the harmony now subsisting between the United States and Spain. But forbearance towards a foreign power may be carried to an extent which is inconsistent with the duty which the President owes to his countrymen. He still trusts that such may not be the case in relation to these American seamen; but the warm interest taken in their fate by persons of high standing and influence in this country, as well as a regard for right and justice, demand, as the President believes, more attention on the part of the Cuban authorities to this case, and a speedy and just settlement of it, if they desire to preserve friendly feelings between the two countries."

I must, therefore, in obedience to the call of duty, request your excellency to have the American seamen before alluded to, without further delay, arraigned before the proper court to be sentenced or acquitted, or order that they be placed at the disposal of this consulate to be sent to the United States. I must also, in obedience to instructions from my government, request of your excellency to be so good as to furnish me authenticated copies of the charges against these American seaman, and the proofs by which it is supposed they can be sustained, for transmission to the Secretary of State, to be laid before the President of the United States.

In the hope that this official letter will meet with more consideration than my last on the same subject, and that a friendly feeling towards my government will prompt your excellency to accede to my requests as above expressed,

I have the honor to remain, with great respect, your excellency's very obedient servant,

WM. H. ROBERTSON,
The Commercial Agent in charge of the Consulate.

His Excellency the MARQUIS DE LA PEZUELA,
Governor, Captain General, &c., &c., of the Island of Cuba.

Mr. Robertson to Mr. Marcy.

[No. 30.] CONSULATE OF THE UNITED STATES, HAVANA,
February 20, 1854.

SIR: My dispatch No. 27 covered a copy of my last communication to the Captain General in behalf of the Jasper's crew. I now have the honor to transmit a copy of his excellency's reply. This will clearly show that the consulate here is reduced to a mere commercial agency; that no rights are conceded to it, and therefore that American citizens are left without protection. The same vigilance, however, will be observed, while I remain in charge of the consulate, that has been practised since I commenced to discharge the duties of the office. I shall continue to remonstrate against any injustice towards my country and countrymen with the authorities here, and report to you the facts. My representations may be disregarded by the Captain General, but I shall in every case try to do my whole duty; and should I meet with rebuke or insult I feel confident that the President will redress the wrong.

I have the honor to be, sir, with great respect, your very obedient servant,

WM. H. ROBERTSON.

Hon. WILLIAM L. MARCY,
Secretary of State of the United States.

P. S.—SIR: Since the foregoing was written, secret notice has been brought to me that the court have rendered their decision in the case of the American seamen, acquitting them, ordering that no costs be paid, and that the prisoners be set at liberty. I believe, however, that they will not be relieved till day after to-morrow.

Very respectfully,

WM. H. ROBERTSON.

[Translation.]

EVER FAITHFUL ISLAND OF CUBA.—OFFICE OF THE GOVERNOR AND CAPTAIN GENERAL, POLITICAL SECRETARY'S OFFICE, SECTION FIRST.

In answer to your official letter, dated 11th instant, relative to the seamen of your nation belonging to the American bark Jasper, I can only say to you that I will give the convenient explanations, and an account of the result of this cause, to her Catholic Majesty's minister at Washington; such being also the instructions that I have from my government for this and any other similar cases.

God preserve you many years. Havana, February 16, 1854.

EL MARQUES DE LA PEZUELA.

The COMMERCIAL AGENT
in charge of the Consulate of the United States.

Mr. Marcy to Mr. Cowperthwaite.

DEPARTMENT OF STATE,
Washington, February 27, 1854.

SIR: I have the pleasure to inform you that a telegraphic dispatch was received at the department this morning, stating that the "Isabel" arrived at Charleston on the 25th instant, bringing the information that the American seamen who have been so long confined in Havana, and for whom you felt so much interest, have been liberated and placed at the disposition of Mr. Robertson, the acting consul.

I am, sir, &c.,

W. L. MARCY.

J. COWPERTHWAITE, Esq.,
Philadelphia, Pennsylvania.

Mr. Robertson to Mr. Marcy.

[Extract.]

[No. 32.] CONSULATE OF THE UNITED STATES, HAVANA,
February 27, 1854.

SIR: I have the honor, as well as the gratification, of informing you that the nine seamen composing the crew of the Jasper, so long and unjustly kept in prison here, have been at last set at liberty. They were released at about one o'clock on the 23d instant, without any notification, official or unofficial from any of the authorities, but were left to find their way to my office as best they could; they were, however, sincerely welcomed, and immediately provided with suitable clothing, &c., of which they were entirely destitute. They were then sent on board the United States steamer "Fulton." Three of them, viz: Harvey C. Parks, William Freeburn, and William Atkins, will proceed in the steamer Black Warrior to New York, where they will be placed in charge of the United States marshal, subject to your orders; the other six, to wit: William Hussy, William Hersey, Charles Robinson, John Radcliffe, John William Leo, and George Hunt, will remain on board the "Fulton" until your directions are received as to the manner of disposing of them.

* * * * * * * *

I have requested the marshal in New York to furnish the captain of the Black Warrior, on his receiving the three seamen, such a document as may enable the captain to recover the passage money (thirty dollars) from the Treasury Department, as I look, of course, upon these seamen as *distressed.*

I have the honor to be, sir, with great respect, your obedient servant,

WM. H. ROBERTSON,
Acting Consul.

Hon. WM. L. MARCY,
Secretary of State, Washington.

Mr. Robertson to Mr. Marcy

[No. 33.] CONSULATE OF THE UNITED STATES, HAVANA,
February 28, 1854.

SIR: The nine seamen liberated from the prison where they were so long and unjustly confined by the authorities of this island have made their protest, and claim damages. They have, at the same time, executed an instrument in favor of D. E. Wheeler, esq., of New York, who is authorized to act for them. I have been requested by said seamen to lay their protest before you, which I now do, enclosing the same herewith;

And remain, sir, with great respect, your very obedient servant,

WM. H. ROBERTSON,
Acting Consul.

Hon. WM. L. MARCY,
Secretary of State, Washington.

Mr. Wheeler to Mr. Marcy.

HAVANA, *February* 28, 1854.

DEAR SIR: At the suggestion of a number of American citizens temporarily in this city, and at the request of the nine unfortunate seamen who have lain in the royal jail here for some time, I drew up the paper which Mr. Robertson, the acting Americal consul, transmits to the Department of State.

These men have suffered beyond description since they were arrested, and been kept in prison for many months against their remonstrance, and against the demands of their government, as made by the consul, and also by your department of the government, and they should, in some form, have redress; and it has seemed to us that this should be sought by them from the government under whose flag they sailed.

This claim has been confided to my hands by them, and I trust it will be regarded as eminently demanding the attention of our government, and that her Catholic Majesty will be required to make such amends as shall be satisfactory to it, and compensate in some measure the unfortunate men whose crime seemed to consist in being American seamen.

The six who do not return to the United States by the "Black Warrior" will remain aboard the steamer Fulton until some disposition shall be made of them by the Department of State, or until they shall recover from the effects of their imprisonment and be able themselves to return home.

I trust, my dear sir, that your multifarious and arduous duties will not prevent you from giving the subject of this letter your early and earnest attention, that Spain at least may know that the American government is not tardy in seeking redress for wrongs which her weakness or indolence inflicts.

I now intend visiting Washington in returning to New York; and if so, I shall do myself the honor to call at the Department of State in relation to this subject.

With the highest considerations of respect, I am your obedient servant,

D. G. WHEELER.

Hon. WM. L. MARCY,
Secretary of State, &c., &c.

To all to whom these presents shall come, greeting: Know ye, that we, the undersigned, now on board the United States steamer Fulton, Captain J. M. Watson, commander, lying in the port of Havana, island of Cuba, this 27th day of February, 1854, do make and set forth the following statement of facts, together with our protest, and our claim, which we believe we are respectively entitled to under the laws and treaties of the United States of America:

We severally and respectively shipped on board the bark Jasper, E. C. Townsend, master, at the port of New York, in the United States, on or about the 12th day of December, 1852, on which day the said bark sailed from New York for a trading voyage to the coast of Africa, taking out a cargo. That we arrived on the coast of Africa some time in the latter part of January, 1853; that nothing occurred on board the bark during the voyage to indicate to us that the voyage was undertaken for any other purpose than that of an ordinary trading voyage. That upon our arrival at Cape Coast, we landed some of our cargo, and the balance of it we landed at Aminia. Here we took in some elephant's teeth and tobacco, and we then sailed southerly along the coast (touching at one or two small places) about fifty miles, and came to anchor on the 2d day of March, 1853. Immediately after dropping anchor Captain Townsend called us into the cabin, paid us our wages to that day, and informed us that he had sold the bark three days previous, at one of the small places we put into, to a Spaniard called Captain Joseph, who came out with the bark from New York as supercargo, as we were informed, and that the bark was going to Cuba, and that we could return in her, and must do so, for if we went on shore we should be murdered. On the same day boats came alongside containing slaves, and were being put on board under the direction of Captain Joseph and two Spaniards, who he appointed mates, and who went out in the bark from New York as passengers. Provision for the slaves and other materials for their confinement were brought on board. There were about three hundred and sixty slaves, and three men to take charge of them and do other work on board the bark; that Captain Joseph then proffered us wages to continue the work, and Captain Townsend urged us to go to work, stating that we could not help ourselves; and we were obliged to do the ordinary duties of sailors on board the bark, as Captain Townsend left and went on shore, having previously discharged the first mate, John Brown, at Cape Coast.

As soon as we could get ready we sailed, and on the 17th day of April we arrived at the southern side of the island of Cuba, and the slaves were immediately sent on shore. On the 19th of the same month the bark was run on a reef, set on fire, and abandoned. Previously to the bark being set on fire we were sent on shore in one boat, leaving on board the bark a number of men who had come on board from the shore and the Spaniard who acted as mate. The captain himself previously left. We were sent on shore without provisions; and we believe it was the intention of those who brought the bark to the island to take our lives. We were not allowed to leave the point of land where we were landed, and were prevented from going away by men who were armed with cutlasses and knives, and everything we had was taken from us except what was upon our backs. On or about the last of April or first of May three of the undersigned found the long-boat of the bark, which had been concealed, and escaped in her, and went to Cape Antonio, where the three, namely, Harvey C. Parks, William Freeburn, and William Atkins, arrived on the 3d of May; and upon the 5th of May the same three were arrested and sent on board the Spanish man-of-war "Habanera," and put in double irons, and kept on board this ship in double irons thirty-five days, and then they were transferred to a merchant schooner and brought to Havana, after a voyage of sixteen days, and then sent on board a Spanish steam man-of-war lying in the Havana bay, and kept there for eight days, and then sent to a prison on shore in Havana, where they remained until they came on board the United States steamer Fulton, lying in the harbor, the 23d day of February, 1854.

The remaining six of the undersigned remained upon the point where we were landed a few days after the above-mentioned three men left, and then were taken by a resident of the island of Cuba to his plantation, and kept there until the middle of July, when we were taken to the north side of the island and there left. Here we remained about two months, and were provided with necessary food by a planter, and prevented from starvation. During this time we were seeking some means to get to Havana; but we did not succeed until we found a Spanish schooner, which came to the shore. We went on board of her, and persuaded the captain to take us to Havana, that we could make known our situation to the American consul at that place, and claim his protection and aid; but before the schooner sailed we were arrested by men from a Spanish man-of-war, and taken on board of her, and on the same day transferred to the same schooner, with orders to the captain of the schooner to deliver us to the captain of the port. Upon our arrival at Havana we were put on board the guard-brig, and kept on board of her twenty-one days, and then were transferred from the brig on the 11th day of September to the prison on shore, where we found the other three of the undersigned, except Wm. Hussy, who was sick, and was sent to the hospital, from whence he was sent to the prison about fifteen days after the other five. That during these various periods, and after the information of the sale of the bark, the undersigned declare ourselves innocent of any crime, and that we sailed from New York under the American flag, and were entitled to the rights and privileges of American seamen. That, after being in prison two or three days, we were separated, or with one or two together taken into court; but no crime was charged against any one of us to our knowledge or belief, but we were remanded to prison, and there confined until we were all discharged on the 23d day of February, 1854. That we were confined in prison, and in one room, with about one hundred and fifty prisoners, charged with all sorts of crimes, and kept with them in a very filthy condition, with scarcely food sufficient to sustain life, and with no clothing except that with which we came from the ship; that we were all turned out of prison with no information how or where to go from those who confined us; that during our imprisonment we were assisted by Mr. Robertson, the acting American consul, and other Americans in Havana, and kept from the last horrors of starvation; that the undersigned have always and universally demanded their rights as American seamen, and denied that they were guilty of any crime whatever, and protested verbally against the treatment that we have received from the Spanish government, without any apparent benefit. The undersigned do now in the most solemn manner set forth this brief statement of facts, and protest against the treatment which we have received from the Spanish government, its authorities and officials, and demand that personal satisfaction as American seamen we are entitled to, and appeal with confidence to the American government for that redress which her citizens or sailors can claim while in pursuit of business under her flag, or are wanderers in a strange land with a still stranger tongue, through the treachery and wickedness of an unworthy captain, or perhaps a still worse Spanish, fraudulent, and surreptitious commander. And while we thus appeal, we cannot forget or cease to record the great kindness received by us from our consul at Havana, and from other American citizens at this port. Our names and places of birth we affix to this instrument, and make them a part of it; and do sign it on board the United States steamer Fulton, Captain J. M. Watson, commander, in the harbor of Havana, this 27th day of February, 1854.

WILLIAM ATKINS, *New York.*
WILLIAM FREEBURN, *Philadelphia, Pa.*
HARVEY C. PARKS,
Marion, Wayne county, N. Y.
his
CHARLES × WM. HERSEY, *New York.*
mark.
his
WILLIAM × HUSSY, *Nantucket, Mass.*
mark.
his
CHARLES × ROBINSON, *Philadelphia, Pa.*
mark.
his
JOHN × RADCLIFFE, *Boston, Mass.*
mark.
GEORCE HUNT, *Baltimore, Md.*
JOHN W. LEO, *Niagara county, N. Y.*

CONSULATE OF THE UNITED STATES,
Havana, Island of Cuba.

On the day of the date hereof, I, William H. Robertson, acting consul of the United States of America for the city of Havana and the dependencies thereof, being on board the United States steamer Fulton, lying in the port of Havana, personally came and appeared William Atkins, William Freeburn, Harvey C. Parks, Charles William Hersey, William Hussy, Charles Robinson, John Radcliffe, George Hunt, and John Wm. Leo, seamen, to me known as the individuals described in the instrument in writing that appears on the two preceding pages of this sheet, and on the four pages of the sheet hereto annexed; and said appearers, being by me severally sworn, did declare and depose that the said instrument contains the truth, the whole truth, and nothing but the truth. The said appearers subscribed their respective names to said instrument in my presence, and declared that they had signed the same as their voluntary respective act and deed.

In testimony whereof, I hereunto set my hand, and affix the seal of my office, (being requested to certify and testify the premises,) [L. S.] at Havana, this twenty-seventh day of February, A. D. eighteen hundred and fifty-four.

WM. H. ROBERTSON.

Mr. Wheeler to Mr. Marcy.

HAVANA, *February* 28, 1854.

DEAR SIR: At the suggestion of a number of American citizens temporarily in this city, and at the request of the nine unfortunate seamen who have lain in the royal jail here for some time, I drew up the paper which Mr. Robertson, the acting American consul, transmits to the Department of State.

These men have suffered beyond description since they were arrested, and been kept in prison for many months against their remonstrance, and against the demands of their government, as made by the consul, and also by your department of the government; and they should, in some form, have redress, and it has seemed to us that this should be sought by them from the government under whose flag they sailed.

This claim has been confided to my hands by them, and I trust it will be regarded as eminently demanding the attention of our government, and that her Catholic Majesty will be required to make such amends as shall be satisfactory to it, and compensate, in some measure, the unfortunate men whose crime seemed to consist in being American seamen.

The six who do not return to the United States by the "Black Warrior" will remain aboard the steamer Fulton until some disposition shall be made of them by the Department of State, or until they shall recover from the effects of their imprisonment, and be able themselves to return home.

I trust, my dear sir, that your multifarious and arduous duties will not prevent you from giving the subject of this letter your early and earnest attention, that Spain at least may know that the American government is not tardy in seeking redress for wrongs which her wickedness or indolence inflicts.

I now intend visiting Washington in returning to New York; and if so, I shall do myself the honor to call at the Department of State in relation to this subject.

With the highest considerations of respect, &c., I am, &c.,

D. G. WHEELER.

Mr. Robertson to Mr. Marcy.

[Extract.]

[No. 36.] UNITED STATES CONSULATE, HAVANA,
March 5, 1854.

* * * * * *

I send you another defence, made in behalf of the prisoners, which contains some interesting facts: it may prove interesting to you. I regret that we have not time to translate it, but we are both nearly broken down with labor night and day.

With great respect, your obedient servant,

W. H. ROBERTSON.

[Translation.]

Don José Perez Ramos, attorney for John Radcliffe, Charles Robinson, and William Hersey, through the acting counsel for the defence, in consequence of criminal proceedings for the introduction of 280 negroes in Bayleu, jurisdiction of Pinar del Rio, according to law, I say:

That there is not one single data in this process by which my clients can be considered as complices in the introduction of negroes from abroad (negroes bozalos) in the island.

The penalty of four years' transportation, (imprisonment in the galleys,) insisted upon in the fiscal pleadings, (by the prosecution,) is not only unusual but enormous, and therefore unjust. Your highness, in the plenitude of your integrity, will not impose such penalty, but order the immediate release of the accused.

In this process there is wanting legal evidence; there is wanting the object with which, or through which, the crime has been committed, (cuerpo del deliz?) and the judgment of the court, so far from condemning, must be for acquittal. If the negroes, who are said to have been brought here, have not been taken, but, on the contrary, not a single one has been met with; if even the names of the owners, the captain, the pilot, and the crew, are unknown; if not even fragments have been found of the ship itself, which is said to have been burnt—since the results of the inquiries made show the impossibility of designating as such the two hulls, the masts and rigging of which cannot be identified; if the allegement of facts is confined to one witness, seeing that everybody pleads ignorance in regard to the same; in short, if nothing of what has been advanced upon this subject can be taken as legal proof, which is, then, the *prima facie* evidence of the crime?

Are impressions, peradventure more or less fallible, sufficient to constitute the basis of an adverse judgment, and to end this noisy trial with the horrors of transportation? However strong conjectures may be, they never can take the place of that which only belongs to the plenitude of proofs. We seek for these in the pages of the indictment, and we do not find them; we examine the same with care, and the only thing that we encounter is the declaration of the American sailors that they have been victims, and nothing more. These declarations are not a confession of the crime, nor do they supply a pretext for condemnation, as we will proceed to demonstrate.

The facts may and do exist in reality; but when these facts come to be dealt with according to law—when the law requires the facts to be clearly sustained, at least with regard to data, and the proofs to be conclusive, and the analysis furnishes nothing of this kind—there is wanting, as we have stated, legal evidence; and without it, no penalty can be imposed, however much moral evidence may float on the surface of the proceedings. What the law requires in order to condemn, is convictions, and not deductions—proofs, and not suspicions. It is proper that in the proceedings which are instituted against the person of an individual, or against his signature, the charges should be proved and ascertained by means of evidence as clear as the light, about which no doubt can exist. From the moment that other principles are adopted, the guarantees of society are attacked and destroyed; and arbitrariness being enthroned, this, and not justice, decides the fate, the honor, and the future welfare of families. This is so evident and reasonable, and so much in conformity with forensic practice, that our tribunals are wont to dismiss a case when the criminality of the party indicted is not proven, although the crime committed be evident—which is equivalent to saying, that the means employed in the investigation were not sufficient to demonstrate the responsibility of the accused, and that for cases of this kind, the courts of judicature have certain doors open, without bringing the matter to a close by an absolute acquitment. In the present instance, there is even less than this. Why? Throughout the whole record of these extensive proceedings, there is no evidence of the introduction of the negroes in question, nor any proof of the crime having been committed. Such is the impartial result which a careful examination of the proceedings has produced.

We are not astonished at this result. The immoral and barbarous negro traffic, which converts men into articles of merchandise, which is degrading and disgraceful to those engaged in it, has unfortunately found numerous advocates, as the fiscal acknowledges, and it is seldom that the action of the tribunals has succeeded in penetrating through the utter darkness with which interest, cupidity, corruptions, and cunning have enveloped this crime, which reason, law, and humanity alike condemn.

For this reason your highness will perceive, that although the collector of the royal revenues asserts in his communication that the rumors about two hundred and eighty negroes having been imported at the point of Bayleu were notorious, there is not one single individual that will certify to the fact. There is not a solitary word in these pages, therefore, with the exception of the declarations of the sailors, that throws light upon the commission of the act. Hence the citations from the communication of her Brittanic Majesty's consul were entirely of a negative character. Hence the existence of the crime has not been proved. We do not allege it, however, as a truth, as it has been set forth in the fiscal pleadings, that the country is in favor of the importation of Africans. In a greater or lesser degree, the same thing occurs in the investigation of grave outrages; they have always taken place—they have been witnessed—are known and referred to; and the same persons who, in private, assert the facts, and give accounts of the minutest details, when they are called upon to testify in a court of justice, have nothing to say, and are ignorant of everything. There is, unfortunately, a certain degree of fear associated with the courts of law, as a public institution, which is fatal in itself, because it affords impunity to crime, and renders the powerful arm of the tribunals useless. It is to this custom, originating in ignorance and in error, and which the efforts of an enlightened public opinion alone can put down, that the profound silence observed on such occasions, and the want of data for judicial decisions, is owing. Shall it be said, on this account, that the country where such things come to pass is in favor of the impunity of crime? Shall it be said that it encourages and desires crime? Certainly not. There are evils which are coeval with the condition of the people; and the people have a social education, which, like their intellectual or private education, influences all their actions. However difficult it may be to note the beginning of this influence, it is nevertheless felt and perceived in all that occurs. To the legislator as well as to the jurist, to the latter as well as to the observing man, the facts which present themselves are never isolated. The obscurity prevailing in these investigations, the useless labors attending the multitude of measures that have been adopted, the silence and the negatives pitted against the activity and skill of the magistrate, do not indicate that the country is for the introduction of Africans, nor for the infraction of treaties, the observance of which is so much insisted upon. It is the result of other causes, the discussion of which would lead us astray from the case before us. It is nevertheless a fact in point; a fact which concerns the defence, and which cannot be allowed to pass unnoticed, when a proper appreciation of the truth is of so much importance in the proceedings.

John Radcliffe, Charles Robinson, and William Hersey, are not complices in the importation of the 280 negroes who are said to have been fraudulently landed at Bayleu: they were the victims, and not the delinquents; the deceived, and not the deceivers; and between the two characters, there is the enormous difference which separates crime from innocence; the fiscal department not being able to find a just cause for indictment, there being not a single article in the penal law which embraces the case in question, inasmuch as these persons have not been detected, either at sea or on land, in the commission of crime; nor did the vessel sail from this island; nor were there any negroes captured, there being not the least indication, with the exception of their own declarations, either of the expedition, owner or captain. The department aforesaid has considered as a confession of the crime, the very exception, which would have acquitted the accused parties of it if the disembarcation had been established, which is not the case. That the sailors sailed from New York in the American bark Jasper, for Africa, for purposes of lawful trade; that as soon as they saw on board negroes for the slave market, they refused to continue on their voyage; that they did not accomplish anything in consequence of the distance they were from any coast where they might find a consul of their nation; that they were conveyed to the southern part of this island; that they proceeded to Cape Listic with a boat, the captain, pilot, and officers of the brig, which the latter set on fire, having gone off; and that while they were trying to procure assistance at Cape San Antonio they were arrested, and taken on board her Majesty's steamer Gaudalquiver—is what appears from their declarations. There is not an article in the penal law which can be applied to the present case. The only charge which has been brought against them, with a show of legal fairness, does not only contain its own reply, but its own refutation. Why did they continue on the voyage, they were asked, when they had ascertained that the object of that voyage was to carry on the prohibited traffic of slaves? Because, the victims of deceit in the first instance, they were subsequently the victims of force and of circumstances.

It is an original mode of proceeding, that whereas, according to law, the charges must be made to rest upon the results of the investigation, the only charges that have been preferred in this case rest solely upon the declarations of the accused themselves. Throughout the whole summary proceedings, almost, there does not appear any legal charge, which is very much in favor of their innocence. These sailors were ignorant of the true object of the expedition; nor did they pause to inquire into the same, bound as they were already, with regard to time, destination and wages; and having likewise been impressed with the legitimate object of the expedition, without any reason on their part for suspecting that they were the victims of circumstances, the combination of which was force, and an invincible force, because in that maritime latitude, at an enormous distance from the coast, and without the support which a consul of their nation might have afforded them, they had to succumb, and did succumb, in so critical a station. If Radcliffe, Robinson, and Hersey had been criminals, as it is supposed, they would have gone with the captain and the other officers of the ship, when, after having landed the negroes and fired said vessel, they could have saved themselves by flight. They prefer, however, to remain; they do not follow in company with those who had vilely deceived them; they suffer hunger and privations; they remain in an unknown land, the language of which they do not speak; they descend in a boat, are arrested, imprisoned. And yet charges are brought against them; still they are indicted for an act in which they did not voluntarily take part; they are unfortunate, and on account of this misfortune an indictment is filed against them, for the purpose of consigning them to prison, with hard labor. We do not know any one, they said; we are strangers in the country; we do not know whither to wend our steps; we did not go to the authorities whom we did not know either, because we might be questioned, imprisoned and prosecuted. The authors of the crime were far away and in safety; the deceived sailors had no means to return to their country, and there to exercise their rights. There is nothing criminal in this; there is no ground for charges, and the facts are satisfactorily explained.

Your highness will see that nothing has been proved in regard to the crime; that not a single negro has been taken; that neither the owners nor the officers of the vessel are known; that it has not even been ascertained who has purchased these slaves; that the investigation has been carried as far as the most interior plantations, causing the magistrate to appear—his dependents, servants, and even the slaves of those plantations—all of whom have been questioned; that the inquiries made about the vessel in those waters by the sub-delegate of marine have not brought forth any evidence, seeing that it is stated in the report that, inasmuch as the masts and rigging of the "Jasper" are not known, the two hulls that were seen there cannot be designated as appertaining to the same—everything remains in obscurity and mystery. Colonel Villers, lieutenant governor of Pinar del Rio, who was the responsible local authority, is acquitted for want of evidence; the petty justice of the district is likewise acquitted; they are both restored to their respective offices; and yet there are other men of low condition, foreigners, who are wandering at random in our seas, without the means of subsistence, and shall the consequences of the process be applied against them only? Your highness will not permit it.

If these declarations are of no validity whatever, as your highness has demonstrated, by acquitting the functionaries of Pinar del Rio, who are responsible for the vigilance of those coasts—if they were not sufficient to convict those officers of neglect of duty, shall they now suffice for the condemnation of these poor men, when, before, they offered no obstacle in the way of an acquittal? It were, at least, absurd to conceive of so invidious a distinction—such a monstrous contrariety, when the rules of judicial action, solemn and severe, are fixed, invariable, and decisive of the rectitude of the magistrate, which is one of the most sacred attributes of justice. These declarations of the sailors, my clients, therefore, are not a confession of the crime, nor is this the spirit of the law of Castile. To be convinced of this fact, let those declarations be read. It is not said, we have committed this crime, but only we were deceived. These declarations allude to the unlawful acts of others, such as the traffic, the introduction of slaves in this island; nor did the will nor the inclination of the deponents take part in that traffic. Let any part of the declarations be cited to prove the foundation for such an assertion.

The law requires, moreover, for the responsibility of the accused, a deliberate disposition to transgress. The actions of men have their origin, their object, and determined ends. To keep these out of view, would be equivalent to condemning the whole human family. All the circumstances by which the sailors found themselves surrounded when the negroes were already on board, and they had ascertained the concealed object of the voyage, exercised in regard to them real violence, a force which they could not overcome; and this force, this violence, were the maritime latitude, the greater number they had to contend with, their miserable condition, the enormous distance, the utter absence of means of escape, or even to rise in rebellion against the captain, for they would have perished in the struggle. The law abstains from inflicting penalty upon the man who labors under the terrible weight of such circumstances; and this is the foundation of the exception to the application of severe measures, according to the opinion of jurisconsults.

It is conclusively inferred that they had no liberty of action, either moral or physical; that the acts cannot be imputed to them under any aspect whatever; and that this most essential requisite being wanting, they are not amenable to law.

Even though the declarations were to be misconstrued so far as to give them a meaning of which, as it has been demonstrated by the acquittal of the local authorities, they are not susceptible, they would be utterly wanting in efficacy, as they would be the declarations of accomplices in the very crime, and such evidence is of no validity whatever in law.

Everything, therefore, tends to convince and to set forth the innocence of the accused and the pressing necessity, because the rectitude with which the administration of justice ought to be conducted demands it, of decreeing the release of my clients, in order that they may be delivered over to the consul of their nation, and be able, in their own country, to prosecute those who have so iniquitously deceived them. With this view of the case, the summary being obscure, inefficient, and without any merit whatever, the criminal proceedings without foundation, seeing that the commission of the crime for which the prosecution has been got up has not been proved, and reproducing, as I do, all that was favorable to the subject in B. 348, on account of the solid foundations it contains, I supplicate your highness that, taking into consideration my reply to the prosecution, as reproduced in all its force, you will acquit my clients of all crime and penalty, by decreeing that they shall be at once set at liberty, as it is proper and should be done according to justice, &c.

JOSE PERES RAMOS.
I. MANUEL COSTALES.

Mr. Marcy to Mr. Robertson.

[Extract.]

DEPARTMENT OF STATE,
Washington, March 7, 1853.

SIR: * * * * * * *
The announcement that the American seamen in whose behalf you have so strenuously exerted yourself have been acquitted, affords much satisfaction.

You will provide for their return to the United States in accordance with previous instructions, taking care that their necessary wants, as destitue American seamen, be supplied.

I am, sir, &c.,

W. L. MARCY.

W. H. ROBERTSON, Esq.,
Acting United States Consul, Havana.

CASE OF THE BLACK WARRIOR.

Mr. Robertson to Mr. Marcy.

[No. 42.] CONSULATE OF THE UNITED STATES,
March 14, 1854.

SIR: Captain Bullock, of the steamship Black Warrior, becoming impatient, as he has a large number of officers and men on his hands at a very heavy expense, and was ignorant of the real charges of complaint that justified the proceedings against him and his ship, made a memorial to the Governor and Captain General, praying that himself, his officers and crew, should be permitted to embark in the Crescent City, expected from New Orleans on her way to New York; and at the same time to be furnished with a statement of the case, that he might report to his owners. Said memorial, at the captain's request, was enclosed in a note from me, calling his excellency's attention to it. Last evening I received a reply, of which the document herewith enclosed is a translation.

How long these proceedings may be continued it is impossible to say.

I have the honor to be, sir, with great respect, your very obedient servant.

WM. H. ROBERTSON, *Acting Consul.*

Hon. WM. L. MARCY,
Secretary of State of the United States.

[Translation.]

[L. S.]

EVER FAITHFUL ISLAND OF CUBA.—OFFICE OF THE GOVERNOR AND CAPTAIN GENERAL, POLITICAL SECRETARY'S OFFICE, SECTION FIFTH.

The jurist to whom belongs the judicial investigation of the case of the steamer Black Warrior, has just reported to me as follows:

"MOST EXCELLENT SIR: The assessor (legal adviser) has just dispatched the process that the preceding petition refers to, advising your excellency in it that the same shall return into the hands of the 'fiscal,' to whom belongs, as the representative of the royal exchequer, to plead the rights of the same; consequently, no decision has as yet been pronounced that is to be communicated to the captain of the steamer detained, and by him spontaneously abandoned; so that the persons of the crew of said steamer, being in the enjoyment of their liberty, can make use of it as they may choose either to remain in or leave this country, your excellency's permission being first obtained. But in regard to the process, it is necessary to go through the opportune proceedings before pronouncing the proper resolution, to the results of which must remain subjected the captain of the steamer; giving to that end the necessary guarantee, as he should be made to understand, should your excellency so ordain it, referring afterwards this petition to the *fiscal*, with all the proceedings upon the matter."

And, in conformity with his report, I transfer the same to your lordship for your information, and in reply to your communication of this date; in the understanding that, as your lordship will perceive, the officers and crew of said steamer are at liberty to transfer themselves where they please; but not so Captain Bullock, for the reasons already expressed.

God preserve your lordship many years. Havana, March 13, 1854,

EL MARQUIS DE LA PEZUELA.

To the CONSUL
of the United States in this city.

Mr. Robertson to Mr. Marcy.

[Extract.]

CONSULATE OF THE UNITED STATES, HAVANA,
March 21, 1854.

SIR: * * * * * *

Enclosed herewith you will find a copy, with translation, of an official letter from the collector of the customs to Mr. Charles Tyng, consignee of the steamer "Black Warrior," restoring to the owners the said steamer and her cargo. The ship has been received under protest, and the fine will be paid under protest. She was taken possession of yesterday in the most filthy condition, and in the greatest disorder, and I am informed that many articles belonging to her are missing. All circumstances bearing upon the case will hereafter appear in the captain's protest. She is now taking in her cargo, and intend to leave for New York on Friday next.

* * * * * *

[Translation.]

ADMINISTRATION GENERAL OF THE MARITIME REVENUE OF HAVANA.

His excellency the superintendent general, delegate of the royal exchequer in this island, under date of the 16th instant, has been pleased to issue the following decree:

"In view of the fiscal's opinion, having before me all the other precedents of the case, and finally concurring in the spirit of benevolence which is evident in the decision of the superior directing board of the royal exchequer, I resolve to fix the fine of six thousand dollars, which is to be paid by the company owning the steamer Black Warrior, without any other disbursement on any account whatsoever, as from the said fine shall be deducted the expenses incurred hitherto and the dues that were defrauded from the royal exchequer"—

Which I transmit to you for your information, that you may be pleased to make effective (hacer efectiva) the said fine, and dispose that the captain of the Black Warrior take charge of her and the cargo, all with the urgency that the case demands.

God preserve you many years. Havana, March 18, 1854.

JOAQUIN ROCA.

CHARLES TYNG, Esq.,
Consignee of the American steamer "Black Warrior."

Mr. Sutherland to Mr. Marcy.

NEW YORK, 54 WALL STREET,
March 28, 1854.

SIR: In the statement of Messrs. Livingston, Crocheron & Co., agents of the New York and Alabama Steamship Company, relative to the seizure of the "Black Warrior," &c., which they had the honor to lay before you on the 11th of March inst., they referred to former unjust demands made by the authorities at Havana, upon the agents of said company there, for certain "tonnage dues," &c., in violation of certain privileges which had been previously conceded and verbally promised, if not authoritatively ordained or decreed, to the steamers of said company, being the same privileges conceded to, and enjoyed by, the steamers of the English Royal Mail Company, and those of the American "Law" line.

The amount which the said agents at Havana were thus compelled to pay, and did pay, under protest, on or about the 17th of February, 1853, was $3,372 50; since then, a demand has been made upon the said agents for two trips more, amounting to $2,197 76.

Upon the first demand being made, Messrs. Tyng & Co., the said agents at Havana, made a memorial to the intendente, requesting that the matter might be referred to the home government at Madrid. In this memorial they not only complained of this demand of these tonnage dues, &c., under the circumstances, as unjust and dishonorable, but insisted on the claim of the steamers of the "New York and Alabama Steamship Company" to enjoy the same privileges as the steamers of the "English Royal Mail Company," and those of the American "Law" line. This request to have the matter referred to the home government having been granted, Messrs. Tyng & Co. wrote to Mr. Barringer, who was then the American minister at Madrid, enclosing a copy of the memorial; and explaining the case, asked his attention to it. To this letter no answer has been received.

Upon the demand being made for the $2,197 76, for two other trips, which was about the 10th of December, 1853, Messrs. Tyng & Co. wrote Mr. Soulé, our present minister at Madrid; and, referring to the said memorial and their letter to Mr. Barringer, fully explained the case to him, and asked his attention to the matter. No reply has been received from Mr. Soulé, nor is it known that the letter has been received by him.

On the behalf and at the request of Messrs. Livingston, Crocheron & Co., I have the honor now to enclose, herewith, a copy of the letter of Messrs. Tyng & Co., to Mr. Soulé, and to ask you, as the chief executive officer of the government having charge of our "foreign affairs," to give the subject-matter of it that attention and action which it may and ought to have, not so much as an isolated case of Spanish agression upon the rights and property of American citizens, as from the fact that it has been followed up by the late unjust seizure of the "Black Warrior" by the same Spanish officials.

I have the honor to be, your obedient servant,

JOS. SUTHERLAND.

Hon. Wm. L. Marcy,
Secretary of State, &c.

Havana, *December* 10, 1853.

The undersigned, agents of the American steamers "Black Warrior" and "Cahawba," which vessels ply regularly between New York and Mobile, stopping each voyage at this port, beg to call your attention to the following facts:

In the month of August, 1852, previous to the establishment of the line, we made a memorial to the intendente, asking that the steamers of this line might be placed upon the same footing and enjoy the same privileges as the steamers belonging to the English Royal Mail Company, and those of the American "Law" line, which run between New York and New Orleans. This request was granted, and the "Black Warrior," the first of the line, commenced making her trips in the month of September following, and has continued to call here, on her voyages out and home, twice per month, ever since. The privileges granted to the above named lines, and which were promised to this line also, are as follows:

1st. They are exempted from the payment of certain port charges levied upon common merchant vessels coming to this port for the purpose of bringing or carrying away cargoes, such as light dues, mud-machine dues, &c., &c.; and, second, they are allowed the privilege of taking merchandise to the extent of three tons, without incurring the charge of tonnage dues paid by merchant vessels.

The Black Warrior had made four voyages, calling at this port twice on each voyage, when, to our astonishment, the custom-house authorities sent us the bills, and demanded payment of the tonnage dues and other port charges for those four voyages, the same as though she had been a common merchant ship, and no promise had been made to consider her as otherwise. These bills for tonnage, dues, &c., amounted in the aggregate to near five thousand dollars, ($5,000.) In answer to our question why they demanded these charges, we received a reply that a royal order had been received from Madrid, in answer to a memorial by the house of Villodo, Wardroff & Co., of this place, asking that the English steamer "Tamaulipas" might be placed upon the same footing as the two first mentioned lines of steamers. This royal order refused the request, on the ground that no merchant vessel should enjoy the privileges granted to the mail steamers, and the custom-house authorities, choosing to consider the Black Warrior as a merchant vessel, not only rescinded the privileges they had before granted, but demanded payment of the past dues which they alleged she had incurred. We objected to paying the amount and made a memorial to the intendente, requesting that the matter might be referred to the home government, at Madrid. This request was granted, and the memorial, (of which we herewith enclose a copy,) was, after much delay, forwarded on the 1st of March last. We also wrote to Mr. Barringer, who was at that time the American minister, explaining the case, and requesting his attention to it, but, having received no reply to our letter, are uncertain whether he received it or not. We beg leave to present to you the following reasons why these steamers should be placed upon the same footing with those of the American "Law" line, and not with the English steamer "Tamaulipas:"

The steamers "Black Warrior," of 1,700 tons, and the "Cahawba," of 1,850 tons, American measurement, are large side-wheel steamers, and are commanded by officers of the United States navy. They merely stop here for from four to six hours on their trips to and from New York and Mobile. They make these stops merely to land mails and passengers, and to take in coals and other necessary supplies; they neither land nor receive cargo. Like the "Law" line of steamers, the only use they have made of the three tons granted, has been to take samples of merchandise, and other small packages, for the accommodation of the commerce of the place. Being side-wheel boats, and using sails only as auxiliaries, they are obliged to steam during the whole passage. Moreover, as a large portion of their holds is taken up by the boilers and other necessary machinery, their carrying capacity is very small in proportion to their tonnage. With the steamer "Tamaulipas" the case is very different. The "Tamaulipas" is a propeller, built in England, with a view to carrying merchandise principally. She is a sailing-vessel, and only uses her propeller as an auxiliary when the winds are unfavorable. She measures very small, but her carrying capacity is very large in proportion. She runs from Liverpool to Vera Cruz, and from there here, bringing cargo and passengers. She lies in port for from three to four days, and receives and discharges cargo, the same as any merchant vessel, and there is no just reason why she should not be considered as such.

We contend that it is an injustice to represent the Black Warrior and the Cahawba to be of the same class and subject to the same duties as the Tamaulipas, being, as they are, of an entirely different build and intended for an entirely different purpose.

We claim that they are of the same class, subject to the same duties and other port charges, and entitled to the same privileges as the "Law" line of steamers before mentioned. More than this, we consider it not only an unjust, but a dishonorable act, on the part of the authorities, that, after having given their consent and admitted these steamers eight different times upon precisely the same footing as the "Law" line, and that consent being one of the inducements for these steamers to stop in this port, then not only to withdraw the permission, but also to demand payment for those past voyages—voyages which would not have been made had that permission not been granted. Had the intendente informed us, in answer to our application before the line was established, that these steamers could not be granted the privileges accorded to the "Law" line, then arrangements would have been made either for them not to stop here at all, or else to load full cargoes as an offset to those expenses; but having given the permission, we consider the government bound both legally and honorably to make good the promise. Within the past few days we have again been called upon to pay the amount of these tonnage and other dues. We have called upon the custom-house officers, to know why the demand is made again, after having been referred last spring to the home government at Madrid. We have been informed by them, that no answer has as yet been received to the memorial then sent; but that it is an order from the intendente to the collector of the port, that the amount *shall* be paid. If these charges are persisted in, it will be necessary for the owners to order these steamers to stop here no more, as the expense thus incurred would be ruinous.

As American citizens ourselves, and as the agents and representatives of large American interests in this port, we would request you, as the American minister plenipotentiary to the court of Spain, to have this matter fairly represented to the proper authorities at Madrid who have charge of those affairs, and see that we, as agents of the owners of these steamers, are protected in our just and legal rights. We would wish you to represent to them that the steamers are not only of great importance to the commerce of the place, as is indeed the case, but also to the government itself, in the way of forwarding dispatches, &c., as has always been done by them without any charge whatever.

We would feel greatly obliged if you would acknowledge the receipt of this letter, and inform us, so far as may be in your power, of the prospects of a speedy settlement of the affair; and beg leave to subscribe ourselves,

Most respectfully, your obedient servants,

CHARLES TYNG & CO.

Hon. PIERE SOULE,
Minister Plenipotentiary of the United States at Madrid.

[Translation.]

Rules and instructions for the custom-house service of the ports of entry in the island of Cuba, ordered to be put in force by royal order of the 13th of February, 1847. Printed in Havana, at the printing office of the government and royal treasury, for her Majesty, on the same year of 1847.

[*Articles concerning what took place with regard to the "Black Warrior."*]

Art. 1. "The operations of the custom-house shall commence from the moment that vessels come into port." (After directing the commandant of carabiniers to be present at the sanitary visit, and to cause the vessel to be watched until she is admitted to free practice, it continues:) "The vessel being admitted to free practice, the aforesaid officer shall go on board and receive from her captain the manifest of the cargo she brings. In doing this, he shall make a note, at the bottom of said document, of the hour when the same was delivered to him, of the lines of writing it contains, stating which have not been corrected, or which have been, and the circumstance of the vessel having anchored, it being necessary for him to sign this note, with the captain and the interpreter, in case of said captain being a foreigner. After this, he shall deliver to the same captain a printed copy, in three languages, according to examplar No. 1, of the obligations with which he is bound to comply, and the penalties he would incur by their infraction; and having done this, he shall take care," &c., &c.

Art. 4. The manifest being presented with the formalities enumerated, the commandant of carabiniers, or whoever may represent him, shall forward the same to the collector of customs, in order that he may hand it to the interpreter, &c., &c.

Art. 5. "During the space of twelve hours, counting from the time that the vessel comes to anchor, (it being understood, for this purpose, the hours intervening between six in the morning and seven in the evening, every day in the year, irrespective of holydays,) the captain shall be at liberty to make additions in his manifest, whether for omissions, irregularities, or errors he may have committed in the same, or in consequence of not having presented it with the formalities required by the foregoing articles."

Art. 6. "The alterations which the captain may have to make, conformably with the privilege granted by the preceding article, shall be comprised in an appendix, which he shall present to the collector, noting down the hour of its delivery, and both signing the same, if it be office hours; if not, he shall present it to the chief of carabiniers that may be on duty at the mole, who, without the least delay, and under the strictest responsibility, shall transmit the same to the collector, with a memorandum, signed by said chief himself and the captain, of the hour when it was delivered."

Chapter V.—Tonnage and arrivals.

Art. 54. "National or foreign vessels entering the ports of the island to trade, with whatever kind of cargo, shall pay, besides consular and municipal duties, the tonnage duties specified by the tariff, according to the results of the guaging effected on the occasion of their first voyage, for all vessels, whether national or foreign."

Art. 56. "If, after having come in ballast, the vessels sail again without a cargo, they shall be exempt from the payment of tonnage duties; but this duty shall be exacted from them if they take the whole or part of their cargo in produce of the country, or in articles of any other kind or derivation, even when they are not worth the duties. In the same manner they shall pay, under all circumstances, the local duties which are levied in each port."

Art. 57. "Nor shall those vessels pay tonnage duties which arrive at a port in quest of water or provisions, or to repair damages; but if such vessels leave the whole or part of their cargo, or ship produce of the country, or articles of any other derivation, they shall pay in full the duty aforementioned."

Chapter XI.—Mercantile depot.

Art. 119. "Articles, produce, or effects, intended for deposite, shall be divided into two classes. Those of the first class shall only enjoy this benefit during the term of one year, not to be prolonged; and those of the second class for two years, not to be prolonged likewise."

Art. 123. "The articles composing the second class are the following: Flax, hemp, cotton, wool, silk, furs, horse-hair in its natural state or manufactured, and every species of texture, &c."

Chapter XII.—Fines, double duties, and seizures.

Art. 160. "The value affixed to effects, produce or articles of trade, shall be the criterion for regulating the fines and double duties, which are not designated in these instructions by a fixed sum."

Art. 162. "At the expiration of the twelve hours specified in article 5th for the rectification or addition of the manifest, all bulks that have not been set down in it shall be seized, a fine being likewise imposed upon the captain of as much more as the value of the same; provided, that the amount of duties which should have been paid for the contents of the bulk, or bulks seized, does not exceed four hundred dollars, because if it should exceed that amount, and the articles belong or be consigned to the owner, captain, or supercargo of the vessel, the fine shall not take effect, and, in its place, the vessel shall be seized, together with her freight and all belonging to her."

Art. 175. "If, upon the visit of the inspector, which must be made to all vessels before the papers with which they have to sail are delivered to them, there should be found any excess in the cargo, this shall be seized, and a fine imposed upon the captain equal to the value of said excess."

Chapter XIII.—General regulations.

Art. 190. "The captain of every vessel, national or foreign, which may enter any of the ports of entry of the island, on her passage out, whether with cargo or in ballast, by stress of weather or in transit, shall present her manifest or register, in the manner and with the formalities prescribed in these instructions, and shall be subjected to the fines and penalties imposed in the same, for any violation of the regulations therein contained."

Art. 193. "From the moment that a vessel in cargo enters a port, until she has discharged the same, or, if either in transit or driven by stress of weather, until she sails again, and from the moment that a vessel in ballast takes in cargo, until her register is closed and she gets under way, there shall be a carabinier, at the utmost two, on board of her, for the purpose of performing the duties allotted to such which are laid down in these instructions, or in the regulations of said body. If this carabinier should be relieved for the convenience of the service, or for other causes, he shall deliver over to the person who may replace him, the memorandum book of the loading and unloading of the vessel, in the presence of one of his immediate superiors, who shall revise the same, in order that, in case of any difference occurring, the responsibility may be thrown upon whom it belongs."

Art. 197. "The collector of customs shall attend to the manifests and registers of foreign or national vessels which may enter in ballast, in distress, or in transit, on the same terms as are established with regard to those that bring imported cargoes."

Art. 203. "None of the provisions contained in these instructions shall be interpreted in a different sense from their literal context. When any doubt or difficulty shall occur in regard to their application, the collectors shall communicate the same for advice to the respective intendent, who will submit them, with his opinion, to the superintendency; and the latter shall decide, by previous agreement with the superior tribunal having control of the finances, the matter being referred to the supreme government for its approbation or correction."

[Translation.]

Exemplar No. 1.—Rules for the guidance of the masters and supercargoes of vessels, Spanish or foreigners, engaged in the importation trade in the ports of entry of the island of Cuba.

1. Masters or supercargoes of transit vessels, entering any of the ports of entry of this island, are obliged, as soon as they have dropped anchor, to present to the officer of the carabiniers who shall come on board, a manifest containing their names, that of the ship, the number of Spanish tons she measures, what her cargo consists of, the name of the place she sailed from, the number of bales of goods or bulks, with the designation of their respective marks, numbers, and names of the persons to whom they are consigned.

If all or part of the cargo should happen to consist of salted beef, salt, cocoa, or other articles put up in bulk, these shall be manifested by weight or Castilian measure, specifying, also, the articles of mess, naval and military stores, and the quantity of hard coals they bring for their own consumption, if the vessel be a steamer.

2. Masters and supercargoes of vessels putting into said ports by stress of weather, are obliged to present the manifest of their cargo, with the same specification as if it were intended for traffic and to be disposed of in the island.

3. Masters and supercargoes of vessels entering in ballast are subject to the same obligation.

4. Those masters who may have been compelled, by bad weather, or by other fortuitous circumstances, to throw overboard part of their cargo, shall likewise set it down in their manifest, specifying, though it were by wholesale, the quantities, bulks, and kinds or species, being obliged to present their declarations to the custom-house, as well as the log-book, in corroboration of their assertions.

5. Those vessels proceeding from Spanish ports with their registers dispatched by the respective custom-houses, are only obliged to manifest the effects they bring which are not inserted in the register, articles of mess, and the stores already mentioned.

6. If the master or supercargo fail to present the manifest at the time prefixed, he shall incur a fine of five hundred dollars.

7. Whosoever shall fail to declare the exact number of Spanish tons his vessel measures, shall be obliged to pay the costs which may be incurred in guaging the same, provided that the excess of tonnage she is found to measure does exceed ten per cent. of what is set down in the manifest.

8. When neither the master nor the supercargo is able to draw up the manifest, that duty shall revert to the consignee of the vessel, or to any of his dependents who may be empowered to that effect.

9. During the twelve hours following that of the delivery of the manifest, reckoned from six in the morning till seven in the evening, he who presented the same shall be at liberty to make such alterations in it as he may deem proper, by waiting personally upon the collector if within office hours, or, in the contrary case, upon the chief of the carabiniers, who is on duty at the custom-house.

10. If, at the expiration of the twelve hours designated by the foregoing regulation, there shall be found on board the vessel any bulks or other effects which have been omitted in the manifest, the same shall be seized, and the master or supercargo mulcted in as much more the amount, of their value, provided that the duties which ought to have been paid for the contents of the bulk or bulks seized do not exceed $400; for if they do exceed that sum, and the effects belong to or be consigned to the owner, master, or supercargo of the vessel, the fine shall not be levied, and, in its place, the aforesaid vessel, with her freights and all that belong to her, shall be confiscated.

11. It shall not be allowed to disembark anything without the permission of the collector, and the knowledge of the officer of the carabiniers who may be on duty at the mole. For the simple act of disembarking anything, although they may be articles of little importance or free of duty, the master or supercargo shall pay a fine of $1,000; and all the effects seized, as well as the boat or launch which conveyed them, shall be confiscated, provided that the amount of duties said articles would have had to pay does not exceed $200; but if it exceed that sum, the fine shall be omitted and the ship confiscated.

12. Nor shall any effects be allowed to be shifted from one ship to another within the bay, either in small or large quantities, without those requisites mentioned in the foregoing rule; the masters or supercargoes of both vessels being, in case of contravention, subject to the penalty specified in the rule aforesaid.

13. If any vessel discharge goods, in either small or large quantities, in a port which is not a port of entry, the vessel and all that appertains to her shall incur the penalty of confiscation.

14. If, after having discharged a vessel, there be found wanting any of the bulks set down in the manifest, it shall be understood that the master or supercargo has committed a fraud against the treasury, by fining them in the amount of $200 for each of the bulks missing.

15. If it should be proved upon the visit of the inspector, which must be made to every vessel before the papers with which she has to sail are delivered to her, that her cargo exceeds the entry, the same shall be seized, and a fine three times the value of said excess be imposed upon the master.

16. The seizures which shall be made of articles, produce, or effects attempted to be shipped in a fraudulent manner, shall be subject to the same confiscation and fine which are mentioned in the foregoing article.

17. If masters or supercargoes should not have the means to pay the amount of their respective penalties, there shall be used for the payment of such, and the costs, the vessels which they command, unless their consignees voluntarily come forward to pay the same.

A true copy.

[Translation.]

Observations.

In order to avoid the delays which are occasioned to steamers that are only occupied in conveying passengers and the mails in the trips they make periodically from one port of the United States of America to the other, touching at Havana—because such delay is incompatible with their regulations, which only allow them to remain a few hours in said port of Havana, (three or four at the utmost)—a custom has been established of asking the consignees, in advance of the entrance of said steamers, for the register, supposing them in ballast, whenever they do not bring cargo for this port, nor come here to take such cargo. Thus it has always been done; because, although it is provided in article 1 of the instructions "that the operations of the custom-houses shall commence from the moment that the vessels enter port," that then, or when they are admitted to free practice, the commandant of the carabiniers is to receive from the captain the manifest of the cargo, taking note of the hour, in order that the aforesaid captain may return to sign, it was understood that these formalities were adopted with reference to national or foreign vessels entering the ports of the island to trade with whatever kind of cargo—an intention which is set forth in article 54, and which coincides with the very remarkable circumstance that in 1847, when the instructions were drawn up, if we are not mistaken, these lines of North American steamers were not established. However this may be, it is a fact that the custom-house has concurred in the custom alluded to.

In her last trip the "Black Warrior" brought from Mobile some bales of cotton—an article which is not of trade, which never enters among the staples of consumption in Havana, and for which, therefore, there are no duties assigned by the tariff. Nor do goods which come here in transit, in a vessel that is taking said goods to another port, pay such duties; consequently it is not to be presumed that the captain of the Wlack Warrior had intended to commit a fraud.

The aforesaid steamer entered this port at seven o'clock in the morning. Supposing the captain to have represented her in ballast in the manifest, it must be taken into consideration that the same instructions, in article fifth, state positively that during the space of twelve hours the captain shall be at liberty to make additions in his manifest, either on account of omissions, irregularities, or errors he may have committed, or in consequence of not having presented the same with the required formalities. In order to allow of no doubt, this same article fifty says, that these twelve hours shall be comprised from the moment that the ship comes to anchor, and that they must be understood as the hours intervening between six in the morning and seven in the evening; therefore there can be no doubt that in asking for the bill of clearance the captain had the unquestionable right of making additions in his manifest, and that this privilege could not and should not have been denied to the consignee, Don Carlos Tyng, when, on being informed of the difficulties that had interposed, he asked for the same of the collector of customs, who founded his refusal upon the fact that this right had been forfeited when Don Felipe Nunez, who signed the request in behalf of the consignees, solicited the visit of clearance. There is not one article in the instructions which establishes such a loss of the right of making additions to the manifest, and there must be borne in mind, above all, the custom of which we have before made mention.

Let it be remembered that the "Black Warrior's" cargo being in transit, she is not subject to tonnage duties, and still less to importation duties; she would only have to pay port duty, (derecho de ponton,) which would amount to about $150. Hence, it must be inferred that under no circumstances did these duties or supposed fraud amount to what occasions the fines, and double as much, which are imposed when the fraud is committed against the royal treasury, and which constitute the rule according to article 160; because that port duty is merely arbitrary, created by the *Real Junta de Fomento*, and not by the *Cajas Reales*, or general expenses of the nation. Between the *Junta de Fomento* and the royal treasury, there is the difference of a corporation purely local, which attends to the encouragement of agriculture and the commerce of the province solely, and the government, which in a monarchy, or central power, is at the head of the nation. Besides these remarks, the consideration which is suggested by article 162 appears conclusive; it says: "At the expiration of the twelve hours designated in article 5," etc.; which words, "at the expiration," do not admit of the least doubt, nor allow of an interpretation calculated to subject those bulks which had not been included in the manifest to confiscation, and to impose upon the captain a fine of as much more the amount of their value, or the confiscation of the vessel, freight, and all belonging to her, before that period of time had expired. There is no doubt but that the act of taking possession of the "Black Warrior" was contrary to the instructions, seeing that it began to be carried out four or five hours after her entrance into port, and that to refuse permission to make additions in the manifest, by inserting in it the cargo which she had brought in transit, when the novelty of interrupting the practice or custom followed until then became palpable, was still more illegal.

In normal cases, and with regard to vessels entering to trade, the provisions of the instructions could not be interpreted in a different sense from their literal context, seeing that article 203 forbids it; the confiscation of a cargo brought in transit by a steamer that only comes to this port to leave and to take passengers and the mails, even though setting aside the custom aforesaid, ought to be considered as much less reasonable. The collector of customs should have explained, in his first communication to the superior authorities, that the twelve hours had not elapsed before he ordered the vessel to be seized for the purpose of discharging and confiscating the bales of cotton. This suppressed fact, although it is not denied, is, fortunately for the master and the owners of the cargo, too well authenticated; because the steamer having entered at seven o'clock in the morning, the aforesaid twelve hours lasted until the same hour in the evening; nevertheless, the captain made his reclamation at midday through the consular agent. Subsequently the consignee called upon the collector, and it was only three o'clock in the evening when said consignee, Don Carlos Tyng, returned to the custom-house, and, in the presence of two individuals, requested of the collector to be allowed to exercise the right granted by the fifth article of the instructions. Tyng showed that he had this right in his first memorial, and it was neither denied nor contradicted; moreover, from the very day of the ship's entrance, it was undertaken to discharge her, and the act was only suspended when the captain abandoned the vessel and left her with all the crew.

OPENING OF THE MAILS OF THE UNITED STATES.

Mr. Sharkey to the Secretary of State.

[Extract.]

[No. 19.] CONSULATE OF THE UNITED STATES, HAVANA,
November 8, 1852.

SIR:

* * * * * * * *

It seems to be difficult to induce either the authorities or people here to believe that our government does not lend its countenance to expeditions against this island, although I have again and again assured them to the contrary. I must inform you that we are not allowed to receive newspapers from the United States through the post office, nor is any one allowed to bring them on the shore, two or three papers being excepted, as I understand, and it may be that other communications are suppressed. This condition, to say the least, is humiliating especially to me.

Mr. Sharkey to Mr. Everett.

[No. 25.] CONSULATE OF THE UNITED STATES, HAVANA,
February 21, 1853.

SIR: In the absence of a postal arrangement with this island, it has been the custom to deposite letters intended for the United States in a letter bag kept for that purpose by the consignee of the mail steamers. This bag is closed at the proper time, and sealed, and it is then taken by a clerk of the house and delivered on board the ship. I have never heard any objection made to this custom, nor have the authorities here, as far as I know, ever heretofore claimed any authority over it. On the 19th instant, however, the mail bag intended for the "Empire City," after it had been regularly closed, was seized as it was being conveyed from the house of the consignee, taken to an office, the seal broken, and the contents examined; after which it was returned to the individual who had charge of it, and by him taken on board the ship. On yesterday a like course was pursued with the mail bag intended for the "Crescent City." The seizure and examination were made, as I am informed, by the chief of police, but of course under the order of the Captain General. It is said that no letters were taken from the bags; I felt it to be my duty to remonstrate against this course as indecorous towards my government, and have the honor to enclose you a copy of my communication to the Captain General on that subject. I believe a like course was attempted with the British mails a few years ago, but it was resisted and abandoned. The British mails, however, are made up at the consul's office. You will see how easily our correspondence, official as well as private, may be obstructed. I was not present at these examinations, but give you the information on reliable authority. There is evidently some alarm existing here, but from what cause I know not.

I have the honor to be, with great respect, your obedient servant,

W. L. SHARKEY,

Hon. EDWARD EVERETT,
Secretary of State of the United States.

CONSULATE OF THE UNITED STATES, HAVANA,
February, 21, 1853.

MOST EXCELLENT SIR: Information has reached me that on the 19th and 20th instant, the mail bags intended for the United States mail steamers Empire City and Crescent City were seized by the public authorities after they had been regularly closed and sealed, as they were being carried from the house of the consignees and agents of those ships (Messrs. Drake & Co.) to the wharf, the seals broken, and the contents of the bags examined. It is not my province to discuss this question as one of national concern, it will be referred to the government at Washington, where, I doubt not, it will be duly considered. But I must nevertheless avail myself of the occasion to express my deep regret at the occurrence, and respectfully, but decidedly, to remonstrate against it as discourteous towards my government, for the following reasons: The United States mail steamers which touch at this port have been running under the employment of the government for more than five years. During that time they have constantly brought regular mails from the United States, and have deposited them in the post office here, and have thus rendered essential service to this government, and have also contributed to the interests of commerce, to the convenience of the inhabitants, and to the interests of the Post Office Department of the island. During the same period, in the absence of a postal arrangement, it has been the uniform custom to deposite letters for the United States in a letter bag kept for that purpose by the consignees of the ships, who at the appointed time, closed and sealed it, and delivered it on board the ship, where it was received as the mail of the United States. If I am not misinformed, the officials of this government have very often availed themselves of this facility. To this custom, although well known, no objection has heretofore been made or restriction imposed. On the contrary, it has been tacitly approved and sanctioned, and had thus assumed the character of a customary regulation.

The sudden interruption in a matter of comity so beneficial, and which has so long existed without any intimation of an intended change, may well be regarded as ground of surprise. The government of the United States has had no intimation whatever that this custom was not altogether agreeable, or I am sure it would have been abandoned. Our Post Office Department must be supposed to have given its approval to this mode of making up the mails here, under the supposition that it was entirely approved here, and it has therefore incurred the responsibility of delivering all such letters as might be mailed here; and it is to be regretted that it was thought necessary to depart from the customary mode, as the government of the United States has in the most unrestricted manner given the full benefit of its mail arrangement to this government, and has, moreover, been steadfast in its friendship towards the government of her Catholic Majesty, and more especially towards this island.

I have the honor to be, with all due respect, your obedient servant,

W. L. SHARKEY,

Consul of the United States.

His Excellency Señor D. VALENTIN CAÑEDO.

Governor and Captain General, &c., &c., &c.

Mr. Sharkey to the Secretary of State.

[Extract.]

[No. 27.] CONSULATE OF THE UNITED STATES, HAVANA,
March 12, 1853.

SIR: In my dispatch No. 25 of the 21st ultimo, I had the honor to communicate the facts in reference to the opening of the mails of the United States by the authorities of this city, and also to forward a copy of my communication to the Captain General on that subject. I have now the honor to forward his reply, and also to state that no other mails have since been subjected to examination.

* * * * * *

I have the honor, &c.,

W. L. SHARKEY.

Hon. SECRETARY OF STATE *of the United States.*

[Translation.]

[L. S.] POLITICAL SECRETARY'S OFFICE, FIRST SECTION,

I have received the communication that your lordship addressed me under date of the 21st ultimo, in consequence of the bags containing the mails made up at the commercial house of Drake & Co., and destined for the United States mail steamers, having been examined by the chief of the police.

Independently of your lordship's (incompetencia) want of authority in the matter which your lordship acknowledges, I must state to you that the said search having been effected within Spanish territory, and at a time especially when they were in possession of private persons, not clothed with any official character, in no manner have the friendly relations between both governments, nor the deference due to their agents, been affected by that act.

Whether the bags were sealed or not, it is evident that on their crossing the line of the custom-house guards established on the coast, and consequently on the wharves of this city, a mere guard would have had sufficient authority to cause them to be opened; and I even add that he would have been obliged to do it, for the purpose of ascertaining if there were among their contents matters on the exportation of which the royal treasury was entitled to duties. And if there can be no doubt in this, much less will there be for acknowledging the same powers in a functionary of infinitely higher station, and who, as the chief of police aforesaid, independent of this office, holds high rank in the service of the State. Your lordship is well aware of the exceedingly temperate manner in which the acts were effected—that the greatest legality presided in them; and finally, that nothing was done but to look, in a few moments, over the addresses of the letters, after adopting the proper precautions to avoid that malice or ignorance should give them afterwards an appearance of violence or irregularity.

Your lordship is no less aware of the good disposition on the part of my authority to attend to your wishes, even in unofficial matters, of which are authentic evidence certain recent acts which I do not suppose your lordship may have forgotten. On this account I am the more surprised at your lordship's entertaining, for an instant, a doubt of my good dispositions, and of the especial care with which I endeavor to avoid all that may offend the sincere and cordial friendship of the respectable American government.

God preserve you many years. Havana, March 2, 1853.

VALENTIN CAÑEDO.

To the CONSUL *of the United States.*

Mr. Robertson to Mr. Marcy.

CONSULATE OF THE UNITED STATES, HAVANA,
August 29, 1853.

SIR: Information has just been brought to me that a royal order has been received here instructing the Captain General to have all the mails for the United States made up at the Spanish post office, and not to allow the present practice for the future. I am also informed that the British mails are exempted from the order—they are made up at the British consulate. I give you this information as a fact not to be doubted.

I have the honor, &c.,

W. H. ROBERTSON.

WM. L. MARCY,
Secretary of State, Washington.

Mr. Robertson to Mr. Marcy.

CONSULATE OF THE UNITED STATES, HAVANA,
August 29, 1853.

SIR: The Spanish post office in this city has been for some time past in the habit of cutting open letters coming from the United States, before proceeding to give them out. It is understood that it is done by order of the Captain General, and that their object is to see if the contents is printed matter; in which case, (it is stated,) the party to whom it is addressed is called to open it in the presence of some officer of the government. Several letters addressed to Hon. Judge Clayton, United States consul at Havana, and to myself, as consul, have been cut open. As such acts on the part of the authorities here are very discourteous, and imply suspicion against this consulate, I have deemed it my duty to remonstrate with the Captain General. The annexed is a copy of my communication to his excellency.

Hoping that my course will meet your approval, I have the honor, &c., &c.,

W. H. ROBERTSON.

WM. L. MARCY,
Secretary of State.

Mr. Robertson to the Captain General.

CONSULATE OF THE UNITED STATES, HAVANA,
August 29, 1853.

MOST EXCELLENT SIR: I regret that I have been disappointed in four different attempts to pay my respects to your excellency, the object of which was to remonstrate with your excellency against the repeated indignities practised in your post office towards the consulate of the United States, in the cutting open of sundry letters directed to the Hon. Judge Clayton, United States consul at Havana, and others directed to the undersigned as consul. Satisfied in my own mind that such an indignity (implying suspicion of this office) cannot meet your excellency's sanction or approbation I communicate the fact to you, in the full confidence and hope that it will not be repeated.

I have the honor to be, &c., &c., your excellency's, &c.,

W. H. ROBERTSON.

His Excellency Señor Don VALENTIN CAÑEDO,
Governor and Captain General of Cuba.

Mr. Robertson to Mr. Marcy.

[Extract.]

[No. 55.] CONSULATE OF THE UNITED STATES, HAVANA,
September 13, 1853.

SIR: Referring to my communication of the 29th ultimo, No. 52, and the document therewith enclosed, I now have the honor to transmit to you a copy of the Captain General's reply to my letter. His excellency gives in detail the reasons that have induced the government to take the measures complained against by me, but assured me that he had given orders to the postmaster of Havana not to effect any examination of the correspondence addressed to this consulate. However, the United States mail steamer El Dorado arrived here on the 6th instant, from New York, bringing among other letters for me, or to my care, a large package addressed "United States consul, Havana," from your department, bearing the seal thereof. This package was cut. I immediately called on the Captain General and showed him the package. Without replying, he rang his bell violently and called his political secretary, of whom his excellency inquired if he had communicated to the postmaster his orders in regard to the correspondence of the American consulate. The secretary said he had. The Captain General desired him to reiterate his orders, and see that the thing did not happen again; then turning to me, he expressed his regret at the occurrence, and assured me that it should not be repeated. I therefore accepted his excellency's assurances, and thanked him for his promptness.

* * * * * * * *

I have the honor, &c.,

W. H. ROBERTSON,
Acting Consul.

Mr. Robertson to Mr. Marcy.

[Extract.]

CONSULATE OF THE UNITED STATES, HAVANA,
October 14, 1853.

SIR: * * * * * *
As my communication of the 13th ultimo, No. 55, must have reached you long before this time it is needless for me to say more on the subject, except that since the day of my interview with the Captain General mentioned in that letter I have had no reason for complaint on that account.

I have the honor, &c.,
W. H. ROBERTSON, *Acting Consul.*

W. L. MARCY,
Secretary of State.

Mr. Marcy to Mr. Pierce.

DEPARTMENT OF STATE,
Washington, February 1, 1854.

SIR: You will receive, prior to the sailing of the next steamer for Havana, a bag directed to your care, containing public dispatches for the United States consul at Havana. This bag will be closed in this department, and is not to be opened until its delivery to the United States consul in Havana.

On the receipt of this bag you will intrust it to some discreet person on board the steamer, who will deliver it to the consul in person. The commander of the steamer would, doubtless, be quite willing to take it in charge.

You are specially instructed that neither this bag nor any others that may be hereafter sent to the United States consul in Havana are to be opened in New York; nor is any matter whatever to be conveyed in it except what is transmitted from this department.

The enclosed dispatch, addressed to the United States consul at Havana, containing the keys of the mail-bag, I will thank you to send by some individual, whom you will request to place it in the hands of the consul.

I am, &c., W. L. MARCY.

J. FRANKLIN PIERCE, Esq.,
U. S. Dispatch Agent, New York.

CASE OF THE CONTOY PRISONERS.

Mr. Campbell to Mr. Clayton.

[Extract.]

CONSULATE OF THE UNITED STATES, HAVANA,
May 19, 1850.

SIR: On the arrival of the steamer Ohio the Captain General ordered that she should not be permitted to occupy her usual anchorage, but ordered her anchored at the mouth of the harbor, and that none of her passengers for Chagres be permitted to land. The captain thought the anchorage unsafe, and protested against it without avail, this government at the same time denying any responsibility for accidents that might happen to the steamer from the insecurity of her position. The cause of the order is only conjectural, but is supposed to proceed from dispatches received from New Orleans by the schooners Fairy and Heroine, that arrived some forty hours in advance of the Ohio, under charter (it is said) by the Spanish consul.

You are better informed of what has passed, and is passing, in relation to the expedition, than we can be in Havana, and I will not, therefore, presume to give you reports, but only observe that great excitement prevails here. Some nineteen armed vessels of the Spanish navy are coasting around various parts of the island to intercept the reported expedition. I do not myself believe them very efficient, and should the invaders be in steamers, doubt not but they will be enabled to effect a landing.

The government is receiving three thousand militia in Havana to garrison and protect the city in the event of the necessity of sending all the troops to the interior. Those officers that are placed in command, with whom I am acquainted, have never discharged a military duty, or fired a gun.

We shall probably have a good deal of disorder in the city, if civil war should break out. The lower classes are ignorant, idle, debased, and only kept in order by the strong arm of the military. When that is removed it is not easy to foretell the consequences, as they may think insults and attacks upon Americans would be acts acceptable to the authorities who are believed to doubt the good faith of the President, the entire government, and suspect the connivance of all Americans.

* * * * *

I enclose herewith a translated editorial of the official marine paper of this day, and of an order published in the Gazette of the 18th instant, by which you will see what the Spaniards think of the expedition. The order exhibits their method of arresting fugitives.

I have the honor to be, &c.,

ROBERT B. CAMPBELL.

Hon. John M. Clayton,
Secretary of State, Washington City.

[Translation.]

Don Francisco Javier Mendoza, knight of the royal American order of Isabel the Catholic, captain of infantry, with a medal of distinction, and one of the *prosecuting attorneys* (fiscal) of the court of the permanent executive military commission of this island.

Whereas Don Cirilo Villaverde, who made his escape from the prison of this capital, Don José Maria Sanchez Isnaga, Don Ambrosio José Gonzalez, Don Juan Manuel Macias, the Licentiate Don Pedro Aguero, Don Victoriano de Arrieta, Don Gaspar de Betancourt y Cismeros (alias el Lugareño,) and Don Cristobal Madán, whom I am prosecuting for the crime of conspiracy against the legitimate rights of her Majesty, (whom God save,) directed to bring on an insurrection in this country and the island of Puerto Rico, to obtain their independence from the metropolis—the two former, who have before been tried, and incurred the penalties of rebels, insisting in their previous criminal projects, have absconded themselves from this city, and other places of the island where they had been residing, exercising the powers conferred by royal ordinances upon officers of the army—I do by this, my first proclamation, cite, call, and summon the above named individuals to present themselves personally, within the precise term of nine days, at the public prison of this place, to produce their pleas and legitimate defences, in the understanding that if it is not complied with in the given time, the actions will be continued against them, and they will be sentenced as rebels by the council of war of this court, without being further called or summoned, for such is her Majesty's will. Let this proclamation be fixed at the customary places, and published in the official Gazette, that it may reach the notice of all.

FRANCISCO JAVIER MENDOZA.

JOSE FERNANDEZ COTA, *Secretary.*

HAVANA, *May* 17, 1850.

Translation from the "Diario de la Marina," of Havana, dated Sunday, May 19, 1850.

It is publicly said that the pirates are about to carry into effect their villanous plans of invasion of this tranquil Antille. The last news from the neighboring continent appear to leave no doubt about the preparations made for undertaking an enterprise, the result of treason, and which could only have met the concurrence of the most ignorant and desperate rabble, that does not mind dangers, does not examine risks, and for whom the most capricious rapacity is the supreme law of action.

In truth, it was time that the pirates should go to sea—that they should come out displaying their forces and vigor; it was time for them to come to try on our coasts that heroism they boast of; it was time that the heroes of the most infamous vandalism should become acquainted with the loyalty, bravery, and discipline of our navy and army—the loyalty, bravery, and patriotism, of the inhabitants of Cuba. And it would really be a pity that they should not reach the coast—a pity that the smell of Spanish powder should frighten away the vultures!—a great pity that those boasts should become reduced to mere sham! Great crimes need a greater chastisement; and we would ambition for our history the honor of inflicting it. Is it not to be permitted a faithful people to wish occasions on which to display to the world with pride their honest and generous heart?

It is true that the quality of the undertaking, and the importance of those who intend to carry it on, do not even present them to us in such a shape that a victory over them could flatter the pride of those who have in their veins the blood of Pelago and Cortés. But small as the glory might be, that rabble being a real plague, in destroying it, would not we do a signal service to humanity? This is precisely the reason why we anxiously desire the villains to attempt coming upon our coast.

On the other part, after so much has been said about the pretty expedition, when an attempt has been making to wound the susceptibility of our race, is it not to be allowed us to anxiously desire that the purity of our blood should be put to the proof, if it is only that of one single man that any one should wish to examine? It is well to consider the forces of the expedition contemptible before our immense resources, and small the honor we might acquire by destroying those pirates; but let them come to our shores, that we may at once know the extent of their madness, and exhibit on them an imperishable chastisement.

Mr. Campbell to Mr. Clayton.

[Extracts.]

CONSULATE OF THE UNITED STATES, HAVANA,
May 22, 1850.

SIR: I have the honor to enclose, herewith, a copy of a short correspondence with the Captain General, growing out of a publication in the Evening Bulletin of the 20th, one of the government papers. The Bulletin stated that the general of marine had captured at Contoy two vessels and some hundred men.

Knowing nothing of the particulars, beyond the report which you will find republished in the paper of the morning of the 21st, herewith transmitted, my letter to the Captain General was written with great caution and respect, as you will see.

* * * * * * * *

I enclose, herewith, a translated proclamation and edict of the Captain General, declaring the island in a state of siege, and proclaiming martial law, &c., &c.; a translated copy of the account given of the capture of two vessels, and about one hundred men at Contoy, with the comments thereon.

* * * * * * * *

I have the honor to be, sir, &c.,

ROBERT B. CAMPBELL.

CONSULATE OF THE UNITED STATES, HAVANA,
May 20, 1850.

SIR: Having understood that his excellency the general of marine had captured, on or near the Isle of Contoy, two vessels, and about one hundred men, I would respectfully ask of your excellency whether the vessels were or not under the American flag. If under the American flag, whether or not they were furnished with regular and proper papers; whether the men were, in whole or in part, American citizens. Should the captured vessels be *bona fide* American, and the men, or any part of them, American citizens, I would at the same time respectfully ask of your excellency to be informed of the circumstances of the capture and arrest, and the nature of the offence charged against them.

I have the honor to be, with considerations of great respect and esteem, your excellency's most obedient servant,

ROBERT B CAMPBELL.

His Excellency the COUNT OF ALCOY,
Governor and Captain General of the Island of Cuba.

[Translation.]

[SEAL.] POLITICAL SECRETARY'S OFFICE.

As the captured vessels referred to in your lordship's communication of yesterday have not arrived in this port, and his excellency the commander-in chief of this naval station is not here, it is not possible for me to give an answer to the particulars embraced in your said letter, which I shall be enabled to do upon having information when his excellency returns. Which I communicate to your lordship in answer.

God preserve your lordship many years. Havana, May 20, 1850.

THE COUNT OF ALCOY.

The CONSUL *of the United States of America.*

GOVERNMENT AND CAPTAIN GENERALCY OF THE ALWAYS FAITHFUL ISLAND OF CUBA, POLITICAL SECRETARY'S OFFICE.

Inhabitants of the always faithful island of Cuba:

The Governor Captain General and commander in chief of her Majesty's army to-day addresses you, to make known to you that some depraved foreigners, without opinions or principles, without country or feelings—the miserable dregs, in their greater part, which the convulsions of Europe have thrown upon America in these last years, and the same who last year attempted to come to the island from the territory of a friendly nation, where they commenced to assemble—are at last this day upon our soil, to try to realize their rash and infamous undertaking—an undertaking unexampled in the annals of the civilized world—a vandalic attempt, having no other object or purpose but pillage, licentiousness, the ruin and destruction of a country a model of happiness, which they barefacedly announce as offering them a better field for enriching themselves than the Californias, with the spoliation of all property, to be distributed among themselves as the recompense of their exploits, with the breaking up of all bonds, and the relaxing of all those ties which constitute society in this precious Antille, and by which means she has arrived to that state of prosperous fortune she now flourishes in. Their vehement desire is to sink her to a state of anarchy, and bring on the horrors of a civil war, but of a civil war, the character and consequences of which I need not enumerate to you.

But keep calm, however. I was prepared to receive them. Their destiny carries them to their goal, and they shall obtain it. I assure you that the sacred rights of nations and of Spanish nationality cannot be violated at a less cost. Your well-known fidelity, more than the interests of family and property, is to me a perfect guarantee. I understand the cry of indignation with which you will repel the villains; but their blindness deceives them, and they perhaps do not hear it. It is on this account that I take charge of the message, with the loyal and brave army under my command, in the same manner that her Majesty's navy will do it on the waters of the island, and anywhere that they should run to hide themselves. Inhabitants! I hope that no one will observe a wrong conduct. Trust to the vigilance of the authorities, and in the forces of the Queen confided to me for your protection, and for the defence of her dominions.

A respect for the laws, and consideration for the noble behavior of every honest resident, will be the soldier's guide. A rigorous and unlimited punishment, mind you, will await those who should forget what the country expects of all her children, let them be Spaniards of one or the other hemisphere.

The hour of combat has sounded, and its effect shall be heard of in these seas, without any human consideration or reflection restraining me. Do not, however, forget that calm will soon awake again.

THE COUNT OF ALCOY.

HAVANA, *May* 19, 1850.

[Translated from the Diario de la Marina of Havana, May 21, 1850.]

Our readers have already seen, in the extra published yesterday by us, the result of the first attempt which our most excellent commander general had with a part of those who no doubt, in a moment of drunkenness, intended to disturb the peace we enjoy. We are informed that such was their fright, the meanness and cowardice displayed in his presence by those who call themselves the heroes of Palo Alta, that they inspired him with the most profound and deserved contempt. They not only surrendered without fighting—not only weakly implored, like miserable women, for an undeserved pardon, but they had no hesitation in resorting to the meanest and most contemptible means. Such are the men who, in their drunkenness, dreamed of conquering the island of Cuba! Compare that conduct to that of our gallant soldiers, and the world will wonder at their stupid attempt. The case is this: they believed they had merely to arrive and reap the profits of their piracy. In their delirium they imagined themselves owners of the thousands of dollars offered them by the traitors, and of the rich soils, the products of which were to furnish them the means of easily enriching themselves. This hope increased their ambition, and they said, *let us go to Cuba;* but they met on their way a man with a Spanish heart, and the sight of him terrified and confounds them, and in his presence they become humiliated, discouraged, and debased. The same will very soon happen with the rest. It is probable that *their worthy chief*, celebrated in other lines of action, will seek, in a shameful flight, the only means of getting out of his difficulties; but uselessly: our worthy authorities have taken the necessary measures, and the hour of expiation has already sounded for him.

We do not know whether any of our brave men have sealed with their blood their loyalty to the throne and their country. Should it be so, we shall mourn for the victims sacrificed on the altars of duty; but besides the consolation that their blood will be revenged, we have that of saying, with a noble pride, that the bravery of the indomitable Spaniard is now the same as in the times of the illustrious Queen that brought to these lands civilization and religion. Still more: that if there exist any deceived persons in the neighboring nation that imagine such undertakings easy, they will be undeceived, now that they have practically viewed, not only a determined and gallant army and navy, but numberless enthusiastic youths, who, when the least danger appeared, hastened to arm themselves for exterminating the banditti. In the place of proselytes, perhaps expected by them in their delirium, they found in all the inhabitants, without distinction, strong hearts ready to repel that loathsome and vile canaille. From this day the queen of the Antilles will march, secure of her future, by the road of prosperity that has been opened to her for some time by the protecting hand of our sovereign, and the solicitude, tact, and care of the authorities that so well govern us.

GOVERNMENT AND CAPTAIN GENERALCY OF THE ALWAYS FAITHFUL ISLAND OF CUBA, MILITARY SECRETARY'S OFFICE.

An edict.

Don Frederico de Roncali, Count of Alcoy, Governor and Captain General of the island of Cuba, and commander-in-chief of the army—I make known that the foreign pirates, who have been assembled and ready for some time, having already landed upon the territory confided to me by her Majesty, for the purpose of carrying into effect their sacreligious designs, in the sacred duty of preserving the interests of the country, as well as of protecting the lives and property of its faithful inhabitants, making use of the extraordinary powers in me vested, and of those to me appertaining as commander-in-chief, I ordain and command:

ARTICLE 1. All the territory of the island of Cuba, its isles and adjacent keys, are declared to be in a state of siege, and thereby subjected to all its legal consequences as long as the circumstances causing it shall continue.

Notwithstanding the active and pre-eminent action which by this declaration the military jurisdiction becomes entitled to, all other tribunals and courts will continue in their respective exercise, having jurisdiction in all common or ordinary business not excluded by this edict.

ART. 2. All the coasts of this island and its waters are declared in a state of blockade by her Majesty's naval forces; and in consequence thereof, all vessels can be required to produce their papers and documents, and be scrupulously examined. Those coming loaded with passengers, whatever the port they come from, or are bound to, may be, are by that fact considered suspicious; but if their papers and registers do not confirm them as such, they will in that case only be ordered to keep away. Should the contrary be the case, such as a marked defect in their papers, having cargoes of arms and ammunition, or effects which in any manner may bring on civil war on the island, they will immediately be declared enemies and treated as pirates, in conformity to the ordinances of the royal navy.

ART. 3. All persons detected in any number belonging to the invading bands will be immediately shot.

ART. 4. Although there is not the remotest expectation that any inhabitant of this country will be found associated with the horde of robbers, forgetting his sacred duties to his queen, country, and family, and unknowing his own interest—should any one, however, by misfortune, commit such an infamous crime, he will be considered as one of the said foreign horde, and subjected to the same penalty mentioned in the previous article.

ART. 5. Any one serving them as a spy, or voluntarily aiding them with news, money, arms, provisions, or doing them any service, will be immediately shot.

ART. 6. To the same penalty will be condemned all those who, by public or hidden and criminal means, should attempt to change the good opinion of the inhabitants, the subordination of the slaves in the plantations, or in the least alter their internal order, or that should not hasten to give aid, advice, and co-operation, with immediate obedience, to the legitimate authorities.

ART. 7. Commandants general of departments, lieutenant governors in their districts, and commanding officers of troops of operations, and also those in garrison in castles and forts, are charged with the most exact and punctual compliance. All public employés, of any rank, belonging to any class or branch of the government, will co-operate for the best of the service. Any negligence or connivance will incur the penalty of death.

THE COUNT OF ALCOY.

HAVANA, *May* 19, 1853.

[Translated from the Official Gazette of Havana, May 21, 1850.]

LONG LIVE QUEEN ISABEL—LONG LIVE SPAIN.

Hardly had the noble cry of indignation burst out from these faithful inhabitants, produced by the news that the vandalic horde that intended to invade this island had already set foot on her; scarcely had the word of our superior authority, in his proclamation and edict, published by us last night, been heard, when we have already the inexpressible pleasure of being able to announce a victory. The arrival of her Majesty's steamer Pizarro, which came in to-day, having on board his excellency Sr. D. Francisco Amero y Penaranda, commander general of this naval station, has furnished us the important news of the event of two vessels belonging to the vandals having been captured.

The steamer had sailed from this port on the evening of the 16th. On the 17th she learned at the light-house on Cape San Antonio that nothing had occurred on that side; and having afterwards met the brig Habanero, she towed the brig, and both vessels went upon Contoy, where a ship and a hermophradite brig were lying, both being merchant vessels. These vessels had on board upwards of one hundred men, of various nations, badly dressed and equipped, who had arrived from the isles of Canto and Mujeres, near Yucatan, and which were the rendezvous of the pirates engaged in the expedition.

The result of this encounter and of the proper measures taken by the most worthy and intrepid General Amero, has been the capture of both vessels, and of all the adventurers that were on board, and likewise of the whole correspondence of D. Narcisso Lopez, the chief of the expedition, that two days before the event we relate had taken a course northward, with some people, to fall into, as doubtless they have fallen at this time, the hands of our brave troops, and paid with a shameful death his detestable conduct. The correspondence taken will furnish very interesting facts for a complete knowledge of that hair-brained and criminal plan; so that we ought on many accounts to consider this event of the greatest importance.

The Pizarro has brought fourteen of the prisoners that exceed a hundred. By their own saying, they appear to be leaders of the expedition; they belong to various nations, and have shown an inexplicable pusillanimity for men who had dreamed of so daring an undertaking.

We have also learned by the Pizarro, that all the force the adventurers rely upon does not exceed five hundred men; that their intention was, to land in the jurisdiction of Matanzas, and direct their steps afterwards to Havana; to this Havana, that had scarcely read the edict of the superior authority, ran to call for arms to help him in case of necessity, for the chastisement of the expeditionists! To this Havana, where twelve hours of voluntary enlistments has placed at the disposition of the government thirteen thousand able men, ready for war! What will those miserable men say at the sight of such enthusiasm, decision and patriotism? But could they expect anything else, being men whose only object was pillage—men who thought to divide among themselves our property—to be able to give to every officer $20,000 and an estate, and to each soldier $4,000 at the end of the campaign?

It is to be hoped that this lesson will undeceive those miserable men, who, being thirsty for gold and blood, undertake adventures in search of booty to satiate their hunger. If there are unfortunate countries existing, in which they might perhaps try with impunity their daring, now they will have perceived that it is impossible in any part of the Spanish monarchy, and less so in this rich and happy island, sensible and loyal, that owes her prosperity and aggrandizement to her undeviating fidelity, and that, contented, proud and grateful, relies for existence and a future on her unalterable union with the metropolis.

Mr. Campbell to Mr. Clayton.

CONSULATE OF THE UNITED STATES, HAVANA,
May 31, 1850.

SIR: I have the honor to enclose herewith, duplicate copies of a correspondence with the Captain General of the 20th instant; an original letter to the Captain General of the 24th instant, which, upon being informed of the subject of which he treated, he declined to receive, on the ground that diplomatic powers were not vested either in himself or me, and the affair could only be treated of, and settled by yourself and Mr. Calderon; a statement of a conversation had in an interview of Captain Randolph and myself, with the Captain General, and general of marine; copy of a telegraphic dispatch to the collector of Mobile, dated, 27th instant, to be sent to you; copy of a letter of the 29th instant, written at the request of Captain Tattnall, and the Captain General's reply thereto; copy of a letter, of the 29th instant, to the Captain General, with extracts from a letter from Judge Marvin, proving that the persons arrested at Contoy had no participation in the expedition of Lopez; copy and translation of a letter from the Captain General, dated 29th instant, being a second letter in reply to my communication of the 20th instant.

The foregoing papers will explain my opinions and acts on the capture made at Contoy. The letter, the reception of which was declined by the Captain General, was written on the morning of the 24th, sealed, and about to be sent, when Captain Randolph arrived in the Albany. Hoping that the verbal interview about to be had with the Captain General would end in the delivery of the ships and prisoners, the letter was not sent, but placed in my pocket, to be delivered in the event of our reasonable requests and (as I believe) just demands being refused. They were refused, and my letter was offered and taken, but returned for the cause before stated.

After our interview with the Captain General, and the general of marine, (who admitted the captured vessels to be American,) Captain Randolph immediately proceeded to sea, (followed the next morning by the Germantown, Captain Lowndes,) with a determination, if possible, to intercept and retake both the vessels and prisoners, should they be alone, or under convoy of Spanish men-of-war. This, in consultation, we agreed he had a right to do under the laws of nations, in conformity to the policy of the United States so ably set forth by Mr. Webster in the Ashburton correspondence, and under the act of Congress authorizing our men-of-war to capture any vessel which should unnecessarily detain an American merchant ship in the Gulf of Mexico. All must admit that these ships were unnecessarily detained after having been demanded to be sent home for trial, and that demand refused.

Captain Tattnall's views of the right or expediency of Captain Randolph's intended course must have been different, as I understood from him, on his return, that he had ordered Captains Randolph and Lowndes temporarily to other cruising ground. Captain Tattnall, however, on his first visit, explicitly informed the Captain General that "if he fell in with the captured vessels, he should feel it to be his duty to overhaul them, interrogate the officer in charge, and then judge for himself of the course to be pursued."

The Saranac, Captain Tattnall, returned from Key West, and yesterday (30th) he, with Judge Marvin, collector Douglass, of Key West, and myself, called on the Captain General; and Captain Tattnall said to the Captain General that "he was about to return to the United States, and should be highly gratified to be able to communicate to his government that he had been permitted to see and converse with the prisoners from Contoy, as, under existing circumstances, it might do much good, and tend to allay any excitement that might exist at home." The Captain General, turning to me, said, "personally he had no objection to permit the prisoners to be seen and conversed with, but the law would not permit it; and were he to grant permission, the audiencia could and would accuse him of violation of the law, and have a right to censure his conduct; that the prisoners here were well treated, and there was nothing of which they could complain, unless it was their not being permitted to go into the streets; that the marine court, before which their trial was pending, consisted of calm and intelligent officers, who would dispassionately weigh the testimony and do full justice." The question being Captain Tattnall's, the answer intended for him, and Captain Randolph with myself having previously, though fruitlessly, demurred to the decision as a violation of the rights of the prisoners under treaty stipulations with Spain, which guaranty to them free access to counsel of their own selection, and that this government, under no circumstances, had a right to bring them to trial, I did not attempt to controvert what he said.

The whole subject is now before you. Your consul, your naval officers, can do nothing for the relief of the parties; and it is left for the President to adopt such measures as his well known firmness patriotism, and devotion to the honor and interest of his country may dictate.

With great respect and esteem, I have the honor to be, sir, your most obedient servant,

ROBERT B. CAMPBELL.

Hon. JOHN M. CLAYTON,
Secretary of State, Washington City.

CONSULATE OF THE UNITED STATES, HAVANA,
May 20, 1850.

SIR: Having understood that his excellency the general of marine had captured, on or near the Isle of Contoy, two vessels and about one hundred men, I would respectfully ask of your excellency whether the vessels were or not under the American flag. If under the American flag, whether or not they were furnished with regular and proper papers; whether the men were in whole or in part American citizens. Should the captured vessels be *bona fide* American, and the men, or any part of them, American citizens, I would, at the same time, respectfully ask of your excellency to be informed of the circumstances of the capture and arrest, and the nature of the offence charged against them.

I have the honor to be, with considerations of great respect and esteem, your excellency's most obedient servant,

ROBERT B. CAMPBELL.

His Excellency the COUNT OF ALCOY,
Governor and Captain General of the Island of Cuba, &c.

[Translation.]

[SEAL.] POLITICAL SECRETARY'S OFFICE.

As the captured vessels referred to in your lordship's communication of yesterday have not arrived in this port, and his excellency the commander-in-chief of this naval station is not here, it is not possible for me to give answers to the particulars embraced in your said letter, which I shall be able to do, with a knowledge of circumstances, when his excellency returns. Which I communicate to your lordship in answer.

God preserve your lordship many years. Havana, May 20, 1850.

THE COUNT OF ALCOY.

To the CONSUL *of the United States of America.*

CONSULATE OF THE UNITED STATES, HAVANA,
May 24, 1850.

SIR: All attempts which were being made to disturb the tranquillity of this island having signally failed, and no present interest or emergency existing to bias the judgment, or prevent a calm and dispassionate view being taken of all the circumstances attendant upon, and connected with, the capture of the two vessels and all on board, at Contoy, by his excellency the general of marine, and that officer having been in port some thirty hours without my receiving the information which, from your excellency's official communication of the 20th instant, I had a right to expect, and was most anxious to receive, before again addressing your excellency: having heard, however, that a portion of the prisoners are placed, or are immediately to be placed, upon trial, I feel it a duty to draw the attention of your excellency to a few suggestions, made for the purpose of avoiding, in certain contingencies, misunderstandings, and possibly difficulties, between the government of the United States and her Majesty the Queen of Spain.

One of the vessels captured at Contoy is said to be the American bark Georgiana. By reference to the New Orleans price-current, I find that the American bark Georgiana, Benson, master, was, on the 25th of April, regularly cleared by G. W. Breedlove, with a cargo of coal for Chagres, which proves the sailing of that particular vessel to have been with the knowledge of the collector of the port, and that her papers were in due order.

Should the Georgiana be one of the vessels captured by his excellency the general of marine, *she* is an American, and could only have been legally captured for the actual or intended violation of law in Spanish waters. To establish this position, I would ask, can Spanish law extend out of and beyond Spanish territory? Can it be enforced on the high seas, or in foreign jurisdiction? Must it not be admitted that the prerogative of her Catholic Majesty cannot legally extend beyond her dominions; and would not any attempt to enforce it beyond such limits be assuming for Spain the exercise of an authority extra-territorial, and which might be exercised, if it has not already been done, to the injury of the persons and property of the citizens of other nations, while on the high seas and under the flag of their country? The doctrine which has been advanced and advocated by one of the greatest statesmen of the age, and which, in my opinion, the government of the United States has held, and is determined to hold in all future time, and at all hazards, is, that every merchant vessel on the high seas is rightfully considered as a part of the territory to which she belongs, and the forcible entry upon any such vessel by a foreign force is *prima facie* a wrong, and the government under which such entry is made must show cause of justification.

There may have been justification in this particular instance for temporary detention of the two vessels; but, for aught I know to the contrary, no overt act has been committed against the Spanish government by the master or those on board the captured vessels. There may have been intention, but that intention may have been repented of and changed. But if even the intention of overt acts against this government was entertained at the time of capture, it cannot vest a power in this government to arrest the parties in a foreign country to be brought to Cuba for trial. To illustrate this it may not be amiss to refer to the case of the Duc d'Enghien, (with which your excellency is familiar,) to prove the opinion of the civilized world on a parallel case. If (so far as appears) offence against any government has been committed by the masters or others on board the captured vessels, (supposing them to be American, with regular papers,) the offence has been against the laws and government of the United States, and to that government alone are they amenable, unless they have, in some way, violated the laws of Mexico.

The foregoing views are briefly submitted to your excellency in the confident belief that they are correct; and if so, that the parties already here with the ship, and others to arrive, will immediately be given up, that they may be sent to the United States for trial, and the legality of the capture and detention be left to the governments of the United States and Spain to be decided upon.

I have the honor to be, with considerations of great respect and esteem, your excellency's most obedient servant,

ROBERT B. CAMPBELL.

His Excellency the Count of Alcoy,

Governor and Captain General of the Island of Cuba, &c.

Statement of a conversation had by Captain Randolph and Mr. Campbell in an interview with the Captain General.

HAVANA, *May* 24, 1850.

The United States sloop-of-war Albany, V. M. Randolph, commander, having this day arrived in the port of Havana, and it having been reported to Captain Randolph that two vessels and several men, said to be Americans, had been captured at or near the island of Contoy, belonging to Yucatan, he, with the consul of the United States for Havana, called upon the Captain General, for the purpose of investigating the matter.

After the usual salutations, Captain Randolph told the Captain General that he had understood that two vessels, reported to be American, had been captured by the general of marine, together with about one hundred men, of whom some fourteen had been brought to this port.

The Captain General replied that two vessels with some men had been captured; that this government had in their possession proofs that those vessels and men were connected with the expedition which left New Orleans for the invasion of this island.

Captain Randolph then desired to know whether the captured vessels had the American colors flying? Whether they were on neutral ground, or on the high seas, or on Spanish waters? Whether the men captured were Americans in whole or in part? Whether any overt act had been committed by them upon Spanish territory?

The Captain General said, that owing to the general of marine's short stay in this port, he had not received official information of the circumstances connected with the capture to enable him to give answers to the questions propounded to him, but observed that pirates could be captured wherever found, whatever flag or papers they might have.

Captain Randolph said to the Captain General, that vessels under American colors could not be stopped on the high seas by a foreign force, unless suspicions were entertained of their being engaged in piracy; and then, if proper papers were found on board, the vessels and men had to be delivered up to the authorities of the United States; and in consequence he, Captain Randolph, demanded from the Captain General the delivery to him of the two vessels and the men captured by the general of marine, that they might be carried to the United States for trial, which the Captain General refused to accede to, saying that he had no jurisdiction over the matter, it being a case which was to be tried by the marine court, over which he had no jurisdiction.

Upon being asked by Captain Randolph for permission to see the prisoners now in the port of Havana, the Captain General answered that he had no authority; that the general of marine, being the judge of the cause, would, if he could, let Captain Randolph see the prisoners; but that, if permission was not granted, the cause would be, that the prisoners, being under the action of law, the summarial proceedings not having come to an end, they, by the Spanish laws, could not be permitted to hold communication but with the court.

On being referred to the general of marine, the consul and Captain Randolph asked the Captain General if he was not the head and chief of this government. He answered "Yes." He was then told that he was the source from which information ought to be sought, and not from his subordinates.

The consul and Captain Randolph explained to the Captain General their views in regard to the policy heretofore pursued by the government of the United States in relation to the right of visit and search, and expressed their opinion that the affair they had been referring to was more serious than his excellency thought of, for it might involve the question of war.

His excellency thought differently, and said that he was personally willing to give all satisfaction, but that he could not give way to threats; and if war was the consequence, he was prepared to meet it, using the expression, "que vengan"—"let them come." The consul and Captain Randolph disclaimed any intention of making threats.

Captain Randolph informed the Captain General, that as he had not been able to obtain any satisfactory information, and was not permitted to see and converse with the prisoners, he would report to his government that two American vessels and several American citizens had been captured on the high seas or on neutral ground, and brought to this port as prisoners, and that, in consequence, war virtually existed between the United States and Spain.

The Captain General said that Captain Randolph might do as he pleased, but the report would not be correct, for the vessels and men captured formed part of the expedition under Lopez, were nothing but pirates, and therefore subjected to the laws of nations, enforced by the power to which the cruiser that captured them belongs.

Captain Randolph observed that he would perhaps think proper to address his excellency a communication upon the subject, and desired to know if it would be received.

The Captain General answered, that if Captain Randolph's letter was in proper terms it would be received, a copy thereof sent to the general of marine to obtain information, and when this was obtained, he, the Captain General, would be happy to answer Captain Randolph's communication, accompanying a copy of the general of marine's report in relation to the capture of the vessels and men, &c., and that he would also forward to Mr. Calderon, the Spanish minister at Washington, a copy of the correspondence, as it was a subject which had to be arranged by the representatives of the two governments, Mr. Clayton and Mr. Calderon, who alone had diplomatic power.

In the course of conversation, the consul took out and presented to the Captain General a sealed communication he had prepared, which his excellency, upon learning from the consul the contents thereof, refused to receive, asserting that the consul had merely commercial functions, and therefore had no right to interfere in the affair; and observed also, that he, himself, nor Captain Randolph had any diplomatic powers.

The Captain General tried to persuade Captain Randolph not to do any more in the business, for that he had already done everything which his duty as an officer of the United States required of him, and more so, when it was in favor of men undeserving of his sympathy, and who had a year ago abused him for the affair at Round Island.

The Captain General was courteous in coversation, and appeared to be trying to impress his opinion upon our minds.

Immediately after the above interview Captain Randolph and the consul called upon the general of marine to investigate the same affair.

Captain Randolph said to the general that he had come to inquire of him whether it was true that he had captured two vessels and some men, to which the general answered that such was the fact.

Captain Randolph then desired to be informed if the vessels had American colors flying, and the men were Americans? The general answered that the vessels had no colors flying, and that the men on board, some sixty or seventy, were partly Americans and the rest of various nations. Captain Randolph asked if the vessels and men were in Spanish or neutral waters? The general replied that they were on neutral ground, it is true, but that having proofs in his possession that they formed a part of the expedition which was about to invade his country, he had gone and captured them as pirates, and that some of the men are now in this port.

The general was asked by Captain Randolph what evidence he had that those vessels and men formed a part of the expedition? The answer was, that he had reliable information, corroborated by the papers found with them, and their own confessions. Whether force or threats had been used to obtain those confessions? The general said that this was a question which he could not accept. Being asked by Captain Randolph whether the vessels and men had any papers, and avowed themselves to be Americans, the general replied that they had not avowed anything; that when his steamer was seen by them approaching, they understood their position, and said nothing; that he had not examined the papers; that his stay there was very short, merely long enough to put the captured vessels and men in charge of a sailing vessel of war to bring them to this port; and that he picked out and brought in the steamer Pizarro such as he considered leaders.

Captain Randolph also inquired what class of vessels they were? The general answered, two brigs; whether one of them is a barque? The general did not think any of them had three masts.

Captain Randolph then said to the general of marine that he had been informed that two American vessels having American flags and papers, had been captured, with a number of men, on the high seas, and beyond Spanish jurisdiction; and he therefore demanded the immediate delivery of the captured vessels and men to him, to take them to the United States for trial by the United States.

The general answered, that he had no authority; that the vessels and men had been captured as pirates; that he had proofs of it; and that the laws of this country would try them.

Captain Randolph requested permission to see and converse with the prisoners that are here, so as to obtain a fair statement, which was refused. Captain Randolph then demanded it as a right. The general refused it again, observing that, as the two captured vessels and the greater part of the men had not yet arrived in this port, no declarations had been taken from them; that the summarial proceedings were not finished; therefore the laws of the country did not permit the prisoners to hold communication but with the court that was to try them; that after that they would be allowed counsel, and all facilities for making their defence.

Captain Randolph said to the general of marine that it was rumored that confessions had been extracted from the men by putting the rope to their necks. To this the general answered that those were vulgarities; that no judicial investigation had yet commenced; that the men in conversation had acknowledged that they formed a part of the expedition which, under the command of Lopez, was to invade this island. After that conversation the general stated that the captured vessels were American, and the men in part Americans.

The consul and Captain Randolph observed to the general that it would be better for him to deliver up the vessels and men; that the laws of nations were plain; that the capturing of the vessels and men on neutral ground was illegal. The case of the Duke d'Enghien, under the empire, was cited by us as a parallel, and to bring to the general's mind the intense excitement produced in Europe and the world by that outrage. The general repeatedly asserted that the cases were not parallel; that the Duc was a gentleman. The consul observed that the Duke d'Enghien had nothing to lose but his life and his soul, if he was not prepared for death, and these men were in the same position. Captain Randolph said the only difference was, that the Duke belonged to the blood royal, and these were obscure citizens. But the general still thought as he had before expressed it, and appeared greatly astonished that we should want to consider the two cases as parallel.

The result of the interview was, that the general of marine refused to deliver up the vessels and men, and denied permission to Captain Randolph to have communication with the prisoners now in this port, observing that, if the captain would remain some days longer in the port, he and the consul could then have the opportunity to learn the result of the trial, and to communicate with the prisoners.

Telegraphic dispatch from the United States Consul at Havana to the Hon. John M. Clayton, Secretary of State, Washington, to be forwarded immediately upon receipt by the Collector of Mobile.

CONSULATE OF THE UNITED STATES, HAVANA,
May 27, 1850.

The Albany and Germantown arrived at Havana on the 24th inst. The steamer Saranac arrived on the 25th instant. Captain Randolph, immediately on landing, called, with the consul, to see the Captain General; and first requested, then demanded, from the Captain General to see the prisoners brought from the island of Contoy, which was refused. Captain Randolph then asked if, upon the arrival of the vessels captured at Contoy, they would be given up with the prisoners, to be tried in the United States, which was answered in the negative by the general of marine. Admitted the captured vessels to be American, and also refused permission to see the prisoners. The consul desires particular instructions in relation to the captured vessels and prisoners. The Albany and Germantown were crusing off the harbor yesterday to intercept the captured vessels, and a Spanish frigate kept near them. The Saranac left port yesterday evening, destination unknown. Four out of the five prisoners taken at Cardenas were shot on Saturday. The Spanish government have on this station about twenty-one vessels of war.

ROBERT B. CAMPBELL.

CONSULATE OF THE UNITED STATES, HAVANA,
May 29, 1850.

SIR: Captain Tatnall, of the United States ship "Saranac," who has this day arrived from Key West, states, that in conversation with some of the persons recently engaged in the expedition to Cardenas, they had mentioned to him that a second expedition of a similar character, but of larger number, was to sail on the 21st instant, destined as the last.

Captain Tatnall does not know whether the report is entitled to credence, but deemed it advisable that your excellency should be placed in possession of it.

I have the honor to be, with considerations of great respect and esteem, your excellency's most obedient servant,

ROBERT B. CAMPBELL.

To his Excellency the COUNT OF ALCOY,
Governor and Captain General of Cuba, &c.

[L. S.] POLITICAL SECRETARY'S OFFICE.

I remain informed of, and feel obliged to your lordship, as well as to the commander of the steamer Saranac, Mr. Tatnall, for conveying to me the intelligence he obtained from the piratical adventurers of the steamer "Creole" themselves, respecting a second expedition which was about to sail on the 21st, with the same destination and object as the first. Both the expeditions must form part of the vast plan, as your lordship is well aware, carried on upon territory of the United States, but as I have in advance information of the whole, I am prepared to receive, as I did the first expedition, those who should again attempt their rash undertaking.

God preserve your lordship many years. Havana, May 31, 1850.

THE COUNT OF ALCOY.

To the CONSUL *of the United States of America.*

CONSULATE OF THE UNITED STATES, HAVANA,
May 29, 1850.

SIR: Notwithstanding your excellency having declined to receive my last communication upon the ground that the subject of the recent capture made by the general of marine must be arranged between Mr. Clayton and Mr. Calderon, who alone have the necessary diplomatic power, I am again induced to address your excellency on behalf of the unfortunate men taken at Contoy, in consequence of receiving from

Judge Marvin, the judicial officer before whom was taken the testimony of the Lopez party at Key West, the following letter:

"Learning, from an investigation had before me into the affair at Cardenas, that the persons left on board the American barque Georgiana, and the brig Susan Loud, at or near the coast of Yucatan, constituted no part of the expedition that were to land at Cardenas, but were persons who had gone on board these vessels at New Orleans in good faith, as passengers bound to Chagres, thence to California; and finding, when the steamer Creole joined them, that they had been deceived, and that a descent was intended to be made by General Lopez and others upon Cardenas, these persons, the passengers of the barque and brig, promptly refused to go on the expedition, said they had been deceived, and never joined in any way any such expedition. I beg to call your attention to these facts, that justice may be done to the innocent. I speak in general terms, and say that it became evident, upon an examination of the persons brought before me, and accused with a violation of our laws, that the persons on board the barque and brig captured by the Spanish vessels never intended to be connected with the expedition to Cuba, but supposed the vessels were bound to Chagres, and they were on board as passengers."

The above letter is in general terms, and may admit of exceptions; but if the representations made upon oath at Key West be true, it is manifest that most, or all, of the prisoners captured at Contoy were innocent, not only in acts, but intention, and abandoned the party as soon as its purposes were discovered, and are, consequently, not only entitled to compassion for their ignorance and credulity, but their immediate discharge.

Nothing contained in this letter is to be construed into an admission of the legal right of his excellency the general of marine to capture American vessels with the persons on board on the high seas, or beyond Spanish territory.

Judge Marvin and the collector of Key West are now in Havana, and if desired, I will, with them, wait upon your excellency, that you may know what has transpired in Key West.

I have the honor to be, with considerations of great respect and esteem, your excellency's most obedient servant,

ROBERT B. CAMPBELL.

To his Excellency the COUNT OF ALCOY,
Governor and Captain General of Cuba, &c.

[Translation.]

[L. S.] POLITICAL SECRETARY'S OFFICE.

To the ends that may be of interest to the commercial affairs of which your lordship has charge, as consul of the United States in this place, and having before me your communication dated the 20th instant, I must say to you, after having obtained the circumstances which the state of the cause prosecuted before the marine court permits, that it is true that, on the morning of the 18th of the present month, were captured by her Majesty's men-of-war in the waters immediate to the generally uninhabited island of Contoy a barque and a hermaphrodite brig, called, as was afterwards discovered, "Georgiana Lincumbly" and "Susan Laud," which vessels had no colors flying, nor did they hoist any, notwithstanding they subsequently presented papers showing them to belong to the United States. Of the individuals arrested, it is not yet possible to assure whether any or all are citizens of the United States; it is, however, notorious that the object of the arrest they now suffer is to ascertain the more or less direct share they have had in the expedition of piratical adventurers that sailed out of New Orleans to invade this island, which was effected upon the defenceless town of Cardenas by those conveyed by the steamer "Creole," and they must form a part of the vast conspiracy planned in the United States, which your lordship is aware of. It appears that the two vessels mentioned sailed out of New Orleans with men, arms, provisions, ammunition, and coal, and both communicated with the steamer "Creole," transferring to this vessel arms, coal, provisions, and the number of men she could take, among whom were the master and cook of the said hermaphrodite brig.

I have already told your lordship all that may be of interest to your character and office, and, although perhaps with too many details, I have been guided by a desire of giving you all possible information in regard to what no doubt has caused in you the most profound indignation, the same as in all the inhabitants of this city, without distinction, whether national or foreign, including all North Americans here residing, because that scandalous attempt of the modern buccaneers is repelled by all civilized nations, and their accomplices condemned by all laws and the law of nations, as were to the face of the world on the last year by the worthy President, General Taylor, those who assembled upon Round island, who are the same wretches precisely, and for the same purpose, that, on the dawn of the 19th instant, succeeded in landing at the defenceless town of Cardenas.

God preserve your lordship many years. Havana, May 29, 1850.

THE COUNT OF ALCOY.

To the Consul *of the United States.*

Mr. Campbell to Mr. Clayton.

Consulate of the United States, Havana,
May 31, 1850.

Sir: You are doubtless informed, from Key West, that the two vessels captured at Contoy were the bark Georgiana and the brig Susan Loud, both of whom cleared at New Orleans for Chagres. The Captain General, in his letter, has not given correctly the name of the bark; he has added, I presume, to her name the place to which she belongs.

The names of a portion of the men shot at Matanzas, so far as I can learn, were George Warner, son of Alison Warner, of Evansville, Indiana; Kelly, a resident of Cincinnati; McGreggor, residence unknown. I have not been able to ascertain the name of the other man who was shot, or of the man whose life was spared, and have no means of getting the information. The consul at Matanzas may, perhaps, be able to obtain their names.

I have the honor to be, sir, with great respect and esteem, your most obedient servant,

ROBERT B. CAMPBELL.

Hon. JOHN M. CLAYTON,
Secretary of State, Washington City.

Mr. Clayton to Mr. Campbell.

DEPARTMENT OF STATE,
Washington, May 31, 1850.

SIR: Your dispatches of the 21st and 22d, *two* of the 28th February, 7th and 8th of March, *three* of the 8th, *three* of the 17th; *two* of the 19th and 27th of April; 8th, 16th, 17th, 19th, and 22d of May, 1850, have been received.

The duties devolving upon you in consequence of the fate of the hostile expedition against Cuba will require the exercise of all the prudence and firmness which you can command. It is the President's determination to sustain the honor of this government by the faithful discharge of our obligations towards Spain. For this purpose, prosecutions will be commenced against any persons within our jurisdiction who may have been concerned in the expedition contrary to the existing laws. Whilst actuated by this spirit of good faith towards our neighbor, however, the President expects that the Spanish authorities will not allow themselves to be misled by exultation or vengeance to injure, in their persons or property, any of our citizens in Cuba against whom no probable cause of proceeding may exist; and he demands that those who may be charged with guilt shall have a fair trial. A different course would be sure to rouse a feeling in this country which might defeat the administration of justice towards such persons as may be arrested for offending against our laws, and, indeed, might render it impracticable to prevent further violation to those laws to an extent much more likely to result in peril to Spanish dominion in that island.

But although your duties will be at once arduous and delicate, you will bear in mind that they must be such as strictly belong to the consular character under the law of nations. The Spanish government has refused to consider your functions as in any respect diplomatic. You will, however, be vigilant in ascertaining who among your countrymen in your consular district are charged with crimes against the sovereignty of Spain. You will see that they have a fair trial; and if in any instance this shall be refused, you will report the fact to the department, in order that the Spanish government may be held accountable.

Foreigners detected on board an American vessel equipped and armed for an invasion of the territory of a friendly nation cannot be allowed to use our flag as a fraud to conceal their purposes, or to protect them in the act of invasion. It is true that the 15th article of our treaty with Spain of 1795 declares: "It is also agreed that the same liberty be extended to persons who are on board a free ship, so that, although they be enemies to either party, they shall not be made prisoners or taken out of that free ship, unless they are soldiers and in actual service of the enemies."

This stipulation expressly acknowledges the right of Spain to take armed enemies out of United States vessels. Inasmuch, however, as this right may be abused, in the event of any abuse of that character coming to your knowledge, you will take suitable steps for obtaining redress.

In general, the protection of governments is due to those only who owe them allegiance. If, therefore, any persons not citizens of the United States shall have been arrested upon a charge of being concerned in the expedition, they will have no right to your interposition in their behalf. There may, indeed, be cases in which humanity might require, and would warrant, the exertion of your personal good offices to save the lives of individuals; still it would not be advisable to interfere, even to this extent, without a reasonable prospect of success; and the expediency of any interference will demand the exercise of your best discretion.

I am, sir, &c.,

JOHN M. CLAYTON.

ROBERT B. CAMPBELL,
United States Consul, Havana.

Mr. Clayton to Mr. Campbell.

DEPARTMENT OF STATE,
Washington, June 1, 1850.

SIR: From various sources of information, I conjecture that the Spanish authorities in Cuba, in their excessive zeal to punish the invaders of that island, and all connected with them, while flushed with victory, may possibly forget the difference between crime and the intention to commit it, and wreak their vengeance on American citizens, either native or naturalized, not guilty of any act of invasion or depredation upon Spanish territory. It is said and believed here, that many such were arrested on an island near the coast of Yucatan, called Contoy, within the territory of a power having friendly relations with the United States. As all the facts are not in our possession, the judgment we may have formed of the capture, abduction, and punishment of these men, may possibly be very erroneous. But let us suppose that the men captured on the Mexican island were American citizens, and had occupied it intending to invade Cuba, still I cannot recognize the right of the Spanish authorities to hang, garote, or shoot them for that intention. There was yet a *locus penitentiæ* left for every man of them; and they might have returned to the United States, guilty, indeed, of a violation of the laws of their own country, but of no law that I am aware of under which Spain could have punished them. The intention to commit crime is not *per se* crime. Some overt act must accompany the intent. A design to commit murder is not murder; nor is it, without some attempt to carry it into execution, punishable by the laws of man, however guilty the offender may be *in foro conscientiæ*, and by the ordinances of his Creator. The President means to claim for the American occupants of the Mexican island, that they were not guilty of any crime for which, by the laws of civilized nations, they should suffer death. They may have been, and probably were, guilty of crimes for which this government ought in good faith to punish them, under the act of Congress of the 20th of April, 1818. But supposing the facts relating to their capture to be as they are represented to us, the President has resolved that the eagle must and shall protect them against any punishment but that which the tribunals of their own nation may award. Tell the Count of Alcoy to send them home, to encounter a punishment which, if they are honorable men, will be worse than any he can inflict, in the indignant frowns and denunciations of good men in their own country, for an attempt to violate the faith and honor of a nation which holds its character for integrity of more value and higher worth than all the Antilles together. But warn him in the most friendly manner, and in the true spirit of our ancient treaty, that if he unjustly sheds one drop of American blood at this exciting period, it may cost the two countries a sanguinary war.

I am exceedingly anxious to ascertain all the facts connected with the capture of our citizens on the Mexican island, and their fate. Write by every possible opportunity. Keep me well advised of everything progressing in Cuba. I learn this morning that there is a rumor afloat that more Americans (some say thousands) have landed on the south side of Cuba.

By this time the frigate "Saranac" must have joined the "Albany" and "Germantown." They ought to be able to protect our countrymen who were not guilty of the invasion.

I am, sir, very respectfully, your obedient servant,

J. M. CLAYTON.

ROBERT B. CAMPBELL, Esq.,
United States Consul, Havana.

Mr. Campbell to Mr. Clayton.

CONSULATE OF THE UNITED STATES, HAVANA,
June 4, 1850, 3, *p. m.*

SIR: The American vessels captured at Contoy by the Spanish steamer Pizarro have not yet arrived in this port. The prisoners now here are still incommunicated, and on trial.

With great respect and esteem, I have the honor to be, sir, your most obedient servant,

ROBERT B. CAMPBELL.

HON. JOHN M. CLAYTON,
Secretary of State, Washington City.

Mr. Campbell to Mr. Clayton.

CONSULATE OF THE UNITED STATES, HAVANA,
June 8, 1850.

SIR: The barque Georgiana and brig Susan Loud, captured by the general of marines at Contoy, both arrived in this harbor on the morning of the 5th instant. They are said to have entered without a national or other flag flying. At the time of their arrival the Saranac, Albany, and Germantown were in or near the habor.

The prisoners captured with the barque and brig are still incommunicated, and the trial progressing. All proceedings under the summarial or first process being secret, it is impossible to obtain reliable information of what is being done by the marine court, before which the case is pending. I take it for granted, from the place at which they were captured and the circumstances connected with it, that the parties and vessels must be released; although report, confirmed by opinion somewhat general, represents that the masters will be executed, and the men, generally, sentenced to a punishment not so severe.

Much excitement prevails in Havana, and great hostility to all Americans is manifested and expressed by the Spanish part of the population, I have not myself seen any exhibition of it, but hear much of it from different American masters.

In saying above that the parties and vessels under trial must be released, I do not design to be understood as meaning that they will, under existing circumstances, be given up to our government. The whole conversation of the Captain General and the general of marines with Captain Randolph and myself is at variance with such a course. They appear determined to try all the parties under and by their own laws and usages, and to follow out those laws either for acquittal or condemnation. I feel it a duty to say this much, (notwithstanding the papers already forwarded establish the fact,) lest from any delay of energetic action at Washington the lives of some of the prisoners be sacrificed to the rigor of this government—a danger which possibly can only be averted by immediately demanding, through me or some other mode, the delivery of the prisoners.

I have the honor to be, sir, with great respect and esteem, your most obedient servant,

ROBERT B. CAMPBELL.

HON JOHN M. CLAYTON,
Secretary of State, Washington City,

N. B.—The steamer Pizarro sailed last evening from this port in pursuit of an expedition said to have sailed, or that was about to sail, from New Orleans. R. B. C.

Mr. Campbell to Mr. Clayton.

CONSULATE OF THE UNITED STATES, HAVANA,
June 19, 1850.

SIR: I had the honor to receive, yesterday, by the steamer Ohio from New Orleans, your telegraph dispatch of the 1st instant. The telegraphic report not appearing entirely correct, and feeling an anxious desire to arrange the subject of which it treated in a manner least offensive to this government, and at the same time fully to carry out the views of the President, I called on the Captain General immediately after its receipt with a faint hope of success, and now report in substance the conversation held, and the result of the interview.

The Captain General was informed that I had received instructions from the Secretary of State in relation to the prisoners captured at Contoy; but from my desire to preserve the friendly and amicable relations existing between the governments of the United States and Spain, I deemed it advisable to call personally, and ascertain if an amicable arrangement could be made, by which he would either send the prisoners to the United States for trial, or deliver them over to me to be so sent.

The Captain General replied that they were being tried here; that he had positive proofs in his possession that the men captured at Contoy formed a part of the expedition of Lopez, and that the capture was in every way justifiable, acknowledging at the same time that their criminality was not so great as that of the individuals who had landed in Cardenas.

I observed that no man should be tried for the intention to commit a crime; intentions were not cognizable before human courts—they could only judge of acts; and if ever an intention of crime existed with these men the crime had not been committed, and the intention may have been abandoned.

The Captain General said that it was more than intention; that these men had already started upon their object; that they belonged to the party who had carried their piratical plans into effect and landed in Cardenas, and were clearly criminal, though not to the same extent, with that portion that landed at Cardenas, but had commenced to act upon their plan, and were awaiting the arrival of reinforcements to carry it out, and were guilty of piracy; and having been found and captured by the forces belonging to this government, it vested a perfect right to try them for the purpose of arriving at the degree of guilt of each individual concerned. I observed that the President of the United States does not admit the right of the Spanish government to capture these men—they never having been on Spanish territory, could not have committed any act violative of Spanish law. Even admitting them to be guilty, their guilt was against the laws of the United States; they are amenable to those laws and to no others.

The Captain General reasserted that these men were pirates, and that the laws against pirates held that they could be captured and punished wherever found; that neither himself nor the general of marine had the power to deliver up men who are on trial under the laws, and that he would not deliver them up, and desired me to inform you that the question was one which ought to be left to time. I then stated to the Captain General that my instructions to demand that the men be sent home were positive, and as he said he would not give up the prisoners, although it was unpleasant to do acts not agreeable to him, I should feel it a duty to send him a copy of my instructions accompanied with a demand; to which the Captain General replied, he would not to deliver up the prisoners, nor would he receive any communication upon the subject. The government of the United States could make their demand upon Mr. Calderon in Washington, or through Mr. Barringer at Madrid; that this government is only a dependency and has no diplomatic power.

After some further conversation, the Captain General agreed to receive the communication, but that he would forward it to Mr. Calderon. The Captain General repeatedly urged, that as the government of the United States had a minister at Madrid, and her Catholic Majesty a minister at Washington, all questions arising between the two governments must be settled through those representatives.

I have this morning addressed a communication to the Captain General with an extended extract from your instructions of the 1st instant. Owing to the inaccuracy before noticed in the telegraphic dispatch, the extract was taken from the instructions as they appeared in a Savannah paper, as copied from the National Intelligencer. The extract would not have been made and sent to the Captain General but for its universal publicity. I should have deemed it sufficient to have said that I had been instructed by my government. A copy of my communication to the Captain General is herewith forwarded.

From the conversation of yesterday, it is fair to infer that the prisoners will neither be sent home or placed at my disposition. The trial will progress to a conclusion, and, if acquitted, the prisoners will probably be placed at liberty to get away as they best can. Should conviction take place, it is difficult to say whether they will be pardoned or punished. If the right to try, which this government assumes and acts upon, be once conceded, we cannot complain of the enforcement of a sentence, for we will have yielded everything.

The Captain General says the prisoners are all well, and I presume he is fully informed. Street report, seldom reliable, represents many of them as sick and harshly treated.

I have the honor to be, sir, with great respect and esteem, your most obedient servant,

ROBERT B. CAMPBELL.

Hon. JOHN M. CLAYTON,
Secretary of State, Washington.

Mr. Campbell to the Count of Alcoy.

CONSULATE OF THE UNITED STATES, HAVANA,
June 19, 1850.

SIR: I have the honor to communicate to your excellency the following extract from a letter of instructions addressed to me by the honorable John M. Clayton, Secretary of State of the United States of America:

"From various sources of information I conjecture that the Spanish authorities in Cuba, in their excessive zeal to punish the invaders of that island, and all connected with them, while flushed with victory, may possible forget the difference between crime and intention to commit it, and wreak their vengeance on American citizens, either native or naturalized, not guilty of any act of invasion or depredation upon Spanish territory. It is said and believed here that many such were arrested on an island near the coast of Yucatan, called Contoy, within the territory of a power having friendly relations with the United States. As all the facts are not in our possession, the judgment we may have formed of the capture, abduction, and punishment of these men may possibly be very erroneous.

"But let us suppose that the men captured on the Mexican island were American citizens, and had occupied it intending to invade Cuba, still I cannot recognise the right of the Spanish authorities to hang, garote, or shoot them for that intention. There was yet a *locus penitentiæ* left for every man of them, and they might have returned to the United States guilty, indeed, of a violation of the laws of their own country, but of no law, that I am aware of, under which Spain could have punished them. The intention to commit crime is not *per se* crime. Some overt act must accompany the intent. A design to commit murder is not murder, nor is it, without some attempt to carry it into execution, punishable by the laws of man, however guilty the offender may be *in foro conscientiæ*, and by the ordinances of his Creator.

"The President means to claim for the American occupants of the Mexican island that they were not guilty of any crime for which, by the laws of civilized nations, they should suffer death, They may have been, and probably were, guilty of crimes for which this government ought, in good faith, to punish them, under the act of Congress of 20th April, 1818; but, supposing the facts relating to their capture to be as they are represented to us, the President is resolved that the eagle must and shall protect them against any punishment but that which the tribunals of their own nation may award.

"Tell the Count of Alcoy to send them home to encounter a punishment, which, if they are honorable men, would be worse than any he could inflict, in the indignant frowns and denunciations of good men in their own country, for an attempt to violate the faith and honor of a nation, which holds its character for integrity of more value and higher worth than all the Antilles together; but warn him in the most friendly manner, and in the true spirit of our ancient treaty, that, if he unjustly sheds one drop of American blood at this exciting period, it may cost the two countries a sanguinary war."

The foregoing extract will inform your excellency of the opinion of the President of the United States in relation to the capture made at or near Contoy, and of the requirements of my government that the prisoners be sent to the United States for trial.

I flatter myself from the long continued harmony which has subsisted between our mutual governments, and the importance to each government that the same friendly relations should be preserved unimpaired, that your excellency will dispassionately view the subject in all its bearings, and spontaneously and promptly comply with the requirement.

I would respectfully ask from your excellency a reply to this communication, at as early a period as your convenience may permit.

With considerations of great respect and esteem I have the honor to be your excellency's most obedient servant,

ROBERT B. CAMPBELL.

His Excellency the COUNT OF ALCOY,
Governor and Captain General
of the island of Cuba, &c., &c., &c.,

Mr. Campbell to Mr. Clayton.

[Extract.]

CONSULATE OF THE UNITED STATES, HAVANA,
June 19, 1850, 7 *o'clock p. m.*

SIR: I have the honor to acknowledge the receipt of your official dispatch of the 31st of May, received by the Georgia, and now delivered.

The dispatch of the 1st of June having been already acted upon, leaves me nothing to do so far as the Contoy prisoners are concerned. In fact, it became manifest as early as the 24th of May, as you are already informed in my communication of the 31st of May, that neither myself or your naval officers could do aught for the relief of the prisoners, then as now upon their trial.

The instructions now received shall be obeyed, as others have been, in all things. So far as I can learn, no American citizen has been recently arrested in the jurisdiction of this consulate, and none in a situation to require my present interference.

In my anxiety to forward an account of my action, under instructions of the 1st instant, by the Isabel, which has sailed, it was not possible to get the time to notice other parts of those instructions without losing the opportunity of that mail. The Falcon, to sail at daylight for New Orleans, enables me to prepare duplicates, and further to notice and obey.

You say "the President has resolved that the eagle must and shall protect them against any punishment but that which the tribunals of their own nation may award." I know the patriotism, the firmness, devotion to principle, and the honor of his country's flag which has prompted, and will prompt, all the acts of the President; and conceding all these, it is still impossible to carry out his determination. He may, and he no doubt will, redress the wrongs heaped upon his countrymen, but he cannot recall the sufferings already endured, and the punishment already inflicted upon the prisoners by close confinement, and possibly in chains, first on board a man-of-war, and then in the prison cell.

* * * * * * *

I have just been informed that Mr. Girau, of New Orleans, has been arrested, imprisoned, and incommunicated at Cienfuegos, where, I believe, Mr. McLean has an agent. When such arrests are made upon political charges the parties have no liberty to communicate by word or letter with their friends, and it is accidental if their condition is known.

* * * * * * *

23

I have the honor to be, sir, with great respect and esteem, your most obedient servant,

ROBERT B. CAMPBELL.

Hon. JOHN M. CLAYTON,
Secretary of State, Washington city.

Mr. Campbell to the Secretary of State.

[Extract.]

CONSULATE OF THE UNITED STATES, HAVANA,
June 27, 1850.

SIR: I have nothing of importance to communicate as having occurred in this consulate since my last.

The situation of the Contoy prisoners, so far as I can learn, remains unchanged. It is believed that the investigation has concluded, and copies of all the proceedings sent both to Madrid and Mr. Calderon. Report represents a difference of opinion as to the propriety of yielding to your demand of a surrender of the prisoners, as existing among the principal officers of this government, and it is presumed no positive action will be had upon the demand until positive instructions are received from Madrid, unless the demand is backed by a strong naval force.

The Germantown was in port for three days, and since yesterday morning has been cruising near the harbor. No other American man-of-war has arrived. Mr. Girau, of whose arrest you were informed by me, has regained his liberty and is now in Havana. As you will receive full accounts from Mr. McLean, it is unnecessary for me to trouble you with them.

I yesterday received a letter from a highly respectable merchant at Cardenas, dated 24th instant, stating that Mr. Edmund Doyle, a native of New York, and Mr. Gustavus Rolando, a native of Charleston, S. C., had been taken from their beds at 11 o'clock p. m. of the preceding night, tied, and carried off, the former to the house of the captain of the partido, and the latter to prison. The arrest was caused, the writer states, by Mr. Rolando bursting a cap while preparing his gun for an intended shooting excursion to the country on the next day.

The consul at Matanzas will undoubtedly do all in his power to have the parties released, and will inform you of all particulars.

Is it not the duty of our government to demand and exact full indemnity to American citizens when arrested and imprisoned by a foreign government without cause, or on frivolous pretexts?

* * * * * * *

I have the honor to be, sir, &c., &c., your most obedient servant,

ROBERT B. CAMPBELL.

Hon. JOHN M. CLAYTON,
Secretary of State.

Mr. Clayton to Commodore Morris.

DEPARTMENT OF STATE,
Washington, June 29, 1850.

SIR: The President directs that you proceed, as soon as possible, to Havana, in the war steamer Vixen; that on your arrival there you request an audience of the Governor and Captain General of Cuba, representing to him that you bear a message to him from the President of the United States, of importance to his country as well as your own. On being admitted to his presence, you will demand of him the immediate release of all the prisoners taken at Contoy, and without the Spanish jurisdiction. When making this demand in the name and by the authority of the President of the United States, you will repeat to the Governor and Captain General of Cuba the assurance heretofore conveyed to him and his government, that the government of the United States has never ceased to perform every duty enjoined upon it by our treaty with Spain, and that it will faithfully continue in the discharge of those duties so long as the peaceful relations of the two countries shall continue. That the President expects, in return for this friendly disposition and conduct, the strictest observance of the rights of the United States and their citizens from Spain; that he recognises no right on the part of the Spanish authorities to try and punish the prisoners taken at Contoy; and that he will view their punishment by the authorities of Cuba as an *outrage* upon the rights of this country. Without enlarging upon the grounds taken in making the demand through the consul, of which you are fully informed, the President is satisfied, from the reports which he has received of the evidence taken before Judge Marvin, at Key West, as well as from other information which he deems entirely reliable, that the men taken at Contoy had embarked to go to Chagres, and if any of them had ever designed to invade Cuba, they had repented of that design and abandoned it. Under these circumstances, the President cannot consent that the lives or liberties of citizens of the United States shall be forfeited, or that the question of the truth of the evidence above mentioned shall be referred to any foreign tribunal.

You will say to the Governor that your mission has been occasioned by intelligence that the demand heretofore made by the consul, Mr. Campbell, in regard to these prisoners, was refused on the ground, among others, that the consul had no diplomatic powers. In reply to the demand made by Mr. Campbell, we learn that he was referred to the Spanish minister in Washington, Don A. Calderon de la Barca, and to the court of Madrid. The views of this government on the whole subject have been fully made known to the Spanish minister residing at Washington, of which he has doubtless fully advised the government at Madrid and the Captain General of Cuba. This government has no reason to suppose that a demand so just and reasonable would not now be acceded to by that minister, who is no less distinguished among us for his humanity than his justice, and who, while zealously on all occasions maintaining and defending the rights of Spain, has never shown himself insensible to the importance of preserving the amicable relations which have so long existed between our respective countries.

As to the reference made by the Governor and Captain General to the court of Madrid, you will say to that distinguished functionary, that, in the judgment of the President of the United States, were he to abandon these prisoners to the consequences of the confinement which they must undergo in prison, in such a climate as that of Havana at this season of the year, until a demand could be made upon the court of Madrid and an answer returned, it would amount to a probable sacrifice of the lives of many of them, and a desertion of the duty of this government to protect its own citizens.

The owners of the bark Georgiana and the brig Susan Loud have exhibited to this department statements to prove the innocence of the captains who chartered those vessels; and you will inform the Governor and Captain General of Cuba, that this government expects those vessels to be returned to their owners, with damages for their capture and detention. Those statements confirm the testimony taken before Judge Marvin of the innocence of the prisoners of any intention to invade Cuba; which testimony has, we learn, been fully communicated to the Governor and Captain General.

Should the Captain General refuse to release the prisoners upon your demand, you will then inquire fully into the manner in which they have been treated; their present and past condition; whether any have died, or are sick, and what attention has been paid to them; and what is that evidence upon which the Spanish authorities rely to establish their guilt. For this purpose you will demand admittance to all the prisoners in the presence of the American consul; and upon your return you will make a full report on all these subjects.

You will also respectfully request of the Captain General all the testimony which he has obtained, to enable this government to prosecute any person or persons in the United States who have been engaged either in invading Cuba or in getting up an expedition for that purpose; and you will say to him that I am encouraged to make this request by Don A. Calderon de la Barca, who assures me that some such testimony is in possession of the Spanish authorities, and will be cheerfully tendered to this government to enable it to maintain its treaty stipulations with Spain.

I am, sir, very respectfully, your obedient servant,

JOHN M. CLAYTON,

Commodore CHARLES MORRIS, *&c.*, *&c.*, *&c.*

Mr. Clayton to Mr. Campbell.

DEPARTMENT OF STATE,
Washington, *June* 29, 1850.

SIR: Your dispatches stating the result of your demands for the American prisoners taken on the island of Contoy have been received. This will be delivered to you by Commodore Charles Morris, who goes to Havana with a special message from the President of the United

States to the Governor and Captain General of Cuba, demanding the immediate release of the prisoners. As the Governor has objected to your blending diplomatic with your consular functions, the President has thought proper to transfer the duties, in regard to these prisoners, heretofore enjoined upon you, to the Commodore. Should he request you, on leave granted for that purpose, you will visit the prisoners with him for the purposes indicated in his instructions, and make full report, in concurrence with him, to this department.

I am, sir, very respectfully, your obedient servant,

JOHN M. CLAYTON.

ROBERT B. CAMPBELL, Esq.,
United States Consul, Havana.

Mr. Campbell to Mr. Clayton.

[Extracts.]

CONSULATE OF THE UNITED STATES, HAVANA,
July 3, 1850.

SIR: * * * * * * *

There is nothing new in relation to the prisoners that are here. The Congress and Germantown are both in port.

* * * * * * * *

I am convinced in my own mind that no American in Havana has been in any way concerned with the late expedition; but they having so long enjoyed the liberty of speech at home, it is possible, nay, probable, that *expressions* unacceptable to this government may have been used. Others may be correspondents of newspapers in the States, and their letters may not always have been unobjectionable to this government. All who have committed the one or the other imprudence may be liable to arrest.

I have the honor to be, sir, with great respect and esteem, your most obedient servant,

ROBERT B. CAMPBELL.

Hon. JOHN M. CLAYTON,
Secretary of State, Washington City.

[Telegraphic dispatch.]

Mr. Campbell to Mr. Clayton.

HAVANA, *July* 8, 1850.

The Congress, Albany, and Germantown are now here; the Contoy prisoners are yet *in statu quo:* it is expected that they will be released in a few days. The American consul asks leave of absence for two months, conditioned upon the release of the Contoy prisoners. Mr. John Morland, an American, for whose acts I shall hold myself responsible, will discharge the duties of the office during my absence. Please communicate your reply by telegraph to the collector of the port of Charleston.

Respectfully,

ROBT. B. CAMPBELL, *U. S. Consul.*

Mr. Campbell to Mr. Clayton.

CONSULATE OF THE UNITED STATES, HAVANA,
July 12, 1850.

SIR: I have the honor to acknowledge the receipt of your dispatch of the 29th ultimo, transmitted by Commodore Morris, who arrived in this port on the afternoon of the 10th instant.

The dispatch states, for reasons given, that "the President has thought proper to transfer the duties in regard to these prisoners, heretofore enjoined upon you, to the commodore."

Future interference on my part would be improper. I feel it a duty, however, to mention that the summarial proceedings, in relation to forty-two of the prisoners, have been concluded; the final decision was given on the 9th, approved on the 10th instant, and published in the paper of to-day officially.

Forty-one of the prisoners are absolved for want of evidence; the forty-second, called Moore, is also at liberty, in consequence of a pardon previously promised by the general of marine. The cause of the promise is left to conjecture. The whole forty-two are, however, sentenced to two years of hard labor, should they hereafter be found on the island of Cuba or Porto Rico. These prisoners are now on board the Albany, to sail in the morning for Pensacola. Rufus Benson, master, and John A. Graffon, mate, of the Georgiana, with Thomas G. Hale, mate of the Susan Loud, are detained for further trial; the remainder of the two crews, consisting of seven persons, are also detained. The vessels, with all their appurtenances, are adjudged to be lawful prizes, and confiscated to the use of the Spanish government. The summing up of the decision, when rendered in English, is as follows:

"In view of all that has been stated, the auditor is of opinion that your excellency be pleased to declare—

"1. Legal, as founded on article 86, treatise 2d, title 5th, of the ordinances of the navy of 1793, the detention at Contoy of the bark Georgiana and the brig Susan Loud; his excellency the commander-in-chief of this station and naval forces, on opening and becoming informed of the correspondence of the pirates, having made use of the authority granted by her Majesty for these cases, in the royal order of January 12, 1803.

"2. That, considering the undoubted illegal occupation of the said vessels detained at Contoy, it having been superabundantly proved that they conveyed men, arms, munitions, and provisions for the piratical expedition of Lopez, that they be confiscated, with all their appurtenances, for the benefit of the State.

"3. That a *nolle prosequi* be entered in relation to the forty-two passengers already named, setting them at liberty, for the reasons before stated, with the consent first obtained of their excellencies the Captain General of the island and the commander-in-chief of the station, upon the particulars before named.

"4. That the descriptions of Captain Pendleton and the three sailors that proceeded in the Creole, be sent to the Captain General.

"5, and last. That the summarial proceedings be returned to the fiscal, that he may continue the prosecution against the above-named Benson, Graffon, and Hale, the before-mentioned sailors continuing detained.

"Your excellency will, however, determine what you should deem most proper.

"VICENTE DE RAMOS.

"HAVANA, *July* 9, 1850."

From the foregoing decision you will discover that this government has acted with consistence, firmness, and pertinacity. The legality of the capture, as also the right to try prisoners, was claimed at the outset. There has been no suspension of proceedings, no giving up of prisoners. The court gives a final decision in the case of forty-two, and recommends to the Captain General that they shall not be permitted to land or select the vessels in which to return to the States. To carry out that recommendation, it is understood that the Captain General, at about six a. m. of the morning of the 11th, informed Commodore McKeever that the prisoners would be sent to the Congress during the morning, and they were sent accordingly. The trial of the remainder, I presume, will be prosecuted to conviction or acquittal, in the absence of, or under the pressure of, a second demand from the President. From the opinions believed to be entertained by the Captain General, I do not think he would admit the right of the President to make any demand upon him, or be induced to enter into a correspondence directly with a foreign government. I may be mistaken, but deem it probable that should Commodore Morris make his demand in writing, the subject will again be referred to Mr. Calderon, as the diplomatic agent of his government.

In conformity to your suggestion, I have this morning, at the request of Commodore Morris, and in his company, seen the forty-two prisoners who were tried and liberated, and held conversations with many of them.

They state generally that they never formed, or intended to form, a part of an expedition against this or any other country; that they were "bona fide" emigrants for California, and had paid their passage money for Chagres; that while confined they had not suffered for want of food, but were ironed for six or more weeks, most of the time in double shackles. They make many other statements, with which it is unnecessary to trouble you, as their affidavits and protests will be made and forwarded to you on their arrival in the States.

I send, herewith, a translated copy of the entire argument of the auditor of marine, and approval of his decision.

I have the honor to be, sir, with great respect and esteem, your most obedient servant,

ROBERT B. CAMPBELL.

Hon. JOHN M. CLAYTON, *&c., &c., &c.*

Argument of the Auditor of Marine.

[OFFICIAL.—Translated from the Diario de la Marina.]

Report of the Auditor of Marine of this station, approved and agreed to by the superior decree of the Admiralty, dated 10th instant, in the proceedings carried on consequent to the detention at Contoy of the bark Georgiana and hermaphrodite brig Susan Loud, on the 18th day of May of the present year, with the fifty-two persons found on board of them.

MOST EXCELLENT SIR: The auditor, with all the care and reflection required by their importance, has examined the present summarial proceedings commenced by your excellency's order in consequence of the communication addressed to you on the 18th of May last from Key Contoy, by his excellency the commander-in-chief of this station and its naval forces, in the waters of which key, making use of the authority granted to her Majesty's fleets and vessels by article 86, treatise 2d, title 5th, of the general ordinances of the navy of 1793, he detained the bark Georgiana and brig Susan Loud, with every person found on board of them, on account of the information and reasons for suspicion minutely expressed by his excellency in the aforesaid communication, a copy of which appears on page 2d, and the original on the 208th. The subscriber deems it his duty, before offering to the consideration of your excellency the merits brought forth in the proceedings, and of the documents thereto annexed touching those particulars, to bring to mind here, that more than two years since, some Spaniards, compelled to seek refuge in the United States—some of them fleeing from the punishment they deserved for common crimes, and others to escape the investigations of the police—commenced to serve as a pretext, or rather were elected by some speculators of that country, to present the appearance of a political party that should give a regular shape to the project of robbery and pillage they had conceived in their heated imaginations. Among the elements required for the success of an undertaking of that kind, they relied upon the portion of the adventurers who, in the recent war with Mexico, had tasted the gay life of a campaign, which, without many dangers or toils, brought them many known advantages. They also relied upon that numerous and almost daily immigration from Europe arriving to the neighboring Union, in which are found, mixed up with the many unfortunate beings who seek shelter and bread by means of the work they cannot find in Europe, and many real emigrants for political causes, not a few wretches stained with enormous crimes, or accused of scandalous frauds, or at least impregnated with all the vices that prepare them to enter into any undertaking promising them lucre or gains.

To prepare public opinion a newspaper was established, written in Spanish and English, but of such small dimensions and little merit as scarce were the talents and resources of the new propagandists. In that newspaper were published, with impudent perseverance, the grossest calumnies against the first authorities of the island, supposing it weighed down by enormous taxes, and in a state of effervescence and general discontent. These gratuitous and ridiculous accusations, and the false charges of oppression, misfortune, and discontent, which impelled the island to a desire of being separated from Spain, soon found echo in other newspapers of the neighboring Union. It is known that for some time past the most irritating rivalry has been fermenting between the provinces of the North and South; and with the intention of interesting the provinces of the South, and to stimulate them, they circulated the malignant clamor that such was the reigning discontent in Cuba, that she was only expecting a first occasion, or any aid to constitute a nucleus, that she might form herself into a republic annexed to the United States. With this fantastic plan many deluded men of the South have undoubtedly dreamt and believed they had found the quickest and easiest means of obtaining over their rivals the preponderance they aspire to.

The project of an expedition against Cuba became so general among adventurers thirsting for gold, and acquired such consistency and almost certainty of an immediate realization, that the illustrous President of the United States believed himself obliged to circulate the world-known proclamation of the 11th of August, 1849, by which, after bringing to mind the duty of observing the faith of treaties, and of preventing any aggression on the part of his fellow-citizens against the territories of friendly nations, he declared that none of those who should take part in the expedition *could calculate upon the American government interfering in their behalf, to whatever extremity they might find themselves reduced in consequence of their conduct and undertaking.*

To this manifestation immediately followed the compelling the expeditionists assembled on Round island to disperse; but the speculators and other chiefs of the project, although they deferred it to a better opportunity, have afterwards boasted of having continued their infamous preparations with more experience and caution, to the point of profusively issuing paper payable in Havana. With this paper, and the distribution of property over the whole island, speculations have been carried on, and, as it is publicly asserted, some fortunes have been made, and large sums offered likewise, payable in Havana. Some being well informed, and others deceived with the promise of being conveyed to California, assembled, numbering about 550, under the command of Don Narciso Lopez at New Orleans: from hence they left in three different days upon those same two vessels detained at Contoy by his excellency the commander-in-chief of this station and its naval forces, and on board of the steamer Creole, the only one that succeeded in reaching Cardenas, the soil of which, selected for their landing, was stained with the crimes known to all. It is notorious that, a few hours after, the expeditionists were compelled to re-embark, routed by the small force which, upon the first notice, went to attack them.

That unexampled and unqualified attempt produced a general cry of indignation in this faithful Antille, the echo of which has been heard in the English chamber and in the Capitol of France. But the auditor, in his capacity as a magistrate, will set aside these demonstrations, to occupy with all the impassability and moderation required by law of the facts springing out of the summarial proceedings, and to conclude afterwards, proposing to your excellency the verdicts which, according to his opinion, be just.

Of the five parts composing the proceedings, the "fiscal" (prosecuting attorney) has made—thereby showing an example of praiseworthy industry—a minute extract, from which it appears that the bark named Georgiana Lincumbily, one of the vessels detained at Contoy, left New Orleans on the 25th of April of the present year, cleared for Chagres with provisions and passengers. On the 27th she reached the Belise, and at night received from a fishing boat several cases, which were said to contain machinery, and afterwards turned out to be munitions and arms. After receiving them she went to sea, and in nine or ten days anchored at the island or key of Contoy, upon which the passengers twice landed with their arms, were engaged in drilling, and afterwards returned to the vessel, which made sail for the island of Mujeres, taking on board, for that purpose, a pilot from among some fishermen they found. Contrary winds did not permit them to reach their place of destination, notwithstanding they were for several days making efforts against those and the currents; for which reason they returned to Contoy, where, in three or four days after, the steamer Creole made her appearance, with an unknown flag, which the accused called Cuban. The so-called Colonel or General O'Hara, who commanded the people on the Georgiana, went on board the steamer, and, after communicating with her, returned to his vessel—the Creole starting for the island of Mujeres, from which she came back to Contoy in two or three days; and when she had anchored, one of the chiefs went on board the Georgiana, and going upon the quarter-deck, spread out the so-called Cuban flag, made a speech to the passengers upon the object of the expedition, and returned to the Creole, from which a short time after another boat came with some twenty-five men, discontented with the expedition. One of the vessels then took a position alongside the other, and the operation of transferring the cases of arms, provisions, and coal from the Georgiana to the Creole commenced; and lastly was effected that of the passengers, who it is said were some two hundred men, well armed and uniformed.

The hermaphodite brig Susan Loud, which is the other vessel detained at Contoy, left New Orleans on the 2d of May of the current year, cleared for Chagres with provisions and passengers, and having laid to when she reached 26 degrees of latitude and 87 longitude, she waited some days for the Creole, which, in effect, joined her to receive on board all the passengers taken out of New Orleans by the brig, excepting the two named John Estille and Joseph Byrnes, who hid themselves not to go on board the steamer, and both vessels afterwards bent their course towards the island of Mujeres, from whence the steamer departed for Cardenas and the brig went to Contoy, where she anchored alongside of the Georgiana.

The steamer Creole also left the port of New Orleans, on the 5th day of the said month of May, with about 140 men as passengers, and on reaching the Belise received arms, provisions, and munitions, distributing them on the day after she left the river, putting on cockades, and those who were called chiefs buckling on swords. Two days after this they met the Susan Loud, and the shifting of men, by means of the boats of both vessels, took place; and after having determined upon the operations of the brig, as already stated, and the transferring of men having been effected, the so-called Colonel Bunche made them a speech on the object of the expedition, offering them that the named General Lopez would subscribe in their favor a document binding himself to the fulfilment of the offer of eight dollars per month, and, besides, four thousand dollars at the termination of the expedition; and immediately afterwards, proclamations and the biography of Lopez were distributed. In the Georgiana and Susan Loud were found, at the time of the detention, fifty-two persons; ten of whom belonged to the crews, and forty-two who embarked in New Orleans as passengers. Their names and surnames, with the expression of class, vessel in which they left that port, and number of pages of the summarial proceedings showing their respective declarations, have been specified in the statement accompanying this report, made to avoid the confusion of quotations which would necessarily be caused by the multiplicity of declarations that have had to be taken from foreigners whose names our copyists easily mistake. Of those forty-two passengers, only the individual called A. B. Moore has confessed that he embarked, being cognizant of the true object of the expedition, of which he formed a part as commissary, with the rank of captain; he has also stated that, on the night previous to his embarking on the Creole, he attended a secret meeting, in which had been discussed several affairs having connexion with the expedition, and among other things about the reinforcements that were immediately to follow them under the command of the United States General Quitman. The remaining forty-one passengers have maintained, in their declarations, that they undertook the voyage in the understanding of being conveyed to Chagres and California; and that, having received notice on board that the true intent of the expedition was to attack the island of Cuba, they had refused to follow it, for which they were left at Contoy to go back to New Orleans.

From the letters and papers forwarded by his excellency the commander-in-chief of the fleet, at the time of the detention of the vessels, which documents form the fifth part, and appear translated from pages 216 to 270, both inclusive, and from the papers found by the fiscal in the desk of the captain of the brig Susan Loud, Simeon Pendleton, (the originals of which are from pages 286 to 301, and the translations thereof from pages 274 to 285,) it is seen that in New Orleans, and several other places in the United States, adventurers were enlisted to invade the island of Cuba. Those papers show that the expeditionists formed companies with their respective officers, and that to each one enlisted of the class of privates was offered from one to four thousand dollars at the end of the year of their engagement, besides the eight dollars per month, payable from the day of sailing, and to the class of officers nineteen to twenty thousand dollars, besides the pay corresponding to the respective rank.

On pages 424, 425, and 428, appear the original testaments of some of the expeditionists, translated on pages the reverse of 236, 237, and 238, by which they bequeath and dispose of the property they expected to obtain in Cuba. On page 440 is found original the appointment as second lieutenant of cavalry in favor of John Herbert, signed by

A. Hisell, at the so-called headquarters of the liberating army of Cuba, by virtue of the authority he believed himself invested with by appointment of General Narciso Lopez, commander-in-chief of said army, in which, besides expressing that the said Herbert was appointed second lieutenant of cavalry, with the pay and honor appertaining to that rank, he was authorised to recruit and bring to the city of New Orleans as great a number of volunteers for the cavalry service, destined for said Hisell's battalion, as he could engage. Those volunteers were to present themselves with arms, the value of which would be paid them in Cuba, and one thousand dollars besides, or their equivalent in lands at the termination of the campaign. The reward to the chiefs would be proportionate to their rank, in cash or estates, without their losing, in case of death, the right to those remunerations which would be religiously paid over to their legitimate heirs. In that remarkable document it is likewise stated, that besides that remuneration the officers and soldiers were to receive, according to their grades, pay equivalent to that recovered by the volunteers of the Mexican campaign, the amount of which was to be paid them by the paymaster-general of the army of Cuba, *where the said funds would be collected*, payable from the day of enlistment.

From page 497 to 504 is found a printed biography of D. Narciso Lopez, and on pages 419, 431, and 432, three copies of the proclamations, likewise printed, which were distributed on board of the steamer Creole the day after she left the mouth of the Mississippi.

That biography or historical notice of D. Narciso Lopez, full of misrepresentations, and of fact, invented to exalt him as a brave and learned hero, full of merit and adorned with all the virtues, exaggerates his great influence in the interior of this island, and states that Lopez had some years ago formed the resolution of making her independent; that the movement was to have commenced in the summer of 1848, but that being discovered and persecuted by the government of this island, Lopez had escaped being arrested by embarking on board a vessel bound to Bristol; finding himself, says the hero, obliged to take this step to avoid the fate which himself and friend would undoubtedly have experienced, of being shot in a few days, for which reason he deferred to some future time the realization of his project, which he had no doubt he could accomplish with the greatest ease when he thought the proper time had arrived for making his voyage to Cuba, as his great popularity, especially in the central department, insured his triumph, the result of which would be the success of his mission—that is, emancipating Cuba from the odious yoke, says Lopez, of Spanish tyranny. It is in fact true that the Captain General having decreed, about the middle of the year 1848, the imprisonment of the then General Lopez, who was residing in one of the interior towns of the island, he succeeded, abusing the good faith and gentlemanly behavior of the governor of Matanzas, in escaping, having to give an account of his operations to the military commission charged with his trial, as he had effected his flight from that port. The proceedings continued, however, against him as a rebel, and the sentence pronounced on the 23d of April, 1849, condemning him to loss of office, rank and crosses, saw the public light in all the newspapers of this capital. Lopez, as was to be expected, having taken refuge in the United States, increased the number of the anarchists, and, forgetting, to his eternal shame, all that he owed to Spain from his most tender years, offered himself, or rather made himself, the chief of the expedition, the preparations for which caused the already mentioned proclamation or manifesto of the 11th of August of the same year, 1849, to the publication of which immediately followed the forcible dispersion of the wretches assembled upon Round island.

It is notorious that the press of all colors in the United States, and the newspapers of this capital, have more or less extensively spoken, from the beginning of April of this year, of the second expedition to invade Cuba, or, be it, that which effected a landing in Cardenas; it being remarkable that there appear in it, as well by the revelations of the original documents, which are of indisputable authenticity, accompanying the summarial proceedings in the said fifth part thereof, as by the newspapers, the names of the North Americans, General Quitman, Judge Pinkney Smith, ex-senator Henderson, the editors Sigur, O'Sullivan, O'Hara, Pickett, and others who need not be specified, when those named are sufficient to prove that that expedition has been set on foot, favored by, and composed of, not only of low men, but also of men whose social position, it appears natural, should keep them away from having connexion with such undertakings; and it is most remarkable and unexampled that persons of that kind should find a civilized country in the streets of which they can appear with their heads high, with offices and rank that in no enlightened country can hold even those who are only supected of such crimes.

From the official communication of his excellency the Governor and Captain General of this island, and the accompanying copy thereof, on pages 316 to 321, both inclusive, appears proved, in the legal form sufficient for proceedings of this nature, the consummation of the attempt on the 19th day of May last, or, be it, the tissue of crimes committed by D. Narciso Lopez, from half-past three of the morning on which he and his followers invaded the port and town of Cardenas, belonging to the territory of this ever faithful island. They forcibly dispossessed and imprisoned the chief authority of the place, burnt the house in which that authority made a heroic resistance, robbed the public funds they could lay their hands upon, invited the inhabitants to rebel, and spilt innocent blood, and finally they hoisted up in the public square an unknown flag. They likewise showed a decided intention of continuing in the exercise of their crimes, by going into the interior of the country, which they did not succeed in realizing, because, as before stated, a few hours after, on the same day, the 19th, they were charged upon and routed by a handful of brave men, who compelled them to re-embark.

That attempt—unexampled in history, on account of the exceptional circumstances attending it—of the actors having assembled, and the means been prepared for its perpetration in a friendly country, leaving one of its principal ports, to attack treacherously, cautiously, and secretly, the territory of a nation then, as now, at peace with all the world—has already been unanimously qualified by the press of all colors, with only some few exceptions, such as the Sun, the Delta, and others, which, for their interests and private views, have confronted the shame of constituting themselves the champions and defenders of

Lopez's piratical expedition. That name has been given to it in the British Parliament, by one of the most distinguished writers and jurists of the House of Lords, and is the same qualification made by the President of the United States, when he issued the before-mentioned proclamation of the 11th August; because, only by considering the organizers of the armed expedition it refers to, as pirates, could have been declared that none of the persons connected with it should expect the interference of the government of the United States in their behalf, however great the extremity they might be reduced to in consequence of their conduct and undertaking, which, in fewer words, means that the chief of the State put beyond the pale of law any inhabitant of the Union connecting himself with the project.

The auditor, according to the strictest principles of the laws of nations, also qualifies the attempt of Lopez as a piratical act, with new and aggravating circumstances, of such a nature that they add a new species to the catalogue of piracy. A pirate, by common law, is he who traverses the seas by his own authority, without a known flag, committing all sorts of misdemeanors by force of arms, in peace or in war, attacking all the vessels he meets, without distinction or difference of flags. The buccaneers, who undoubtedly were pirates, and were as such treated, increased piracy with their particular class, in the same manner as Lopez has done it with his expedition against Cuba.

The buccaneers did not merely commit robberies and infamous acts upon the vessels they met on the seas, but extended their acts to attacking some ports and coasts, which they plundered, set fire to, and destroyed in several ways. The pirates and buccaneers never attempted to palliate their iniquity with political pretexts, nor aspired to obtaining a great name or fame; nor had they newspapers to defend them, nor general and judges that would so degrade themselves as to be connected with them, wishing to share their pillage and robbery: all these are peculiarities of the so-called expedition of Lopez, which, doubtless, will constitute an era in history, inasmuch as it has been organized in a friendly country, leaving one of its ports to go and burn, rob and kill, upon the territory of another friendly nation, at the same time that there was flying on the building of a newspaper office established in one of the most public streets of New York, hoisted on a pole, a painted piece of bunting, with emblems and colors, to which was given the name of Cuban flag, and was the same taken by Lopez to Cardenas. In the punishment of that new species of piracy, invented by a few speculators of our neighboring republic, and headed by Lopez, are interested, at the same time as Spain, all other nations of the world, without distinction of hemispheres or flags; for, in the same manner that Spain was attacked, on the 19th of May, in the port and town of Cardenas, any other day, under equal or similar pretexts, might England be attacked in Canada or the Barbadoes; France, in Guadalupe or Martinique; Holland, in Curacoa; Denmark, in St. Thomas; Sweden, in St. Bartholomew; and the Spanish American republics in any parts of their territories; and, in one word, all the other nations without exception. It is not necessary to establish that it exclusively belongs to the jurisdiction of marine courts all that relates to privateering, prizes pirates, mutiny, and any other crime committed on the seas; and as the crime, or rather the combination of crimes, perpetrated in Cardenas, unquestionably constitute piracy, the vessels and persons detained at Contoy must be tried by the marine court, and agreeably to the dispositions of the ordinances of the navy, and subsequent laws. In conformity, therefore, to the existing sovereign dispositions, the proceedings which are now under consideration must be divided into two parts, entirely distinct in themselves—one of them to embrace the condemnation or acquittal of the vessels, having beforehand effected the most necessary investigations to prove their occupation, or place they came from, which, in conformity to article 13th of the royal order of 20th June, 1801, has to be decided by the military courts of the navy, and therefore by that of your excellency, with the subscribing auditor, who constitute the court for this station. The persons must be tried by the forms established by the royal order of the 8th January, 1830, in all that they can be adapted to the present case. To decide of the fate of the Georgiana and Susan Loud, there exist more facts than are needed in the summarial proceedings; for it appears evidently established that those vessels, although they cleared from New Orleans with the apparent object of conveying passengers to Chagres, were engaged in carrying men, arms, provisions, and munitions to attack the island of Cuba, as was effected by the landing of Lopez and some five hundred of his followers in Cardenas, where they perpetrated the crimes already related, and to which place they arrived in the steamer Creole. This vessel was dispatched with the same pretext as those mentioned before, there appearing and being manifest that, although they left New Orleans on different days, they held communication with one another on the high seas, and at Contoy transferred arms and men from one to the other, and acted in a manner that shows that they had made a previous combination, and appointed as a place of rendezvous the island of Mujeres, which the Georgiana could not reach, in spite of her repeated efforts, having been prevented by currents and contrary winds; for which reason she had to go back to Contoy, to which place the Creole went for the arms and men she had taken out of New Orleans, and which was the same place where the Susan Loud afterwards joined them. Although what is above stated is sufficient to prove the true intent of the voyage of these vessels, it will be well to copy here the original document of page 295, translated on page 283, which says:

"This expedition has been perfectly combined, as they have given us tickets for Chagres, so that in case of search by the authorities they may not do anything to us; we took on board of our bark, at the mouth of the Mississippi, a quantity of arms, and being at sea, a revenue vessel passed by our side at night; but they knew what we were, for all the world is in favor of the expedition; we are armed with musket, short sword, and revolving pistols—the officers in the same manner; we are confident of success. General Lopez is at the head of five hundred of us, and if we come out victorious we shall receive our four thousand dollars, and live in peace."

It appears, also, that the Susan and Creole recognised each other by signals, which necessarily must have been previously agreed upon as also that, during the night, they sailed together, keeping lights up to preserve them together; and above all, as it appears, that in the log-books of one and the other vessel no remarks have been made which in any manner could excuse the faults already observed; and as there does not appear that the Georgiana had the proper license to ship the arms and munitions she received at the Belise, there is no doubt left that, according to article 28th, and others agreeing with it, of the royal order of June 20, 1801, they must be declared by your excellency good prizes, and confiscated to the benefit of the State, with all their apparel, sails, instruments, boats, provisions, the rest of the arms found on board, and every other thing belonging to the same, giving an account of the same to her Majesty, that they may be applied to the uses her Majesty should deem best, unless, to avoid the loss or damage they might suffer before the sovereign's resolution can descend, your excellency should prefer to sell them at auction, or in any manner employ them for the benefit of the State. The auditor having concluded, with the statement in the preceding paragraph, touching the vessels detained at Contoy, passes now to occupy himself with the forty-two passengers who were found on them, named Edward B. Davis, John Finch, William Penton, David Flinger Smith, James M. Gowan, John W. Winter, John Gibbs, Thomas M. Armstrong, William B. Smith, William M'Intosh, James Folger, John Cranin, Levi Brown, Alexander Miller, Henry Stevens, Wm. S. Lake, James M. Martin, Henry Smith, John Estell, Joseph Byrnes, Antonio Francisco, Finny S. Welsh, Phill O'Connor, Alexander M. Snelly, Joseph Reed, A. B. Moore, Charles N. Paris, William J. Holland, James O'Donnell, Arthur M'Guire, John M. Coolson, Joel D. Hoag, Stephen Havenstrow, John L. Carter, Allen P. Coolson, James Bannon, Wm. L. Hardy, John Blackstone, Chas. B. Matthews, James Japley, George M. M'Daniel, William Brown. The first seventeen left New Orleans in the Georgiana, the eight following in the Susan Loud, and the remaining seventeen in the steamer Creole. Of all these, A. B. Moore alone has clearly confessed his participation in the undertaking; but taking into consideration the statement of his excellency the commander-in-chief of the station, in his communication dated the 5th instant, at the margin of which this report commences, it is necessary that your excellency should confirm the pardon expressly granted to Moore, in the name of her Majesty, without entering into any observations which are foreign to this place.

Whether the statements of the remaining forty-one passengers be true or false, neither in the summarial proceedings, nor elevating those to a prosecution, nor carrying them arbitrarily to a court where a great extension might be given to the evidence, could anything be obtained that would contradict their assertions, or that would establish that only fear for the consequences of the crimes that were about to be committed in Cardenas, or the want of room in the Creole to convey them, was what detained them at Contoy. The fact proved and undoubted is, that they remained many leagues from our coast; there appearing also, from the documents numbered 12, 15, 28, 55, 60, and 63, the translations of which are shown on pages 226, 227, 240, 257, 260, and 263, that claims were brought against Lopez for deception; that disagreements had occurred among the expeditionists, and, in one word, that the chief, Lopez, placed the Georgiana at the disposition of all the disaffected of the expedition, that they might return to New Orleans. What is moral conviction for a man is not enough for a judge. Without offending common sense, and according to all the rules of reasoning, it may be supposed that when those men engaged or enlisted in the United States, they must have known, if not positively, at least by inference, that the object of the expedition was not lawful or permitted, they being conveyed gratis, and offered a remuneration which did not appear proportionate to any undertaking not offering great risks. The greater part of these passengers can write; the avidity with which the North American people read the public papers is well known; and it is notorious that long before the expedition was carried into effect, the project was spoken of, and especially in the principal southern towns, where the majority of those people were recruited. All this, however, is nothing but opinion more or less founded; so that in the conviction that nothing will be obtained by elevating the summarial proceedings to a prosecution, the auditor deems it strictly just that a "*nolle prosequi*" shall be entered in relation to the passengers, and that they be set at liberty.

Be it, however, permitted to the subscriber, before going further, to express his humble opinion to your excellency that it would not be prudent, under the present circumstances, to allow those men to walk the streets and select the vessel and moment for returning to the United States. It will not be out of place to draw your excellency's attention to the fact that such mercenary beings, disposed to enter into and form part of any undertaking without stopping to examine into its morality, it is to be presumed, would easily increase the number of a new expedition that might reckon upon more resources and a larger number; and although in the private opinion of the auditor such a new and reinforced expedition would have no other result but that of giving a greater occupation to those whose duty it would be to try and punish them, the government, however, cannot neglect, it being their duty, adopting all the precautions which their wisdom may suggest for preserving order and public tranquility, such as that of forbidding all those concerned in this affair from ever returning to the territory of this island and that of Puerto Rico, in the understanding that in case of non-compliance they will be condemned to public works for two years; to which end their "description" may be taken for the information of the government. But nothing of this belongs to your excellency's jurisdiction; the auditor thinks that your excellency should propose to the superior chief of the station to have an understanding with the principal civil and military authority of the island upon the means of conveying those men, and the precautions with which they are to be permitted to return to the Union, delivering, upon that being effected, their money and other private property to them belonging, for, as stated before, the vessels and their appurtenances, together with the captured provisions and arms, must remain confiscated for the benefit of the State, of which duty the fiscal may be put in charge, to have it effected with all possible dispatch by means of a verbal investigation.

The captain that was of the Susan Loud, and the three sailors that proceeded to Cardenas in the Creole, have been declared as beyond the pale of the law by the Captain General's edict of the 19th of May last; therefore it will be proper to furnish his excellency the Captain General the descriptions of those individuals, as they appear upon the crew-lists of the vessels, that the law may be carried into effect in case that their persons be obtained.

The subscriber intentionally abstains, himself, from entering into observations and particulars of any kind respecting Rufus Benson, master of the Georgiana, and her mate, Jos. A. Graffon, and the sailors belonging to the same, Nathan Dawson, Robert J. Burely, James Nowyes; the mate of the Susan Loud, Thomas G. Hale, and sailors of the same, James Stewart, Daniel Blair, John Hamer, Andrew Jinkhantz—as the proceedings respecting Benson, Graffon, and Hale, must continue according to the form prescribed in the royal order of the 8th of January, 1830; to which end the summarial proceedings will return to the fiscal, as soon as what has been determined before shall have been effected, the sailors continuing detained until a further determination.

Recapitulating: In view of all that has been stated, the auditor is of opinion that your excellency do declare—1st. The detention of the bark Georgiana and brig Susan Loud, at Contoy, legal, it being founded on article 86, treaties 2, tit. 5, of the royal naval ordinances of 1793; his excellency the commander-in-chief of this station and of the naval forces having made use, on opening and becoming informed of the correspondence of the pirates, of the authority granted by her Majesty for these cases in the royal order of the 12th of January, 1803. 2d. That, considering the undoubted illegal occupation of the said vessels, detained at Contoy—it having been superabundantly proved that they conveyed men, arms, munitions, and provisions for the piratical expedition of Lopez—they be confiscated, with all their appurtenances, for the benefit of the state. 3d. That a "nolle prosequi" be entered in relation to the forty-two passengers already named, setting them at liberty for the reasons before stated, with the consent first obtained of their excellencies the Captain General and commander-in-chief of the station as to the particulars before named. 4th. That the descriptions of Captain Pendleton and the three sailors that proceeded in the Creole be sent to the Captain General. 5th, and last. That the summarial proceedings be returned to the "fiscal," that he may continue the prosecution against the above-named Benson, Graffon, and Hale, the before-mentioned sailors continuing detained.

Your excellency will, however, determine what you shall deem most proper.

HAVANA, *July* 9, 1850.

MOST EXCELLENT SIR, *Vicente de Ramos:* I conform to it, and let it be fulfilled, the forty-two passengers named in the proceeding report remaining at liberty, placing them at the disposition of their excellencies the Captain General and commander-in-chief of this station for the purpose expressed in the same report; that portion of which relating to it will be conveyed in a polite communication to those authorities; the fiscal being charged with the delivery of the effects and property in the form specified by the auditor; and as such fiscal, attending and being present, to the delivery of the forty-two individuals, stating in the said proceedings the manner in which it has been effected. And issue a correct certificate of the report of the auditor and of this decree, for their insertion in the official part of the Diario de la Marina, in three consecutive numbers, returning the proceedings to the said "fiscal" for the fulfilment of the part appertaining to him, after having passed through the secretary's office the communications and certificate ordained. TABLADA.

Note.—That part of the preceding superior decree having relation to the secretary's office has been complied with. (Date as above.)

JOSE ANTONIO NIRTO.

Mr. Campbell to Mr. Clayton.

Consulate of the United States, Havana,
July 16, 1850.

Sir: The captain, two mates, and seven seamen, detained by this government, have not yet been relieved from incommunication; but permission being granted to Commodore Morris for him and myself to see the prisoners, we first called at the military hospital at 10½ a. m. of this day to see Captain Benson, who had been placed in the hospital, as was understood, on account of his indisposition. We found him in a room with grated windows; and had the pain and mortification that to discover that his intellect was entirely destroyed, and he had become a raving maniac. The madness is manifestly real, and not assumed. The acts and words of a madman it would be idle to report, and I therefore pass them unnoticed.

Being informed by the fiscal that our visit to the prisoners was only permitted from courtesy, it would be expected of the commodore and myself to ask no questions in relation to the trial or circumstances attendant upon their capture. We thus found ourselves limited to the questions of their health, treatment, and whether or not all were alive. They answered that all were well except the captain and one man who had been sent to the hospital; that they had been well treated, and none were dead. We understood from the officers that the seaman in the hospital was convalescent. The questions were asked and answers given in the presence of the fiscal, interpreter of the captain of the port, and other Spanish officers.

After leaving the Soberano, 74, on which were the two mates and six seamen, Commodore Morris and myself called on the general of marine. After some observations of courtesy, &c., the commodore inquired of the general of marine when he thought the trial of the prisoners would terminate. He answered, in about ten days. The commodore stated that he was about to leave the port, and it would be well to give the prisoners, when released, in charge to the consul. The general replied that he could not do so, for the parties would then be at full liberty to select the time and mode of leaving. I observed to the general of marine that certain forms were necessary to enable sailors and others to depart; I therefore hoped he would deliver to them such papers as would remove all difficulties at their departure. This he promised to do.

The answer of the general of marine to Commodore Morris furnishes additional evidence that this government is determined exclusively to direct everything connected with the capture, and that the prisoners shall not have even the appearance of being given up to any official of our government.

My feelings have been so harassed and wounded by the melancholy and hopeless condition of Captain Benson, and the conviction that, with the strongest desires, I have been impotent to save him from so sad and cruel a fate, that I hope I shall be excused by the President should I for a time visit the States, even in advance of permission being received. A few days, however, may lessen the present intensity of feeling. Should they not, I shall leave by an early opportunity.

I have the honor to be, sir, with great respect and esteem, your most obedient servant,

ROBERT B. CAMPBELL.

Hon. JOHN M. CLAYTON,
Secretary of State, Washington city.

Mr. Campbell to Mr. Clayton.

[Extract.]

CONSULATE OF THE UNITED STATES, HAVANA,
July 19, 1850.

SIR: * * * * * * *

The trial of the Contoy prisoners is, I suppose, being proceeded with. Captain Benson, of the Georgiana, it is believed has been removed to a lunatic hospital. I feel a deep interest in his fate, and very much fear that his mind cannot be restored so long as he continues in a situation where he never hears his native language or sees a familiar face. Should anything occur by which, officially or personally, I can in any manner serve him, the contingence will be immediately availed of.

It is believed that the Georgiana and Susan Loud have been hauled into a dock, and are unloading preparatory to taking in cargoes of timber for Spain.

With great respect and esteem, I have the honor to be, sir, your most obedient servant,

ROBERT B. CAMPBELL.

Hon. JOHN M. CLAYTON,
Secretary of State, Washington city.

Commodore Morris to Mr. Clayton.

WASHINGTON, *July* 23, 1850.

SIR: I have the honor to report that, in compliance with your instructions of the 29th ultimo, I embarked in the United States steamer

Vixen on the 1st and arrived at Havana on the 10th instant. I immediately addressed a note to the Governor and Captain General of Cuba, requesting an audience, as directed by your letter, and received a verbal message that he would receive me the next day at noon.

I found in the harbor of Havana the United States frigate Congress, with Commodore McKeever, and the Albany, Commander Randolph. From Commodore McKeever I learned that he had held several conversations with the Captain General respecting the persons captured at Contoy, and had been assured by him that a part of them would be released before the 12th of the month.

Early in the morning after my arrival, Commodore McKeever received a note from the Captain General, dated the 10th, informing him that forty-two of those persons had been liberated, and would be sent to any vessel that he might designate. A translation of this note, accompanied by a list of the men, was sent to me by Commodore McKeever for my directions. He was instructed to receive them on board the Congress, and then to transfer them to the Albany; and Commander Randolph was directed to receive them. Copies of these communications are annexed, and numbered 1, 2, 3, and 4.

At noon of the same day, I waited upon the Governor and Captain General, taking with me Mr. Forelhouse, a gentleman from New Orleans, as an interpreter. When the main object of my visit and the authority under which I was to make communications to him were stated, the Captain General declined receiving any communication as an official one from the government of the United States, because he had no authority to act in any manner upon diplomatic subjects. At the same time he expressed his readiness to receive any communications I might make in my official character of an officer of the navy, and to give to them the same consideration as though they had emanated from a higher authority.

In reply, he was informed that I could only act in conformity with my instructions, and that any communications which I might make must be made as under the authority, and by the direction, of the President of the United States. The consideration and weight which he might give to these communications must, of course, depend upon his own views of his duty.

When declining to receive the communications in the manner indicated, he expressed the highest personal and official respect for the President, and his entire confidence in the intentions of the President to cause all the obligations which were due to Spain from the United States to be faithfully performed.

In the course of the conversation which followed, all the communications required by my instructions were made to the Captain General, with the exception of a formal demand for the captured persons who were still detained. I was induced to defer this until I could commune with those who had been released.

The Captain General had stated, in the course of the conversation, that the persons who were still detained were beyond his lawful control until the judicial proceedings upon them, which were then in progress, should be completed.

The interview was closed after he had again stated that he could not receive the communications which I had made as official communications from the government of the United States, and I had replied that I had made them as from, and by the authority of, the President.

On the morning of the 12th instant the United States consul went with me to the Albany, where we saw and conversed with the forty-two persons who had been liberated the day before. From the statement of these persons, it appeared that, from the time of their capture until quite recently, they had been more or less confined by leg-shackles, and generally on the lower gun-deck of the ship-of-the-line, the Soberano. In other respects none of them made any complaint to me of gross ill-treatment. None of their original number had died, but were all present. When any had been sick, they had been sent to the hospital until they were well enough to return to the ship. All of them appeared to be in good health, excepting the one who returned from the hospital the day they were liberated.

Two of them complained of a loss of money and clothing, and one of a passage ticket to Chagres. I subsequently addressed a note to the general of the marine on this subject, a copy of which, and of his answer, are annexed, and numbered 5, 6, and 7.

The Albany sailed for Pensacola, with these men, on the morning of the 13th instant, under orders, of which a copy is annexed and numbered 8.

On the 15th instant I had another interview with the Governor and Captain General, when I made the formal demand required by my instructions for tne ten men who were still detained of those who had been captured at Contoy.

The Captain General, in reply, stated that these individuals were now in the possession and under the control of the judicial tribunals, and that until those tribunals should decide on the guilt or innocence of the parties, he could not lawfully interfere in any manner with them. He stated, however, that the master of the Georgiana, the mate of that vessel, and the mate of the Susan Loud, were all that were upon trial, and that the seamen were only detained as witnesses. He concluded by repeating assurances of his great respect for the President of the United States, and of his own desire to preserve the most friendly relations between Spain and the United States, by all means that were consistent with his duties to his own country.

By an arrangement with the general of marine, the United States consul and myself visited, on the morning of the 16th, all the persons who are still detained.

We were informed that the master of the Georgiana, Mr. Benson, had been sent to the hospital about the 14th instant, in consequence of symptoms of insanity. We found him there, suffering from mania of a violent character.

Although he recognised the consul and a Spanish officer who accompanied us, he was evidently unable to comprehend, and did not notice anything which was said to him. His mind appeared to dwell upon Lopez, whom he considered to be with us, and on whom he was frequently calling; and upon his Bible, to which he often referred as being in his possession. Nothing which he said gave any other indications of the cause of his insanity. The chief of the hospital promised to have him placed in the ward for the insane, and that every attention should be given to alleviate his unfortunate condition.

The two mates and the seamen, excepting one at the hospital, were on board of the Soberano. On being questioned as to the treatment they had received, they said they had no complaint to make; that when any of them had been sick, they had been sent to the hospital until they were well enough to return on board; and that none of them had died.

The permission to visit the master and mates was granted to us as a favor; for, by the Spanish laws, those persons were not allowed, in the existing stage of their trials, to communicate with any but the officers of the law. We were in consequence requested not to question them on the subject of their capture and trial, but every liberty was granted to question them respecting their condition and treatment.

We were also authorized to inform the seamen that they were only detained as witnesses, and would be released as soon as their testimony should be closed.

The "dictamen" of the Auditor of War and Navy, which decided the case of the two captured vessels, Susan Loud and Georgiana, and of the passengers who were taken with them, was first published on the 12th instant, and again on the 13th and 14th. I annex one of the newspapers which contain it.

It appears by this decision that the authorities of Cuba have considered the capture of those vessels authorized by the law of nations, and have regulated all their proceedings accordingly.

On being questioned, the fiscal of the marine said that the evidence to be used on the pending trials would be the testimony of the seamen, the declarations of the parties, and the papers found in the vessels. I was also assured that those trials would be closed without other delay than was due to their great importance.

Believing that my longer stay at Havana could not be productive of any advantage, I embarked and sailed in the Vixen on the afternoon of the 16th instant.

With much respect, I have the honor to be your obedient servant,

CHAS. MORRIS,
United States Navy.

Hon. JOHN M. CLAYTON,
Secretary of State.

No. 1.

UNITED STATES FRIGATE CONGRESS,
Havana, July 11, 1850.

SIR: I have the honor to enclose, herewith, the translation of a communication of yesterday's date, which I have just received from his excellency the Governor and Captain General of Cuba, and request your instructions thereon.

I am, sir, very respectfully, your obedient servant,

J. McKEEVER.

No. 2.

[Translation.]

On the 7th instant, when you paid me the attention of calling to take leave of me before sailing, I expressed the regret which your departure occasioned me, as well on account of the personal esteem I have for you, as because of an announcement which had already been made known to me by the most excellent commander general of marine, to the effect that, by virtue of summary proceedings held in the tribunal of the garrison, such persons, out of the whole number of those taken at Contoy, who it appears were only passengers on board of the vessels, would soon be declared free; and I had intended to ask you, if it were convenient, to order that one of the vessels under your command should receive on board those individuals who, at the time of receiving their liberty, (under the restriction, however, that they should not remain on the island, which was necessary, for many reasons,) should desire to go to the United States; and as you immediately consented to delay your departure for four days, which was the time I thought would still be necessary for the tribunal to issue its declaration, with a view of your receiving those who might choose to embark in your vessels, if in that time they should be liberated, I now inform you that the moment has arrived in which a decision has been made in regard to the individuals named in the enclosed list, and who, on being asked, have voluntarily said their wish was to return to the country from which they came.

Under these circumstances, I hope you will be pleased to inform me if you are disposed to receive them, in order that, to-morrow, I may give proper orders in relation to the subject.

I avail myself of this occasion to renew to you the assurances of faithful and special esteem as a man and worthy officer in the navy of a nation with which Spain always maintains good relations.

AL CONDE DE ALCOY.

HAVANA, *July* 10, 1850.

List of the individuals detained on board her Majesty's ship-of-the line "Soberano," who, on being placed at liberty, expressed a desire to return to the United States.

A. B. Moore	David Kingler Smith
William J. Holland	James M. Gowan
Charles N. Paris	John W. Winter
James O'Donnell	John Gibbs
Arthur Maguire	Thomas M. Armstrong
John Atwalson	William B. Smith
Joel D. Hoag	Wm. M. McIntosh
Stephen Havenstown	James Fogler
John L. Carter	John Cronin
Allen P. Coalson, (sick in hospital.)	Levi Browne
	Alexander Miller

James Bennon
William L. Hardy
John Blackstone
Charley B. Matthews
James Fagsley
George W. McDaniel
William Brown
Edward B. Davis
John French
William Penton
Henry Stevens
William L. Lake
James M. Martin
Henry Smith
John Estill
Joseph Byrnes
Antonio Francisco
Franc S. Wechser
Philip O'Conner
Alexander M. Snelly
Joseph Reed.

The total number comprising this list is forty-two (42,) one of whom is confined to the hospital by sickness.

ALCOY.

HAVANA, *July* 10, 1850.

No. 3.

UNITED STATES STEAMER VIXEN,
Havana, *July* 11, 1850.

SIR: I have to acknowledge the receipt of yours of this date, covering translation of a communication which you have received from the Governor and Captain General of Cuba, informing you of the release of a part of the persons taken by Spanish vessels of war from American vessels near the island of Contoy, and requesting you to designate some vessel of war to receive them.

You will please, in reply to the Governor, to state you will be ready to receive them on board the Congress as early to-day as may suit his convenience.

After these men shall have been thus received by you, you will cause them to be immediately transferred to the United States sloop Albany. Commander Randolph will be directed to receive them from you.

With much respect, &c.,
C. MORRIS, *U. S. Navy*.

Com. J. MCKEEVER,
U. S. Frigate Congress, *Havana*.

No. 4.

UNITED STATES STEAMER VIXEN,
Havana, *July* 11, 1850.

SIR: Commodore McKeever will send on board the Albany, under your command, a number of the persons who were captured at Contoy in American vessels, and who have been this day released by the governor and authorities of Cuba.

You will receive and provision these men, spirits excepted, and will give them as comfortable accommodations as circumstances will permit, until otherwise directed.

You will keep the Albany prepared to sail at the shortest notice.

With much respect, your obedient servant,

C. MORRIS.

Commander V. M. RANDOLPH,
U. S. Sloop Albany, Havana.

No. 5.

UNITED STATES STEAMER VIXEN,
Havana, July 13, 1850.

SIR: When the consul of the United States and myself were on board the Albany yesterday, to see the persons who have recently been liberated by the authorities of this place, one of them, named A. B. Moore, stated to us that whilst he was under the control of the Spanish authorities, three hundred and ten dollars, a belt, and some clothing, were taken from him; and that on his release he received back only two hundred and twenty dollars, without his belt or clothing.

Another of them, named W. J. Holland, stated that money to the amount of eight hundred and five dollars and fifty cents, and a belt, were thus taken, and only five hundred dollars were returned to him.

Henry Stevens, another of the persons, stated that a passage ticket in his favor, stating, in substance, "This ticket entitles the bearer to one steerage passage to Chagres on the bark Georgiana," was taken from him and was not returned.

Although these statements rest entirely on the simple assertion of the individuals interested, which is owing in part to their inability to make affidavits on oath at the office of the consul of the United States, I have deemed it proper to present them for your consideration.

If it should be found that, from any cause, these articles have been overlooked, when the men were sent on board the frigate Congress, and can now be supplied, they may be sent to the office of the United States consul, to be forwarded for the parties interested.

With much respect, I have the honor to be, your obedient servant,

C. MORRIS,
Commodore United States Navy.

His Excellency the GENERAL OF MARINE, *Havana.*

No. 6.

[Translation.]

HAVANA, *July* 14, 1850.

MR. COMMODORE: I have had the pleasure to receive your note of yesterday, in which you speak of what was said in your presence by three of the individuals who were detained at Contoy, and finally set at liberty by the tribunals.

Being desirous to gratify you, and to acquaint you with what has been ascertained relative to the matter in question, I have gathered from the fiscal officer that, when these men were arrested, an inventory was taken on board of the vessels, in order to collect such arms, papers and money as were to be found. As soon as this inventory was taken, the men under arrest were distributed on board different vessels, leaving all their luggage on board the Georgiana, and the money, with some watches that were found, were deposited in the charge of the steward of the steamer Pizarro. As soon as all the vessels and the men had been assembled at Havana, the latter were presented with the luggage that had come by the Georgiana, and each selected what he said belonged to him. With regard to the money, it was necessary, according to law, for each man to prove the amount he had brought with him, and that the same was his own private property, and not belonging to the expedition, nor to other individuals among those who had committed the crime of aggression. Notwithstanding that none of them produced the evidence aforementioned, the fiscal, taking into consideration that no particular account had been taken of what had been found upon the person of each individual, did the same with the money and the watches that had been collected at Contoy as he had done in regard to the luggage; which is to say, he placed at the disposal of all who were assembled the total amount of articles that had been collected, in order that they might divide it among themselves according to the claims, more or less just, that each might present. This was in fact done, and the accompanying copy of a document showing the legal action of the fiscal officer, which I enclose for your information, proves it.

I have the honor to remain, with the greatest consideration, your obedient, faithful servant,

W. K. Y. H.,

FR. NAMEN.

Commodore Morris, *of the United States.*

No. 7.

We the undersigned, declare, in due form, that we have received the money and jewels, and clothing, and everything that belongs to us and was in our possession at the time we were detained by her Majesty's steamer Pizarro, at the island of Contoy; and we further declare, also, that all the others that are in the same case are also satisfied with their properties.

A. B. MOORE,
W. PRESTON,
W. J. HOLLAND,
E. B. DAVIS,
JOHN ESTILL,
J. D. HOAG,
HENRY STEVENS,
JOHN FINCH.

Havana, *July* 10, 1850.

This is a true copy of the original which is in the process.

In testimony thereof, I, the officer of the navy acting as judge in this case, have signed my name, in company with the interpreter.

FRANCISCO MURIAS,
Juez de la Causa.

RAMON DE ANARTI,
Interpreter.
HAVANA, *July* 13, 1850,

No. 8.

UNITED STATES STEAMER VIXEN,
Havana, July 12, 1850.

SIR: You will proceed with all dispatch, in the United States sloop Albany, under your command, to the harbor of Pensacola, for the purpose of taking to that place the persons who were sent yesterday to the Albany from the Congress, and who have recently been liberated from confinement by the authorities of Cuba.

It is desirable that these persons should remain on board the Albany until the directions from the government can be received in relation to them.

If, on your arrival at Pensacola, you should not, on referring to the commandant of that yard and station, find directions from the Secretary of the Navy respecting them, you will immediately send an officer to Mobile, with a dispatch for the Secretary of the Navy, to be transmitted by telegraph, informing him of the number of persons liberated by the authorities of Cuba, which you have on board, and requesting his instructions in relation to them, and to the future movements of the Albany.

Should you receive no instructions from the Secretary of the Navy respecting the future employment of the Albany, you will be governed by unexecuted instructions which you may have received from Commodore Parker, as the service hereby ordered is only intended to suspend his orders till this service shall have been performed.

Respectfully, your obedient servant,

C. MORRIS,
U. S. Navy.

Com. V. M. RANDOLPH,
United States Sloop Albany, Havana.

www.ingramcontent.com/pod-product-compliance
Lightning Source LLC
LaVergne TN
LVHW020126110826
845151LV00001B/292